LE PONT NEUF

D0077672

LE PONT NEUF

FRENCH GRAMMAR IN REVIEW

FOURTH EDITION

EDWARD M. STACK

PRENTICE HALL   Englewood Cliffs, New Jersey   07632

Library of Congress Cataloging-in-Publication Data

Stack, Edward M.
   Le Pont Neuf : French grammar in review / by Edward M. Stack. --
4th ed.
      p.   cm.
   Includes index.
   ISBN 0-13-530031-2
   1. French language--Grammar--1950- 2. French language--Textbooks
for foreign speakers--English.   I. Title.
PC2112.S68 1991
448.2'421--dc20
                                                            90-49101
                                                            CIP

Acquisitions Editor: Steve Debow
Editorial Assistant: Maria Garcia
Editorial/production supervision and interior design:
   Sabrina Fuchs and Judi Wisotsky
Cover design: Diane Conner
Prepress buyer: Herb Klein
Manufacturing buyer: Dave Dickey

 © 1991, 1978, 1971, 1966 by Prentice-Hall, Inc.
A Division of Simon & Schuster
Englewood Cliffs, New Jersey 07632

All rights reserved. No part of this book may be
reproduced, in any form or by any means,
without permission in writing from the publisher.

Printed in the United States of America
10 9 8 7 6 5 4 3 2 1

ISBN 0-13-530031-2

Prentice-Hall International (UK) Limited, *London*
Prentice-Hall of Australia Pty. Limited, *Sydney*
Prentice-Hall Canada Inc., *Toronto*
Prentice-Hall Hispanoamericana, S.A., *Mexico*
Prentice-Hall of India Private Limited, *New Delhi*
Prentice-Hall of Japan, Inc., *Tokyo*
Simon & Schuster Asia Pte. Ltd., *Singapore*
Editora Prentice-Hall do Brasil, Ltda., *Rio de Janeiro*

CONTENTS

PREFACE

Students who have learned principles of French inductively will benefit from systematic review in the form of clearly stated structures, followed by guided practice in both oral and written formats. I have tried to write the grammatical principles as clearly and simply as possible, avoiding undue technical jargon. I have included mnemonic devices when possible, and sometimes provided a framework on which students can determine usage for themselves.

Each main topic is followed by oral and written applications, starting with fragmentary exercises to demonstrate the application of a particular feature of French grammar, and followed by more complete expressions of thought.

Le Pont Neuf is intended as a university-level review. Each chapter is divided into two or three sections, each dealing with an important grammatical topic, and identified by a section number and title. Section numbers are used so that the student will be able to pinpoint the explanation of a grammatical rule more specifically than would be possible with only a page number, and teachers can more easily direct students' attention to a point (as when marking a correction on written work). For this reason the Index refers the reader to section numbers rather than pages.

Students are encouraged to turn freely to other parts of the book when information is needed. The chapters are generally self-contained and independent, so that reference from one place to another is easily done. Teachers may assign sections or chapters out of the printed order without undue sequencing difficulties.

The new spelling rules[1] adopted in 1990 by the *Conseil supérieur de la langue française* have been implemented in this edition, such as the elimination of the circumflex accent in certain words, such as "aout", and the inclusion of hyphens in all elements of numbers.

All exercises and activities are designed for use entirely in French in the classroom. The explanations of grammar are in English to enable students to prepare work efficiently out of class using their native language and to avoid misunderstandings that might occur if the explanations were in technical French. The need for classroom explanations will thus be reduced to a minimum, preserving valuable class time for the practical application of French in class.

[1] *Les Rectifications de l'orthographe*, Premier Ministre. Paris: Hôtel de Matignon, 19 juin 1990.

A supplementary reading text may be used in conjunction with *Le Pont Neuf* so that examples of literature may serve as a demonstration of grammar in action, and as a source of topics for conversation and composition[2]. The selections in the text called *Reflets*—short, topical and informative readings—are intended to serve as springboards for controlled composition as students strive to improve their writing skills. It is recommended that students provide themselves with dictionaries, which will be useful both in general reading and in finding words needed in compositions.

A separate workbook contains additional exercises and activities for written practice and correlates to each chapter in the main text. I recommend that a student do these exercises for review before attempting the exercises in the text because the workbook provides narrowly structured work as well as a general vocabulary. This book also contains rules of punctuation and division of words, a gallery of cognates and *faux amis*, a listing of some of the excellent dictionaries available, and other reference material.

The publisher and I are grateful to the following persons for their review and comments: Peter Hagiwara, The University of Michigan; Ariel Clignet, Alliance française, Washington, D.C.; Christiane Morin, Chemetka Community College; Hampton Morris, Auburn University; John Westlie, William Jewell College; Etienne André, University of Texas at Austin; Walter Chatfield, Iowa State University.

I would also like to express my appreciation to the following editors and staff of Prentice Hall for their help and attention to detail in the production of this book: Steve DeBow, Louise B. Capuano, Sabrina Fuchs, Maria Garcia, Judi Wisotsky.

Edward M. Stack
Raleigh, North Carolina

[2] I recommend George Simenon's various detective novels under the title "Maigret" for interest, practicality, voluminous conversational material, and cultural content. Students also enjoy the short stories of Aymé, the writings of Camus, and other modern writers that teachers may suggest.

1

Article défini
aller
Destinations

ARTICLE DÉFINI

In French, the definite article (**le, la, l', les**) is ordinarily used with each noun or noun cluster (a noun and its accompanying modifiers) unless replaced by: (a) the indefinite article (**un, une, des**); (b) a possessive adjective (**son, mon,** etc.); (c) an expression of quantity (**beaucoup de**); or (d) a number.

la voiture	ARTICLE + [NOUN]
une voiture	(a) INDEFINITE ARTICLE + [NOUN]
ma voiture	(b) POSSESSIVE ADJECTIVE + [NOUN]
beaucoup de voitures	(c) EXPRESSION OF QUANTITY + [NOUN]
trois voitures	(d) NUMBER + [NOUN]

As a general rule, the French definite article is *always* required when the English equivalent uses *the*. In addition, the French article is required in many cases where English uses no article; these cases will be indicated below.

1.1 Forms of the definite article

The French definite article has four forms:

le (*masculine singular*) before a masculine singular noun beginning with a consonant: **le professeur, le livre, le cours.** Note that most nouns ending in **-ment** are masculine.

la (*feminine singular*) before a feminine singular noun beginning with a consonant: **la faculté, la bibliothèque, la conférence.** All nouns ending in **-tion** are feminine.

l' (*masculine* or *feminine singular*) before any singular noun beginning with a *vowel* sound, including mute **h** (**l'homme, l'hiver**). This is called the "elided" form, in which the vowel of *le* or *la* is replaced by an apostrophe before a vowel: **l'école, l'université, l'histoire.**

les (*masculine* or *feminine plural*) before *any* plural noun: **les cours, les conférences, les hommes, les étudiants.**

1.2 Elision

Elision is the dropping of **-e** in two-letter words when the next word begins with a vowel or mute **h.** Examples are:

je	j'arrive	**me**	il m'écoute
te	il t'aime	**se**	il s'est levé
le	je l'ai	**de**	il vient d'arriver
ne	ils n'ont pas	**ce**	c'est (*only form*)

One three-letter word (**que**) elides, as do its many compounds such as **jusque, lorsque, puisque, quoique, est-ce que, qu'est-ce que.** (Be careful *not* to elide **qui,** which can *never* become **qu'.**)

jusque	jusqu'au commencement
lorsque	lorsqu'elle arrivera

In addition, **si** becomes **s'il** or **s'ils** in those two forms only; **la** becomes **l'** before a vowel sound. These are the only times **i** and **a** are elided.

There are two categories of **h,** mute and aspirate. The letter **h** itself is never pronounced. When a word begins with mute **h** (the more usual), elision occurs:

l'homme   **l'hôpital**   **l'hôtel**   **l'hérédité**   **j'habite**

Some words begin with *aspirate* **h**, marked in most dictionaries with a star or other special symbol. Treat these words as though they begin with a consonant. Neither elision (in writing) nor linking (in speech) occurs before an aspirate **h**:

le héros   les héros [le ero]   **la honte   le hibou**

1.3   Contractions

When the preposition **à** or **de** is used before the definite article **le** or **les**, the contracted forms must be substituted:

INSTEAD OF	USE		
à + le	**au**	*to the, at the*	**au** début
à + les	**aux**		**aux** conférences
de + le	**du**	*of the, from the, some*	**du** professeur
de + les	**des**		**des** théories

No contraction is used when the definite article is **la** or **l'**:

Donnez-moi **de la** viande.

Je veux **de l'**eau.

and no contraction is used when the word **le** (meaning *it, him*) is a pronoun:

Voilà Jacques. Je suis contente **de le** revoir.

Mise en œuvre 1 A

Emploi de l'article défini et des contractions

Complétez les phrases suivantes en remplaçant le tiret par l'article défini ou la contraction convenable:

1. _____ professeur donne les notes _____ étudiants.
2. _____ élève rend ses devoirs _____ institutrice.
3. _____ étudiants qui savent la réponse _____ question lèvent _____ main.
4. _____ craie est sur _____ rebord _____ tableau noir.
5. _____ étudiant ouvre _____ manuel français _____ page indiquée.
6. _____ école est près _____ musée mais assez loin _____ bibliothèque.
7. _____ chauffeur stationne sa voiture derrière _____ immeuble.
8. Tous _____ élèves disent bonjour _____ professeurs.

9. Janine aime _____ fromage, _____ salade et _____ fruits.
10. _____ jeunes gens étudient _____ langue anglaise, et ils commencent à _____ parler et comprendre.

1.4   Required use of the definite article

In French the definite article is required in the following cases where English omits it:

A.   General categories and abstract qualities.

J'aime **le tennis** et **le basket**.	*I like tennis and basketball.*
Les rayons cosmiques sont dangereux.	*Cosmic radiation is dangerous.*
La patience est une qualité admirable.	*Patience is an admirable trait.*

B.   Geographical names (except cities). Names of countries, provinces, states, continents, rivers, mountains, and other geographical names (except cities) include the definite article when they are used as subjects or direct objects:

La France, la Suisse et **le Portugal** sont des pays européens.

L'Europe, l'Australie et **l'Amérique** sont des continents.

La Seine, la Loire et **la Garonne** sont des fleuves français.

Les Alpes, les Pyrénées, les Vosges et **le Jura** sont des montagnes.

Paris, Le Havre, Londres et **Bruxelles** sont de grandes villes.

Nous allons visiter **la Suède** et **le Danemark**.

Cities including an article. A few cities *do* include the article as part of the name. Among them are **Le Caire** (*Cairo*), **Le Havre**, **La Haye** (*the Hague*), **La Havane**, **La Nouvelle-Orléans.**

Le Havre, Le Caire et **Paris** sont des villes intéressantes.

> DESTINATION OR LOCATION. When a noun in one of the above categories is used as part of a prepositional phrase (for *destination*, *location*), the article is replaced by one of the prepositions in section 1.7.

C.   Modifier with proper name. Proper nouns accompanied by an adjective will include the article as part of the noun cluster:

Paris est charmant.	BUT	**Le vieux Paris** est charmant.
Il cherche **Denise**.	BUT	Il cherche **la petite Denise**.

D. Titles and family names. The definite article is used with people's titles in French:

> Voilà **le professeur** Foulet.
>
> **Le colonel** Chabert vient d'arriver.
>
> Je vais poser cette question **au commandant.**
>
> —Bonjour, monsieur **le maire.**

Military titles are preceded by **mon** in addressing superior officers, but omitted in addressing inferior ranks:

> —Oui, **mon colonel,** a répondu le lieutenant.
>
> —Qu'est-ce que vous en pensez, **capitaine?** questionna le commandant.

Family names are not made plural as in English (*We are going to visit the Smiths*). In French the definite article **les** is used, but the spelling of the name remains unchanged: do not add **-s** to proper names:

> Nous avons vu **les Smith** au concert.

No article is used before the titles **monsieur, madame, mademoiselle.** Notice that the noun **le monsieur** means *the gentleman* (or sometimes simply a polite way of saying *the man*).

1.5 Omission of article

The definite article is not used in the following instances:

A. Names of persons and cities. No article is used with names of persons or cities (except the few cities whose names include an article[1]):

> **Marie, Paul** et **Mme Lefèvre** sont allés à Nice.
>
> J'ai visité[2] **Paris, Londres** et **Venise.**

B. Nationality, profession, religion, political preference.
1. *Unmodified designation.* When the name of a *nationality, profession, religion,* or *political preference* follows a form of **être** directly, there is no article:

> Paul est **américain.**
>
> Il est **professeur.**

---

[1] **Le Caire** (*Cairo*), **Le Havre, La Haye** (*the Hague*), **La Havane, La Nouvelle-Orléans.**

[2] Notice that **visiter** is followed directly by the place, and no preposition is used. This verb is used only for places and things. For visiting people, use **rendre visite à** [PERSON], or **faire une visite à** [PERSON].

Marie est **catholique.**

Ils sont **communistes.**

2. *Modifier included.* The use of any modifier with the designation of a nationality, profession, religion or political preference requires the inclusion of the indefinite article (**un, une**) as well:

Paul est **un** médecin **renommé.**   *Paul is **a famous** doctor.*

Gérard est **un bon** catholique.   *Gérard is **a good** Catholic.*

See 5.12 B and 5.13 B for more details on this point.

C.   Academic topics. The preposition **de** is used after **cours, classe, professeur** without an article or contraction:

la psychologie: Je suis un **cours de psychologie.**

la biologie: Voilà mon **professeur de biologie.**

la médecine: **L'École de Médecine** est à Paris.

BUT: **la faculté des sciences:**   *The College of Science*

Distinguish between **le professeur de français** and **le professeur français.** The first teaches French (but is not necessarily French), and the second is a French person who is a teacher (but we do not know what subject he teaches).

Students in a particular specialty are indicated using **en:**

Je suis étudiant **en médecine.**   I am a medical student.

C'est une étudiante **en économie.**   She's a student in economics.

Il se spécialise **en anglais.**   He majors in English.

D.   Names of languages. All names of languages are masculine, and are not capitalized as in English. The article **le** is normally included as with all ordinary nouns:

J'étudie **le chinois** et l'espagnol.

Marie comprend **l'allemand** et le russe.

The article is omitted after any form of **parler**, and after **en** (meaning *in*):

1. *Omission of article after* **parler.** When the name of a language directly follows a form of the verb **parler**, omit the article:

Je parle **chinois.**

Henri ne parle pas **espagnol.**

But this does not apply to other verbs:

Je comprends **le** chinois.

2. *Use of* **en.** The preposition **en** is used with names of languages when *in* is meant:

Il a composé la lettre **en français.**
Hans a répondu **en allemand.**

> Notice that the name of a language is often the same as the masculine form of the adjective applying to a country.

E.   Days of the week, names of the months.
1. *Next or last.* When *next* or *last* (name of the day) is implied or indicated by the verb tense, the article is not used with the name of the day of the week.

Nous sommes allés à Dijon **jeudi.**   PAST TENSE: *last Thursday*
Nous irons à Dijon **jeudi.**   FUTURE TENSE: *next Thursday*

2. When *habitual action* is indicated, use the article **le.** All names of days of the week are masculine.

Nous allons à Paris **le jeudi.**
*We go to Paris **on Thursdays.** (every Thursday)*

J'ai un cours de maths **le lundi et le vendredi.**
*I have a math course **Mondays and Fridays.***

Nous allions au bord de la mer **le samedi.**
*We used to go to the beach **on Saturdays.***

3. *Months.* Use **en** with the name of a month to express *in.*

Il fait froid **en janvier, en février** et **en mars.**

F.   Seasons. All four seasons are masculine. If you wish to say *in* a season, use **en** for the three beginning with a vowel, and **au** for **le printemps.**

L'été est beau.	Je fait des promenades	**en été.**
L'automne commence.	Les feuilles tombent	**en automne.**
L'hiver est dur.	Je fais du ski	**en hiver.**
Le printemps me plaît.	Je fais des voyages	**au printemps.**

To indicate *this* or *that* season, use the demonstrative adjective **ce** [5.7]:

cet été	*this summer*	**cet** automne	*this fall*
cet hiver	*this winter*	**ce** printemps	*this spring*

G.   Addresses, headings. The article is usually omitted in postal addresses and in headings:

Chapitre 4   7, boulevard des Italiens

Thème

place Vendôme   Il habite 34, rue Palatine

NOTE: Use **dans** la rue, **sur** le boulevard, l'avenue or la place:

Marie habite **dans** la rue Royale.

Elle se trouve **sur** la place de l'Étoile.

Mise en œuvre 1 B

Langues

Faites des phrases en combinant les mots de la liste A (énoncés par le professeur) avec les mots de la liste B, à tour de rôle. Utilisez toutes les phrases de la liste A avant de changer le nom de la langue.

EXEMPLE

P: Je parle . . .	ÉTUDIANT 1:	Je parle français.
P: Jean ne parle pas . . .	ÉTUDIANT 2:	Jean ne parle pas français.
P: Paul comprend . . .	ÉTUDIANT 3:	Paul comprend **le** français.

A	B
1. Je parle . . .	français
2. Je ne parle pas . . .	espagnol
3. Jacques comprend . . .	allemand
4. Je ne comprends pas . . .	russe
5. Voici une lettre composée . . .	italien
6. Voilà mon professeur . . . [matière]	chinois
7. Nous suivons un cours . . .	portugais
8. J'aime bien . . .	

Mise en œuvre 1 C

Nationalité, profession ou métier, domicile, langue

Faites des phrases qui comprennent les éléments indiqués:

1. le **métier** ou la **profession** de la personne dont on parle
2. la **ville** et le **pays** où elle[3] habite
3. la **langue** qu'elle parle et la langue (en *italique*) qu'elle comprend aussi

EXEMPLE

Charles / agriculteur // Baton Rouge / Louisiane // anglais . . . *français*

Charles est agriculteur. Il habite à Baton Rouge, en Louisiane.
Il parle anglais, mais il comprend aussi le français.

1. Jean-Paul / ingénieur // Paris / France // français . . . *italien*
2. Hans-Dieter / mécanicien // Stuttgart / Allemagne // allemand . . . *russe*
3. Cécil / chauffeur de taxi // Londres / Angleterre // anglais . . . *gallois*
4. Pavel / ouvrier // Omsk / Russie // russe . . . *anglais*
5. Giuliano / pilote // Torino / Italie // italien . . . *français*
6. Chen / cuisinier // Beijing / Chine // chinois . . . *japonais*
7. Mlle Suzuki / violiniste // Tokyo / Japon // japonais . . . *anglais*
8. M. Sikora / professeur d'histoire // Varsovie / Pologne // polonais . . . *russe*
9. Stéfan / athlète // Stockholm / Suède // suédois . . . *danois*
10. Pete / cowboy // La Grange[4] / Texas, États-Unis // anglais, texan . . . *espagnol*

VERBE IRRÉGULIER *aller*

1.6   Verbe irrégulier *aller*.

Review the verb **aller** in the **présent, imparfait,** and **passé composé** in Appendix C, Verb Table 1. Notice that in the compound tenses, the auxiliary verb for **aller** is **être**, hence the past participle agrees in gender and number with the subject, e.g., **Elle est allée** [10.2] au cinéma.

A.   Prepositions used with means of travel. Use **en** with the name of most conveyances:

---

[3] **La personne** refers to a person of either sex.
[4] **Est-ce que** *la grange* a une signification en français? en anglais? (Voir le dictionnaire.)

	en auto/ en voiture.	*by car (driving).*
	en avion.	*by plane (flying).*
Ils vont à Marseille	en bateau.	*by boat (sailing).*
	en chemin de fer.	
	par le train.	*by train.*

For the three slowest ways of going, the preposition **à** is used:

	à **pied.**
Il va en ville	à **bicyclette.**[5]
	à **cheval.**

Hier je **suis allé** à Boston **en voiture.**   *Yesterday I drove to Boston.*

Nous **allons** souvent à Genève **en avion.**   *We often fly to Geneva.*

Elle **est allée** en ville **à pied.**   *She walked downtown.*

The verb **prendre** (*to take*) may be used as in English with **l'auto, un taxi, le métro, le train, l'avion, le bateau:**

Jean **prend le train** pour aller à Berne.

Jeanne **a pris un taxi** pour aller de l'hôtel à la gare.

B.   Immediate future (le futur proche). Use **aller** [+ INFINITIVE] to indicate action that is expected to happen very soon. The structure corresponds exactly to English usage:

Je **vais** *étudier* ce soir.   I am **going** *to study* *this evening.*

Nous **allons** *partir* maintenant.   *We* **are going** *to leave* *now.*

Notice that if the action is not imminent, the future tense [24.1–24.5] is preferred:

Nous **partirons** en janvier.   *We will leave in January.*

If the meaning *was going to* (*do something*), *but did not do it* is intended, use the imperfect tense [13.1] of **aller** plus the infinitive:

J'**allais étudier,** mais j'ai dû aller en ville.
I *was going to study, but I had to go downtown.*

---

[5] Also use **à** with **motocyclette** and analogous two-wheeled or three-wheeled vehicles.

DESTINATIONS AND LOCATIONS

1.7   Destinations and locations: *at, to,* or *in* (a place).

To indicate *to* or *in* a geographical location such as a city, state, province, or country, the prepositions selected depend on the gender of the location, on the type of location, and on whether the name begins with a vowel.

à is used before names of cities:

>   à Londres   à Paris   à Washington   à Mexico

as well as before cities that have an article as part of the name:

Le Havre	Le Havre	**au** Havre
Cairo	Le Caire	**au** Caire
Havana	La Havane	à La Havane

en is used before all names of countries and states that are of feminine gender:

en France	**en** Suisse
en Italie	**en** Suède
en Russie	**en** Grèce
en Pologne	**en** Autriche
en Chine	**en** Hollande

NOTE: All major European countries are feminine, except for

>   **le** Portugal   **le** Danemark   **le** Luxembourg

The following U.S. states of feminine gender:

en Californie	**en** Floride
en Caroline du Nord	**en** Caroline du Sud
en Georgie	**en** Louisiane
en Virginie	**en** Pennsylvanie

NOTE: States whose English names end in **-a** change this letter to **-e** in French, and are feminine. *Dakota* is an exception, being masculine.

all names beginning with a vowel (except cities) and all continents:

en Amérique   **en** Afrique   **en** Australie   **en** Asie

and states beginning with a vowel regardless of gender:

en Alaska   **en** Arizona   **en** Ohio   **en** Utah

au is used before names of countries of masculine gender:

au Portugal   **au** Danemark   **au** Luxembourg

au Japon   **au** Mexique   **au** Canada

aux États-Unis

names of states with masculine gender:

au Minnesota   **au** Nevada   **au** Texas

or use **dans le:**

dans le Dakota du Nord (Sud)

dans l'État de [name of state] may be used to distinguish state from city:

dans l'État de Washington   *BUT:*   à Washington

dans l'État de New York   à New York

dans l'île de for islands:

dans l'île de la Cité   **dans l'île** de Malte

TO VISIT A PLACE: The verb **visiter** is followed directly by the name of the place, including the article. No preposition is used:

Il a visité la France.   Il a visité Paris.   Il a visité Le Havre.

TO VISIT PEOPLE: Use **faire une visite** à or **rendre visite** à:

Nous **avons rendu visite** à des parents en Belgique.

1.8   Replacements for English *to go* statements.

Basic English is provided with many expressions using *to go* plus another word to describe certain actions. There are specific French verbs for these actions, and they must be used, because the combinations in English cannot be made in French.

BASIC ENGLISH	FRENCH EQUIVALENT	EXAMPLE
to go in	**entrer** (**dans** [N])	Il **entre dans** la salle.
to go out	**sortir** (**de** [N])	Ils **sortent du** laboratoire.
to go up[stairs]	**monter**	Pierre **monte** au premier.
to go down[stairs]	**descendre**[7]	Elle **est descendue** à midi.
to go with [P]	**accompagner**	Il **a accompagné** son père.
to go across [N]	**traverser**	Il **a traversé** la place.
to go to bed	**se coucher**[8]	Il **s'est couché** à minuit.
to go to sleep	**s'endormir**	Il **s'est endormi** tout de suite.
to get along without [N]	**se passer de** [N]	Je **me passe d'**auto.
to go by [N]	**passer par**	Jean **est passé par** une petite route.

Mise en œuvre 1 D

Conversation sur la géographie

In exercises such as this, calling for a personal response on your part, your answer should consist of (a) a direct reply to the question, and (b) a second sentence or more in which you explain or elaborate on your reply. If you forget to continue on with this elaboration, your teacher might remind you to do so by saying something like **"Tiens!"** which means approximately *"Well, that's interesting. Tell me more!"*

Répondez aux questions suivantes par des phrases complètes. Employez les réponses indiquées; ensuite ajoutez au moins une phrase explicative.

EXEMPLE

Quel pays veux-tu visiter?
 Je voudrais[9] visiter la Suisse.
 Je m'intéresse à l'alpinisme, et j'ai entendu dire que le pays est très beau. Et j'ai des parents à Berne.

1. Quel continent veux-tu visiter?
Europe / Amérique / Asie / Australie

2. Quel ville voudrais-tu visiter . . .
en France?[10] / en Espagne? / au Canada? / en Angleterre? (Londres?) / en Italie? / en Russie? (Moscou?)

---

[7] **Descendre** also means to stay at a hotel: (**Il est descendu à l'Hôtel Lutetia**); and *to get out of* any vehicle, or *off* a horse or bicycle: **Elle est descendue de la voiture.**

[8] **aller au lit** is also correct.

[9] **Je voudrais** *I would like to* . . . conditionnel de **vouloir.**

[10] **Je voudrais** *visiter* **Paris,** or **Je voudrais** *aller à* **Paris. Visiter** is followed directly by the name of the locality, while **aller** requires one of the prepositions in [1.7]. Remember that **visiter** cannot be used for *people* (use **faire une visite à** or **rendre une visite à**).

3. Quelle langue parle-t-on . . .
   en Belgique? / en Espagne? / en Italie? / en Suisse? / au Québec? / en Égypte? /
   au Japon? / en Chine? / au Brésil? / au Maroc?

4. Où est-ce qu'on parle . . .
   français? / portugais?/ arabe?/ latin? / suédois? / russe? / hindi?

5. Quelle est une destination convenable pour . . .
   les individus qui aiment le ski?
   les professeurs qui font des recherches?
   les gangsters?
   les législateurs de votre état?
   les cosmonautes?
   les nouveaux mariés?

6. Où vas-tu pour visiter . . .
   le gratte-ciel[11] qui s'appelle « Empire State »?
   l'Alamo?
   Hollywood?
   les chutes du Niagara?
   une base de lancement d'une fusée NASA?
   le Vatican?

7. Quels cours suis-tu à l'université? (—Je suis[12] un cours de . . .)
   français / informatique / histoire / anglais / psychologie / économique / maths /
   chimie / politique / [autres?]

Mise en œuvre 1 E

Récit

Composez une ou deux phrases indiquant **qui** va faire un voyage, **à quelle destination, quand** et **comment.**

EXEMPLE   Mme P / Belgique / vendredi / chemin de fer

Le vendredi Madame Piplet va en Belgique en chemin de fer. Elle va faire une
visite à sa cousine.

QUI	DESTINATION	QUAND	MOYEN
1. M. Duplessis	Londres	aout	avion
2. Moi, je	université	mercredi	métro

---

[11] **le gratte-ciel** *skyscraper*
[12] **suivre** *to follow, to take [a course]*

3. Professeur Léman   Portugal   printemps   voiture

4. M. et Mme LeClerc   Le Havre   les lundis   autocar

5. Pierre et Claude   Suède   semaine prochaine   bateau

6. docteur   hôpital   mardi et jeudi   bicyclette

Mise en œuvre 1 F

Thème facultatif

1. Mr. Lecoultre takes the subway from the Gare du Nord to the Cité universitaire every Monday, Wednesday, and Friday.
2. Marguerite is going to write a paper[13] for her history class.
3. Gérard is a newspaper reporter. He lives in Courbevoie, a suburb of Paris.
4. Pierre is a watchmaker who[14] lives in Geneva[15] (Switzerland).
5. He would like to visit Spain, Portugal, and the United States in the fall.

---

[13] une communication
[14] qui
[15] Genève

2

Temps présent
depuis, pendant, pour
Impératif

TEMPS PRÉSENT

2.1 Uses of the present tense

The present tense has the following main functions:

A. Action at the present moment.

— Que **faites-vous**?   *"What are you doing?"*
— Je **prépare** un examen.   *"I'm getting ready for an exam."*

B. Habitual action still in effect.

D'habitude je **vais** à l'église le dimanche.
Usually I go to church on Sundays.

Nous **étudions** toujours à la bibliothèque.
*We always **study** at the library.*

C. Conditional sentences with *si*. In conditional sentences, when the result clause is in the *future* or *imperative*, use the present tense after **si** (*if, whether*):

CONDITION   RESULT (FUTURE)

Si vous **parlez** français, je vous comprendrai[1].
If you **speak** French, I'll understand you.

CONDITION   IMPERATIVE

Si vous **allez** à pied, partez de bonne heure.
If you **are walking**, leave early.

The si-clause need not be first in the sentence, but the present tense stays with it:

Je vous comprendrai **si** vous **parlez** français.

D.   Actions in the immediate future. The present tense may be used to indicate future actions, as in the English equivalents:

Demain je **pars** pour le Mexique.   *Tomorrow I am leaving for Mexico.*

Je **passe** mon examen **cet après-midi**.   *I am taking my exam this afternoon.*

E.   With *depuis* statements (*have been doing something*). To indicate that a certain action, now in progress, has been going on for a certain length of time, use the present tense with **depuis** [2.4A].

J'attends **depuis** vingt minutes.   *I have been waiting for twenty minutes.*

Alternatively, the present tense is used with $\boxed{\textbf{Il y a} \; [\text{TIME}] \; \textbf{que}}$ to avoid confusion of *clock time* with *duration* of the activity. The ambiguity is possible because **depuis** means either *since* or *for a time*.

AMBIGUOUS:

Je **suis** ici *depuis* une heure.   *I have been here for an hour.* OR
                                         I have been here since one o'clock.

CLEAR:

Il y a une heure **que** je suis ici.   *I have been here for an hour.*

2.2   Formation of the present tense

Regular verbs can be formed mechanically, by rule (**par la règle**). The present tense of *irregular* verbs should be memorized because of the lack of consistency in the stems (and occasionally in the endings).

[1] **comprendrai,** FUTURE TENSE [24.1 ff]

To form the present tense of regular verbs, (1) drop the ending of the infinitive to get the stem (**le radical**) and (2) add the present tense endings for the six forms. The ending system follows:

	VERB TYPE		
	-er	-re	-ir
je	-e	-s	-is
tu	-es	-s	-is
il (elle, on)	-e	-	-it
nous	-ons		-issons
vous	-ez		-issez
ils (elles)	-ent		-issent

	parler	**vendre**	**finir**
je	parl **e**	vend **s**	fin **is**
tu	parl **es**	vend **s**	fin **is**
il	parl **e**	vend	fin **it**
nous	parl **ons**	vend **ons**	fin **issons**
vous	parl **ez**	vend **ez**	fin **issez**
ils	parl **ent**	vend **ent**	fin **issent**

For a complete display of the three types of verbs (*conjugations*), see Appendix B (Model Regular Verbs). As you proceed with the text, you should freely consult other sections of the book for immediate information. Cross-references to other sections are given by numbers in square brackets.

2.3   Meanings of the present tense

There are two main meanings in English which are equivalent to the present tense in French. In most instances the two-word equivalent is appropriate. If it does not sound right, try the one-word equivalent. In English, the two-word present is for action going on *right now*, the one-word present is for *habitual* action.

PRESENT TENSE (FRENCH)	PRESENT TENSE (English)	
	TWO-WORD (RIGHT NOW)	ONE-WORD (USUALLY)
il **travaille**	*he is working*	*he works*
elle **étudie**	*she is studying*	*she studies*
nous **arrivons**	*we are arriving*	*we arrive*
il **va**	*he is going*	*he goes*

The two-word English equivalent (*present progressive form*) is not usable for certain verbs, such as **il comprend, il sait, il est,** which must be given the one-word equivalents *he understands, he knows, he is*.

The distinction between an immediate action and a habitual action is determined by the context or by adverbial expressions:

Il travaille **maintenant.**   IMMEDIATE ACTION

Il travaille **tous les jours.**   HABITUAL

When a **depuis**-phrase completes the sentence, the English equivalent is *has (have) been doing* something:

Il travaille **depuis vingt minutes.**   *He **has been working** for 20 minutes.*

Je vous attends **depuis longtemps.**   *I **have been waiting** for you for a long time.*

Mise en œuvre 2 A

Formation du présent

Composez une phrase en employant les mots donnés. Ajoutez une seconde phrase d'explication.

EXEMPLE (je) travailler—bibliothèque

Je travaille à la **bibliothèque** tous les soirs.
J'étudie mes leçons dans la salle de lecture.

1. (nous)   travailler—université
2. (vous)   préparer—devoirs
3. (ils)   étudier—leçon de français
4. (tu)   visiter—musée
5. (elle)   assister—conférence
6. (je)   jouer (à)—tennis

7. (tu)	jouer (de)—guitare (*f.*)		19. (vous)	écrire—lettre
8. (Paul)	aller—théâtre		20. (nous)	lire—roman
9. (nous)	aller—cinéma		21. (il)	finir—travail
10. (Marie)	faire—camping		22. (nous)	obéir (à)—agent
11. (elles)	parler—italien		23. (ils)	bâtir—maison
12. (je)	être de retour		24. (vous)	réussir (à)—examen
13. (Pierre)	fermer—fenêtres		25. (Jean)	vendre—auto
14. (elle)	trouver—dictionnaire		26. (Marie)	faire—cuisine
15. (tu)	passer—examen		27. (tu)	rendre—devoirs
16. (ils)	gagner—argent		28. (je)	perdre—patience (*f.*)
17. (il)	penser (à)—voiture		29. (nous)	attendre—professeur
18. (je)	habiter—banlieue (*f.*)		30. (Alain)	échouer (à)—examen

Activité de groupe

Posez à votre voisin ou à votre voisine une question basée sur les mots de l'exercice précédent, par exemple:

—Travaillez-vous souvent à l'université le soir?

La personne qui répond ajoutera une seconde phrase d'explication:

—Mais oui, je travaille souvent à l'université le soir.
Je prépare mes devoirs pour le lendemain.

Ensuite cette personne posera à l'étudiant suivant (ou à l'étudiante suivante) une question basée sur le numéro 2 de l'exercice, et ainsi de suite.

depuis, il y a [TIME], pendant, pour

2.4   *depuis*–construction, present and imperfect tenses

A.   With the present tense (*has been* [*doing something*]). Actions that are still in progress when the speaker makes a statement about them can be described using **depuis** [TIME] and a verb in the present tense.

Jacqueline *travaille* depuis quinze minutes.
*Jacqueline **has been working** for fifteen minutes.*

Since the action is still going on, it makes sense to use the present tense, even though the English equivalent uses *has been*. Notice that the **depuis**-expression is always at the end of the sentence.

NOTE: If the action is *still in progress*, use the present tense with **depuis** [TIME].

B.   With the imperfect tense (*had been* [*doing something*] *when something else happened*). If the action has already been completed when something else happened, there are two clauses. The first clause contains the imperfect tense with the **depuis** time indicator, telling what *had been* going on when the action in the second clause occurred.

IMPERFECT	PASSÉ COMPOSÉ

Jeanne *lisait* **depuis quinze minutes** / quand Paul est arrivé.
*Jeanne **had been reading** for fifteen minutes / when Paul arrived.*

The sequence of the two events is the order in which they appear in the sentence. The **depuis**-clause is always the *earlier* event, in progress when the second event (in the passé composé, here) happened.

In summary, for *has been doing*, use the *present tense* before the **depuis**-construction. The action is still in progress.

For *had been doing*, use the *imperfect tense* before the **depuis**-construction, and indicate the other action in a second clause using the passé composé. Both actions are in the past, and the action with the **depuis**-construction occurred before the **quand**-clause.

2.5   Il y a [TIME] que

Ambiguity sometimes arises when the **depuis**-phrase can be interpreted either as a specific clock time, or as a span of time. For example, *Je suis ici **depuis deux heures*** has two possible meanings:

> *I have been here **since two o'clock.***
> *I have been here **for two hours.***

If you mean a span of time *two hours*, use **Il y a** [TIME] **que** at the *beginning* of the sentence:

> **Il y a** *deux heures* **que** je suis ici.   *I have been here two hours.*

This cannot mean *since two o'clock*. Notice that **Il y a** [TIME] **que** always comes at the *beginning* of a sentence.

2.6   Completed and future action: *pendant, pour* [TIME]

When the action is *not* continued into the present, use **pendant** or **pour** (as appropriate) to express *for* [TIME].

A.   **pendant** *(during)* for a completed action of some duration in the past:

Nous sommes restés en France **pendant quinze jours.**
We stayed in France for two weeks.

B.   **Use pour** for future actions:

Jean-Paul va en Suisse **pour** un mois.
Jean-Paul is going to Switzerland for a month.

2.7   Questions with *depuis*

To inquire how long something has been going on, the present tense is used after one of the following forms:

A. Use **depuis quand** + PRESENT TENSE to elicit a date or the day something began:

— **Depuis quand** étudies-tu le français?
— *J'étudie le français **depuis le 20 septembre (samedi, l'anné passée).***

B. Use **depuis combien de temps** + PRESENT TENSE to find out the *duration* of an event now in progress:

— **Depuis combien de temps** étudies-tu le français?
— *Je l'étudie **depuis trois ans (un trimestre, un mois).***

Notice that the answers, as well as the questions, show that the action is still going on, since the present tense is used.

Mise en œuvre 2 B

Expressions de durée

Composez une phrase pour chaque groupe de mots ci-dessous, en employant **pendant, depuis, il y a** ou **pour** selon le cas. Évitez l'ambiguïté.

1. Jean / étudier / trois heures[2]
2. Marie / travailler / 2 octobre
3. Les Brun / voyager / Afrique du Nord / deux mois
4. M. et Mme Bonnet / visiter / Suède / quinze jours / 1990
5. Nous / aller / séjourner / Portugal / un mois / année prochaine
6. Robert / se reposer[3] / 15h
7. Robert / se reposer / trois heures
8. Ces étudiants / étudier japonais / le 28 août
9. Ils / écrire / thème / quarante-cinq minutes
10. Nous / faire / devoirs / une heure et demie

Mise en œuvre 2 C

Thème facultatif

Donnez l'équivalent en français:

1. I have been working here since eight o'clock.
2. It is eight fifteen[4], and I have been working for fifteen minutes.
3. Georges has been working for eight hours.
4. We are going to Cannes for two weeks.
5. Roger has been lying on the beach for twenty minutes.
6. Suzanne has been in the department store[5] since nine o'clock.
7. She has been looking at a red dress for an hour.
8. These[6] students are going to France for two years.

L'IMPÉRATIF

2.8   Use of the imperative

The imperative (command) forms of a verb are used for giving directions or orders. They are derived from the present tense **tu-, vous-** and **nous-** forms. The three imperative forms are:

---

[2] Expliquez la différence entre les deux façons d'écrire cette idée.
[3] Au cas de besoin, référez-vous à la section 12.1.
[4] Au cas de besoin, référez-vous à la section 8.12.
[5] **Le grand magasin:** À Paris il y a la Samaritaine, les Galeries Lafayette, le Printemps, par exemple.
[6] **Ces** [5.7]

A. The **tu**-form (*familiar form*), used for giving orders to *one* individual who is a member of the family, a close friend, a child, or an animal. (If an order is directed to *more than one* individual in these categories, the *vous*-form is used.)

B. The **vous**-form, for giving orders to one or several people not in the categories above; or to more than one individual in the familiar category.

C. The **nous**-form, for suggesting that something be done by the speaker along with others addressed.

Finis le travail, Brigitte.	*Finish the work, Brigitte.*	**(tu)**
Finissez le travail, monsieur.	*Finish the work, sir.*	**(vous)**
Finissons le travail, mes amis.	*Let's finish the work, my friends.*	**(nous)**

2.9   Formation of the imperative

The imperatives consist of the **tu**-, **vous**-, and **nous**-forms of the present tense, after dropping the personal pronouns.

IMPERATIVE	DERIVED FROM	MEANING
Parle!	**tu parles**	*Speak!*
Parlez!	**vous parlez**	*Speak!*
Parlons!	**nous parlons**	*Let's speak!*

Notice that the final **-s** is dropped from the **tu**-form when the preceding letter is **e** or **a**. (Before the pronouns **y** and **en**, final **-s** is retained. EXCEPTION: **Vas-y; Penses-y; Cherches-en.**)

2.10   Imperative of irregular verbs

Irregular verbs form the imperative in the same ways as regular verbs (with the exception of **avoir, être,** and **savoir**).

	TU-FORM	VOUS-FORM	NOUS-FORM
faire	**fais**	**faites**	**faisons**
mettre	**mets**	**mettez**	**mettons**
prendre	**prends**	**prenez**	**prenons**
dire	**dis**	**dites**	**disons**

EXCEPTIONS. The three irregular verbs that do *not* form the imperative in the same way as regular verbs are the following:

INFINITIVE	IMPERATIVES	MEANING
avoir	aie	*have (be)*
	ayez	*have (be)*
	ayons	*let's have (be)*
être	sois	*be*
	soyez	*be*
	soyons	*let's be*
savoir	sache	*know, be aware of*
	sachez	*know, be aware of*
	sachons	*let's know*

Ayez confiance en l'avenir.	*Trust the future.*
N'**aie** pas peur, mon enfant.	*Don't be afraid, my child.*
Soyons prudents.	*Let's be careful.*
Sachez la vérité.	*Know the truth.*
Sois sage.	*Behave yourself. (Be good.)*

2.11   Negative imperatives

Make a command negative by placing it between **ne** and **pas** in the usual way:

Parlez!	**Ne** parlez **pas**!	*Don't speak!*
Mets la table!	**Ne** mets **pas** la table!	*Don't set the table!*
Allons en ville!	**N'**allons **pas** en ville!	*Let's not go downtown!*
Dites quelque chose!	**Ne** dites **rien**!	*Don't say anything!*

2.12   Imperative form of reflexive (pronominal) verbs

You are already familiar with many everyday commands using reflexive verbs, such as:

Levez-vous!	Lève-toi![7]	Levons-nous!
Asseyez-vous!	Assieds-toi![8]	Asseyons-nous!
Dépêchez-vous!	Dépêche-toi!	Dépêchons-nous!

[7] The reflexive pronoun **te** becomes **toi** when inverted.
[8] Remember, the **-s** of the **tu**-form is dropped in commands when the infinitive ends in **-er**.

These forms are derived from the present tense of reflexive verbs [12.1–12.3]. To create the imperative of these "pronominal" verbs, the subject pronoun is eliminated, and the reflexive pronoun is placed *after the verb*[9], and joined to it by a hyphen:

1. STATEMENT	2. DROP SUBJECT PRONOUN	3. COMMAND
vous vous levez	~~vous~~ vous levez	Levez-vous!
nous nous pressons	~~nous~~ nous pressons	Pressons-nous!
tu te dépêches	~~tu~~ te dépêches	Dépêche-**toi**!

NOTE: **te** becomes **toi** in inverted position. Remember also that the **-s** of the **tu**-form is dropped in *commands* when the preceding letter is **-e** or **-a**.

2.13   Negative commands of reflexive verbs

Negative commands are formed by using the form in column 2 above, and enclosing the result between **ne** and **pas** (or other negative completion).

~~vous~~ vous levez	Ne **vous levez** pas!
~~nous~~ nous pressons	Ne **nous pressons** pas!
~~te~~ te dépêches	Ne **te dépêche** pas!

Mise en œuvre 2 D _____

Impératif

Complétez les idées suivantes en ajoutant un impératif, suivant les exemples:

EXEMPLE

Tu veux *traverser* la rue?
Traverse la rue!

Vous voulez *vous reposer?*
Reposez-vous!

1. Tu veux *poser* une question?
2. Vous voulez *acheter* un dictionnaire?
3. Nous voulons *visiter* le Louvre.
4. Tu veux *entrer* dans cette salle?

[9] When the pronoun follows the verb, it is said to be "inverted," or in "inverted position."

5. Nous avons envie de *parler* français.
6. Vous préférez *commander* du vin blanc?
7. Vous voudriez *quitter* la conférence?
8. Tu veux *savoir* la vérité?
9. Vous voulez *être* courageux?
10. Tu ne veux pas *avoir* peur?
11. Nous voulons *aller* au cinéma.
12. Tu ne veux pas *accompagner* les autres?
13. Tu veux *rentrer* à la maison?
14. Tu ne veux pas *rester* en classe?
15. Tu veux *te reposer?*
16. Nous ne pouvons pas *expliquer* le problème.
17. Nous préférons *déjeuner* avec les Lebrun.
18. Vous avez envie de *visiter* la Suède?
19. Il faut *monter* au premier étage.
20. Il faut que tu *te couches*.

Mise en œuvre 2 E

Impératif des verbes

A. Demandez à un inconnu[10] ou à une inconnue de:

> EXEMPLE monter au second
>> Montez au second, monsieur.

1. monter au second
2. chercher la police
3. téléphoner au professeur
4. donner un message à votre camarade de chambre
5. dire au professeur que vous êtes souffrant(e)
6. mettre le formulaire sur la table
7. faire le nécessaire
8. prendre soin

B. Posez les mêmes demandes à un copain (*forme familière*).

> EXEMPLE monter au second
>> Monte au second, mon ami.

C. Proposez les mêmes actions à tout le monde, vous-même y compris.

[10] **Un inconnu** = *a stranger*. Il faut donc vouvoyer. N'employez pas la forme familière (**tu**).

EXEMPLE monter au second
Montons au second.

Reflets

La philosophie canine: Pensées de Riquet

I. Les hommes, les animaux, les pierres grandissent en s'approchant et deviennent énormes quand ils sont sur moi. Moi non. Je demeure toujours aussi grand partout où je suis.

VII. Tout passe et se succède. Moi seul je demeure.

X. Méditation. J'aime mon maître Bergeret parce qu'il est puissant et terrible[11].

XI. Une action pour laquelle on a été frappé est une mauvaise action. Une action pour laquelle on a reçu des caresses ou de la nourriture est une bonne action.

XVI. Les hommes exercent cette puissance divine d'ouvrir toutes les portes. Je n'en puis ouvrir qu'un petit nombre. Les portes sont de grands fétiches qui n'obéissent pas volontiers aux chiens.

XVIII. On ne sait jamais si l'on a bien agi[12] envers les hommes. Il faut les adorer sans chercher à les comprendre. Leur sagesse est mystérieuse.

XX. Il y a des voitures que des chevaux traînent par les rues. Elles sont terribles. Il y a des voitures qui vont toutes seules en soufflant très fort. Celles-là aussi sont pleines d'inimitié. . . . Le monde est plein de choses hostiles et redoutables.

Sujets de composition ou de discussion: Riquet

1. Qui est Riquet? Quelle est sa place dans le monde?
2. Qu'est-ce qu'il y a de permanent dans le monde de Riquet? Qu'est-ce qui change d'un moment à l'autre?
3. Quelle est la règle de moralité et de justice? Comment sait-on la différence entre les bonnes et les mauvaises actions?
4. Pourquoi Riquet regarde-t-il les hommes comme des dieux? Que peuvent-ils faire qui est impossible aux autres?
5. De quelle façon Riquet adore-t-il son maître? Comment sait-on qu'il a peur aussi?
6. Les portes, qu'est-ce qu'elles représentent?
7. Qu'est-ce que Riquet pense des machines? Quelles deux sortes de machines est-ce qu'il contemple?
8. Riquet paraît-il heureux, malheureux? Est-ce qu'il se sent en sécurité dans le monde?

---

[11] **terrible**-*qui inspire de la terreur.*
[12] **agir** = *to act, to behave.*

3

Pluriel des noms
Partitif
Possession

PLURIEL DES NOMS

3.1 Sign of the plural is *les* and NOUN + *s*

To form the plural of a noun, change the singular definite article to **les**[1] and add -s to the singular noun.

la fille	**les** filles
le livre	**les** livres
le héros	**les** héros[2]
l'église	**les** églises

The main exceptions to this system are nouns ending in **-u, -al, -s, -x,** and **-z.**

---

[1] **Les** is pronounced [le] before consonant sounds, and [lez] before vowels and mute **h.**

[2] Since this is an aspirate **h,** there is no liaison: pronounce this [le ᴇʀᴏ]. Aspirate **h** is usually indicated in dictionaries by an asterisk before the word: ***héros, *hache, *hibou.**

3.2 Nouns ending in *-u*

A.   Add *-x* to form the plural:

le château	les châteaux	*castles*
le bateau	les bateaux	*boats*
le feu	les feux	*fires, (traffic) lights*
le jeu	les jeux	*games*
l'eau	les eaux	*waters, fountains*
le genou	les genoux	*knees*
le *hibou	les hiboux	*owls*
le bijou	les bijoux	*jewels*

B.   Exceptions: add *-s* to the following nouns ending in *-u:*

le pneu	les pneus	*tires*
le sou	les sous	*sous (money)*
le matou	les matous	*tomcats*
le clou	les clous	*nails*

Notice that the plural forms of these nouns are pronounced the same as the singular. Only the pronunciation of the definite article **les** indicates that the noun is plural.

3.3 Nouns ending in *-al* change to *-aux.*

le journal	les journaux	*newspapers*
le cheval	les chevaux	*horses*
le général	les généraux	*generals*
l'animal	les animaux	*animals*
l'hôpital	les hôpitaux	*hospitals*

3.4 Nouns ending in *-s, -x, -z* remain the same in the plural

le fils	les fils	*sons*
le nez	les nez	*noses*
le choix	les choix	*choices*

3.5   Irregular plurals of certain nouns

l'œil	*the eye*	les **yeux**	*the eyes*
le **ciel**	*the sky*	les **cieux**	*the skies, heavens*

3.6   Titles

Ordinary forms of address (M., Mme, Mlle) are usually spelled out only if there is a possibility that the person designated may see the writing. The common abbreviations are shown. (Notice that no period is used with abbreviations that end in the same letter as the word fully spelled out.)

SINGULAR	PLURAL
Monsieur (M.)	Messieurs (MM.)
Madame (Mme)	Mesdames
Mademoiselle (Mlle)	Mesdemoiselles

Mise en œuvre 3 A

Pluriel des noms

Composez des phrases en mettant les noms au pluriel.

EXEMPLE

Robert a acheté / trombone[3] / cahier / crayon

Robert a acheté **des trombones, des cahiers et des crayons.**

1. Jacques a visité / musée / château / palais / usine
2. Il regardait / tableau / mur / fontaine / machine
3. Les touristes ont entendu / explication du guide / ruisseau / son / bruit
4. François admire / Français / fille / héros militaire / parc
5. Nous avons cherché / professeur / billet / crayon / agent de police
6. Marie a / œil bleu[4] / cheveu blond / disque / auto
7. Au jardin zoologique nous avons vu / ours / hibou / tigre / autre animal
8. Mon amie admire / bijou / chapeau / robe / garçon
9. Dans le garage il y a / matou / pneu / clou / bicyclette
10. Nous aimons / cheval / chat / chien / oiseau

[3] **trombone** *m.* = *paper clip*
[4] Pluriel irrégulier: **yeux bleus**

Mise en œuvre 3 B _____

Pluriel des noms en contexte

Mettez au pluriel les mots en italique, en faisant les autres changements nécessaires, selon l'exemple.

EXEMPLE

Mon neveu est à Paris.

Mes neveux sont à Paris.

1. Jean-Paul voudrait voir *le château.*
2. *L'homme* du bureau parle très lentement.
3. *Le héros* du voyage dans la lune est très modeste.
4. Fermez *l'œil.*
5. Ma voiture a *un pneu* usé.
6. *Le général* va à Londres en avion.
7. Complétez *le travail* aussitôt que possible.
8. *Le journal* annonce le mariage de ma cousine.
9. *Le bateau* part de Bâle.
10. *Le fils* de M. Leduc est très intelligent.

ARTICLE PARTITIF

3.7   Use

The partitive article (**le partitif**) means *some.* It is used to differentiate between a *whole category* of objects [3.8] and merely a *part* (or *personal share*) of the objects. Notice the distinction between the following:

I **like** coffee. (= *the whole category*)	J'aime **le café.**	GENERAL ARTICLE
I **am having** (some) coffee. (= *a share*)	Je prends **du café.**	PARTITIVE

When the English equivalent contains *the,* use the general article (**le, la, les**); when it contains or implies *some,* use the partitive (**du, de la, des**).

3.8   General class

The general class (designated by the definite article and the plural noun of countable items) means *"in general."* It is found after statements of *liking, disliking,* or other generalities. Suppose we represent the general class by a circle:

Since one can have an attitude towards a whole class of things, one can say, "I like books (in general)," or "I like meat (in general)." If the words *in general* can be added to a statement, the general article should be used.

If, however, only a part of the general class could be involved, as would be the case with any form of consumption by an individual, use the partitive. Verbs of *having, taking, eating, looking at,* and the like, obviously could not apply to *all* of a class. The partitive is formed by prefixing **de** to the general class, resulting in the partitive article (*some*), just an individual *share* (or *slice*) of the whole:

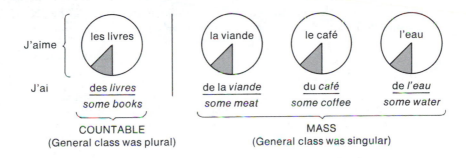

3.9   Personal ownership or consumption: partitive required

A.   Use. After verbs indicating personal ownership or consumption (that is, where *some* rather than *all* would be appropriate before the noun), use the partitive. The word *some* is often omitted in English, so you must test to see if it is appropriate.

GENERAL	O	J'aime les disques.	*I like records.*
PARTITIVE	▲	J'*ai* **des** disques.	*I have (some) records.*
GENERAL	O	Il s'intéresse aux films.	*He is interested in movies.*
PARTITIVE	▲	Il *a vu* **des** films.	*He has seen (some) movies.*
GENERAL	O	Il déteste les chats.	*He hates cats.*
PARTITIVE	▲	Sa mère *a* **des** chats.	*His mother has (some) cats.*

B.   Cues. The partitive is usually expected after such verbs as **avoir (il y a), acheter, apporter, boire, commander, demander, dépenser, donner, porter, regarder, voir.**

J'ai vu **des** tableaux admirables.

Nous regardions **des** animaux.

Il y a **des** verres sur la table.

When the noun after such verbs is followed by some qualifier that identifies the noun as a *specific* one, the definite article is used:

J'ai vu **les** tableaux | *dont vous m'avez parlé.* | RELATIVE CLAUSE

Nous regardions **les** animaux | *dans le jardin zoologique.* | PREPOSITIONAL PHRASE

Henri cherche **l'argent** | *qu'il a perdu.* | RELATIVE CLAUSE

Since **les tableaux, les animaux,** and **l'argent** are all specific things (not generalities) identified by the clauses that follow, the definite article is used. The clauses need not be expressed, but may be understood or clearly required by the context.

3.10   Cues from English

If *the* appears in the English equivalent, the reference is specific, hence the French requires the definite article **le, la, l', les.**

I like the meat. Give me the meat, please.
J'aime **la** viande. Passez-moi **la** viande, s'il vous plaît.

If *the* does not appear in English, the problem in French becomes that of selecting the general or partitive. Test yourself on the following examples:

GENERAL OR PARTITIVE?

1. *He wants coffee.*
2. *Give me orange juice, please.*
3. *Books are useful.*

ANSWERS

1. He wants (some) coffee. PARTITIVE
   Il veut **du café.** (He would not want *all* the coffee there is.)
2. Give me (some) orange juice, please. PARTITIVE.
   Donnez-moi **du jus d'orange,** s'il vous plaît.
3. Books (in general) are useful. GENERAL.
   Les livres sont utiles.

If you want to say "*Some* books are useful," begin with **Il y a** (which calls for the partitive):

Il y a **des** livres qui sont utiles.
There are (some) books which are useful.

Il y a **du** café que j'aime.
There is some coffee that I like.
= *I like **some** coffee (not other coffee).*

(The relative pronouns **qui** and **que** are dealt with in Chapter 22.)

3.11   Table of typical partitives

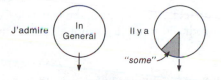

PLURAL IN THE GENERAL CLASS (COUNTABLE NOUNS)			
ITEM (WITH *THE*)	GENERAL CLASS (WITHOUT *THE*)	PARTITIVE (*SOME*)	FORM OF PARTITIVE
le soldat	**les** soldats	**des** soldats	
le frère	**les** frères	**des** frères	
le château	**les** châteaux	**des** châteaux	
la maison	**les** maisons	**des** maisons	
la forme	**les** formes	**des** formes	**des**
la bouteille	**les** bouteilles	**des** bouteilles	*(plural partitive*
l'école	**les** écoles	**des** écoles	*for* **countable**
l'homme	**les** hommes	**des** hommes	*nouns)*
l'avion	**les** avions	**des** avions	

SINGULAR IN THE GENERAL CLASS (MASS OR UNCOUNTABLE NOUNS)		
le vin	**du** vin	
le café	**du** café	**du** (*m.s.*)
le sucre	**du** sucre	
la viande	**de la** viande	**de la** (*f.s.*)
la bière	**de la** bière	
l'eau	**de l'**eau	**de l'** (*m.* or *f.*)
l'argent	**de l'**argent	(*before vowels*)

Generally, French and English are identical with regard to whether a noun is singular or plural when the general class is designated. The majority of nouns are plural in the general class, and the French partitive for them always uses **des.** Other nouns, most of which are names of liquids, granular material (**le sucre**), or other items not thought of as a collection of individual items (**e.g. la viande, l'eau, l'argent**) are singular in the general class. These "mass," or "uncountable" nouns add **de** before the singular article to form the partitive, resulting in the partitives **du** *(m.)*, **de la** *(f.)*, or **de l'** (for mass nouns beginning with a vowel sound).

3.12   Partitive becomes *de* after a negative verb

A.   Partitive article. After a verb in the negative form, the partitive article (**des, du, de la, de l'**) is reduced to **de** (**d'** before a vowel sound).

POSITIVE		NEGATIVE	
J'ai acheté	**de la** viande.	Je n'ai **pas** acheté	**de** viande.
Nous avons	**des** livres.	Nous n'avons **pas**	**de** livres.
Georges a	**de l'**argent.	Georges n'a **pas**	**d'**argent.
Donnez-moi	**du** café.	Ne me donnez **pas**	**de** café.
	FULL PARTITIVE		**de** ONLY

B.   General or definite article is unchanged. When a noun with the definite article follows a negative verb, use the same article as after a positive verb. Notice that there is never **de** in this construction.

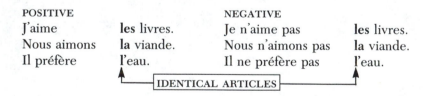

POSITIVE		NEGATIVE	
J'aime	**les** livres.	Je n'aime pas	**les** livres.
Nous aimons	**la** viande.	Nous n'aimons pas	**la** viande.
Il préfère	**l'**eau.	Il ne préfère pas	**l'**eau.

IDENTICAL ARTICLES

Mise en œuvre 3 C _____

Partitif ou article général?

Combinez les éléments de la liste A avec les noms de la liste B à tour de rôle, selon l'exemple.

EXEMPLE

PROFESSEUR: le livre. J'aime . . .
1ᵉʳ ÉTUDIANT: J'aime **les livres.** [3.8]

PROFESSEUR:	Je n'aime pas . . .
2e ÉTUDIANT:	Je n'aime pas **les livres.** [3.8]
PROFESSEUR:	J'ai . . .
3e ÉTUDIANT:	J'ai **des livres.** [3.9]
PROFESSEUR:	Je n'ai pas . . .
4e ÉTUDIANT:	Je n'ai pas **de livres.** [3.12]

Après avoir épuisé la liste A, le professeur recommencera en utilisant le second nom de la liste B, et ainsi de suite.

A	B
1. J'aime . . .	le livre
2. Je n'aime pas . . .	la pomme
3. J'ai . . .	le disque
4. Je n'ai pas . . .	le café
5. J'ai beaucoup . . .	le vin
6. Donnez-moi . . .	les petits pois
7. Ne me donnez pas . . .	le timbre-poste
8. Sur la table, il y a . . .	la viande
	le gâteau
	l'argent

Mise en œuvre 3 D

Partitif

Remplacez les blancs par **l'article partitif**, **l'article général**, **l'article défini** ou **de**, selon le cas.

1. Il y a _____ étudiants qui ont toujours raison.
2. Mon cousin adore _____ autos, mais il attrape souvent _____ contraventions (*tickets*), beaucoup _____ contraventions.
3. _____ médecins d'un grand hôpital ont trop _____ malades à visiter.
4. Il y a _____ architectes locaux qui ont _____ maisons originales.
5. Au restaurant j'ai commandé _____ vin mais je n'ai pas commandé _____ eau. En plus, j'ai pris _____ soupe (*f.*), _____ salade (*f.*), _____ rosbif (*m.*), _____ pommes frites (*f.*), _____ petits pois, et, comme dessert, _____ fruits.
6. Je préfère _____ restaurants où il y a _____ musique (*f.*).
7. Nous aimons _____ vin, aussi (*therefore*) buvons-nous beaucoup _____ vin.

8. Vous autres Américains aimez _____ eau (*f.*); eh bien, commandez _____ eau.
9. _____ dictionnaires sont _____ livres très utiles.
10. Les chats sont _____ animaux familiers.

POSSESSION

3.13   Possessive adjectives

As the table shows, possessive adjectives agree in gender and number with the noun modified. Notice that the choice of gender of the adjective depends entirely upon the gender of the noun, and not of the person possessing.

	Before **FEMININE SINGULAR** nouns beginning with a consonant	Before **MASCULINE SINGULAR** nouns and **FEMININE SINGULAR** nouns that begin with a vowel sound	Before **ALL PLURAL** nouns (pronounce final -s as [z] before nouns starting with a vowel sound)
my	**ma** table	**mon** { livre (*m.*) / école (*f.*)	**mes** { livres (*m.pl.*) / écoles (*f.pl.*)
your	**ta** table	**ton** { livre (*m.*) / idée (*f.*)	**tes** { livres (*m.pl.*) / amis (*m.pl.*) / idées (*f.pl.*)
his *her* *its*	**sa** { table / maison	**son** { livre (*m.*) / ami (*m.*) / école (*f.*)	**ses** { livres (*m.pl.*) / amis (*m.pl.*) / écoles (*f.pl.*)
	BEFORE ALL SINGULAR NOUNS		
our	**notre** table		**nos** livres
your	**votre** livre		**vos** tables
their	**leur** ami		**leurs** amis

Notice the use of the masculine forms **mon, ton, son** with feminine singular nouns beginning with a vowel sound. This makes for ease of pronunciation. Students often forget to use the masculine possessive adjective with a feminine singular noun that begins with a vowel sound:

une école   **mon** école (*not* "ma école")

une amie   **mon** amie (*not* "ma amie")

EXEMPLES

Voilà Lucien. **Son** livre et **sa** montre sont sur la table.
*This is Lucien. **His** book and **his** watch are on the table.*

Voilà Marie. **Son** livre et **sa** montre sont sur la table.
*There is Marie. **Her** book and **her** watch are on the table.*

—Va chercher **tes** cahiers, dit le père.
*"Go and get **your** notebooks," said the father.*

3.14   Required repetition of possessive adjectives

Unlike English, which permits the omission of a second "my" in *My father and brother are arriving*, French requires that the possessive adjective be repeated before *each* noun modified:

> *Mon* père et *mon* frère arrivent.
>
> *Ma* tante et *mon* oncle voyagent.
>
> *Vos* cahiers et *votre* stylo se trouvent sur la table.

3.15   *de +* [NOUN] **forms the possessive of proper nouns**

French has no device quite so convenient as the English apostrophe and *-s* (*John's, the teacher's*, etc.) to indicate ownership. Instead, French employs a prepositional phrase: **de** + name of possessor. If the name of a person or the title **Monsieur, Madame** or **Mademoiselle** [1.04D] is used, there is no article:

Voilà la maison **de Paul.**	*There is Paul's house.*
Le livre **de Suzanne** est là.	*Susan's book is there.*
C'est l'amie **de Madame Antoine.**	*She is Mrs. Antoine's friend.*

If a common noun is used after **de,** the article is included. Contractions are required when the article is **le** or **les.**

l'appartement **de l'**ami	*the friend's apartment*
la maison **du** professeur	*the teacher's house*
l'intelligence **des** étudiants	*the students' intelligence*

When a family name is used in the plural sense, the article **les** is contracted with **de** to form **des.** You will recall that no *-s* is added to the family name in French:

l'auto **des Dupont**	*the Duponts' car*

3.16   Possession using *être à* [NOUN or DISJUNCTIVE PRONOUN[5]]

This is an additional way of expressing possession:

Cette voiture **est à** Monsieur Martin.	*This is Mr. Martin's car.*
Ces livres **sont à** Hélène.	*Those are Hélène's books.*
Ce billet **est à** moi.	*This is my ticket.*

3.17   Parts of the body, articles of clothing

When it is obvious that the arm, leg, hand, or other part of the body, or an article of clothing, belongs to the subject of the sentence, use the *definite article* to indicate possession instead of the possessive adjective (**mon, ton, son,** etc.):

Elle se lave **les mains.**	*She is washing **her** hands.*
Il a **les** yeux bleus.	***His** eyes are blue.*
Van Gogh s'est coupé **l'**oreille.	*Van Gogh cut off **his** (own) ear.*
Tu as **les** pieds sur la chaise.	*You have **your** feet on the chair.*
Elle se peigne **les** cheveux.	*She is combing **her** hair.*
Je me suis brossé **les** dents.	*I brushed **my** teeth.*

The part of the body is left in the singular even if several people are indicated, provided each individual uses only one:

Les élèves lèvent **la** main.   *The pupils raise **their** hands.*

Mise en œuvre 3 E _____

Possession

Complétez les phrases en ajoutant les adjectifs possessifs convenables.

EXEMPLE

Jean a fermé (porte et fenêtres).

Jean a fermé **sa** porte et *ses* **fenêtres.**

1. Jean a fermé (porte et fenêtres).
2. Paul ouvre (livre et cahiers).

---

[5] The disjunctive pronouns are listed in 17.4.

3. Je fais une visite à (oncle et tante).

4. (beau-père et belle-mère) habitent à Vichy.

5. (père et mère) vont souvent au bord de la mer en été.

6. Nous sommes fiers de[6] (bibliothèque et musée).

7. Cette petite voiture est à moi. C'est (voiture).

8. Cette chemise est à toi. C'est (chemise).

9. Cette maison est à nous. C'est (maison).

10. Voilà la famille de Marie et de Jean. C'est (famille).

Récrivez les phrases suivantes pour y incorporer le nom du propriétaire indiqué entre parenthèses. Ajoutez une seconde phrase selon l'exemple.

EXEMPLE

(Charles) Voilà le dictionnaire.

Voilà le dictionnaire **de Charles. C'est son dictionnaire.**

11. (Marie)   Voilà **le stylo.**

12. (Rémi)   La jeune fille là-bas est sa **petite amie.**

13. (mon oncle)   **L'appartement** se trouve rue de la Grenouille.

14. (votre père)   **La voiture** est dans le parking.

15. (the Duponts')   Nous allons à **la soirée.**

Complétez en ajoutant l'article ou l'adjectif possessif, selon le cas. Ajoutez une seconde phrase personnelle.

EXEMPLE

Anne se brosse (dents). Et vous?

Anne se brosse *les* dents. **Moi, je *me* brosse *les* dents après chaque repas.**

16. Anne se lave (mains et figure). Et vous?

17. Il a (chapeau sur tête). Et vous?

18. Le professeur a (main dans poche). Et vous?

19. Marie a (yeux bleus). Et vous?

20. Alexandre a (cheveux blonds). Et vous?

---

[6] Répétez la préposition **à** ou **de** avec chaque nom.

Mise en œuvre 3 F

Révision: Emploi du partitif

Combinez tous les éléments de chaque problème en une seule phrase.

1. A la pharmacie / j'ai acheté / savon / dentifrice / brosse à dents
2. Au marché j'ai acheté / poires / pommes / laitue (*f.*)
3. Au grand magasin j'ai acheté / chemises / chaussures / pantalons (*m.*)
4. J'aime / viande / petits pois / café
5. Au restaurant j'ai commandé / viande / petits pois / café

4

Expressions de quantité
mettre, prendre

4.1 Adverbs of quantity using *de* alone

The following adverbs of quantity require **de** before the following noun. No article or contraction is used; it does not matter whether the noun is singular or plural:

assez de	*enough*	trop de	*too much, too many*
beaucoup de	*many, much*	peu de[1]	*very little, very few*
pas mal de	*many, much*	combien de [N][2]	*how many [N]*

Il a **assez d'**argent.	*He has enough money.*
Ils ont **beaucoup de** livres.	*They have a lot of books.*
J'ai **pas mal de** travail à faire.	*I have a lot of work to do.*
Il a **trop de** travail.	*He has too much work.*
Combien de disques as-tu?	*How many records do you have?*

[1] Note that **un peu de** means *a little.* Contrast the following:
　　J'ai **peu d'**argent.　*I have very little money.*
　　J'ai **un peu d'**argent.　*I have a little money.*
[2] The notation [N] indicates that a noun would be placed in this location.

4.2   Specific measures use *de* alone

When a specific measure such as a quart, a kilo, a pound, a slice, etc. is used, **de** is used *without an article* (and therefore *without a contraction*) before the noun. This is the same as English usage.

un **kilo de** pommes	*a kilo^3 of apples*
une **tasse de** café	*a cup of coffee*
dix **litres d'**essence	*ten liters of gasoline*
une **bouteille de** vin	*a bottle of wine*
une **grappe de** raisin	*a bunch of grapes*
un **morceau de** fromage	*a piece of cheese*
une **tranche de** pain	*a slice of bread*

4.3   Repetition of *de* for extension of quantity to another noun

An adverb of quantity may modify several nouns that follow it, without repetition of the adverb itself. By repeating just the preposition **de,** the previously mentioned adverb remains in effect:

Il a **beaucoup de** disques et **beaucoup de** livres. *becomes*
Il a **beaucoup de** disques et **de** livres.
He has lots of records and books.

Combien de frères et **de** sœurs avez-vous?
How many brothers and sisters do you have?

4.4   Exceptions: plusieurs (*several*) and quelques (*a few*)

These two expressions of quantity are followed directly by the noun modified, without an article or **de:**

Jeanne a **plusieurs dictionnaires.**
Jean has several dictionaries.

Elle a **quelques disques** classiques.
She has a few classical albums.

---

^{3} Ten kilo(gramme)s are figured as 22 pounds. The demi-kilo (half-kilo) is the French **livre** (*f.*), or a pound and one-tenth.

4.5   *quelque chose de* [adj.], *rien de* [adj.] *something, nothing*

These expressions are followed by an adjective in the masculine singular form:

Voici **quelque chose de nouveau!**
Here is something new!

Je **ne** vois **rien d'intéressant** dans le journal.
I don't see anything interesting in the paper.

Mise en œuvre 4 A _____

Expressions de quantité

Faites une phrase complète, en combinant l'expression de quantité de la liste A avec le nom de la liste B. Utilisez le verbe qui convient et ajoutez quelques mots pour compléter l'idée.

EXEMPLE

(**beaucoup**)   château / leçon / animal

Il y a **beaucoup de châteaux** en France.

Nous avons **beaucoup de leçons** à préparer aujourd'hui.

J'ai vu **beaucoup d'animaux** au jardin zoologique.

A	B
1. **beaucoup**	château / leçon / animal / vin
2. **assez**	café / fruit / travail / temps
3. **trop**	monde[4] / travail / voiture / impôt[5]
4. **peu**	argent / voyage / difficulté / nouvelle
5. **plusieurs**	solution / problème / rapide / ordinateur
6. **un kilo**	pommes / tomates / sucre / charbon
7. **deux bouteilles**	vin / bière / coca / eau de vie[6]
8. **quelques**	ami / étudiante / problème / billets
9. **un peu**	essence / encre / café / difficulté
10. **une livre**	beurre / viande / raisin / thé

[4] **le monde** = *people*
[5] **un impôt** = *tax*
[6] **une eau de vie** = *brandy*

Mise en œuvre 4 B _____

Expressions de quantité

A. Répondez aux questions au sujet de Michel en employant une des expressions de quantité de la liste à droite, sans duplication.

Michel est vedette de cinéma. Il compose des chansons et il danse.

1. Est-ce qu'il a des maisons?	assez
2. Il a des voitures?	beaucoup
3. Il gagne de l'argent?	énormément
4. Il a des animaux familiers?	juste assez
5. Il a des gants blancs?	peu
6. Il a des amis?	plusieurs
7. Est-ce qu'il dit beaucoup en public?	très peu
8. Connaît-il d'autres chanteurs?	quantité

B. Désignation de quantités par catégorie. Demandez à un autre individu s'il possède la chose qui se trouve dans la liste A. Utilisez le partitif. L'autre répond en choisissant l'expression de quantité qui convient dans la liste B.

EXEMPLE

raisin—Tu as *du* raisin?
    —Mais oui, j'ai **une grappe** *de* **raisin.**

A	B
1. fromage	un demi
2. essence	une grappe
3. pain	trois litres
4. eau minérale	une tasse
5. viande	un verre
6. café	un kilo
7. croissants	une boîte
8. bière	un mètre
9. pommes de terre	une tranche
10. bananes	un morceau
	une bouteille
	une douzaine

Mise en œuvre 4 C

Une entrevue avec une vedette

Mettons que vous êtes journaliste, et que vous posez plusieurs questions à une vedette de cinéma[7] parce que vous préparez un article à son sujet pour votre revue. Votre voisin(e) en classe jouera le rôle de vedette.

À tour de rôle, posez à la vedette une question susceptible d'une réponse contenant un adverbe de quantité. Employez les verbes signalés (ou d'autres si vous voulez). La vedette répondra en employant une expression de quantité ou l'équivalent, en ajoutant quelque détail intéressant pour les fanatiques d'Hollywood.

JOURNALISTE: Combien de voitures avez-vous?

VEDETTE: J'ai six voitures: cinq Rolls et une Benz.

JOURNALISTE: Est-ce que vous gagnez beaucoup d'argent?

VEDETTE: Mais oui, je gagne pas mal d'argent. Mais je ne suis pas riche: je n'ai que treize millions de dollars.

Si la vedette réplique négativement, il faut qu'elle explique.

JOURNALISTE: Combien d'éléphants avez-vous à la maison?

VEDETTE: Vous rigolez[8]! Bien entendu, je n'ai pas d'éléphants à la maison. Mais je connais un chanteur pop qui a une girafe.

SUJETS

1. ami(e)s célèbres
2. maisons (posséder)
3. disques classiques
4. disques rock (produire)
5. investissements
6. assister aux concerts
7. animaux familiers
8. voyages à l'étranger
9. lettres des fanatiques
10. chevaux (dans l'écurie)
11. argent (dépenser)
12. casinos / boîtes de nuit

---

[7] **la vedette** = *movie star*. Since this is a feminine noun, the pronoun **elle** refers to a star of either gender.

[8] **rigoler** = *to kid, to joke*

VERBES IRRÉGULIERS *mettre* ET *prendre*

4.6   mettre (*to put*)

Several verbs conjugated in the same way are shown in section 4.8.

PRÉSENT	je **mets**	nous **mettons**
	tu **mets**	vous **mettez**
	il **met**	ils **mettent**

IMPARFAIT   STEM: **mett-** from present tense form 4.
Autrefois ma sœur **mettait** la table.

PASSÉ COMPOSÉ   PAST PARTICIPLE: **mis**   AUXILIARY VERB: **avoir**
Hier **j'ai mis** une heure à faire mes devoirs.

PASSÉ SIMPLE   STEM: **m-** + **is** system of endings.
Il **mit** ses livres sur la table.

FUTUR   FC STEM: **mettr-** (+ future endings)
Demain je **me mettrai** en route pour Nice.

CONDITIONNEL   FC STEM: **mettr-** (+ imperfect endings)
Si j'avais le temps je **mettrais** cette lettre à la poste.

SUBJONCTIF   STEM: **mett-** (1-stem verb)

que je **mette**	que nous **mettions**
que tu **mettes**	que vous **mettiez**
qu'il **mette**	qu'ils **mettent**

Je doute **qu'il se mette en colère.**
I doubt that he will get angry.

NOTE: Though an irregular verb, **mettre** follows regular formation for the **imparfait, futur, subjonctif** and **conditionnel**.

4.7   Idioms using *mettre*

Notice the following special uses of this verb:

mettre la table	*to set the table*
mettre [TIME] à [INF]	*to take* [AMOUNT OF TIME] *to* [DO SOMETHING]
mettre une lettre à la poste	*to mail a letter*

se mettre à [INFINITIVE][9] to begin to [DO SOMETHING]

se mettre en route (pour [N]) to set out (for [PLACE])

se mettre en colère (contre)[10] to get angry (at [PERSON])

Ma mère met la table.

Mettez cette lettre à la poste, s'il vous plaît.

Claude **se met à préparer** le déjeuner.

Le chauffeur **se mit en colère** contre l'agent.

J'ai mis trois heures **à composer** cet essai.

4.8   Verbs conjugated like *mettre*

The following verbs are merely compounds of **mettre**. By learning **mettre**, you automatically know the following compounds:

permettre (à [P] **de** [I]) *to permit* [PERSON] *to* [DO SOMETHING]

promettre (à [P **de** [I]) *to promise* [PERSON] *to* [DO SOMETHING]

remettre [N] à [P] *to give* [SOMETHING] *to* [SOMEONE]

transmettre [N] *to transmit* [SOMETHING]

NOTE: It is important to retain the word-order as indicated in the above formulas. The **à** and **de** expressions must appear in the order shown. There are similar indicators in the vocabulary to guide you.

Le professeur **permet aux** étudiants **de chanter** en classe.
The teacher allows the students to sing in class.

J'ai **promis** à mon père **d'étudier** dur.
I promised my father to study hard.

Les élèves **ont remis** leurs copies au professeur.
The pupils handed in their exercises to the teacher.

Direct and indirect object pronouns [6.3, 7.3] may be substituted. In the first example **aux étudiants** may be replaced by the indirect object pronoun **leur**:

Le professeur **leur** permet de chanter en classe.

In the third example, both direct and indirect object pronouns may be substituted:

Les élèves **les lui** ont remises. [AGREEMENT 9.4].
     INDIRECT OBJECT (au professeur)
    DIRECT OBJECT (les copies)

---

[9] Se mettre à = commencer à
[10] se mettre en colère (contre) = se fâcher (avec)

Mise en œuvre 4 D

Le verbe irrégulier *mettre*

Révision des adverbes temporels:

demain   *tomorrow*
aujourd'hui   *today*
hier   *yesterday*
  la semaine passée   *last week*
  la semaine prochaine   *next week*
   autrefois   *in the past, formerly*
   maintenant ⎫
   en ce moment⎬   *now*
   à présent   ⎭

Récrivez les phrases suivantes en ajoutant l'expression entre parenthèses. Mettez le verbe au temps qui convient. (Review the imperfect [13] and passé composé [9].)

EXEMPLES

   (demain)   Jeanne **met** la table.
            Jeanne **mettra** la table *demain.*
   (autrefois) Papa me **permet** de conduire la voiture.
            Autrefois papa me **permettait** de conduire la voiture.

  1. (demain)   Elle **se met au** travail.
  2. (hier)   Paul **mettra** votre lettre **à la poste.**
  3. (autrefois)   Je **mets** toujours une heure à déjeuner.
  4. (demain)   Nous **nous mettons en route** pour Chartres.
  5. (en ce moment)   **J'ai mis** mes devoirs sur le bureau.
  6. (hier)   Nous **remettons** ces devoirs au professeur.
  7. (la semaine passée) Nous **promettons de** travailler dur.
  8. (hier)   Ils **mettent** deux heures à faire le voyage.
  9. (autrefois)   Je **mets** la table pour ma famille.
10. (hier)   Je **permets** à mon camarade **de** conduire ma voiture.

Mise en œuvre 4 E

Emploi pratique des verbes de la famille de *mettre.*

Répondez à la question. Ajoutez ensuite une seconde phrase pour expliquer votre réponse.

EXEMPLE

Mettez-vous longtemps à faire votre travail?

Mais oui, je **mets** deux heures à faire mon travail.

Les exercices sont intéressants, vous savez.

1. Combien de temps mettez-vous à écrire un thème français?
2. Est-ce que vous remettez vos devoirs à temps tous les jours?
3. Le professeur permet-il aux étudiants de chanter en classe?
4. À quelle heure vous mettez-vous en route pour votre premier cours?
5. Est-ce que le professeur se met quelquefois en colère?
6. Avez-vous promis à quelqu'un de bien travailler ce semestre?
7. En rentrant à la maison où mettez-vous vos livres?
8. À quelle heure vous mettez-vous à étudier le soir?

4.9   Verbe irrégulier *prendre* (*to take*)

Several verbs conjugated in the same way are shown in section 4.12.

PRÉSENT

je **prends**	nous **prenons**
tu **prends**	vous **prenez**
il **prend**	ils **prennent**

} NO **-d** IN PLURAL

⬆ —— NOTICE DOUBLE **nn** IN FORM 6

IMPARFAIT   STEM: **pren-** from present tense form 4.
D'habitude nous **prenions** quelque chose à minuit.

PASSÉ COMPOSÉ   PAST PARTICIPLE: **pris**   AUXILIARY VERB: (**avoir**)
Hier **j'ai pris** le métro pour aller en ville.

PASSÉ SIMPLE   STEM: **pr** + **is** system of endings.
Il **prit** les livres qui étaient sur la table.

FUTURE   FC STEM: **prendr-** (+ future endings)
Demain je **prendrai** l'avion pour Nice.

CONDITIONNEL   FC STEM: **prendr-** (+ imperfect endings)
S'il pleuvait **je prendrais** mon parapluie.

SUBJONCTIF   STEMS: **prenn-** / **pren-** (2-stem verb)

que je **prenne**	que nous **prenions**
que tu **prennes**	que vous **preniez**
qu'il **prenne**	qu'ils **prennent**

Je doute **qu'il prenne** les billets.

I doubt that he will buy the tickets.

4.10   Idioms using *prendre*

prendre un billet (pour [N])	to buy[11] a ticket (for [N])
prendre la décision (de [I])	to make the decision (to [DO SOMETHING])
prendre la parole	to take the floor (to speak)
prendre quelque chose	to have a snack
prendre garde (de [I])/ (à [N])	to be careful, to watch out for
prendre le petit déjeuner	to have breakfast

Jacques **a pris les billets** au guichet.
Jacques bought the tickets at the ticket window.

Allons **prendre quelque chose.**
Let's go have a bite to eat.

Prends garde de ne pas tomber.
Be careful not to fall.

Prenez garde aux voitures.
Look out for the cars.

4.11   Meaning distinctions: *to take*

Be careful to avoid using **prendre** when the English *to take* occurs in the following expressions:

to *take* a course	**suivre** un cours (vt 28)
to *take* a walk	**faire** une promenade (16.3)
to *take* (AN HOUR) to do something	**mettre** (une heure) à (I) (4.7)
to *take* (PERSON) somewhere	**emmener°** (P) (19.11)
to *take* (A THING) somewhere	**emporter** (N)

EXEMPLES

Je **suis** un cours de psychologie.
I am taking a psychology course.

J'**ai mis** deux heures à faire mes devoirs.
I took two hours to do my homework.

Mme Durand **a emmené** les enfants au parc.
Mrs. Durand took the children to the park.

Ce client **a emporté** mon stylo à bille.
That customer took my ball-point pen.

---

[11] **Prendre un billet** is preferred to **acheter un billet.**

4.12   Compounds of *prendre*

The following verbs are compounds of **prendre** using prefixes. They are conjugated in the same way as the basic verb.

*app*rendre [N] à [P]	*to learn* [N]; *to teach* [N] *to* [P]
*com*prendre	*to understand; to include*
*entre*prendre	*to undertake*
*re*prendre	*to take back*
*sur*prendre	*to surprise*

Nous **apprenons** des verbes irréguliers en français.

Le professeur **a appris** une chanson **aux** étudiants.

Il **a repris** nos compositions.

Mise en œuvre 4 F _____

prendre, mettre

Complétez les questions en utilisant **prendre, mettre** ou un des composés de ces verbes, selon le cas. Ensuite répondez aux questions.

EXEMPLE

Les touristes _____ le petit déjeuner à l'hôtel. Et toi?

Les touristes **prennent** le petit déjeuner à l'hôtel.

Moi, je **prends** le petit déjeuner chez moi.

1. Jean est toujours généreux: il _____ les billets. Et toi?
2. François n'hésite pas à _____ la parole quand il a une idée. Et toi?
3. Après mes cours j'ai envie de _____ quelque chose. Et ton camarade de chambre?
4. Mon ami _____ vingt minutes à lire ce chapitre. Et toi?
5. Après le petit déjeuner je me _____ en route pour la bibliothèque. Et toi?
6. Quand j'arrive en classe je _____ ma place tout de suite. Et votre ami(e)?
7. Le professeur _____ aux étudiants à résoudre un problème en maths. Et le professeur d'anglais?
8. Ils _____ l'explication du professeur. Et toi?
9. L'instituteur se _____ en colère si les élèves ne _____ la leçon. Et les parents?
10. Georges _____ une demi-heure à déjeuner. Et toi?

Reflets _____

l'Informatique

La machine la plus importante depuis l'invention de la presse d'imprimerie est sans doute l'ordinateur. La machine à calculer du philosophe Blaise Pascal au dix-septième siècle et la machine de Charles Babbage au dix-huitième siècle ont beaucoup contribué au développement de l'ordinateur. Cependant c'est à Johann von Neumann de l'université de Princeton que l'on doit la première machine comprenant une mémoire intégrale, essentielle au fonctionnement des ordinateurs d'aujourd'hui.

Pour faire marcher l'ordinateur et ses périphériques il faut un **logiciel,** un ensemble de programmes nécessaire pour effectuer un traitement sur un ordinateur. L'ordinateur comprend un **tableau de bord,** un **moniteur,** et des périphériques tels qu'une **imprimante** et un **modem.** Un très grand ordinateur central s'appelle un **ordinateur universel.**

La science qui a pour but les ordinateurs et leur usage s'appelle **l'informatique.**

Thème

1. Computer science is essential for today's business.
2. There are many computers in our Paris office.
3. The software includes programs for word processing and data processing.
4. There is a hard disk, but there are several diskettes on the manager's desk.
5. Our boss uses his computer for desktop publishing; he writes a newsletter.
6. My roommate is taking a data-processing course at the university.
7. He has spent several days learning something important about (on the subject of) scientific applications.
8. Most of the English students work in the laboratory, where they use word-processing programs for their reports and compositions.
9. The university library uses computers for the card catalogue, and to locate books that are in other libraries.
10. Be careful not to erase the diskettes.

VOCABULAIRE

les affaires *m.pl.*	*business*
le fichier	*card catalogue*
l'informatique	*computer science*
le traitement des données	*data processing*
l'édition électronique *f.*	*desktop publishing*

la disquette	*diskette*
effacer	*erase, to*
essentiel,-le	*essential*
le disque fixe	*hard disk*
retrouver	*locate, to*
le gérant	*manager*
le bulletin d'informations	*newsletter*
la programmation	*programming*
le rapport	*report*
le logiciel *m.*	*software*
universitaire	*university* adj.
le traitement de texte	*word processing*

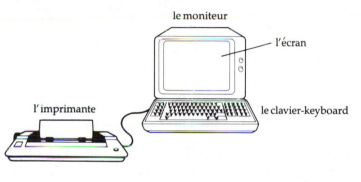

le moniteur

l'écran

l'imprimante

le clavier-keyboard

Ordinateur

5

Accord de l'adjectif
Place de l'adjectif
C'est ou *Il est*

ACCORD DE L'ADJECTIF

An adjective helps define the size, shape, color, or other qualities of a noun. In English the adjective usually precedes the noun it qualifies. In French, on the contrary, the usual place of an adjective is *following* the noun, with the exception of about fifteen common ones.

In dictionaries (and in the end vocabulary of this book) you will find the adjective listed in its masculine singular form. The notation **grand,-e** means that the masculine singular form is **grand,** that **-e** is added to make the feminine form **grande.** If the feminine or the plural is formed in an irregular way, it will be indicated.

5.1   Agreement in gender and number

An adjective must agree in gender and number with the noun it qualifies. There are usually four forms of the adjective, so that it can be made to take on the same gender and number as the noun:

	MASCULINE	FEMININE
SINGULAR	intéressant	intéressante
PLURAL	intéressants	intéressantes

The masculine singular form (*m.s.*) is converted to feminine singular (*f.s.*) by adding -**e.** Either masculine *or* feminine singular is made plural by adding -**s.**

The main exceptions to this rule are: (1) adjectives already ending in -**e** in the masculine singular form (**facile, jeune,** etc.), to which nothing is added for the feminine singular; (2) adjectives ending in a consonant which is doubled before adding the feminine ending -**e** (**actuel, actuelle**); (3) adjectives ending in -**er** and -**ier,** which add a grave accent before adding the feminine -**e** (**dernier, dernière; premier, première**); and (4) adjectives ending in -**x** in the basic (*m.s.*) form, which remain the same in the masculine plural, but which change -**x** to -**se** in the feminine (**heureux, heureuse**).

Pronunciation note: In spoken French, it is helpful to learn the feminine form first. Then, by dropping the final consonant sound, the sound of the masculine form is obtained (compare the phonetic transcriptions below):

FEMININE	MASCULINE	DROPPED SOUND
évidente [evidãt]	évident [evidã]	[t]
curieuse [kyrjǿz]	curieux [kyrjǿ]	[z]
étroite [etrwat]	étroit [etrwa]	[t]
blanche [blãʃ]	blanc [blã]	[ʃ]

There are a number of exceptions to this general principle of pronunciation. For example **bonne, bon** [bɔn] [bɔ̃], **brune, brun** [bʀyn] [bʀœ̃] in which nasalization occurs in the masculine form; and **dernière, dernier, première, premier** with the pronunciations [jɛr] (*f.s.*), [je] (*m.s.*).

5.2   Adjectives ending in *-e* in the masculine singular

These adjectives have only one pronunciation, and only two written forms.

	MASCULINE	FEMININE
SINGULAR	facile	facile
PLURAL	faciles	faciles

Here are some common adjectives of this type (the dagger indicates adjectives which *precede* the noun modified):

facile	*easy*	**difficile**	*difficult, hard*
riche	*rich*	**pauvre**	*poor*
agréable	*pleasant*	**ridicule**	*ridiculous*

jeune†	young	admirable	admirable
malade	ill	faible	weak
moderne	modern	utile	useful
même†	same	autre†	other
célèbre	famous	possible	possible
rouge	red	jaune	yellow
large†	wide	politique	political

5.3   Adjectives ending in *-l, -n, -et* and *-s*

With these adjectives the final consonant is doubled before adding **-e** to form the feminine.

actuel, actuelle	*current, present*
cruel, cruelle	*cruel*
naturel, naturelle	*natural*
spirituel, spirituelle	*witty*
nul, nulle† [+NOUN]	*no, not any* [N]
ancien, ancienne	*ancient; former* [5.11]
bon, bonne†	*good*
net, nette	*neat, clean*
bas, basse	*low*
épais, épaisse	*thick*

5.4   Adjectives ending in *-er*

These adjectives change **-er** to **-ère** for the feminine.

premier, première†	*first*
dernier, dernière†	*last*
léger, légère†	*light, slight*
cher, chère	*dear, expensive*

5.5   Adjectives ending in *-x*

These adjectives usually change the **-x** to **-s**, then add **-e** for the feminine.

heureux, heureuse	*happy, fortunate*
généreux, généreuse	*generous*

jaloux, jalouse	*jealous*
BUT **vieux, vieille†**	*old*
doux, douce	*sweet, gentle*

5.6   Alternate masculine adjectives, irregular forms

A.   Alternate masculine adjectives.

Bel, vieil, nouvel [6.01] are *masculine singular* only, and are used (instead of **beau, vieux, nouveau**) only in front of a masculine singular noun beginning with a *vowel* sound. These alternate forms are pronounced just like the feminine forms.

MASCULINE

SINGULAR	PLURAL
un **bel** arbre	de **beaux** arbres
un **vieil** homme	de **vieux** hommes
un **nouvel** avion	de **nouveaux** avions

Notice that the *regular* plural form is used with plural nouns, regardless of the sound they begin with.

B.   Irregular forms.

neuf, neuve	*(brand) new*	**ma voiture** *neuve*	*my new car*
blanc, blanche	*white*	**la robe** *blanche*	*the white dress*

5.7   Demonstrative adjective *ce*

The demonstrative adjective **ce** (**cet, cette, ces**) precedes the noun. Like **beau, nouveau,** and **vieux,** it has an alternate masculine form (**cet**) for use before a masculine singular noun beginning with a vowel sound (**cet arbre, cet homme**):

	MASCULINE	FEMININE	MEANING
SINGULAR	ce (cet + vowel)	cette	*this, that*
PLURAL	ces	ces	*these, those*

Ce livre est très intéressant.

Cet homme habite à Lyon.

Cette pièce est très longue.

Ces garçons et **ces jeunes filles** habitent à Genève.

The appropriate form of **ce** is repeated with each noun, just as the article or posses-sive adjective must be repeated:

> **Ce** sofa et **ce** fauteuil sont bleus.
>
> **Ce** garçon et **cette** jeune fille sont heureux.
>
> **Ces** hommes et **ces** femmes dansent bien.

5.8   Suffixes *-ci, -là*

Some ambiguity exists with such a phrase as **ce livre,** which may mean either ***this book*** or ***that book.*** In conversation it would be clear from the speaker's distance from the book. To eliminate doubt in writing, add a suffix to the noun (attached with a hyphen).

-ci (from **ici**)	*this*	ce livre-**ci**	*this book*
-là	*that*	ce livre-**là**	*that book*
		cette maison-**là**	*that house*

J'aime **ce livre-ci,** mais je n'aime pas **ce livre-là.**
*I like **this** book, but I don't like **that** book.*

Cette maison-ci est chère; **cette maison-là** est bon marché.
***This** house is expensive; **that** house is cheap.*

Notice that without these suffixes, there would be no way to distinguish between the identical nouns (**ce livre . . . ce livre**).

Mise en œuvre 5 A

Accord de l'adjectif

Employez l'adjectif entre parenthèses avec les noms qui le suivent.

EXEMPLE

(intelligent)   un homme / une femme / des enfants
C'est un homme intelligent.
C'est une femme intelligente.
Ce sont des enfants intelligents.

1. (intéressant)   un article / une peinture / des livres / des personnes
2. (neuf)   un livre / une robe / une voiture / des maisons
3. (actuel)   la situation / son emploi / le gouvernement

4. (spirituel)   un homme / une femme / un ouvrage / des auteurs
5. (cher)   un livre / une maison / un hôtel / des voitures
6. (heureux)   un étudiant / une jeune fille / un événement / des femmes
7. (blanc)   un éléphant / une rose / une voiture / des maisons
8. (facile)   un devoir / une leçon / une solution / des examens
9. (étroit)   une rue / un chemin / une porte / des portes
10. (large[1])   une salle / un boulevard / une avenue

PLACE DE L'ADJECTIF

5.9   Preceding adjectives

Most French adjectives *follow* the noun they modify. The adjectives in the list below are exceptions because they usually precede the noun, as in English. Learn them well, because they are very commonly used, and because if you are very familiar with this list, you will know that any adjective that does *not* appear on it will normally come *after* the noun.

To aid in memorization, these adjectives are grouped according to meaning (similar, opposite, or related meanings) insofar as possible. When two forms are shown, the first is the "basic" *m.s.* form, and the second is the *f.s.* form. If only one form is given, the masculine and feminine forms are identical. Notice the four adjectives which have an alternate masculine form when used before a vowel sound:

PRECEDING ADJECTIVES

bon, bonne	*good*	**mauvais, mauvaise**	*bad*
grand, grande	*big*	**petit, petite**	*small*
long, longue	*long*	**court, courte**	*short*
haut, haute	*high*	**beau (bel), belle**	*beautiful, fine*
joli, jolie	*pretty*		
jeune	*young*	**vieux (vieil), vieille**	*old*
nouveau (nouvel), nouvelle	*new*		

Not grouped by meaning are these preceding adjectives:

ce (cet), cette [5.7]	*this, that*
autre, un(e) autre	*other, another*

[1] **large** = *wide*

même [N]	*same* [N]
large	*wide*
propre [N]	*own* [N] (*my **own** book*)
cher, chère	*dear*
premier, première	*first* (all numbers precede)
dernier, dernière	*last*

EXEMPLES

Elle a une **nouvelle**[2] secrétaire.	*She has a new (= another) secretary.*
J'ai une **nouvelle**[2] voiture.	*I have a new car.*
C'est une **longue** rue.	*It's a long street.*
Voici ma **dernière** cigarette.	*Here is my last cigarette.*
On a construit un **autre** pont.	*Another bridge has been built.*

INTERVENING ADJECTIVE: **des** becomes **de.**[3]

When an adjective from the above list is inserted into a noun phrase beginning with **des,** then **des** becomes **de:**

Jacques a **des disques.**

Jacques a **de** *nouveaux* disques.

Il y a **des rues** intéressantes dans le quartier.

Il y a **de** *vieilles* rues intéressantes dans le quartier.

5.10   Two adjectives with a single noun

A.   Adjectives having different places. Place each adjective in its normal position. Usually one of the adjectives will be a preceding adjective. As a result, one precedes and one follows. It is important to know the list of preceding adjectives for this reason.

un **petit** livre **rouge**	*a small red book*
une **nouvelle** revue **française**	*a new French magazine*

It is possible for two or three adjectives to precede a noun, especially with **ce, même,** and **autre:**

---

[2] Notice the meanings of **nouveau: une nouvelle voiture** is a car that is new to the owner, yet may be old. It could mean *another car.* By contrast, the adjective **neuf, neuve** is a following adjective, and means *brand-new.* **Ma voiture neuve** is *my brand-new car.*

[3] Sometimes **des** is tolerated, but here we use the rule indicated.

cet **autre jeune** homme	*that other young man*
la **même petite** voiture	*the same small car*

When there are two or more preceding adjectives, the ones likely to be closest to the noun are **jeune, vieux,** and **nouveau.** The adjectives **même** and **autre** are farthest from the noun.

Certain noun groups are considered to be a single unit: **les petits pois** (*peas*) and **la jeune fille** (*girl*).

B.   Two following adjectives. If there are two adjectives that both follow the noun, they are joined by **et** if they are similar in nature, or by **mais** if they contrast:

une femme **charmante** *et* **spirituelle**

un homme **riche** *mais* **malheureux.**

5.11   Word order and alternate meanings

Certain adjectives may be placed either before or after the noun modified. Care must be taken with these adjectives, because the meaning differs depending on the position. The usual position is marked with a star [★]:

ADJECTIVE	MEANING BEFORE NOUN	MEANING AFTER NOUN
ancien, -ne	*former*	*old, ancient*★
brave	*good, worthy, fine*	*brave*★
certain, -e	*particular*	*unquestionable*★
cher, chère	*dear* (cherished)★	*expensive*
dernier, dernière	*last* (of a series), *final*★	*last* (most recent)
grand, -e[4]	*great, large*★	*tall*
même	*same*★	*very, itself*
pauvre	*poor* (unfortunate)	*poor* (no money)★
propre	*own*	*clean*★

Compare the following examples:

mon **ancien** professeur	*my old (former) teacher*
l'histoire **ancienne**	*ancient history*

[4] **Grand** means *great, important* only when applied to people, particularly with **un homme, une femme, un général,** etc. Otherwise **grand** simply means **big, large.**

| un **brave** garçon | *a fine boy* |
| un homme **brave** | *a brave man* |

| un **certain** monsieur | *a certain (particular) gentleman* |
| une chose **certaine** | *a sure thing* |

| ma **dernière** cigarette | *my last cigarette* |
| la semaine **dernière** | *last week* |

| un **grand** homme | *a great man* |
| un homme **grand** | *a tall man* |

| le **même** film | *the same movie* |
| le film **même** | *the film itself* |

| le **pauvre** malade | *the poor patient (we're sorry for him)* |
| l'étudiant **pauvre** | *the poor student (no money)* |

| ma **propre** chambre | *my own room* |
| une chambre **propre** | *a clean room* |

Mise en œuvre 5 B

Accord et place de l'adjectif

Combinez l'adjectif (ou les adjectifs) entre parenthèses avec les noms de la liste. Commencez par **C'est** ou par **Ce sont**:

EXEMPLES

(petit)   une maison / un chat / des voitures

C'est une **petite** maison.

C'est un **petit** chat.

Ce sont de(s) **petites** voitures.

1. (mauvais)   un moment / une note / des films
2. (facile)   une leçon / un travail / des exercices
3. (beau)   un château / un arbre / une jeune fille

4. (vieux)   un soldat / un ami / une dame / un homme
5. (ce)   garçon / dame / étudiant / professeurs
6. (même, jeune)   le professeur / la femme / les gens
7. (long)   un boulevard / une rue / des exercices / un passage
8. (étroit)   une porte / une rue / des fenêtres
9. (grand)   un appartement / une maison / des familles
10. (dernier)   le paragraphe / ma cigarette / l'exemple

Mise en œuvre 5 C

Ordre de deux adjectifs

Composez une phrase en commençant par **C'est** ou par **Ce sont**, incorporant les deux adjectifs selon l'exemple ci-dessous.

EXEMPLES

(autre, intéressant)   un livre / une nouvelle (*news*)

C'est un **autre** livre **intéressant.**

Ce sont **d'autres nouvelles intéressantes.**

(même, blanc)   la maison

C'est la **même** maison **blanche.**

1. (même, spirituel)   la femme / l'homme / les professeurs
2. (agréable, petit)   une soirée / une maison / un appartement
3. (beau, intelligent)   un chien / un homme / une dame
4. (vieux, riche)   un monsieur / un homme / une personne
5. (petit, blanc)   des maisons / des chats / une voiture
6. (court mais difficile)   un exercice / une leçon / des instructions
7. (pauvre mais heureux)   un homme / des jeunes gens / un enfant
8. (sympathique et spirituel) un ami / une amie / un conférencier

EMPLOI DE *c'est* OU DE *il est*

Autotest: Est-ce *C'est* ou *Il est?*

C'EST, IL EST OU ELLE EST . . . ?	COVER THIS COLUMN AND TRY THE PROBLEM.	
	SOLUTION	REFERENCE
petite	**Elle** est petite.	5.13 A
Jacques	**C'est** Jacques.	5.12 A
moi	**C'est** moi.	5.12 A
médecin	**Il** est médecin.	5.13 B
facile à faire	**C'est** facile à faire.	5.12 C
facile de parler anglais	**Il** est facile de parler anglais.	5.13 C
petit livre	**C'est** un petit livre.	5.12 B
un bon professeur	**C'est** un bon professeur.	5.12 B
un cahier	**C'est** un cahier.	5.12 B

5.12   Summary of uses of *C'est*

When the verb is **est** (or **sont**), use **C'est** (or **Ce sont**) if what follows is a (A) proper name, (B) modified noun, or (C) dependent sentence with an adjective or adverb.

A.   Proper name or disjunctive pronoun:

C'est **Denis.**

C'est **Monsieur Legrand.**

C'est **moi.**

B.   Modified noun or noun-adjective group. Note that even *articles* alone count as modifiers:

C'est *une petite* voiture.

C'est *un* match *intéressant.*

C.   Dependent sentence. A *dependent* sentence is one that has no meaning without a preceding statement.

> **C'** is for *Contingent* on a foregoing sentence: **C'est . . .**

[ouvrir cette grande porte]   C'est **difficile à faire.**[5]

[J'ai gagné le match!]   C'est **bien!** C'est **formidable!**

　　　　　　　　　　　　└─DEPENDS ON PREVIOUS STATEMENT FOR MEANING

5.13 Summary of uses of *Il est* and *Elle est*

Use a regular subject pronoun when a form of **être** is followed by (A) an adjective referring to one specific noun previously mentioned, (B) the name of a religion, profession, nationality or political preference without a modifier, (C) a self-sufficient sentence, or (D) a prepositional phrase.

A. An adjective alone[6] having a specific noun antecedent:

La table. **Elle** est **ronde.**

Voilà Jean.   **Il** est **charmant.**

Tu vois Marie là-bas? **Elle** est **très**[6] **intelligente.**

B. An unmodified name of a *profession, nationality, religion* or *political persuasion:*

Voilà M. Sequin. **Il** est **ingénieur.**[7]　　　[PROFESSION]

J'ai parlé à Sven. **Il** est **suédois.**[8]　　　[NATIONALITÉ]

Tu connais Mme Jacotin? **Elle** est **catholique.**[9]　　[RELIGION]

Voilà Georges. **Il** n'est pas **communiste.**　　　[POLITIQUE]

Ces garçons? **Ils** sont **étudiants.**　　　[MÉTIER]

C. An independent sentence. These are self-contained, and do not depend on a previous context for meaning.

I is for **Independent:** Il est . . .

Il est **difficile** d'*apprendre* le chinois.

Il est **amusant** de *jouer* aux dames.[10]

D. A prepositional phrase:

Elles sont **devant la porte.**

---

[5] If this statement were made in isolation, the question «*Qu'*est-ce qui est difficile à faire?» would arise, because the statement is not self-sufficient, but depends on a previous statement like the one shown in brackets.

[6] The word **très** may be included without violating this principle.

[7] BUT: C'est *un* ingénieur *extraordinaire.* [5.12 B]

[8] BUT: C'est *un* Suédois très connu. [5.12 B]

[9] BUT: C'est *une bonne* catholique. [5.12 B]

[10] **dames** = *checkers*

5.14 Comparative chart

The information from the two preceding sections is summarized in this table.

C'est[11] + MODIFIER + NOUN	Il est[12] + ADJECTIVE
C'est **une table**.	Il est **petit**. Elle est **petite**.
C'est **mon** père.	Il est **sympathique**.
Ce sont **nos amis**.	Elles sont **charmantes**.

	+ PROFESSION, NATIONALITY, RELIGION *"Honorary" Adjectives*
C'est **un bon** catholique.	Il est **catholique**. RELIGION
C'est **un** médecin **renommé**.	Il est **médecin**. PROFESSION
Ce sont **de riches** Américains.	Ils sont **américains**. NATIONALITY
C'est **un ancien** communiste.	Il est **communiste**. POLITICS

C'est + PROPER NOUN OR DISJUNCTIVE PRONOUN.	Il est + PREPOSITIONAL PHRASE
C'est **Robert**. C'est **lui**.	Robert. Il est **avec son frère**.
Ce sont **les Smith**. Ce sont **eux**.	La table. Elle est **dans la cuisine**.

GENERAL ANTECEDENT	SPECIFIC ANTECEDENT
[ ] C'est **bien!** (*What is?*)	[la table] Elle est **ronde**.
CONTINGENT PHRASE	INDEPENDENT PHRASE
[ ] C'est **difficile à faire**. (*What is?*)	Il est **difficile de parler russe**.

5.15 Les couleurs

Les adjectifs de couleur s'accordent en nombre et genre:

blanc, blanche	gris, grise	rose
bleu, bleue	noir, noire	jaune
brun, brune	vert, verte	rouge

[11] **C'est** or **Ce sont**.
[12] **Il est, Elle est, Ils sont, Elles sont**.

Les couleurs composées sont invariables:

une robe bleu clair[13]	un veston bleu foncé[14]
une voiture gris fer[15]	un costume[16] bleu-noir

NOTE:

un poisson rouge	*a goldfish*
un chien marron	*a brown dog*
les cheveux roux	*red hair*

Mise en œuvre 5 D _____

Bleu, blanc, rouge

Répondez aux questions suivantes.

1. Quelles sont les couleurs du drapeau français[17]?
2. De quelle couleur est le ciel?
3. De quelle couleur est le gazon[18]?
4. Quelles sont les couleurs officielles de votre université?
5. En indiquant leurs couleurs, nommez les vêtements que vous portez maintenant. (la chemise ou le chemisier, le veston, le pantalon, le jean, la jupe, la robe, le costume, le pull-over, les chaussures, la cravate, etc.)

Mise en œuvre 5 E _____

Emploi de *C'est* ou de *Il est*

Faites une phrase complète en commençant par **C'est, Ce sont, Il (Elle) est,** ou **Ils (Elles) sont.**

EXEMPLE

le facteur

C'est le facteur.

---

[13] *light blue*
[14] *dark blue*
[15] **fer** = (*steel gray*) = *iron*
[16] **costume (veston, pantalon, gilet)** *suit of clothes*
[17] The colors are named in order, starting at the flagpole.
[18] *grass*

1. mon professeur	11. mathématicien
2. une femme sportive	12. bon étudiant
3. française	13. petit chat
4. un Français	14. petit
5. un soldat allemand	15. maisons magnifiques
6. soldat	16. charmante
7. un bon catholique	17. élégants
8. intelligent	18. médecin
9. un homme très connu	19. avocat célèbre
10. très spirituelle	20. mon frère qui habite à Lyon

Mise en œuvre 5 F

C'est ou Il est

Complétez la phrase en commençant par **C'est facile (difficile) de . . .** ou par **Il est facile (difficile) de . . .** [5.12 c, 5.13 c].

EXEMPLES

voir   **C'est facile à** voir.

jouer aux cartes   **Il est facile de** jouer aux cartes.

1. flatter une personne peu intelligente
2. faire
3. comprendre cette théorie
4. comprendre
5. répondre aux questions du professeur
6. croire
7. croire que René est très intelligent
8. trouver l'entrée du métro
9. trouver
10. oublier un numéro de téléphone

Mise en œuvre 5 G

Accord des adjectifs / C'est ou Il est

Répondez aux questions suivantes selon l'exemple, en employant l'adjectif entre parenthèses une fois sans le nom, et ensuite avec le nom.

EXEMPLES

(intéressant)   Comment trouvez-vous cette pièce? / ce film?

Elle est intéressante. **C'est une** pièce **intéressante.**

Il est intéressant. **C'est un** film **intéressant.**

1. (long)   Comment trouvez-vous ces discours? / cette conférence?
2. (charmant)   Comment trouvez-vous cet appartement? / cette maison?
3. (cruel)   Que penses-tu de cette loi? / de ce juge?
4. (épais)   Comment est ce mur? / cette planche?
5. (incroyable) Comment trouvez-vous cet accident? / cette excuse?
6. (bon)   Comment est ce film? / cette pièce de théâtre?
7. (heureux)   Comment est cet étudiant? / cette étudiante?
8. (vieux)   Comment sont ces églises? / ces monuments?
9. (spirituel)   Comment trouvez-vous cet acteur? / cette actrice?
10. (large)   Comment est ce boulevard? / cette rivière?

6

Pronom complément d'objet direct
Pronom *en*

PRONOM COMPLÉMENT D'OBJET DIRECT

6.1 Identification of direct object

To determine the direct object, quote the subject and verb, then ask *what?* The noun that answers this question is the direct object. (Notice that a prepositional phrase cannot be the answer.)

> Paul rend ses devoirs au professeur.
> TEST: Paul rend (*what?*)   ANSWER: **ses devoirs** = DIRECT OBJECT

The prepositional phrase **au professeur** is an *indirect object*.

6.2 Position of the direct object pronoun (La place du pronom complément d'objet direct)

    A.   **Pronouns appear before the inflected verb.**

> Paul **rend** *ses devoirs* au professeur.
> Paul *les* **rend** au professeur.   *(Before a simple verb)*
> Paul *les* **a** rendus au professeur.   *(Before the auxiliary verb)*

B.   Before a dependent infinitive. When the meaning is most closely attached to an infinitive, the pronoun precedes the infinitive:

Nous allons **voir le professeur.**
Nous allons *le* voir.

Je commence à **comprendre la leçon.**
Je commence à *la* comprendre.

C.   Before a negative imperative. When a command is negative, the pronoun appears in the usual place, before the verb.

Ne fermez pas **les fenêtres.**
Ne *les* fermez pas.

D.   After a positive imperative. This is the only time the object pronoun follows a verb. It is attached to the verb with a hyphen.

Fermez **les fenêtres.**
Fermez-*les*.

E.   Before *voilà, voici.*

Voilà la porte.   **La voilà.** *(There it is.)*
Voici le professeur.   **Le voici.** *(Here he is.)*

6.3   Table of direct object pronouns

me (moi)*	*me*	nous	*us*
te (toi)**	*you*	vous	*you*
le (l')	*it, him*		
la (l')	*it, her*	les	*them*

* **moi** is used only after a positive imperative.

Regardez-**moi.**   Cherchez-**moi.**

When the command is negative, **me** is used before the verb.

Ne **me** regardez pas.   Ne **me** cherchez pas.

** **toi** is used only after a positive imperative. In all other cases **te** is used in front of the verb.

> Lève-**toi.**   Couche-**toi.**

6.4   Neuter direct object supplied

The neuter direct object pronoun **le** is used when the verb demands a direct object, and none is in evidence other than a general idea. It may represent a noun, an adjective, or a whole clause.

—Monsieur Dupont va arriver demain.	
—Je **le** sais.	*I know (it).*
—Êtes-vous fatigué?	
—Je **le** suis.	*I am. (I am **it**. [= tired])*
—Êtes-vous étudiant?	
—Je **le** suis.	*I am.*
—Est-elle contente?	
—Elle l'est.	*She is.*

6.5   Verbs requiring a direct object

The following verbs are followed directly by a noun in French. This contrasts with English, where a prepositional structure *(for, to, at* [N]*)* is used.

attendre [N]	*to wait **for** (= to await* [N]*)*
chercher [N]	*to look **for***
demander [N]	*to ask **for***
écouter [N]	*to listen **to***
envoyer° chercher [N]	*to send **for***
payer° [N]	*to pay (**for**)*
regarder [N]	*to look **at***

J'**attends** l'autobus.	*I am waiting **for** the bus.*
Il **cherche** son thermos.	*He is looking **for** his thermos.*
Il **demande** un journal.	*He is asking **for** a newspaper.*
Nous **écoutons** la radio.	*We are listening **to** the radio.*
Jean **paie** le repas.	*Jean is paying **for** the meal.*
Papa **a payé** le voyage.	*Dad has paid **for** the trip.*
Envoyez chercher le médecin.	*Send **for** the doctor.*
Je **regarde** la télévision.	*I am looking **at** (watching) television.*

Pronoun substitution. The direct object pronoun may replace the direct object [N]:

L'autobus? Je l'attends.	*I am waiting for it.*
Le cahier? Je le cherche.	*I am looking for it.*
Le journal? Le client le demande.	*The customer is asking for it.*
La radio? Nous l'écoutons.	*We are listening to it.*
Le repas? C'est Jean qui le paie.	*It's John who is paying for it.*

6.6   Verbs requiring a preposition

Certain verbs cannot take a direct object in French, although they can in English.

A.   Requiring *à* [N]

obéir à [N]	*to obey*	J'obéis à mon père.
jouer à [N: *game*]	*to play*	Henri joue au tennis.
plaire à [N]	*to please*	Cela plaît à ma mère.
promettre à [N]	*to promise*	Il a promis à Jean de venir.
répondre à [N]	*to answer*	Je réponds à la lettre.
ressembler à [N]	*to resemble*	Vous ressemblez à votre frère.
écrire à [N]	*to write*	J'ai écrit à mon oncle.

B.   Requiring *de* [N]:

s'apercevoir de [N]	*to perceive*	Je m'apercevais de sa timidité.
s'approcher de [N]	*to approach*	Il s'approche de la table.
douter de [N]	*to doubt*	Je doute de son succès.
se douter de [N]	*to suspect*	Je ne me doute de rien.
jouer de [N: *instrument*]	*to play*	Elle joue de la guitare.
se souvenir de [N]	*to remember*	Je me souviens de votre oncle.
se servir de [N]	*to use*	Il se sert d'un ordinateur.

Mise en œuvre 6 A

Pronom complément d'objet direct

Répondez aux questions suivantes affirmativement et ensuite, négativement, en remplaçant les mots en italique par le pronom complément d'objet direct approprié.

EXEMPLE

Comprenez-vous *cette leçon?*
Oui, je **la** comprends.   Non, je ne **la** comprends pas.

Est-ce que vous lisez *ce roman de Balzac?*
Oui, je **le** lis.   Non, je ne **le** lis pas.

1. Comprenez-vous *l'allemand?*
2. La nuit fermez-vous *toutes les fenêtres?*
3. Aimez-vous regarder *la télévision?*
4. Regardez-vous souvent *la télévision?*
5. Vos amis écoutent-ils *la musique de Gounod?*
6. Le soir demandez-vous *la permission de sortir?*
7. Est-ce que vous trouvez *cette leçon* difficile?
8. Est-ce que les étudiants visitent *le musée?*
9. Est-ce que vous cherchez *le bureau du professeur?*
10. Avez-vous *les livres pour vos cours?*
11. Êtes-vous *fatigué* après vos classes?
12. Votre chambre est-elle *agréable?*
13. Avez-vous envie de voir *le nouveau film italien?*
14. Avez-vous besoin d'étudier *la grammaire?*

Mise en œuvre 6 B

Objet direct avec l'impératif

Répétez les impératifs suivants affirmativement et négativement, en remplaçant le complément d'objet direct par le pronom approprié.

EXEMPLE

Fermez *la porte de la salle de classe.*
Fermez-**la.**   Ne **la** fermez pas.

1. Fermez *les fenêtres.*
2. Cherchez *le dictionnaire français-anglais.*
3. Visitez *la cathédrale de Notre-Dame.*
4. Prenons *la voiture de votre père.*
5. Regardons *ces étalages.*
6. Étudions *les règles de grammaire.*
7. Finissez *le travail.*

8. Accompagnons *ma mère* en ville.
9. Lisez *cet article* dans le journal.
10. Mettez *la lettre* sur la table.

PRONOM **EN**

6.7 Use

En replaces a previously mentioned noun governed by a form of **de** (**du, des, de la, de l'**). The English meaning depends upon the context.

Il arrive	**de Paris.**	Il	**en**	arrive.
Jean parle	**de la leçon.**	Il	**en**	parle.
Il voit	**des touristes.**	Il	**en**	voit.
Elle a	**des livres.**	Elle	**en**	a.
	de-PHRASE		**en**	

The various contextual meanings for the examples are, in order, (1) *from there*, (2) *about it*, (3) and (4) *some*, replacing partitives [3.7].

A.   If de + [N] represents a *thing*, the whole prepositional unit may be replaced by en before the verb.

Il s'est approché **de la table.**	He approached the table.
Il s'**en** est approché.	He approached it.
Je doute **de votre sincérité.**	I doubt your sincerity.
J'**en** doute.	I doubt it.
Je me souviens **de cette gare.**	I remember this station.
Je m'**en** souviens.	I remember it.

B.   If de + [N] represents a *person*, do not use en. Instead, retain the *de* and add the appropriate disjunctive pronoun [17.4].

Paul s'approche **de l'agent.**	Paul is approaching the policeman.
Paul s'approche **de lui.**	Paul is approaching him.
Je parle **de mon amie.**	I'm talking about my girlfriend.
Je parle **d'elle.**	I'm talking about her.

However, if the partitive *(some)* is used, **en** may replace even persons:

| Je cherche **des** clients. | I'm looking for some customers. |
| J'**en** cherche. | I'm looking for some. |

6.8   *En* required

When a French sentence ends with a *number* or *expression of quantity*, **en** is required before the verb.

Il a deux autos.	Il **en** *a* deux.	*He has **two**.*
Elle a plusieurs chats.	Elle **en** *a* plusieurs.	*She has **several**.*
Il a vu trois amis.	Il **en** *a* vu trois.	*He saw **three**.*
Il lui reste une bouteille.	Il lui **en** *reste* une.	*He has **one** left.*

6.9   Quelques [N] *becomes* en [VERB] . . . quelques-un(e)s

If the expression of quantity is **quelques**, add **-uns** or **-unes** when it is at the end of the sentence, and replace the [N] by **en**.

J'ai vu **quelques** acteurs.	*I saw a few actors.*
J'**en** ai vu quelques-**uns**.	*I saw some.*
Michel a **quelques** amies.	*Michael has a few friends.*
Michel **en** a quelques-**unes**.	*Michael has a few.*

6.10   Word order with *en*

A.   Inflected verbs. The pronoun **en** precedes the inflected verb (the *auxiliary* in compound tenses).

Il voit **des amis.**	Il **en** voit.
Il a vu **des cousins.**	Il **en** a vu.

B.   Main verbs followed by dependent infinitives. When the main verb is followed by a dependent infinitive, **en** precedes the infinitive rather than the inflected verb:

Il **veut acheter** des livres.	*He wants to buy some books.*
Il **veut** *en* **acheter.**	*He wants to buy some.*

C.   Negation and inversion. In negatives and inversions, **en** clings to the verb, and becomes part of the verb unit.

Il voit **des avions.**	Il	en voit.	
NEGATIVE	Il n'	en voit	pas.
INVERSION	N'	en voit	-il pas?
		VERB UNIT	

Il a vu **des avions.**	Il	en a	vu.
NEGATIVE	Il n'	en a	pas vu.
INVERSION	N'	en a	-t-il pas vu?
		VERB UNIT	

NOTE: There is *never agreement* of a *past participle* with **en**, even though it may be a preceding direct object.

Mise en œuvre 6 C

Emploi du pronom *en*

Remplacez la partie convenable de chaque phrase par **en**, tout en faisant les autres changements nécessaires.

EXEMPLE

Donald a beaucoup *d'argent.*
Donald **en** a beaucoup.

1. Ce vin vient *de France.*
2. Ce camion-là est chargé *de marchandises japonaises.*
3. Je prendrai *du café,* s'il vous plaît.
4. Il y a *quelques étudiants* qui ont toujours raison.
5. Zut alors! Je n'ai pas *d'argent* sur moi!
6. Jacques a commandé *quelques livres* à la librairie.
7. Nous sommes en train de lire *des poèmes.*
8. Actuellement le professeur nous parle *de l'économie.*
9. Marcel Aymé a écrit *des contes fantastiques.*
10. J'ai lu trois *contes d'Aymé*[1].

Mise en œuvre 6 D

Emploi d'*en* en conversation

Répondez aux questions suivantes affirmativement et négativement, en remplaçant toujours le nom complément d'objet par le pronom qui convient.

[1] Do not make a substitution for **d'Aymé**, but rather for the whole phrase **contes d'Aymé**.

EXEMPLE

Cherchez-vous des renseignements?
Mais oui, j'**en** cherche.
Mais non, je n'**en** cherche pas.

1. As-tu commandé du café?
2. As-tu des vidéo-cassettes?
3. As-tu un magnétoscope[2]?
4. Est-ce que la serveuse a apporté un cendrier?
5. Est-ce que ton père a gagné de l'argent à la Bourse?
6. Ton père a-t-il acheté des actions de Michelin?
7. Il a fait trois voyages d'affaires en Suisse.
8. As-tu demandé de l'argent à tes parents pour tes frais scolaires?
9. Est-ce que tu écris des lettres au journal local?
10. Est-ce que Suzanne est déjà sortie de la maison?

Reflets

Le Voyage en avion

1. **une aérogare.** Les passagers peuvent se rendre à l'une des aérogares au centre de la ville pour commencer leur voyage. Il y a deux aérogares à Paris: l'aérogare des Invalides et l'aérogare de la Porte Maillot. Des autobus transportent les passagers de l'aérogare jusqu'à l'aéroport.

2. **l'aéroport.** Les passagers peuvent arriver en autocar ou dans leurs propres voitures qu'ils laissent dans le parking. **Les salles d'attente** sont spacieuses et confortables. En attendant leur **vol,** les voyageurs ont à leur disposition une librairie, un restaurant, une pharmacie, un bureau de poste, un bureau de change et de nombreuses boutiques.

   Il y a trois aéroports qui desservent Paris: l'aéroport Charles de Gaulle, situé à Roissy, à environ 27 kilomètres au nord-est de la capitale, est le plus grand et le plus moderne. Orly au sud, et Le Bourget au nord, desservent également Paris.

3. **le vol.** Au moyen de hautparleurs qui se trouvent partout dans le bâtiment, on annonce les arrivés et les départs. Par exemple, l'on pourrait annoncer: « Mesdames et messieurs: Air France annonce l'arrivée du vol 437 en provenance de Barcelone. Le vol 324 à destination de Marseille est prêt à partir. »

4. **l'embarquement.** Les passagers qui se sont rassemblés à la porte d'embarque-

---

[2] **un magnétoscope** = *a VCR*

ment sont enfin invités à monter à bord de leur avion en traversant la passerelle téléscopique.

5. **le personnel.** Dans l'aérogare se trouvent des représentants des diverses compagnies (Air France, SAS, Lufthansa, British Airways, Aéroflot, American Airways et d'autres) qui contrôlent les billets et s'occupent des passagers et des bagages. Le personnel de sécurité surveille électroniquement et visuellement les bagages et tous les individus qui circulent dans l'aéroport pour protéger les avions contre le sabotage et la piraterie aérienne.

6. **L'équipage** de l'avion comprend le pilote, le copilote, le navigateur (ou officier mécanicien navigant) dans le poste de pilotage. Le tableau de bord de l'avion moderne est muni de toutes sortes d'instruments sophistiqués, y compris un radar et des ordinateurs. Les avions les plus récents sont entièrement informatisés. Dans la cabine il y a des hôtesses qui circulent pour s'occuper des rafraîchissements, des repas et du confort des voyageurs.

7. **la piste.** Les avions **atterrissent, roulent au sol** et **décollent** de la piste. Un avion chargé qui est prêt à décoller attend sur une piste de circulation. En recevant l'autorisation de la tour de contrôle, l'avion s'avance sur la piste d'envol (ou d'atterrissage), accélère les réacteurs, et s'envole à toute allure avec un bruit assourdissant.

8. **la douane et l'immigration.** Les passagers internationaux qui débarquent doivent passer la douane et l'immigration pour le contrôle des bagages et des passeports.

Thème

1. There are three airports near Paris. The Charles de Gaulle airport located at Roissy is the most modern.

2. Passengers arrive there by car or by bus, and wait for their flights in the waiting rooms.

3. At this moment there is a jet liner for Barcelona at the end of the runway.

4. The pilot is waiting on the runway for the control tower to give authorization to take off. He has been waiting for ten minutes.

5. Air France's flight 542 left Paris at noon. It is going to arrive at its destination about two o'clock.

6. The arrival of a flight from London is announced, and the passengers who are getting off the plane are passing through immigration before they go to get their baggage.

7. Jacques and Suzanne Mornet took this flight so that they can visit the exhibition[3] at the Louvre tomorrow.

8. The trip took an hour, and they brought several suitcases; their friend Pierre brought two.

[3] **l'exposition** (*f.*)

9. Some of the travelers in the airport were waiting for a flight to Geneva. They spent some time in the shops or in the restaurant. It was important for them to listen[4] to announcements of departures.

10. Our car was in the parking lot. We had been looking for it for ten minutes when we finally found it.

Sujets de conversation ou de composition

1. Quelles sont les avantages et les inconvénients d'un voyage en avion? (le trajet à l'aéroport / le stationnement / l'attente / la sécurité / les dangers de navigation / le prix / la vitesse / le confort, etc.)

2. Si vous n'aimez pas voyager en avion, quel moyen de transport préférez-vous? Quels sont les avantages et les inconvénients de ce mode de transport? (le T.G.V., l'autocar, la voiture, l'hélicoptère, etc.) Faut-il considérer aussi la distance à parcourir en choisissant un moyen de transport?

3. Quels changements dans les modes de transport est-ce que vous prévoyez pour l'avenir? Comment vont-ils changer la vie de tous les jours? (les trains de haute vitesse comme l'aérotrain[5], les véhicules à sustenation magnétique, etc.)

---

[4] *"that they listen . . ."*

[5] Soutenu et guidé par les coussins d'air, l'aérotrain glisse sur une voie de béton en forme d'un T inverse.

7

Pronom complément d'objet indirect
Pronom *y*
venir et *tenir*

PRONOM COMPLÉMENT D'OBJET INDIRECT

7.1   Identification of indirect object noun

To determine the indirect object, quote the subject and verb of the sentence, and then ask *to whom?* (**à qui?**). The indirect object *noun* will invariably be preceded by the preposition **à** (**au, aux**).

> Paul rend ses devoirs au professeur.
>
> TEST: Paul rend (**à qui?**)   ANSWER: **au professeur** = INDIRECT OBJECT

In English the preposition *to* is often omitted, but by inserting it with the various nouns following the verb, the indirect object can be found:

> *I gave my father the newspaper.*
>
> TEST: *I gave (**to whom?**)   to the newspaper?   to my father?*

Obviously the indirect object is *my father* in this sentence. Remember that in French, a form of **à** is *always* present in front of the *indirect object noun*.

7.2   Position of the indirect object pronoun

The indirect object pronoun is placed before the verb:

A.   In front of the *inflected verb:*

SIMPLE TENSE:	Je *parle* à cette personne.	Je lui *parle*.
COMPOUND TENSE:	J'*ai parlé* à cette personne.	Je lui *ai parlé*.

B.   In front of a *dependent infinitive:*

Je voudrais *parler* à cette personne.   Je voudrais **lui** *parler*.

C.   In front of a *negative command* (negative imperative):

Ne *répondez pas* à l'agent.   Ne **lui** *répondez pas*.

D.   After a *positive command*. This is the only case in which object pronouns are placed *after* the verb. They are joined to the verb (and to each other, if there are two) by a hyphen. See 7.6 for the order when there are two pronouns after the imperative form.

Suivez-**moi**.   Regardez-**le**.
Posez ⏍ la **question** *au prof.* ⏍   Posez-la-*lui*.

7.3   Table of indirect object pronouns

me (moi)	*to me*	**nous**	*to us*
te	*to you*	**vous**	*to you*
lui	*to him* / *to her*	**leur**	*to them*

NOTE: The form **moi** replaces **me** in positive commands [7.6]:

Le professeur **me** rend ma composition.	STATEMENT
Ne **me** posez pas cette question.	IMPERATIVE, NEGATIVE
Donnez-**moi** ce livre, s'il vous plaît.	IMPERATIVE, POSITIVE

NOTE: The form **leur** is invariable when it means *to them*, unlike the possessive adjective which agrees in number (**leur auto, leurs amis**).

7.4   Structures requiring an indirect object

Indirect objects are always nouns designating persons, preceded by **à**. The indirect object pronoun therefore replaces **à** + PERSON. The following verbal structures take an indirect object in French, but often do not in English. (The notation [P] indicates the designation of a person.)

poser une question à [P]	*to ask* (someone) *a question*
obéir à [P]	*to obey* (someone)
répondre à [P]	*to answer* (someone)
dire (quelque chose) **à** [P]	*to say* (something) *to someone*
dire à [P] **de** [I]	*to tell* (someone) *to (do something)*
demander (quelque chose) **à** [P]	*to ask* (someone) *for* (something)
demander à [P] **de** [I]	*to ask* (someone) *to (do something)*
écrire à [P]	*to write* ([to] someone)

EXAMPLES

PRONOUN REPLACEMENT

L'avocat pose une question **au témoin.**
The lawyer asks the witness a question.

Il **lui** pose une question.
He asks him a question.

Le pilote obéit **aux directeurs.**
The pilot obeys the executives.

Il **leur** obéit.
He obeys them.

La tour répond **au pilote.**
The tower answers the pilot.

Elle **lui** répond.
It answers him.

On dit **au pilote** de décoller.
The pilot is told to take off.

On **lui** dit de décoller.
He is told to take off.

Je demande **à maman** de lire.
I ask mother to read.

Je **lui** demande de lire.
I ask her to read.

Paul demande un billet **à la caissière.**
Paul asks the cashier for a ticket.

Il **lui** demande un billet.
He asks her for a ticket.

7.5 Multiple object pronouns (two pronouns with one verb)

When there are two pronouns before one verb, the order is as follows:

1	2	3	4	5

$$
\begin{matrix} \text{me} \\ \text{te} \\ \text{se} \\ \text{vous} \\ \text{nous} \end{matrix} \quad \text{BEFORE} \quad \boxed{\begin{matrix} \text{le} \\ \text{la} \\ \text{les} \end{matrix} \ \text{BEFORE} \ \begin{matrix} \text{lui} \\ \text{leur} \end{matrix}} \ + \ [\text{y} \ + \ \text{en}] \ + \ \boxed{\text{verb}}
$$

L'S LINKED TO VERB

This order applies to all sentences except *positive* imperatives [7.6]. As an aid to memory, remember: if two pronouns begin with *l*, they go in *"Lphabetical"* order and if one begins with *l* and the other does not, the one with *l* is *last* (or *linked* to the verb). This disregards **y** and **en,** *always* last.

Il **me la** rend.
On **nous les** donne.   L-WORD COMES LAST
Ne **me le** demandez pas.

Elle **m'en** a parlé.   **en** (AND **y**)[1] ALWAYS LAST

When negative imperatives are used, the same rule applies.

Ne **me la** rendez pas.	*Don't give it to me.*
Ne vous **en** servez pas.	*Don't use it.*
Ne **leur en** parlez pas.	*Don't talk to them about it.*
Ne **m'en** demandez pas.	*Don't ask me for any.*

7.6 Positive imperatives: pronoun order

When a verb has both a direct and an indirect object, the corresponding pronouns are placed *after* the verb. They are joined to the verb and to each other by hyphens.

	1	2	3
POSITIVE IMPERATIVE VERB		-moi	[m'en]
	-le	-lui	
Donnez-	-la	-nous	-en
	-les	-leur	

[1] Elision occurs when **me, te,** or **se** appears before **y** or **en.**

The following examples show how the pronouns replace noun objects. The negative imperative [2.11], which uses normal order, is shown for comparison.

Donnez ces livres à Bernard.

Donnez-*les*-lui.   NEGATIVE: Ne **les lui** donnez pas.

Rendez *cette machine* à ce client.

Rendez-*la*-lui.   NEGATIVE: Ne **la lui** rendez pas.

Apportez-*moi* de la salade.

Apportez-*m'*en.   NEGATIVE: Ne **m'en** apportez pas.

Notice that the sequence of pronouns is essentially the same as for positive statements and negative imperatives; the difference is mainly in the placement of the pronouns after the positive command, and the use of hyphens.

Mise en œuvre 7 A

Pronom complément d'objet indirect

Remplacez le complément d'objet indirect par le pronom approprié.

EXEMPLE

Luc obéit *à ses parents.*

Luc **leur** obéit. / Il **leur** obéit.

1. François obéit toujours *à son père.*
2. Obéissez tout de suite *à l'agent de police.*
3. Obéissons *aux agents de police.*
4. L'agent répond poliment *au touriste.*
5. Paul pose une question technique *au pilote de notre avion.*
6. Robert désire poser des questions aux députés.
7. Michel est un étudiant sérieux: il plaît à ses professeurs.
8. Jean-Paul demande de l'argent à sa mère.
9. M. Lefort demande à cet étudiant de lire un paragraphe.
10. Le pilote dit aux passagers de rester assis.

Mise en œuvre 7 B

Place des pronoms multiples

Remplacez les mots en italique par les pronoms appropriés.

EXEMPLE

Charles écrit *des lettres à des amis en Angleterre.*
Charles **leur en** écrit.

1. Les étudiants posent *des questions difficiles aux ingénieurs.*
2. Les passagers demandent *des renseignements à l'employée.*
3. Le professeur demande *à cette étudiante* de lire *la poésie.*
4. Le facteur nous apporte *une lettre recommandée* (registered).
5. Le jeune architecte nous parle *de problèmes techniques.*
6. Nous rendons *nos devoirs au professeur* tous les jours.
7. Remettez *cette lettre à l'avocat,* s'il vous plait.
8. N'apportez pas *le journal au patron* en ce moment.
9. Apportez-moi *les billets* demain, s'il vous plait.
10. Ne dites jamais *la vérité aux espions.*

PRONOM **Y**

7.7   Use

The pronoun **y** replaces either a prepositional phrase indicating location, an à-phrase generated by a verbal structure, or **là.** It is used *only* for things, *never* for persons. It appears before the inflected verb or dependent infinitive, like object pronouns:

Jean est **dans la maison.**	Jean **y** est.	LOCATION
Il répond **à la question.**	Il **y** répond.	VERBAL STRUCTURE
Il reste **là.**	Il **y** reste.	(**là**)

When the prepositional phrase to be replaced by **y** follows an infinitive, **y** appears before that infinitive instead of before the inflected verb:

Je $\boxed{vais}$ en ville.	J'y $\boxed{vais}$.	INFLECTED VERB
Je voudrais $\boxed{aller}$ en ville.	Je voudrais y $\boxed{aller}$.	INFINITIVE

If the object of a prepositional phrase to be replaced is a PERSON, regular indirect object pronouns must be used [7.3] rather than **y**:

Jean répond **à cette lettre.**	Jean **y** répond.	THING
Jean répond **à son amie.**	Jean **lui** répond.	PERSON

In some cases such as **penser à** [PERSON], the preposition is retained, and a disjunctive pronoun (17.4) is substituted for the noun. See 7.10 for other such verbs.

Dominique pense **à son grand-père.**

Dominique pense **à lui.**   (à + DISJUNCTIVE PRONOUN)

7.8   Locations replaced by *y*

Prepositional phrases designating locations may be replaced by **y**. Such prepositional phrases may begin with **à, dans, en, devant, derrière, sur,** etc.:

Nous entrons **dans la salle.**	Nous y entrons.
Il retourne **en ville.**	Il y retourne.
L'autocar est **devant la gare.**	L'autocar y est.
La tasse est **sur la table.**	La tasse y est.

It is assumed that the location has already been mentioned, so that the meaning of **y** will be clear to the listener.

7.9   *y* and *là*

These two words are synonymous only if *there* is meant. Word order is different, in that **là** comes at the end of a sentence:

—Est-elle dans la cuisine?

—Mais oui, elle est **là.** (Elle y est.)

Informally, **là** sometimes means *here,* as in the following telephone conversation:

—Est-ce que Marie est **là**?   *Is Marie there?*

—Oui, mademoiselle, elle est **là.**   *Yes, she is (here).*

7.10   Verbal structures requiring *à* (Régimes)

The following verbal structures include **à** + NOUN. If the noun refers to a thing (and has been mentioned already as an antecedent), the pronoun **y** may replace that prepositional phrase (**à** + NOUN). *If the noun is a person, use the indirect object pronouns [7.3]:*

assister à	*to attend (a function)*
jouer à[2]	*to play (a game)*
obéir à	*to obey (a person or thing)*
renoncer° à	*to give up; to renounce*

[2] **jouer de** = *to play (a musical instrument)*

répondre à	*to answer (a person or thing)*
réussir à (un examen)	*to succeed in; to pass (an exam)*

The following may replace à [N] by the pronoun **y**; but if a *person* is involved, the prepositional phrase cannot be replaced. Instead, keep **à** and use a disjunctive pronoun after it:

faire attention à	*to pay attention to*
s'intéresser à	*to be interested in*
penser à	*to think about*
songer° à	*to think about*

Je m'intéresse **à la langue française.**	Je m'**y** intéresse.
Je m'intéresse **à cette actrice.**	Je m'intéresse **à elle.**
Pierre pense **à la loi.**	Pierre **y** pense.
Pierre pense **à sa mère.**	Pierre **lui** pense **à elle.**
Gérard répond **à la question.**	Gérard **y** répond.
Gérard répond **au professeur.**	Gérard **lui** répond.

7.11   Idioms using *y*

A.   y être   *to understand; to be "with it"*

Y êtes-vous?	{*Do you follow me?* / *Are you with me?*}
Vous y êtes!	*You've got it!*
Ah, j'y suis!	*Now I understand!*

B.   y compris [N] (*fixed form*)   *including* [N]

J'ai étudié les langues, **y** compris le russe.
I have studied languages, including Russian.

Mise en œuvre 7 C _____

Pronom *y*

Remplacez une partie de chacune des phrases suivantes par le pronom y:

EXEMPLE

Le patron répond *à la lettre du candidat.*
Le patron y répond.

1. Pierre va *au Havre*.
2. Je prends toujours l'autobus pour aller *à l'université*.
3. Nous allons *à Londres* en avion.
4. Son livre et sa montre sont *sur la table*.
5. J'ai envie d'aller *au Bois de Boulogne*.
6. Nous regardons les animaux *au jardin zoologique*.
7. *Au restaurant*, Roger a commandé du vin.
8. Il est commode d'aller *en ville* par le train.
9. Le bureau de mon père se trouve *dans une tour*.
10. Il faut faire attention *à la leçon*.
11. Claude obéit à la loi.
12. Je réponds poliment aux questions du touriste.
13. Mon camarade de chambre joue au tennis tous les jours.
14. Hier soir nous avons assisté à un concert de Mozart.
15. Est-ce que vous pensez aux prix qui montent?
16. Je renonce complètement aux cigarettes.
17. Suzanne Masson s'intéresse aux grands musées de Paris.
18. Les livres sont dans l'étagère [bookcase].
19. Je réussis toujours à mes examens.
20. La grand-mère du Petit Chaperon Rouge demeurait dans une chaumière.

Mise en œuvre 7 D

Pronoms complément d'objet, *y* et *en*

Remplacez les mots en italique par les pronoms appropriés:

EXEMPLE

Les passagers demandent *des renseignements à l'hôtesse*.
Les passagers **lui en** demandent. / Ils **lui en** demandent.

1. Paul répond tout de suite *à la question*.
2. Paul répond *au professeur* sans hésiter.
3. Est-ce que vous avez besoin *de mon dictionnaire*?
4. Je n'ai plus *de cigarettes*, je regrette.
5. Pierre donne *des cigarettes à ses amis*.
6. Paul met *les livres sur le bureau du professeur*.
7. Voilà *la jeune fille anglaise*. Je voudrais parler *à cette jeune fille*.
8. Je vais *à l'aéroport* en autocar. Voilà *l'aéroport*.
9. J'ai beaucoup *de valises*; j'ai trois *valises*.
10. Allez chercher *le médecin* tout de suite!

VERBES IRRÉGULIERS **VENIR** ET **TENIR**

7.12   Review *venir* (verb table 30) and *tenir (verb table 29)*

Since these verbs are very similar in formation, a parallel presentation will help you remember them.

PRÉSENT	je **viens**	je **tiens**
(2 stems:	tu **viens**	tu **tiens**
vien / ven;	il **vient**	il **tient**
tien / ten)	nous **ven**ons	nous **ten**ons
	vous **ven**ez	vous **ten**ez
	ils **vienn**ent	ils **tienn**ent
IMPARFAIT (regular)	il **ven**ait	il **ten**ait
PARTICIPE PASSÉ	**venu** (être)	**tenu** (avoir)
PASSÉ COMPOSÉ	Elle est **venue**	Elle a **tenu**.
PASSÉ SIMPLE (regular endings minus the vowel) Note accent in **nous-** and **vous-**forms.	je **vin**s	je **tin**s
	tu **vin**s	tu **tin**s
	il **vin**t	il **tin**t
	nous **vîn**mes	nous **tîn**mes
	vous **vîn**tes	vous **tîn**tes
	ils **vin**rent	il **tin**rent
FUTUR	je **viendr**-ai	je **tiendr**-ai
CONDITIONNEL	je **viendr**-ais	je **tiendr**-ais
SUBJONCTIF 2 stems: **vienn / ven;** (**tienn / ten**)	que je **vienne**	que je **tienne**
	que tu **viennes**	que tu **tiennes**
	qu'il **vienne**	qu'il **tienne**
	que nos **venions**	que nous **tenions**
	que vous **veniez**	que vous **teniez**
	qu'ils **viennent**	qu'ils **tiennent**

7.13   Idioms with *venir*

venir [1]   **to come** *[for the purpose of **doing something**]*

Jean-Jacques **vient voir** le professeur.
*Jean-Jacques **has come to see** the teacher.*

venir de [1]   *to have just (**done something**)*

Jean **vient de voir** le professeur.
*Jean **has just** seen the teacher.*

In the imperfect tense, **venir de** [1] means *had just* [1].

Jean **venait de** *voir* le professeur quand je suis arrivé.
*Jean **had just** seen the teacher when I arrived.*

NOTE: *Only* the present and imperfect tenses can be used with this idiom.

7.14   Verbs conjugated like *venir*

revenir	to come back	Il **revient** demain.
devenir	to become	La situation **devient** difficile.
se souvenir (**de**)	to remember	Je **me souviens de** votre sœur.

CAUTION: Distinguish between the following meanings:

*to **come** back*	**revenir**	(The subject is *approaching* the speaker.)
*to **go** back*	**retourner**	(The subject is *going away from* the speaker.)

Les Beatles **viennent** aux États-Unis. (Speaker is in the U.S.)
Plus tard ils **retournent** en Angleterre.
Les Beatles **reviennent** (deuxième voyage) aux États-Unis.
Ils **retournent** ensuite en Angleterre.

If the speaker were in England, the account of the trips would be as follows:

Duran Duran **vont** aux États-Unis.
Ils **reviennent** en Angleterre.
Ils **retournent** aux États-Unis.
Ils **reviennent** ensuite en Angleterre.

Notice the special use of **devenir** for *become of*:

—Et Georges Brun, qu'**est-il devenu?**   *"And what has become of George Brun?"*

—Il a déménagé.   *"He moved."*

7.15   Idioms with *tenir*

tenir à [I]   *to be eager (anxious) to do something*
tenir à [N]   *to value* [N] *highly; to prize* [N]

Je **tiens à** *obtenir* une bonne note en physique.
I am eager to get a good grade in physics.

Jean-Paul **tient à** *sa voiture.*
Jean-Paul thinks so much of his car (that he would never part with it).

7.16   Verbs conjugated like *tenir*

retenir   *to remember; to retain*

obtenir   *to obtain*

contenir   *to contain*

appartenir (à)   *to belong (to)*

maintenir   *to maintain*

Il est difficile de **retenir** tout cela.
It is difficult to remember all that.

J'**obtiendrai** le renseignement que tu veux.
I will obtain the information you want.

Ce livre **appartient** à Marie.
This book belongs to Marie.

Mise en œuvre 7 E

venir and *tenir*

Répondez à la question et ajoutez une deuxième phrase.

EXEMPLE

Pourquoi est-ce que le professeur vient en classe?

Il **vient** en classe pour apprendre le français aux étudiants.

Les étudiants **tiennent à** parler une langue étrangère.

1. Pourquoi venez-vous en classe?
2. Comment venez-vous à l'université?
3. Est-ce que vous venez en classe le samedi?
4. Est-ce que les autres étudiants viennent en classe tous les jours?
5. A quelle heure retournez-vous à la maison?
6. Est-ce que votre mère est contente de voir revenir son fils (ou sa fille)?
7. Quand revenez-vous à la classe de français?
8. Combien d'étudiants viennent en classe tous les jours?
9. A quelle heure faut-il revenir en classe?
10. Est-ce que vous retenez bien la poésie?
11. Est-ce que ce livre appartient au professeur?
12. Avez-vous envie de devenir riche?
13. Tenez-vous à obtenir une bonne note en français?
14. Qu'est-ce que vous tenez à la main en ce moment?
15. Qu'est-ce que vous venez de faire en classe?

Mise en œuvre 7 F

Thème

1. Charles is writing a letter to his parents because he needs money. He is asking them for it to pay his college expenses.
2. His father is ready to help him, and he has money; he gives him some every week.
3. His mother and father have just returned from Zurich, in Switzerland; you remember that he has investments there.
4. Before[3] they take a flight from de Gaulle, they consult a travel agent and they obtain some information about[4] Geneva.

---

[3] **avant de** + [INFINITIF]. Voir 18.6.

[4] **au sujet de**

5. They are interested in[5] the Swiss railways, and would like to speak to him about them. He was interested in them too.

6. They have been staying at the Hôtel du Parc for three days, but they intend[6] to leave[7] it this evening.

7. I know that they are returning to Paris before they take a pleasure trip on the Swiss National Railways.

8. As for[8] the money, Mr. Mouret turned[9] to his son and said, "Don't be afraid. Calm down[10]. I am going to send you some by air mail."

---

[5] **s'intéresser à** (qqch)
[6] **avoir l'intention de** + [INFINITIF].
[7] **partir, sortir, quitter,** ou **laisser?** Voir 10.8.
[8] **quant à**
[9] **se retourner**
[10] **se calmer**

8

Négation
Chronologie
Voix passive

NÉGATION

8.1 Verb unit identification

An easy solution to some word-order problems is the use of the "verb unit." This is especially helpful for negation and questions.

> The VERB UNIT is the *inflected verb*[1] together with all the preceding words *except* the subject.

The verb unit is enclosed in a box:

Il ⟦**les lui donne.**⟧

Il ⟦**les lui a**⟧ donnés ce matin. (PARTICIPLE IS NOT PART OF VERB UNIT.)

Aussi ⟦**est-elle**⟧ restée à la maison.

Nous ⟦**nous sommes**⟧ levés de bonne heure.

In *negation*, **ne** precedes the *verb unit*, and **pas** (or other negative word) follows it:

Il **ne** *les lui donne* **pas.**

[1] The inflected verb is any form except the infinitive or the past participle. When an infinitive is adjusted for tense or agreement with a particular subject, this change is an inflection.

97

In *questions* by inversion, the *subject* is placed after the verb unit, and a hyphen is inserted:

> ⟦ **Les lui a** ⟧ -t-il donnés ce matin?

8.2   Simple negation. ne [VERB UNIT] pas.

To change a statement, command, or question to the negative, place **ne** in front of the verb unit, and **pas**[2] after it.

STATEMENT	Ils **la lui** rendent.	Ils ne **la lui** rendent pas.
	Ils **la lui ont** rendue.	Ils ne **la lui ont** pas rendue.
COMMAND	**Fermez** la porte.	Ne **fermez** pas la porte.
QUESTION	**Est-elle** venue hier?	N'**est-elle** pas venue hier?
	S'est-il dépêché?	Ne **s'est-il** pas dépêché?

Notice that when a verb has a hyphen joining it to a pronoun, the hyphenated form is considered to be an inseparable unit, as in the last two examples.[3]

8.3   Alternate negative words replacing *pas*

To obtain other negative meanings, **pas** may be replaced by one of the following. Note that **ne** is always retained:

ne . . . **jamais**	*never*	Il n'étudie **jamais**.
ne . . . **rien**	*nothing*	Il **ne** dit **rien**.
ne . . . **plus**	*no longer*	Il **ne** travaille **plus**.
ne . . . **guère**	*scarcely*	Il **ne** comprend **guère**.
ne . . . **pas encore**	*not yet*	Il n'a **pas encore** compris.

Notice that **pas encore** is inseparable; these two words should remain together. Do not use both **pas** and one of the other negative words. Doing so will create a double negative.

---

[2] An alternative to **pas** is **point**. There is really no difference in meaning, although **point** is slightly more emphatic.

[3] An exception to this is in the case of *commands* where there are object pronouns. The object pronouns are placed before the verb unit:

Fermez-la.	Ne **la** fermez pas.
Donnez-les-moi.	Ne **me les** donnez pas.
Dépêchons-nous.	Ne **nous** dépêchons pas.

8.4   Alternate negatives that follow the past participle

The alternate negative words in the following list *follow the past participle* in compound tenses:

ne . . . personne	*nobody, not . . . anyone*
ne . . . que [NOUN]	*only* [NOUN]; *except* [NOUN]
ne . . . aucun(e) [NOUN]	*no* [N]; *not any* [N]
ne . . . nul(le) [NOUN]	*nothing* [N], *not any* [N]
ne . . . ni [N] . . . **ni** [N]	*neither* [N] . . . *nor* [N]

In the case of **aucun(e)** and **nul(le),** the gender of the noun following **aucun(e)** or **nul(le)** determines whether to use the masculine or feminine form:

Je ne vois **aucune maison** blanche.   (*Feminine,* to agree with **maison.**)

For **ni . . . ni,** the following nouns include the article or possessive if specific things are mentioned, and omit the article for generalities:

Je n'ai vu **ni** le professeur **ni** le doyen.	SPECIFIC (use article)
Je n'ai **ni** mon cahier **ni** mon stylo.	SPECIFIC (use article)
Je n'ai **ni** raquette **ni** balles.	GENERALITY (no article)
Je n'ai vu **ni** mon frère **ni** ma sœur.	SPECIFIC (use possessive)
Je n'ai **ni** frère **ni** sœur.	GENERALITY (no article)

Ne . . . personne, ne . . . rien, ne . . . que:

Il n'y a **personne** dans la salle.

Il n'a parlé **à personne.**

Nous n'avons **rien** trouvé.

Elle n'a dépensé **que** cent francs.

When using **ne . . . que,** you should place the word **que** at the location in the sentence where it shows the limitation. It need not appear directly after the verb unit:

Nous **n'avons** trouvé **que** trois cartes géographiques dans ce livre.
We found only three maps in this book.[4]

---

[4] This is correct, in spite of the tendency in English to place *only* in a location that does not show the real limitation: *We only found three maps in this book.* In this statement, the limitation is not really on *found,* but rather on the number of maps.

8.5 *Rien* and *Personne* as subjects

When one of these words is the subject of a clause or sentence, it is placed at the beginning (as in the English equivalent). The word **ne** must appear at the usual location in front of the verb to validate the meaning:

Rien ne me trouble.   *Nothing is bothering me.*

Personne n'a compris la question.   *Nobody understood the question.*

The words **rien, jamais,** and **plus** may also be used alone in answers to questions:

—Qu'est-ce qui se passe?   **—Rien.**
—Tu vas souvent à l'opéra?   **—Jamais.**

8.6 Multiple negative elements

It is possible to use more than one negative expression after the verb to multiply the meanings. Only one **ne** is needed, and **pas** is omitted when an alternate negative element is used. Following the verb there are such combinations as:

Il ne dit **plus rien.**
He doesn't say anything any more.

Nous **n'**allons **plus jamais** au café.
We never go to the café any more.

Elle **ne** parlait **jamais plus** à **personne.**
She never spoke to anyone any more.

Je **n'**ai **jamais rien** entendu à propos de cela.
I never heard anything about that.

Personne, ni en récréation **ni** en classe, **ne** nous adressa **plus** la parole[5].
Nobody spoke to us any more, either in recreation period or in class.

Jamais personne ne vient la voir.
Nobody ever comes to see her.

Vous **ne** comprenez **jamais rien.**
You never understand anything.

8.7 Infinitive negation

Infinitives are made negative by placing **ne pas, ne rien, ne jamais,** or **ne plus** together before the infinitive:

[5] Jacques de Lacretelle, *Silbermann*. Paris: Gallimard, 129th ed. 1922. p. 97.

Je vous demande de **ne pas** *sortir*.   *I am asking you not to go out.*

Il s'amuse à **ne rien** *faire*[6].   *He has fun doing nothing.*

The expressions in section 8.4, however, straddle the infinitive:

Il a promis de **ne** *voir* **personne**.   {*He promised to see nobody.*
{*He promised not to see anybody.*

8.8   Partitive *des* becomes *de* after a negative

When a partitive follows a negation, **des** becomes **de**, as indicated in [3.12]:

Nous avons *des* **livres** techniques.
Nous n'avons **pas** *de* **livres** techniques.

Je prends *du* **sucre** dans mon café.
Je ne prends **pas** *de* **sucre** dans mon café.

Mise en œuvre 8 A

Négation

Mettez les phrases suivantes à la forme négative. Imaginez une seconde phrase pour compléter la pensée.

EXEMPLE

Jean étudie sa leçon.

Jean **n'**étudie **pas** sa leçon. Il regarde la télévision.

1. La première représentation a commencé. (Elle commence à . . .)
2. Paul prend les billets. (C'est Bernard qui . . .)
3. Paul a pris son billet.
4. Le film est français.
5. La vedette du film était Paul Newman.
6. Il y a beaucoup de monde dans la salle.
7. Mon père va souvent à Londres.
8. Il fait le trajet en bateau.
9. Ma mère prend le petit déjeuner à six heures.
10. Mon frère fait la cuisine.
11. Je fais la vaisselle.
12. Est-ce que vous faites la cuisine?

[6] As an extreme example, **Il décida de** *ne jamais plus rien* **dire à** *personne*. *He decided never to say anything to anyone any more.*

13. Fermez la porte, s'il vous plaît.
14. Écrivez une longue lettre au maire.
15. Nous arrivons en retard.
16. Nous avons posé des questions difficiles.
17. Le directeur est de retour.
18. Vous avez fini le travail.
19. J'ai envie de faire une promenade.
20. Cette jeune fille est toute seule.

Négation de l'infinitif [8.7]. Mettez les infinitifs en italique à la forme négative.

21. Être ou *être*, voilà la question.
22. Elle demande aux étudiants de *faire* du bruit.
23. On nous demande de *fumer*.
24. Le professeur demande aux étudiants d'*écrire* des phrases compliquées.
25. Il est difficile de *comprendre* ces phrases simples.

Mise en œuvre 8 B

Autres termes de la négation

Répondez négativement aux questions suivantes en employant le mot négatif indiqué entre parenthèses.

EXEMPLE

(pas encore)   Allez-vous en ville maintenant?

Je **ne** vais **pas encore** en ville.

1.	(pas encore)	Vous allez déjeuner maintenant?
2.	(jamais)	Vous jouez au tennis?
3.	(aucun, -e)	Alain a-t-il beaucoup d'amis?
4.	(rien)	Que faites-vous ce soir?
5.	(plus)	Allez-vous souvent au cinéma?
6.	(guère)	Est-ce que le film est amusant?
7.	(personne)	Qui cherchez-vous?
8.	(plus)	Est-ce que vos parents visitent toujours l'Italie?
9.	(ni)	Avez-vous des frères et des sœurs?
10.	(pas encore)	Écrivez-vous votre composition?
11.	(jamais)	Avez-vous fait la connaissance de cet auteur?
12.	(aucun, -e)	Y a-t-il une exception à la règle?

CHRONOLOGIE

8.9 Time divisions

Review the following **divisions du temps:**

le siècle	*century*
au XIXe siècle	*in the 19th century*
l'an,[7] **l'année**	*year*
le mois	*month*
quinze jours	*two weeks*
la semaine, huit jours	*week*
la semaine prochaine	*next week*
la semaine passée	*last week*
le jour,[7] **la journée**	*day*
le matin	*morning*
midi, minuit	*noon, midnight*
l'après-midi (*m.* ou *f.*)	*afternoon*
le soir	*evening*
la nuit	*night*
une heure	*hour*
une minute	*minute*
une seconde	*second*

---

[7] **un an, un jour.** The masculine forms are used for a fairly precise measure of time, and especially when a number above one is included:

> Il a passé **trois jours** à Nice.
> Jean habite à Paris depuis **trois ans.**

une année, une journée. These are used when the main interest is in the social activity involved, rather than in exact times. Often the "year" or "day" is merely approximate:

> Claude a passé **l'année scolaire** à Grenoble.
> Nous avons passé **la journée** au bord de la mer.

The academic year is obviously not an exact measurement of a year, often being just nine months; and a day at the beach may be only 18 hours.

8.10   Days of the week

Review **les jours de la semaine:**

lundi	*Monday*	**vendredi**	*Friday*
mardi	*Tuesday*	**samedi**	*Saturday*
mercredi	*Wednesday*	**dimanche**	*Sunday*
jeudi	*Thursday*		

NOTE: Do not use the article with the name of a day when a *specific day* is meant. For habitual action (*on Mondays, Saturdays,* etc.) use the singular article **le.** [1.5 E]

8.11   Months

Review **les mois de l'année:**

janvier	*January*	**mai**	*May*	**septembre**	*September*
février	*February*	**juin**	*June*	**octobre**	*October*
mars	*March*	**juillet**	*July*	**novembre**	*November*
avril	*April*	**aout**	*August*	**décembre**	*December*

To say *in (month)* use **en** or **au mois de:**

En juillet, nous ne serons plus à la maison.

Je fais du ski **au mois de** janvier.

8.12   Dates

In writing dates (**la date**), no capital letters are used for the days of the week or the months of the year. The definite article is often dropped:

le 14 novembre 1991   or, informally,   **14 novembre 1991**

In stating the year, one can say either *nineteen hundred ninety-one* or *one thousand nine hundred ninety-one:*

dix-neuf-cent-quatre-vingt-onze⎫
mil-neuf-cent-quatre-vingt-onze⎭ 1991

To ask the date:

> —**Quel jour sommes-nous aujourd'hui?**   *What is today's date?*
> —Nous sommes le 23 novembre.   *It's the 23rd of November.*
> *or* —**Quelle est la date aujourd'hui?**   *What is today's date?*
> —C'est aujourd'hui le 3 avril.   *It's the 3rd of April.*

Notice that only cardinal numbers are used in French (with the one exception of the *first*), whereas the ordinal numbers are commonly used in English.

> —C'est aujourd'hui **le premier avril.**   *Today is April 1st.*

To ask the day of the week:

> —**Quel jour de la semaine est-ce?**   *What day of the week is it?*
> —C'est aujourd'hui mardi.   *Today is Tuesday.*

For a complete review of numbers, see Appendix A.

8.13   Clock time (*l'heure* f.)

The general way of stating the time (o'clock) is "**Il est — heures.**

A.   The half-hour is expressed by Il est — heures *et demie.* (f.) Notice how this is abbreviated numerically:

> Il est sept heures **et demie** (7 h 30).

The masculine form **et demi** is used after **midi** (*noon*) and **minuit** (*midnight*):

> Il est **midi et demi** (12 h 30).
> Il est **minuit et demi** (0 h 30).

B.   The quarter-hour is expressed by *et quart.*

> Il est deux heures **et quart** (2 h 15).

C.   The quarter *before* the hour is expressed by *moins le quart.*

> Il est dix heures **moins le quart** (9 h 45).
> *It is **quarter of ten.*** *or   It is **nine forty-five.***

The number of minutes *before* the hour is **moins** [*number of minutes*]:

> Il est midi **moins vingt** (11 h 40).
>
> Il est huit heures **moins cinq** (7 h 55).

D.   The number of minutes *past* the hour is expressed:

> Il est dix heures **trois** (10 h 03).
>
> Il est onze heures **seize** (11 h 16).

E.   To indicate A.M. **and** P.M. Add **du matin** for morning hours, and **du soir** to indicate evening hours (if it is not obvious from the context):

> Il arrivera à huit heures vingt **du soir.**
> *He will arrive at eight-twenty* P.M.
>
> Il est sept heures **du matin.**
> *It is seven o'clock in the morning* (A.M.).

F.   The twenty-four-hour system. This is used by railroads, airlines, theaters, military services, etc., and makes the indicators A.M. and P.M. superfluous. For example, here is a typical schedule of departure times for trains from Paris to Le Havre:

Départ		*Departures*
9 h 11	*that is:*	9:11 A.M.
11 h 10		11:10 A.M.
14 h 11		2:11 P.M.
16 h 44		4:44 P.M.
19 h 56		7:56 P.M.

G.   *Exactly* and *Approximately:*

> Il est neuf heures **précises.**   *It is **exactly** nine o'clock.*
>
> Il arrivera **vers** dix heures.   *He will arrive **around** ten o'clock.*

Mise en œuvre 8 C

Chronologie

Répondez aux questions suivantes.

EXEMPLE

Quel jour est-ce aujourd'hui?

C'est aujourd'hui mardi le 7 novembre.

1. Quel jour est-ce aujourd'hui?
2. Quelle heure est-il?
3. Quels sont les mois de l'année?
4. Combien de mois y a-t-il dans une année?
5. Combien de jours y a-t-il dans une semaine?
6. Quels sont les jours de la semaine?
7. Quels sont les mois de vacances en France?
8. Combien d'années y a-t-il dans un siècle? (Employez **ans** dans la réponse.)
9. Quelle est la date du commencement du XXIe siècle?
10. Quels sont les trois parties de la journée?
11. Quand dormez-vous?
12. Combien de secondes y a-t-il dans une minute?
13. Quelle heure est-il à midi?
14. Quel est l'équivalent anglais de *quinze jours*?
15. Quel est l'équivalent anglais de *huit jours*?
16. Quelle heure est-il maintenant?
17. Quel temps fait-il en hiver? (16.3)
18. Quel sport faites-vous en automne?
19. Quel temps fait-il en été?
20. Que faites-vous depuis cinq minutes?

Mise en œuvre 8 D _____

La date et l'heure

Répondez aux questions suivantes.

A. Quelle heure est-il?
(6 h 00)   Il est **six heures précises.**

1. 7 h 00	11. 8 h 35	21. 2 h 06
2. 7 h 15	12. 8 h 40	22. 14 h 07
3. 7 h 30	13. 8 h 45	23. 14 h 15
4. 7 h 45	14. 8 h 50	24. 14 h 45
5. 8 h 00	15. 8 h 55	25. 15 h 00
6. 8 h 05	16. 9 h 00	26. 17 h 09
7. 8 h 10	17. 9 h 03	27. 18 h 17
8. 8 h 15	18. 12 h 00	28. 20 h 20
9. 8 h 20	19. 24 h 00	29. 22 h 30
10. 8 h 30	20. 0 h 05	30. 23 h 35

B. Quel est la date aujourd'hui?
(January 23)   **C'est aujourd'hui le 23 janvier.**

1. September 3rd	7. December 5th
2. June 9th	8. February 22nd
3. April 1st	9. July 14th
4. May 19th	10. March 30th
5. October 10th	11. December 25th
6. November 7th	12. January 1st

LE PASSIF ET LE PRONOM **ON** _____

8.14 Passive Construction

A. Identification of the passive. The passive is much more frequently used in English than in French. Avoid passive constructions by rephrasing your thought into an active form. In the passive, the subject is acted upon, whereas in active constructions the subject is the doer of the action indicated by the verb.

PASSIVE	*Our dog was killed by a car.*	
ACTIVE	*A car killed our dog.*	Une voiture a écrasé[8] notre chien.
PASSIVE	*He is admired by all the professors.*	
ACTIVE	*All the professors admire him.*	Tous les professeurs l'admirent.
PASSIVE	*French is spoken in Canada.*	
ACTIVE	*They speak French in Canada.*	**On parle** français au Canada.

If there is no clear performer of the action (like the car and the professors above), then there is a French volunteer who will do anything: it is **on,** used with a form 3 verb. The last of the preceding examples demonstrates its use. If, for example, we did not know what killed our dog, then we could say:

On a tué notre chien.   (**Someone** *killed our dog. Our dog was killed.*)

B.   Suggestions using *on*. Suggestions and questions are often framed with the subject **on**:

On va en ville?   { *Shall we go downtown?*
{ *Are you going downtown?*

On doit payer?   *Do we have to pay?*

8.15   Use of pronoun *on* to avoid a passive

Most sentences which occur to the English mind in the passive form can be recast into the active form. If the agent (doer of the action) is not mentioned, the pronoun **on** can be used as a subject:

The house is seen in the distance.	PASSIVE
=*One sees the house in the distance.*	ACTIVE
On voit la maison dans le lointain.	

The doors were closed at 1:30.	PASSIVE
=*One closed the doors at 1:30.*	ACTIVE
On a *fermé* les portes à 1 h 30.	

The teacher was given a prize.	PASSIVE
=*They gave the teacher a prize.*	ACTIVE
On a offert un prix au professeur.	

If the agent *is* mentioned, simply use that agent as the subject and recast the sentence into active construction. (**On** is not needed.)

[8] **écrasé**   *run over,* literally *crushed.*

*John was given a book **by the teacher**.*
= ***The teacher*** *gave John a book.*

Le professeur a donné un livre à Jean.

8.16   Reflexive verbs replacing the passive

Certain verbs are sometimes used reflexively to avoid the passive. Among these are **se composer de** (*to be composed of*), **se diviser en** (*to be divided into*), **se dire** (*to be said*), **se vendre** (*to be sold*).

La symphonie **se divise en** quatre mouvements.
*The symphony **is divided into** four movements.*

Cela ne **se dit** pas.
*That **is not said**.*

Le livre **se compose de** douze chapitres.
*The book **is composed of** twelve chapters.*

Les portes **se ferment** à midi.
*The doors **are closed** at noon.*

Le tabac **se vend** ici.
*Tobacco **is sold** here.*

L'électricité **s'utilise** partout.
*Electricity **is used** everywhere.*

The last three examples could just as well be made active by using **on**:

On ferme les portes à midi.

On vend le tabac ici.

On utilise l'électricité partout.

8.17   True passive voice

The passive may be formed (as in English) by using any tense of **être** + [PAST PARTICIPLE]. The past participle agrees in gender and number with the subject.

être + PAST PARTICIPLE

Il **a été aidé** par son père.

Elles **ont été aidées** par leur père.

La maison **a été construite** en 1986.

8.18   Use of *de* or *par* as agent with the passive

When the passive voice is used, **de** + [AGENT] usually indicates a static situation; **par** + [ACTIVE AGENT] indicates action:

Notre chien **a été écrasé** *par* un camion. (*action*)
Our dog was run over by a truck.

M. Leclerc **est admiré** *de* tout le monde. (*static*)
Mr. Leclerc is admired by everybody.

La maison **était entourée** *d'*un mur. (*static*)
The house was surrounded by a wall.

Les voitures **sont examinées** *par* leur propriétaire. (*action*)
The cars are examined by their owner.

Les arbres **ont été couverts** *de* neige. (*static*)
The trees have been covered with snow.

Mise en œuvre 8 E

Moyens d'éviter la voix passive

Mettez les phrases suivantes à la voix active.

EXEMPLES

M. Leclerc est admiré.
On admire M. Leclerc.

Notre maison a été construite en 1989.
On a construit notre maison en 1989.

1. Ma voiture a été réparée.
2. Mon vélo a été perdu par mon frère.
3. Les portes ont été fermées avant neuf heures.
4. Cette symphonie a été composée au dix-neuvième siècle.
5. Ma bicyclette a été volée (*stolen*).
6. Notre voiture a été réparée par le mécanicien.
7. Cette pièce a été représentée pour la première fois à Paris.
8. Cette pièce a été représentée par la Comédie-Française.
9. Ma composition a été corrigée par le professeur.
10. Ma composition a été corrigée.
11. Les phrases anglaises ont été répétées.

12. Les phrases italiennes ont été répétées par les étudiants.
13. La machine à écrire a été vendue.
14. Le tabac est vendu ici.
15. Cette fenêtre a été ouverte ce matin.
16. L'enfant a été retrouvé.
17. Les boutiques sont fermées au mois d'aout.
18. Un livre a été offert au meilleur élève.
19. La ville est divisée en vingt arrondissements.
20. L'heure de la réunion a été fixée.

Mise en œuvre 8 F

Thème

1. The Duponts never go to the movies because they don't like contemporary films.
2. I don't fly to London because I am afraid of planes.
3. Nobody takes the boat to New York because the trip is too expensive.
4. I have only a week for my visit to London. I am leaving for London on Wednesday.
5. Nothing seems as interesting as the beautiful châteaux of the Loire.
6. René scarcely studies his books; he does nothing but loaf.[9]
7. I don't find any maps on this shelf; they have been taken by one of the teachers.
8. Our theater was admired by the Swiss tourists.
9. I attend history class on Mondays, Wednesdays, and Fridays at twenty minutes of nine.
10. My roommate promises not to smoke; I can't stand cigarettes or cigars.[10]

Sujets de conversation ou de composition

1. Parlez des choses que vous préférez ne pas faire, et pourquoi.
2. Comparez les activités de deux de vos connaissances, en signalant les différences remarquables. Employez quelques négatifs.

---

[9] *to loaf* = **flâner;** use **ne faire que** [I] *to do nothing except* [I] cf. Mise en oeuvre 9C, no. 11.
[10] *to stand* = **tolérer**

9

Passé composé (*avoir*)
Verbe irrégulier *avoir*

PASSÉ COMPOSÉ (AUXILIAIRE **AVOIR**)

9.1 General

The passé composé is a verb tense dealing with completed events in the past. The form consists of two parts (i.e. *composé*).

The two parts of the passé composé are (1) the *auxiliary verb* (**avoir** or **être,** depending on the verb) in the present tense, and (2) the *past participle* of the main verb.

Most verbs use the auxiliary *avoir*. The verbs using the auxiliary *être* should be learned [10.3]; then any verb you do not recognize as being in *"la maison d'être"* is assumed to use the auxiliary *avoir*[1].

9.2 Use of the passé composé

This tense is used for an action that happened in the past, is *fully completed*, (over and done), and occurred only once at a time specifically indicated or strongly implied:

[1] Reflexive verbs all use *être*, but are easily distinguished by the reflexive pronoun *se* in the infinitive form.

L'employé **a ouvert** la porte à midi.

Les touristes **ont quitté** le musée à trois heures.

The passé composé is *not* used for actions that were habitual or recurrent in the past, nor for actions that were in progress but not completed at a given past time. Actions and descriptions of that kind are a function of the imperfect tense (**l'imparfait**) [13.1].

9.3   Formation of the passé composé with *avoir*

This tense consists of the auxiliary verb **avoir** in the present tense, plus the past participle of the main verb.

Nous **avons travaillé**   à la bibliothèque.
— PARTICIPE PASSÉ
— AUXILIAIRE (avoir)

A.   Past participle. The past participle (**participe passé**) is formed by dropping the infinitive ending (**-er, -ir,** or **-re**) and replacing it by the participle endings as follows:

VERB TYPE	DROP	ADD	PAST PARTICIPLE	EXAMPLE	MEANING[2]
parl/**er**	**-er**	**-é**	**parlé**	**ils ont parlé**	*they spoke*
fin/**ir**	**-ir**	**-i**	**fini**	**nous avons fini**	*we finished*
vend/**re**	**-re**	**-u**	**vendu**	**j'ai vendu**	*I sold*

NOTE: The past participle *cannot be used alone*. It must be used in conjunction with the auxiliary verb.

B.   Irregular past participles. You cannot form the past participles of *irregular* verbs using the method above. You will need to look them up until you have used them enough to have them firmly in mind.

Some of the most commonly used ones are:

VERB	PAST PARTICIPLE	EXAMPLE	MEANING
avoir	**eu**	**J'ai eu** faim.	*I was hungry.*
être	**été**	**Il a été** étonné.	*He was astonished.*

[2] Notice that the one-word past in English is preferred in most cases to a literal two-word meaning. Thus *They spoke Spanish.* is preferred to *They have spoken Spanish.*

N.B.

VERB	PAST PARTICIPLE	EXAMPLE	MEANING
faire	**fait**	Ils **ont fait** une promenade.	They took a walk.
lire	**lu**	Elle **a lu** la lettre.	She read the letter.
voir	**vu**	Nous **avons vu** ce film.	We saw that movie.
devoir	**dû**	Il **a dû** partir.	He *had to leave* / *must have left*.
écrire	**écrit**	Jean **a écrit** la lettre.	*Jean wrote* / *has written the letter*.
dire	**dit**	Il m'**a dit** de faire cela.	He told me to do that.
prendre	**pris**	Elle **a pris** un taxi.	She took a taxi.
comprendre	**compris**	J'**ai compris** la situation.	I understood the situation.
mettre	**mis**	Elle **a mis** la table.	She set the table.
ouvrir	**ouvert**	Il **a ouvert** la porte.	He opened the door.
souffrir	**souffert**	On **a** beaucoup **souffert.**	There has been a lot of suffering.
offrir	**offert**	Il **a offert** des fleurs à son amie.	He gave some flowers to his friend.

Learn the past participles of other irregular verbs as you need them.

9.4   Agreement of the past participle (Accord du participe passé)

The past participle for verbs compounded with **avoir** is invariable *unless* a direct object stands before it. If the direct object *follows* the verb, there is no agreement.

Il **a** acheté *une voiture neuve.*

└── DIRECT OBJECT FOLLOWS VERB. (NO AGREEMENT)

Voilà *la voiture* qu'il a achetée.

└── DIRECT OBJECT PRECEDES VERB.

(PAST PARTICIPLE AGREES—FEM. SINGULAR)

The past participle agrees with the *preceding direct object* (PDO) in gender and number, just like an adjective. The only words that can affect the ending of the past participle in this way are (1) **que** [22.3], the relative pronoun used as a direct object; (2) direct object pronouns (**le, la, les, me, te, se, nous, vous**)[3], and (3) **combien de,**

---

[3] Be sure that you are *not* dealing with an indirect object pronoun in the case of **me, te, nous** and **vous,** which can mean *to me, to you, to us,* and are therefore used both as direct and indirect object pronouns. Test to see if *to* is meant, in which case the past participle does not agree.

quel, lequel des, with which the following noun determines number and gender. In the following examples, the PDO is underlined.

(1) Voilà la personne que vous **avez rencontrée** hier.

(2) Ces chaises? Madeleine **les a achetées** hier.

(3) Combien de chaises **as-tu pris*es*?**

NOTE: **Identification of the direct object.** To find out what the direct object is, say the subject and the verb, then ask —**Quoi?** (*What?*). The answer is the direct object. Notice that the answer cannot be a prepositional phrase. Sometimes there is no direct object. What is the direct object in the following?

Mes amis ont compris la leçon.[4]

Nous avons parlé au touriste américain.[5]

Nous avons parlé espagnol quand nous étions à Madrid.[6]

Jacques nous a donné deux billets pour l'opéra.[7]

Elle s'est levée avant six heures du matin.[8]

THE MECHANICS OF AGREEMENT:

Agreement is made with a PDO in gender and number, using the same method as for agreement of adjectives [5.1]. Add **-e** to the basic form to make it feminine; add **-s** to the basic form to make it masculine plural; add **-es** to the basic form to make it feminine plural. Since the past participle agrees only with a direct object that stands before it in the sentence, the participle is invariable when a direct object *follows* it.

J'ai vu **cette personne** en ville.	INVARIABLE
Voilà la personne que j'ai vue en ville. PDO	AGREEMENT WITH PDO
J'ai vu **ces étudiantes** hier.	INVARIABLE
Les étudiantes? Je les ai vues hier. PDO	AGREEMENT
Nous avons quitté **les jeunes filles** à midi.	INVARIABLE
Les jeunes filles? Nous les avons quittées à midi. PDO	AGREEMENT

[4] —**Mes amis ont compris** *quoi?* **La leçon** is the direct object.

[5] —**Nous avons parlé** *quoi?* There is no answer, hence no direct object. The expression *to the American tourist* answers the question—"**À qui?**", which is not applicable unless you are seeking the indirect object.

[6] —**Nous avons parlé** *espagnol.* **Espagnol** is the direct object.

[7] —**Jacques a donné** *quoi?* **Billets** is the direct object.

[8] —**Elle a levé** *quoi?* She raised *what? Herself* (s') is the direct object.

Other examples of preceding direct objects:

Paul ⟦nous⟧ a **regardés.**
Combien de ⟦livres⟧ avez-vous **achetés?**
Quelle ⟦pièce⟧ as-tu **vue** en ville?
Lesquels de ces ⟦films⟧ ont-ils **préférés?**

TEST YOURSELF: **Agreement of the Past Participle**

Supply the correct form of the past participle in the following problems. Cover the answer that appears on the line below each problem until you have written the necessary form.

1. Jean a ⟦trouver⟧ la lettre.
   Jean found *what?* DO is **la lettre.** It follows the verb, so there is *no* agreement: Jean **a trouvé** la lettre.
2. Les lettres? Je les ai ⟦finir⟧.
   I finished *what?* **les** is the DO, and since it comes before the verb, there *is* agreement: Je les **ai finies.**
3. Voilà la lettre que Jean a ⟦écrire⟧.
   Jean wrote *what?* DO is **la lettre.** Since it appears *before* the participle, there *is* agreement: Voilà la lettre **que** Jean **a écrite.**

9.5 Invariable past participle

In addition to the rule that past participles using the auxiliary **avoir** agree only if there is a PDO, notice the following two cases:

A.   Agreement is never made with *en*, even though it may be a PDO:

Il a vu **de belles statues.**   Il **en** a **vu.**
He saw some fine statues.   *He saw some.*

J'ai acheté **des cassettes.**   J'**en** ai **acheté.**
I bought some cassettes.   *I bought some.*

B.   When the past participle is followed by an infinitive (expressed or implied), there is no agreement.

La dame **que** nous avons **entendu** *chanter* s'appelle Martine Brun.
Voilà la voiture **que** le douanier **a laissé** *passer.*

Mise en œuvre 9 A

Une crise scolaire

Complétez ce commentaire sur la lettre de Robert en ajoutant à la phrase incomplète l'expression entre parenthèses. Mettez le verbe au passé composé. Notez que les phrases qui commencent par un tiret (—) sont des citations directes. Faites les élisions nécessaires.

EXEMPLE

(**raconter** sa vie à l'université)

Dans une lettre à son père, Robert . . .

Dans une lettre à son père, Robert lui a raconté sa vie à l'université.

1. (écrire une lettre à ses parents) Hier soir, il . . .
2. (devoir leur demander de l'argent) Malheureusement, il . . .
3. (dire la vérité) Dans sa lettre, il . . .
4. (dépenser tout mon argent)—J'avoue que je . . .
5. (ne pas gaspiller cet argent)—Naturellement, je . . .
6. (payer mes frais scolaires)—J' . . ., affirme-t-il.
7. (résister à réclamer encore de l'argent) Bien sûr, il . . .
8. (oser aborder le sujet) Vers la fin de la lettre, il . . .
9. (expliquer sa situation) D'abord, il . . .
10. (mentionner modestement ses qualités) Et il . . .
11. (assister à tous mes cours)—Il faut dire que je . . .
12. (ne pas sécher un seul cours)—Soyez certains que je . . .
13. (finir mes recherches en histoire)—A la bibliothèque, je . . .
14. (écrire ma composition)—Pour mon cours d'anglais, je . . .
15. (même promettre de ne plus fréquenter le bistrot) Pour plaire à son père, il . . .
16. (faire ses devoirs) A partir de ce jour-là, il . . .
17. (passer ses examens du mi-semestre)—En plus, je . . .
18. (même réussir à quelques examens) Notez qu'il . . .
19. (mettre la lettre à la poste) Plein d'espoir, Robert . . .
20. (boire un verre au bistrot du coin avec des copains) Ensuite, pour se détendre un peu, il . . .

Mise en œuvre 9 B

Accord du participe passé

On commente la lettre de Robert. Remplacez les infinitifs en italique par le passé composé. Faites attention à l'accord et à l'élision nécessaires.

1. Les parents (*recevoir*) la lettre que Robert (*écrire*).
2. —Nous la (*lire*) tout de suite, (*dire*) le père de Robert.
3. Combien d'argent Robert (*demander*) à son père? [21.6]
4. —Il nous (*demander*) un supplément d'argent.
5. Les 200 francs qu'il (*dépenser*) sont au bistrot du coin maintenant.
6. Robert (*téléphoner*) à ses parents. Il leur (*poser*) la question suivante:
7. —Est-ce que vous (*comprendre*) ma situation?
8. —Nous la (*comprendre*) avec difficulté, (*répondre*) son père.
9. Les frais scolaires que tu (*payer*) sont une dépense nécessaire.
10. La question que Robert (*poser*) était épineuse.[9]
11. —Robert nous (*chercher*) pour emprunter de l'argent, (*dire*) quelques-uns de ses amis.
12. Il nous (*expliquer*) en détail son besoin d'argent.
13. Les qualités qu'il (*énumérer*) étaient admirables.
14. Malheureusement, il (*ne pas réussir*) à tous les examens qu'il (*passer*).
15. D'ailleurs, il (*reprendre*) sa place au bistrot du coin!

VERBE IRRÉGULIER avoir

9.6   avoir (*to have*)

Review the present, imperfect, future, and passé composé tenses of the verb **avoir** in Appendix C, Table 2.

Note the following important idioms using **avoir**:

avoir raison	*to be right*
avoir tort	*to be wrong*
avoir envie de [I]	*to feel like [doing something]*
avoir faim	*to be hungry*
avoir soif	*to be thirsty*
avoir mal à [PART OF BODY]	*to have a pain in / [PART] hurts*
avoir besoin de [N or I]	*to need*

---

[9] **Une question épineuse** = an uncomfortable (touchy) question, lit. "thorny"

avoir sommeil	*to be sleepy*
avoir beau [FAIRE qqch[10]]	*to do something in vain*
avoir l'air [ADJECTIF[11]]	*to seem* [ADJECTIVE]
avoir [N°] **ans**	*to be* [No.] *years old*
avoir peur [**de** qqch]	*to be afraid* [*of* something]
avoir le trac	*to be scared, to have stage fright*
avoir du toupet	*to have a lot of nerve* (impertinence)
avoir rendez-vous avec . . .	*to have an appointment / date with*
avoir le cafard	*to have the blues*
avoir l'intention de [+ INF]	*to intend to* [*do* something]

J'**ai beau** étudier, je n'apprends rien.
There's no use in my studying; I don't learn anything.
No matter how much I study, I don't learn anything.

Marie et Georges **ont envie** d'aller au cinéma.
Marie and George feel like going to the movies.

Jacques **a** dix-neuf **ans.**
Jacques is nineteen (years old).

J'ai **mal aux** dents.
I have a toothache.

J'ai **rendez-vous avec** Suzanne à 10 heures.
I have a date with Suzanne at ten o'clock.

9.7   avoir [qqch] à [FAIRE] (*to have* [something] *to* [do])

The word order shown must be followed. The infinitive **faire** may be replaced by any other infinitive as desired.

J'**ai** une composition à écrire.
I have a composition to write.

Nous **avons** un examen à préparer.
We have an examination to get ready for.

Jacques n'**a** rien à faire ce soir.
Jacques has nothing to do this evening.

---

[10] The abbreviation **qqch** stands for *quelque chose* (*something*); a noun would appear at this position in a structure. When the infinitive [**faire**] or the small cap [I] is shown in brackets, this means that any infinitive could be used at that position.

[11] Since **air** is masculine, the masculine form of the adjective must be used, even when describing a feminine noun: **Marie a l'air fatigué.**

9.8 Special cases: avoir (*to be the matter*) / C'est que . . . (*the thing is that . . .*)

— Qu'est-ce que **tu as?**   *What's the matter with you?*

— Qu'est-ce qu'**il y a?**   *What's going on? What's the matter?*

RÉPONSES POSSIBLES:

— **C'est que** je suis fauché.   *(The thing is) I am broke.*

— **C'est que** j'ai mal à la tête.   *I have a headache.*

9.9 Il y a vs. Voilà   *there is, there are*

Use **il y a** when the object you refer to is *not in view*. Add a prepositional phrase to indicate its location. Use **voilà**[12] when you can point to it. It does not matter whether the noun is singular or plural.

Il y a des dictionnaires *dans la bibliothèque.*

Voilà un bon dictionnaire.

Voilà mon professeur de français.

9.10 Interrogative form y a-t-il   *is there, are there?*

Y a-t-il assez de place pour tout le monde?

Y a-t-il des ordinateurs dans le laboratoire?

9.11 Time ago il y a [TIME]; voilà [TIME]

J'ai passé mon examen **il y a** une semaine.
I took my exam a week ago.

Nous avons fini le travail **voilà** une heure.
We finished the work an hour ago.

9.12 avoir lieu   *to take place*

This expression is used for important events such as **une cérémonie, une réunion, une fête, un concert, une conférence.** The place and/or time is usually mentioned.

[12] **Voilà** is related to the theoretical command **Vois là** (*See there*).

La fête **va avoir lieu (aura lieu)** à Cannes.
The festival will take place in Cannes.

Les Jeux Olympiques **ont lieu** tous les quatre ans.
The Olympic Games take place (are held) every four years.

Mise en œuvre 9 C

Idiotismes avec *avoir*

Répondez aux questions, ou commentez en utilisant le mot entre parenthèses.

 1. (faim)   Pourquoi cherchez-vous un restaurant?
 2. (tort)   Jean croit que Séville est la capitale de l'Espagne. A-t-il raison?
 3. (mal)   Cet homme veut consulter le dentiste. Pourquoi?
 4. (sommeil)   L'enfant veut aller au lit.
 5. (ans)   Denis est né en 1979. Quel âge a-t-il?
 6. (ans)   Quel âge avez-vous?
 7. (envie)   Nous avons assez étudié. Que veux-tu faire?
 8. (besoin)   Je veux écrire une carte postale, mais je n'ai pas de stylo.
 9. (trac)   Claude va passer un examen demain.
10. (cafard)   Luc me semble très malheureux.
11. (beau)   Jacques ne fait qu'étudier, mais il ne réussit pas aux examens.
12. (air)   Suzanne semble fatiguée.

Reflets

L'Université

1. L'année passée les étudiants de l'université **ont suivi des cours** (de maths, d'anglais, de physique, d'économie, de journalisme et de gestion[13], entre autres). Pour **se distraire**[14] ils ont fait du sport, ou bien ils sont allés au théâtre, au cinéma pour voir les films italiens, ou dans les boites de nuit[15]. Parfois ils ont **pris quelque chose** dans une brasserie ou dans un bistrot. De temps à autre ils ont **assisté aux réunions** des cercles et des clubs (tels que le Club sportif, le Club Alpin).

[13] **gestion** = *management*
[14] **se distraire** = *to relax, to find amusement.* The noun is **la distraction**, *diversion, amusement.*
[15] **boites de nuit** = *night clubs*

2. Avant d'assister à un cours, ils ont dû **s'inscrire au cours.** Les étudiants ont été à **la librairie** pour acheter leurs **manuels** et d'autres livres, et à **la papeterie** pour se procurer du papier, des stylos et des cahiers. A la différence des États-Unis, les étudiants ne sont pas obligés d'assister aux cours. L'assistance est **facultative.**

3. Le laboratoire de langues, équipé de magnétophones spéciaux, de téléviseurs et d'ordinateurs, a beaucoup facilité l'étude des langues étrangères. Pendant l'année scolaire nos étudiants ont commencé à comprendre et à parler une autre langue vivante.

   Il existe aussi une **formation technique:** les instituts de biologie appliquée, d'informatique, de chimie; et les écoles d'ingénieurs par exemple.

   La date de l'ouverture des cours s'appelle **la rentrée;** en général, la rentrée a lieu début septembre.

4. Hier matin le professeur **a fait l'appel** comme d'habitude. Ensuite il y a eu une présentation et beaucoup d'exercices à faire. Le cours de langue a consisté en exercices structurels, faits **à tour de rôle,** suivis de conversations. Parfois le professeur a demandé aux étudiants d'aller **au tableau noir** pour écrire des phrases **à la craie.** Quand ils ont fait des fautes, ils ont dû les **effacer** et les récrire correctement. (Est-ce que c'est possible de faire cela dans la vie réelle?)

Mise en œuvre 9 E

A l'école

Répondez aux questions en y ajoutant un commentaire.

1. Quelle est la date de la rentrée chez vous?
2. Combien de cours avez-vous suivis l'année passée? Quels ont été les cours?
3. Qu'avez-vous dû faire avant d'assister aux cours?
4. Où a-t-on acheté les manuels? Les cahiers, les crayons, le papier?
5. Quelle est la différence entre une librairie et une bibliothèque?
6. Quand et pourquoi allez-vous à la bibliothèque?
7. Quelle méthode d'enseignement est-ce que votre professeur de français a employée?
8. Quelles méthodes d'enseignement est-ce que vous trouvez les plus efficaces? (la conférence, la discussion, la démonstration, le laboratoire?)
9. Qu'est-ce que le professeur fait pour vérifier la présence des étudiants?
10. Qu'avez-vous fait pour vous distraire la semaine passée?

11. Quels autres cours ont des laboratoires? Comment est-ce que leur fonctionnement contraste avec le laboratoire des langues?
12. Est-ce que vous participez aux activités des clubs? Expliquez.

Sujets de conversation ou de composition

1. Avez-vous un cours favori? Pourquoi est-ce qu'il vous plait? Décrivez les procédés d'un de vos cours, en indiquant ce que font le professeur et les étudiants.
2. Commentez les activités d'un club, d'un cercle, d'un groupe spécial, ou d'un sport qui rend votre vie à l'université plus agréable.

10

Passé composé (*être*)
Verbe irrégulier *être*
Distinctions de vocabulaire

PASSÉ COMPOSÉ AVEC L'AUXILIAIRE **ÊTRE**

10.1 Formation of the passé composé

The passé composé of the 15 intransitive[1] verbs listed below is formed by combining the present tense of **être** and the past participle of the main verb. (All reflexive verbs also use the auxiliary **être** [12.1].)

The past participles of these verbs are formed in the regular way [9.3 A] except for three:

VERB	PAST PARTICIPLE	EXAMPLE
naître	**né**	Il **est né** à Paris.
mourir	**mort**	Elle **est morte** à Nice.
venir	**venu**	Ils **sont venus** nous voir.

The past participle agrees with the *subject* in gender and number, with these verbs using the auxiliary **être:**

[1] *Intransitive* means that there can be no direct object.

MODEL VERB: sortir[2] in the **passé composé**
PAST PARTICIPLE: **sorti** (regularly formed)

je **suis sorti(e)**[3]	nous **sommes sorti(e)s**[4]
tu **es sorti(e)**	vous **êtes sorti(e)(s)**
il **est sorti**	ils **sont sortis**
elle **est sortie**	elles **sont sorties**

NOTE: The past participle **sorti** is shown with feminine and plural endings, where they are possible. Those in parentheses indicate the various possibilities of agreement[5] with the subject. Notice that the final **-s** with the **nous**-form (form 4) is obligatory, since **nous** is plural by definition. On the other hand, **vous** can be singular or plural, masculine or feminine; and **tu** can be either gender, but never plural.

When writing French, select the appropriate agreement depending upon who the subject is. For example, if the person you are addressing as **tu** is a male, use the basic (*m.s.*) agreement. If **nous** or **vous** is the subject, use the masculine plural agreement (unless the subjects are all female).

Examine Appendix C for further examples such as **venir** (Verb Table 30) and **partir** (Verb Table 20).

10.2   Agreement of the past participle

The past participle of intransitive verbs compounded with **être** must agree with the SUBJECT in gender and number. Agreement is made as though the past participle were an adjective: the basic past participle is masculine singular. Add **-e** to make it feminine singular, add **-s** to make it masculine plural, and add **-es** to make it feminine plural.

Il est **arrivé.** (*m. s.*)	Ils sont **arrivés.** (*m. pl.*)
Elle est **arrivée.** (*f. s.*)	Elles sont **arrivées.** (*f. pl.*)

You might visualize the situation as though the form of **être** were an equal sign (=). **Elles = arrivées** shows both sides of the equation to be feminine plural.

NOTE: There is a different rule for reflexive verbs (**verbes pronominaux**) [12.4], and for verbs listed in 10.5 where there is a direct object.

---

[2] Irregular verbs are listed in Appendix C.

[3] Letters in parentheses show alternate possible agreements. Use only the appropriate one in any given sentence.

[4] The agreement here *must* be plural, although either masculine or feminine is possible.

[5] *Agreement* refers to **l'accord du participe passé.**

10.3   Verbs compounded with *être*

The following verbs form the compound tenses using the auxiliary **être**. If you learn to recognize these verbs, then you will know that any unfamiliar verb will use the *other* auxiliary, **avoir**.

INFINITIVE	PAST PARTICIPLE	MEANING (*has* +)
aller	**allé**	*gone*
venir	**venu**	*come*
revenir	revenu	*come back*
devenir	devenu	*become*
arriver	**arrivé**	*arrived*
partir (de)	**parti**	*departed, left*
entrer (dans)	**entré**	*gone in, entered*
sortir (de)	**sorti**	*gone out, left*
monter (dans)	**monté**	*gone up; gotten into*[6]
descendre (de)	**descendu**	*gone down, gotten out of*[7]
naître	**né**	*born*
mourir	**mort**	*died*
rester	**resté**	*remained, stayed*
tomber	**tombé**	*fallen*
retourner	**retourné**	*gone back, returned*

A helpful device for remembering which verbs are formed with **être** in the compound tenses is "La Maison d'**être**."

The words with opposite meanings are contrasted by being on the opposite sides of the house (e.g. *going in* the front door (**entrer [dans]**) contrasted with *going out* the back door (**sortir [de]**). There are only three irregular past participles: **venu, né, mort,** shown in brackets; the bedrooms on the **premier étage** (*second floor*) represent two of these "irregular" happenings in life (being born and dying); they have irregular past participles. The third is **venir** and its compounds.

Make the distinction between **revenir** (*to come back*) and **retourner** (*to go*

---

[6] **Monter** is also used for getting into or on a means of transportation: **Il est monté dans sa voiture.**

[7] **Descendre** is also used for *to stay* at a hotel; *to descend* or *get out of*, or *off of*, a vehicle.

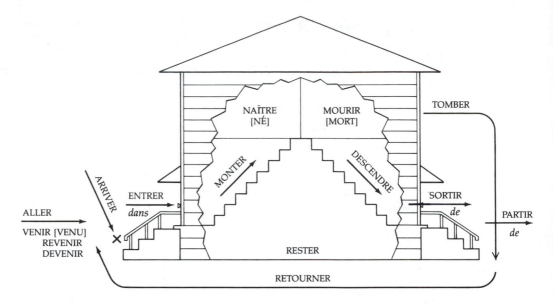

back). With **venir** and its compounds, the person or thing mentioned is conceived to be *approaching* the speaker, whereas with **retourner** the subject is *going away* from the speaker:

> Jeanne **est venue** chez nous hier soir.
> *Jeanne **came** to our place yesterday evening.*
>
> Elle **est retournée** chez elle après la soirée.
> *She **went back** home after the party.*

Finally, notice that all compounds of the verbs in this group also use the auxiliary **être**: *re*venir, *de*venir, *r*entrer, *re*partir, *re*naître for example. The prefix *re-* means *again.*

10.4 Prepositions required: *entrer dans, sortir de,* and *partir de*

If a *location* is mentioned after these verbs, the preposition shown is required before the name of the location:

Il est entré.	BUT	Il est entré **dans la salle.**
Elle est sortie.	BUT	Elle est sortie **de la maison.**

10.5   Transitive use of *monter, descendre, rentrer* and *sortir*

These four verbs can be used with a direct object[8] with the meanings shown below. They are then conjugated with the auxiliary **avoir** in the compound tenses. The noun symbol [N] represents the direct object:

monter [N]	*to take (something) upstairs*
descendre [N]	*to take (something) down*
sortir [N] **de**	*to take (something) out (of)*
rentrer [N]	*to bring (something) back*

The direct objects are underlined in the following examples.

J'ai **monté** le journal au patron.	*I took the paper up to the boss.*
Les touristes **ont descendu** les valises.	*The tourists took their bags down.*
Robert **a sorti** un stylo du tiroir.	*Robert took a pen out of the drawer.*
Il **a rentré** les chaises du jardin.	*He brought the chairs back in from the garden.*

The rule for agreement using **avoir** now applies [9.4]. If there is a PDO (a direct object in front of the past participle), unlike English order, there is agreement:

Les tourists **ont descendu** les valises.	DIRECT OBJECT FOLLOWS **descendu.** NO AGREEMENT.
Les touristes *les* **ont descendues.**	DIRECT OBJECT **(les)** IS A PDO. AGREEMENT.

NOTE: If the order is unlike English, there is probably an agreement problem. In English, one wouldn't say, *"The tourists **them** took down,"* or *"I **it** took upstairs."*

Mise en œuvre 10 A

On a cherché des renseignements

Vous et un ami ou une amie voulez faire un voyage. Vous avez contacté une visite à un agent de voyages. Pour décrire ce qui est arrivé, mettez les phrases au passé composé en faisant les changements nécessaires. Faites attention à l'auxiliaire.

EXEMPLE

Mon ami(e) et moi / aller / ville / hier matin

Mon ami(e) et moi, nous **sommes allé(e)s** en ville hier matin.

---

[8] That is: "transitively."

1. nous / besoin / renseignements / pour arranger / voyage
2. nous / aller / agence de voyages
3. nous / arriver / devant / bureau / vers neuf heures
4. on / ouvrir / porte / neuf heures et demie
5. nous / entrer / bureau / et / monter / premier étage
6. une charmante employée / nous / inviter[9] / entrer / son / bureau
7. elle / sortir / crayon / tiroir / et / faire / note
8. je / expliquer / que / nous / avoir / idée de / aller / Espagne
9. ma sœur / déjà visiter / Madrid / année dernière
10. quand elle y / aller / elle / fait / voyage / avion[10]
11. nous / rester / bureau / pendant une heure
12. je / devenir / un peu frustré(e) / à cause de / prix du voyage
13. nous / décider[11] / rester / Paris
14. nous / remercier / employée / et / sortir / bureau
15. nous / quitter / agent / vers dix heures
16. nous / descendre / rez-de-chaussée / et / sortir / bâtiment
17. lui (elle) / me / quitter / pour / aller / cinéma
18. je / retourner / maison / pour / feuilleter[12] / brochures
19. nous / ne pas retourner / agence de voyage
20. Et les bicyclettes? / nous / les / sortir / garage

VERBE IRRÉGULIER ÊTRE

10.6   Review the forms of the verb *être* [*to be*]

Review the forms of **être** in Appendix C, Verb Table 13. Note the meaning of these tenses:

PRÉSENT	Vous **êtes** très gentil.
IMPARFAIT	Elle **était** belle quand elle **était** jeune. (*used to be, was*)
PASSÉ COMPOSÉ	Il **a été** à Lyon en 1988. (*was*)
PASSÉ SIMPLE	Il **fut** à Lyon en 1988. (*was*: literary)

Formation: **f-** + **-us** system of endings, section 20.2.

[9] Souvenez-vous de la préposition qu'on emploie entre **inviter** et un infinitif suivant. [18.4] (Il faut mettre à devant l'infinitif suivant.)

[10] Employez **en avion** pour les personnes, **par avion** pour les lettres.

[11] Attention à la préposition qu'on emploie entre **décider** et un infinitif suivant [18.5].

[12] *to leaf through*

FUTUR	Ils **seront** contents de le savoir. (*will be*)
	Formation: **ser-** + future endings, section 24.4.

CONDITIONNEL	Ils **seraient** contents s'ils étaient riches. (*would be*)
	Formation: **ser-** + imperfect endings, section 25.2.

SUBJONCTIF	Je doute qu'elle **soit** contente. (*is*) (*will be*)
	Formation: Section 14.9.

10.7   Idioms using *être*

Learn the following special uses of this verb:

être d'accord (avec [P[13]]	*to agree* (*with* [P])
être de retour	*to be back*
être en train de [INFINITIF]	*to be* [*doing something*] *at the moment*
être à [N][14]	*to belong to* [N[15]]
être de bonne humeur	*to be in a good mood*
être de mauvaise humeur	*to be in a bad mood*
être bien	*to be comfortable* (*persons only*)
être en panne	*to be broken down* (*machines*)

Ma voiture **est en panne**; elle ne marche plus.
My car is broken down. It's not running any more.

Je suis de ton avis. Nous **sommes d'accord.**
I am of the same opinion as you. We agree.

M. Leboutiller **est de retour** depuis une semaine.
Mr. Leboutiller has been back for a week.

Je ne peux pas sortir; je **suis en train de** faire mes devoirs.
I can't go out. I'm right in the middle of doing my homework.

Ce manuel **est à** Lucien. Ce n'**est** pas à moi.
This textbook is Lucien's. It's not mine.

Mise en œuvre 10 B

Idiotismes avec *être*

Complétez les phrases en employant une expression avec **être**. Ajoutez une explication logique pour justifier la constatation:

[13] The symbol [P] indicates that a noun representing a *person* should appear at this location.
[14] Synonym for **appartenir*** à.
[15] The symbol [N] indicates that a noun should appear at this location.

EXEMPLE

Le patron n'est pas heureux aujourd'hui. Il . . .

Il est de mauvaise humeur.

C'est que sa voiture est en panne.

1. Votre amie a l'air content. Elle . . .
2. Laure a été en vacances, mais maintenant elle . . .
3. Le professeur ne peut pas vous voir en ce moment. C'est que . . .
4. Je ne peux pas sortir parce que . . .
5. J'ai manqué une classe, mais ce n'est pas ma faute. C'est que ma bicyclette . . .
6. L'ordinateur ne marche pas, donc le programmeur est . . .
7. Marie et Gérard ont les mêmes opinions politiques. Ils sont . . .
8. Vous êtes assis sur une chaise en mauvais état. Est-ce que vous . . .
9. Cette voiture n'est pas à moi; c'est . . .
10. M. Duval a terminé son voyage. Il est . . .

DISTINCTIONS DE VOCABULAIRE

10.8   Semantic differences: *partir, sortir, quitter, laisser.*

A.   **Partir** (**de** [N]) means *to leave* or *to depart.* If the place left is mentioned, it is obligatory to use **de.**

Il est parti à midi.   BUT   Il est parti **de la maison** à midi.

A related expression is **à partir de** [TIME OR PLACE] which means *starting with:*

Elle travaille à la librairie **à partir d'aujourd'hui.**
She works at the bookstore beginning today.

Commençons à lire **à partir de** la page 108.
Let's begin reading starting at page 108.

B.   **Sortir** (**de** [N]) means *to leave, to go out of* (*a place*). This verb is used only for *to leave* in the sense of *going out* of some "container" like a house or room. If the place is mentioned, **de** must precede it. The action starts *inside.*

Il est sorti.   *He has gone out.*

Il est sorti **de la maison.**   *He has left the house.*

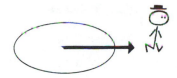

C.   Quitter [N] means *to leave (a person or place), to go away from (a person or place)*. This verb cannot be used alone like **partir** or **sortir**; the person or place left must be mentioned. No preposition is used.

Il **a quitté son ami** à la gare.   *He left his friend at the station.*
J'ai quitté mon hôtel à midi.   *I left my hotel at noon.*
Nous **l'avons quitté** à midi.   *We left it (or him) at noon.*

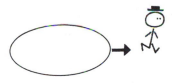

D.   Laisser [N] means *to leave (something)*. This verb indicates that some object has been placed and left behind. That object must be mentioned (it is the direct object).

J'ai laissé mon livre sur la table.   *I left my book on the table.*
Robert **laisse le pourboire.**   *Robert is leaving the tip.*

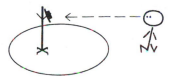

The structure **laisser** [I] + [N] means *to allow (something* [N]) *(to be done* [I]). Notice the reversal of order from the English equivalent.

Le professeur **a laissé partir** *les étudiants.*
The teacher allowed the students to leave.

Le douanier **laisse passer** *les voyageurs.*
The customs officer allows the travelers to pass.

Some common combinations of **laisser** and an infinitive lend themselves to simpler translation. For example, **laisser tomber** [N] may be given the equivalent *to drop:*

Bernard **a laissé tomber** le dictionnaire.
Bernard dropped the dictionary.

This structure may be compared with *causative* **faire** [17.1].

Mise en œuvre 10 C

Distinctions de vocabulaire [10.8]

Mettez les verbes en italique au passé composé. Faites attention au choix de l'auxiliaire (**avoir** ou **être**), et à l'accord du participe passé.

EXEMPLE

Nous *allons* à la Gare du Nord. Nous *prenons* le train de 6 h.

Nous **sommes allés** à la Gare du Nord. Nous **avons pris** le train de 6 h.

1. Je *pars* de la maison à midi, et après le travail je *quitte* le bureau vers cinq heures.
2. —Je *vais* à la bibliothèque, dit-il, pour consulter des œuvres de référence.
3. Elle *reste* dans la salle de lecture pendant une heure; elle *met* ses livres sur une table.
4. Elle *consulte* l'article intitulé «Italie» parce qu'elle cherchait des renseignements sur Venise, ville bâtie sur un groupe d'ilots.
5. En 1834, George Sand *tombe* amoureuse d'Alfred de Musset. Ils *voyagent* à Venise où ils *restent* pendant un certain temps.
6. Après avoir lu cet article, j'*arrive* à l'article sur Vienne, la capitale de l'Autriche.
7. Je *sors* de la bibliothèque et je *trouve* que la circulation devenait intense.
8. Des voyageurs *entrent* dans la gare; d'autres en *sortent* au moment où j'y *arrive*.
9. Ma grand-mère *vient* à Paris nous rendre visite, mais elle *retourne* chez elle dans l'après-midi.
10. Heureusement elle *revient* une seconde fois, et elle *descend* de l'autobus près de notre immeuble.

11

Adverbes
ouvrir

ADVERBES

11.1   Place de l'adverbe: général

An adverb[1] usually *follows* a verb to fine-tune its meaning. An adverb may also modify an adjective, a past participle, or another adverb; the adverb then *precedes* the modified word:

MODIFYING THE:	
VERB:	Il ⸢*écrit* **bien**⸣ le français.
ADJECTIVE:	Elle est ⸢**extrêmement** *intelligente.*⸣
PAST PARTICIPLE:	Il semble ⸢**très** *fatigué.*⸣
	La porte était ⸢**partiellement** *ouverte.*⸣
	J'ai ⸢**complètement** *oublié*⸣ la clé.
	La concierge a ⸢**beaucoup** *parlé.*⸣
ADVERB:	Cette voiture marche ⸢**trop** *vite.*⸣

[1] Adverb = add(ed to the) verb

135

11.2   Short adverbs follow the verb

A short adverb is placed in the sentence *after* the inflected verb (the simple verb or the auxiliary verb):

MODIFYING A:	ADVERB IS PLACED:	EXAMPLE:
Simple verb	After the one-word verb	Il travaille **bien.**
Compound verb	After auxiliary	Il a **bien** travaillé.

Adverbs of this type are:

déjà	*already*	**beaucoup**	*much, a lot*
bien	*well*	**souvent**	*often*
trop	*too much*	**toujours**	*still, always*
assez	*enough*	**bientôt**	*soon*
pas encore	*not yet*		

SIMPLE TENSE	COMPOUND TENSE
Elle part **déjà.**	Elle est **déjà** partie.
Il m'écrit **souvent.**	Il m'a **souvent** écrit.
Ils se lèvent **bientôt.**	Ils se sont **bientôt** levés.

11.3   Adverb in negation

These adverbs *follow* the negative block that begins with **ne** and ends with **pas:**

Il ne m'écrit pas *souvent.*   Il ne m'a pas *souvent* écrit.

NOTE: The negative of **déjà** is **pas encore** (*not yet*):

Elle comprend **déjà.**   Elle **ne** comprend **pas encore.**

Elle est **déjà** partie.   Elle n'est **pas encore** partie.

11.4   Long adverbs ending in *-ment*

The ending **-ment** is equivalent to **-ly** in English. There is some flexibility regarding the placement of adverbs ending in **-ment**. Such adverbs may be placed at the beginning or end of the sentence:

Il est entré **silencieusement.**	*He entered silently.*
Elle parlait **rapidement.**	*She was speaking rapidly.*
Lentement[2] il s'approcha de la porte.	*Slowly he approached the door.*

[2] The position following the verb is equally acceptable: Il s'approcha **lentement** de la porte.

A.   Regular formation of adverb in *-ment*. Some adverbs may be formed from the feminine adjective, to which **-ment** is added:

ADJECTIVE	FEMININE	ADVERB	MEANING
actuel	actuelle	**actuellement**	*currently*
complet	complète	**complètement**	*completely*
doux	douce	**doucement**	*softly*
égal	égale	**également**	*also, likewise*
léger	légère	**légèrement**	*slightly*
malheureux	malheureuse	**malheureusement**	*unfortunately*

B.   Irregularly formed adverbs in *-ment*. The following adverbs have a slight spelling change from the normal formation. Notice the underlined portion:

assidument	*assiduously*
poliment	*politely*
absolument	*absolutely*
assurément	*certainly*
énormément	*greatly, tremendously*
forcément	*necessarily, inevitably*
précisément	*precisely, exactly*
notamment	*notably, particularly*
récemment	*recently*
évidemment	*obviously*

C.   Adverbial expressions using *avec*. Certain prepositional phrases with **avec** are the equivalent of adverbs:

PHRASE	ADVERB	MEANING
avec élégance	**élégamment**	*elegantly*
avec grâce	**gracieusement**	*gracefully, graciously*
avec soin	**soigneusement**	*carefully*
avec patience	**patiemment**	*patiently*
avec bruit	**bruyamment**	*noisily*
avec douceur	**doucement**	*gently, softly*
avec vigueur	**vigoureusement**	*vigorously*

11.5   Adverbs of time

The adverbs of time usually appear at the *beginning* or *end* of a sentence or a clause. These *do not* follow the inflected verb. The most common adverbs of time are:

hier	*yesterday*
avant-hier	*day before yesterday*
demain	*tomorrow*
le lendemain	*the next day*
aujourd'hui	*today*
maintenant	*now*
en ce moment	*now*
à présent	*now, at present*
d'abord	*first of all*
enfin	*finally*
d'habitude	*usually*
d'ordinaire	*usually*
à [x] heures	*at [x] o'clock*

Days of the week:

lundi, mardi, mercredi, jeudi, vendredi, samedi, dimanche

Hier Jacques a vendu son vélo. (*ou* Jacques a vendu son vélo **hier**.)
Robert est parti jeudi, et **le lendemain** il a visité Dijon.
D'habitude je fais mes devoirs avant sept heures.
Il va partir **demain**.
Ils sont à la bibliothèque **aujourd'hui**.

11.6   Glossary of often-used adverbials of time

A.   Relating to a fixed appointment or time of an event:

à l'heure	*on time*
en retard	*late*
en avance	*early (in advance)*
de bonne heure[3]	*early*

[3] Note the idiomatic expression **A la bonne heure!** meaning *Fine! Good for you!*

Le train arrive **toujours** à l'heure.

Carole arrive **de bonne heure** pour la conférence.

B.   Relating to a personal concept of what is late or early:

tôt   *early*

tard   *late*

Le train part à cinq heures du matin. Il part **tôt**[4].

Le passager arrive à cinq heures sept. Il est **en retard**[5].

Pierre se couche vers une heure du matin. Il se couche **tard**[6].

Un jour il s'est couché à dix heures du soir. Il s'est couché **tôt**.

The words **tôt** and **tard** may be modified by **très**, **trop**, or **si**, and may be used in comparisons:

Le passager est arrivé **trop tard** à la gare.

Il est venu *aussi* **tôt** *que* possible.

C.   Days with relation to the present or past:

RELATIVE TO THE PRESENT MOMENT		RELATIVE TO THE PAST	
aujourd'hui	*today*	**ce jour-là**	*that day*
hier	*yesterday*	**la veille**	*the preceding day*
demain	*tomorrow*	**le lendemain**	*the next day*
après-demain	*day after tomorrow*		
avant-hier	*day before yesterday*		

Nous sommes arrivés au Havre le 12 octobre 1987. **Le lendemain**[7] nous sommes allés voir des cousins.

D.   Adverbs indicating habitual action. The following adverbs have meanings that refer to habitual action. They are therefore signals to use the present tense (for actions still habitual) or the imperfect tense (for actions that were habitual in the past).

[4] It is generally thought that 5 A.M. is an early hour, so this train leaves early, at 5 A.M.

[5] Although this passenger arose early (**tôt**), he is late for the train, i.e., with relation to a fixed time that has been set. (See A)

[6] That is, **tard** for the people who consider ten or eleven in the evening the time to retire. When Pierre retires at ten, that is early for him, hence **tôt**. It could be **tard** for some other people.

[7] The next day, i.e., **le 13 octobre**.

toujours	*always, still*
souvent	*often*
d'habitude	*usually*
d'ordinaire	*usually*
tous les jours	*every day*
toutes les semaines	*every week*

E.   Synonyms [=] and Antonyms [≠]

SYNONYMS

parfois	= quelquefois	*sometimes*
ensuite	= puis	*then, next*
tout de suite	= immédiatement	*immediately*

ANTONYMS

déjà	≠ pas encore	*already / not yet*
après	≠ auparavant	*after / previously*
tôt	≠ tard	*early / late*
souvent	≠ rarement	*often / seldom*
d'abord	≠ enfin	*first of all / finally*
toujours	≠ ne . . . (plus)(jamais)	*still, always / no longer, never*

—Elle est **toujours** là?   *"Is she still there?"*
—Non, elle **n'**y est **plus**.   *"No, she is no longer here."*

11.7   *Très* and *si*

Très and **si** may *not* be used to modify adverbs of quantity [4.1] such as **beaucoup, assez, trop**. The intensified form of **beaucoup** is **énormément**.

Cet étudiant est **bien fatigué**. *(very tired)*

Il a **très peu de** fautes. *(very few)*

Je ne savais pas que cette voiture marchait **si vite**. *(so fast)*

Jean-Paul a **énormément de** talent. *(very much, tremendous)*

11.8   Day precedes time

When both a day and a time are mentioned, the day precedes the time. This is logical movement from larger to smaller units of identification.

Claude est arrivé **hier** *à trois heures.*

11.9   Inversion required after *aussi* (therefore), *peut-être* (perhaps, maybe), and *à peine . . . que* (scarcely . . . when)

When a sentence or clause begins with one of these three expressions, inversion of subject and verb is required. Notice that **aussi** takes on the meaning *therefore, so:*

> Marie est née à Paris, **aussi** *parle-t-elle* français.
> *Marie was born in Paris, so (therefore) she speaks French.*

> Jean n'est pas venu aujourd'hui; **peut-être** *viendra-t-il* demain.
> *John didn't come today. Perhaps he will come tomorrow.*

> **A peine** *était-il* entré **que** Gérard a commencé à parler.
> *He had scarcely entered when Gérard began to speak.*

When positioned after the verb, **aussi** retains its usual meaning *also*. The meaning of **peut-être** remains the same in both possible positions.

> Maria parle italien et elle comprend **aussi** l'anglais.

> Jean viendra **peut-être** demain.

Mise en œuvre 11 A _____

Place de l'adverbe

Placez l'adverbe correctement dans la phrase.

EXEMPLE

(déjà) Il part. / Il est parti.

Il part déjà. / Il est déjà parti.

1. (déjà)   La pièce commence. / La pièce a commencé.
2. (bien)   Paul parle. / Il a parlé.
3. (trop)   Vous travaillez. / Vous avez travaillé.
4. (en retard)   Nous arrivons. / Nous sommes arrivés.
5. (demain)   Ma tante partira. / Georges va partir.
6. (assez)   Ils travaillent. / Ils ont travaillé.
7. (doucement)   Il ferme la porte. / Il a fermé la porte.
8. (très)   Mon cousin est intelligent. / Il parle vite.
9. (bruyamment)   Il entre. / Il est entré.
10. (beaucoup)   Ma belle-mère parle. / Elle a parlé.
11. (à midi)   Mon oncle est arrivé hier.

12.	(aujourd'hui)	Le train arrivera à sept heures.
13.	(légèrement)	C'est un dessin irrégulier.
14.	(si)	Pourquoi le patron est-il irrité?
15.	(peut-être)	Il est de mauvaise humeur.
16.	(aussi)	Elle est malade; elle reste à la maison.
17.	(hier)	Le journal a annoncé le mariage de ma cousine.
18.	(entièrement)	Vous avez raison.
19.	(hier)	La conférence a eu lieu à vingt heures.
20.	(à l'heure)	Le professeur arrive. / Je suis arrivé.

Mise en œuvre 11 B

Adverbes temporels

Complétez la phrase en vous servant des locutions suivantes: **en avance, de bonne heure, en retard, à l'heure, tôt** ou **tard.**

1. Mon train part de la gare à cinq heures du matin. J'arrive à la gare à 5 h 05. Le train part très _____ le matin, mais je suis arrivé _____.

2. Je suis arrivé trop _____ pour prendre le train.

3. J'ai rendez-vous avec mon professeur de sociologie à dix heures. J'arrive à son bureau à dix heures précises: je suis donc _____.

4. J'arrive à ma classe d'histoire à dix heures et demie, mais elle a déjà commencé. Je suis _____ pour la classe, malheureusement.

5. Jean est arrivé à cette même classe à dix heures vingt. Il est arrivé plus _____ que moi. Mais nous sommes tous les deux _____.

Complétez en vous servant de la liste suivante: **aujourd'hui, demain, hier, le lendemain, la veille.**

6. _____ je suis en train de travailler dans mon jardin; _____ j'ai fait une visite à mon oncle qui habite à Courbevoie; _____ je vais visiter le musée.

7. Le lundi 6 juin nous avons quitté Paris pour aller à Genève; _____ nous sommes arrivés dans cette ville magnifique en Suisse. C'était le 7 juin.

8. J'ai passé un examen d'anglais le 31 mars, donc j'ai beaucoup étudié _____.

Mise en œuvre 11 C

Révision des adverbes

Répondez aux questions suivantes en employant les mots indiqués:

EXEMPLE

Aimez-vous la musique?

beaucoup / énormément / toujours

Mais oui, j'aime **beaucoup** la musique.

Mais oui, j'aime **énormément** la musique.

Mais oui, j'aime **toujours** la musique.

1. Avez-vous des disques?
   beaucoup / plusieurs / trop
2. Aimez-vous les disques de Johnny Hallyday?
   beaucoup / bien / enormément
3. Connaissez-vous des avocats à Paris?
   plusieurs / quelques / très peu
4. Lisez-vous des romans policiers?
   souvent / énormément / parfois
5. Voudriez-vous du vin?
   un verre / une bouteille / un peu
6. Aimez-vous le vin?
   un peu / beaucoup / parfois
7. Combien de vos amis sont partis en vacances?
   plusieurs / beaucoup / la plupart
8. Quel cours suivez-vous maintenant?
   français / psychologie / physique
9. Est-ce que vous étudiez le soir?
   toujours / parfois / rarement
10. Comment préparez-vous vos devoirs?
    avec soin / patiemment / lentement
11. D'où vient-il?
    France / Canada / États-Unis [20.7]
12. De quoi le verre est-il rempli?
    vin / eau / fleurs [20.8]

VERBE IRRÉGULIER **OUVRIR**

The following verbs are completely regular except in the present indicative and the past participle:

ouvrir	to open	**rouvrir**	to open . . . again
couvrir	to cover	**découvrir**	to discover; to reveal
offrir	to give, to offer, to present		

11.10   Present tense (-er endings)

These **-ir** verbs are irregular in that they use the present tense endings for **-er** verbs.

	ouvrir	couvrir	découvrir	offrir	rouvrir
j'	**ouvr**|e	couvr|e	dćouvre	offre	rouvre
tu	**ouvr**|es	couvr|es	découvres	offres	rouvres
il	**ouvr**|e	couvr|e	découvre	offre	rouvre
nous	**ouvr**|ons	couvr|ons	découvrons	offrons	rouvrons
vous	**ouvr**|ez	couvr|ez	découvrez	offrez	rouvrez
ils	**ouvr**|ent	couvr|ent	découvrent	offrent	rouvrent

11.11   Past participle

These verbs form the past participle in **-ert.** All are conjugated with **avoir.**

VERB	PP.	EXAMPLE
ouvrir	ouv**ert**	Il **a ouvert** les fenêtres.
couvrir	couv**ert**	Il **a couvert** son visage.
découvrir	découv**ert**	Il **a découvert** ce procédé.
offrir	off**ert**	Il m'**a offert** une cigarette.

Mise en œuvre 11 D _____

ouvrir et verbes apparentés

Mettez les verbes en italique au passé composé.

1. On *ouvre* les portes maintenant. (hier à midi)
2. On *couvre* cent kilomètres en une heure et demie.
3. Dominique *découvre* des fautes dans ses phrases.
4. Les élèves *offrent* un livre au meilleur professeur.
5. Nous *offrons* un cadeau à notre père pour son anniversaire.

Mettez les verbs en italique au présent.

6. Nous *avons rouvert* les yeux. Nous les *avons rouverts*.
7. Les astronautes *ont découvert* des planètes. Ils les *ont découvertes*.
8. Le garçon *a couvert* le plat d'un couvercle.

9. Je lui *ai offert* une place près de la porte.

10. Mon oncle nous *a offert* ses billets d'opéra.

Reflets

La Bourse

La Bourse des valeurs est un service public qui permet aux individus de participer financièrement à l'expansion des entreprises commerciales. Le ministère de l'Économie exerce un contrôle sur le marché. Un individu qui achète des actions est un **actionnaire,** parce qu'il est propriétaire de **valeurs mobilières** (actions ou obligations).

D'habitude le client étudie le cours et examine les entreprises pour les évaluer avant de **placer ses fonds.** Enfin il choisit parmi les corporations et passe **la commande d'achat** à **un courtier.** Celui-ci exécute la commande selon les instructions du client, et fait **la livraison des titres** dans les trois ou quatre **jours ouvrables** après la conclusion de l'achat.

Ayant acquis des valeurs mobilières, le client commence à surveiller le **cours de la bourse** dans les journaux pour savoir si le prix monte ou baisse. S'il a de la chance, il passe la commande de vendre quand **la cotation** est élevée, afin de gagner. S'il doit vendre au moment où la cotation n'est pas favorable, il perdra une partie de **son investissement.**

Les transactions de la Bourse se font très rapidement, surtout depuis l'installation des ordinateurs centraux pour faciliter les opérations.

VOCABULAIRE DE LA BOURSE

achat *m.*	*purchase*
acquis *pp.* acquérir	*acquired*
action *f.*	*stock*
actionnaire *m.*	*stockholder*
baisser *v.*	*to drop*
Bourse[8] **(de valeurs)** *f.*	*stock exchange*
commande *f.*	*order*
cotation *f.*	*quotation*
cours *m.*	*market value, price*
courtier *m.*	*broker*
disponible *adj..*	*available, at one's disposition*

[8] **Une bourse** is also the word for an academic scholarship grant of money.

investissement *m.*	*investment*
livraison des titres *f.*	*delivery of certificates*
obligation *f.*	*bond*
ouvrable *adj.*	*business days [open]*
particulier *m.*	*private citizen*
selon *prep.*	*according to*
surveiller	*watch closely*
valeurs mobilières *f.*	*stocks and bonds*

Sujets de composition ou de causerie

1. Est-ce que vous avez des valeurs mobilières? Si vous n'avez pas d'actions, pourquoi est-ce que vous renoncez à en acheter? Si vous en avez, de quelles entreprises êtes-vous actionnaire? Est-ce que leurs actions montent ou baissent? Pourquoi?

2. Quelles sont les conditions qui font monter ou baisser les cotations? Le cours de la bourse est-il sujet aux événements politiques? économiques? Quels événements font changer le cours de la bourse?

3. Est-ce que vous connaissez des individus qui ont beaucoup gagné en valeurs mobilières? Quels sont les milliardaires qui ont eu des succès, et comment ont-ils agi pour y parvenir? Qu'est-ce qu'ils ont tendance à faire avec l'argent gagné?

12

Verbes pronominaux
sortir et verbes apparentés

VERBES PRONOMINAUX

Reflexive verbs are called **pronominaux** in French because they require an extra pronoun before the verb. A reflexive verb has *two* pronouns: the subject pronoun and the reflexive pronoun, always in the same combinations (**je me, tu te, il se**, etc.). The action is said to be *reflexive* because it is reflected upon the doer: **il se lave** = *he is washing **himself**.* Sometimes the action is reciprocal: **ils se parlent** = *they are talking to each other;* **ils se battent** = *they fight **with each other**;* **ils s'entendent** = *they get along **together**.*

Many reflexive verbs also can be used non-reflexively, but the meaning is altered: **se lever°[1]** means *to get up,* whereas the non-reflexive **lever°** means *to raise.*

Il se lève vers sept heures du matin. REFLEXIVE
He gets up around seven o'clock in the morning.

Il lève la carafe.   NOT REFLEXIVE
He raises the carafe.

Some verbs exist only reflexively, although no reciprocal or reflexive action is involved. They simply require the reflexive form. Among these are **s'en aller** *(to go away),* **se souvenir de** *(to remember),* and **s'écrier** *(to exclaim).*

[1] The symbol ° after an infinitive indicates a stem-changing (orthographic-changing) verb [26.1–26.7].

Il s'en va.   Je me **souviens** de lui.

He goes away.   *I remember him.*

12.1 Commonly used reflexive verbs

Many of the verbs dealing with our everyday activities are reflexive. Some of these are listed below in an assumed possible order of events in the course of a day:

se **réveiller**	*to wake up*
se **lever**°	*to get up*
se **laver**	*to wash up, to get washed*
se **peigner** (les cheveux)	*to comb (one's hair)*
se **maquiller**	*to put on makeup*
s'**habiller**	*to get dressed*
se **presser** (**de** [INF])	*to hurry (to do something)*
se **dépêcher** (**de** [INF])	*to hurry (to do something)*
se **demander** (**si**)	*to wonder (whether)*
s'**occuper** (**de** [N])	*to be busy (with something)*
se **servir de** [N]	*to use (something)*
s'**intéresser à** [N]	*to be interested in (something)*
se **promener**°	*to go for a walk*
se **produire**	*to happen*
se **passer** [=arriver]	*to happen*
s'**adresser à** [P]	*to speak to, to address (a person)*
se **rendre à** [N]	*to go to (place)*
se **diriger**° **à** (**vers**)	*to go to (towards)*
se **procurer** [N]	*to get (something)*
se **fâcher** (**de** [N])	*to get angry (about [something])*
se **plaindre** (**de** [N])	*to complain (about [something])*
se **distraire**	*to amuse oneself*
s'**amuser** (**à** [INF])	*to have a good time (doing something)*
se **reposer**	*to rest*
se **déshabiller**	*to get undressed*
se **brosser** (les dents)	*to brush (one's teeth)*
se **coucher**	*to go to bed*

NOTE: When the infinitive is used, the reflexive pronoun must agree with the noun or pronoun affected by the action [18.9]:

Il nous a dit de **nous dépêcher.**   *He told us to hurry.*

12.2   Reflexive pronouns

The double pronoun combinations required with reflexive verbs are shown below. (The third-person pronouns **ils** and **elles** can, of course, be replaced by nouns in ordinary use.)

je **me** demande   nous **nous** demandons ⎫
tu **te** demandes   vous **vous** demandez   ⎬   *I wonder, you*
il **se** demande   ils **se**   demandent ⎭   *wonder*, etc

└────────REFLEXIVE PRONOUNS────────┘

Elision occurs with reflexive pronouns before a vowel sound.

Je m'adresse à Jean.   Nous nous adressons à Jean.

Tu t'adresses à Jean.   Vous vous adressez à Jean.

Il s'adresse à Jean.   Ils s'adressent à Jean.

12.3   Negative forms of reflexive verbs

Identify the verb unit in the sentence. This is the inflected verb (in compounds, just the auxiliary verb) and all preceding words except the subject. The verb unit (VU) is enclosed between **ne** and **pas**.

Nous │ nous **promenons** │ dans le parc.   POSITIVE
        VERB UNIT

Nous *ne* │ **nous promenons** │ *pas* dans le parc.   NEGATIVE

Elles │ **se sont** │ levées   POSITIVE
        VERB UNIT

Elles *ne* │ **se sont** │ *pas* levées   NEGATIVE

One exception is the case of **déjà**. In the negative it becomes **ne . . . pas encore** (*not yet*):

Ils **se sont déjà** installés à l'hôtel.   POSITIVE

Ils *ne* se sont *pas encore* installés à l'hôtel.   NEGATIVE

Mise en œuvre 12 A _____

Présent des verbes pronominaux

Complétez les phrases suivantes en ajoutant les mots entre parenthèses; mettez l'infinitif à la forme appropriée.

EXEMPLE

Quand je suis en retard, je *(se dépêcher)*.

Quand je suis en retard, je **me dépêche.**

1. Quand je suis fatigué, je *(se reposer* un peu).
2. Hier les étudiants *(se réunir* à deux heures).
3. En arrivant, nous *(s'installer* dans la chambre).
4. Est-ce que vous me comprenez? Je *(se le demander)*.
5. Mes parents me demandent de *(se passer* d'auto).
6. Les touristes viennent à Paris pour *(s'amuser)*.
7. Nous sommes allés à la pharmacie pour *(se procurer* des médicaments).
8. L'homme se lève et il *(s'approcher* du bâtiment).

Mise en œuvre 12 B

Verbes pronominaux

Répondez aux questions suivantes.

EXEMPLE

Nous nous amusons bien. Et vous?

Moi, je **m'amuse** bien aussi.

1. Nous nous adressons au professeur. Et vous?
2. L'étudiante s'approche de la table. Et vous?
3. Les autres s'arrêtent de parler. Et vous?
4. Paul se demande si le professeur le comprend. Et vous?
5. Nous nous dépêchons de finir le repas. Et vous?
6. Le professeur se fâche. Et vous?
7. Paul se lève à sept heures du matin. Et vous?
8. Nous nous habillons à sept heures et quart. Et vous?
9. Nous nous dépêchons de prendre le petit déjeuner. Et vous?
10. Nous nous excusons de notre hâte. Et vous?
11. Nous nous occupons de nos recherches. Et vous?
12. Nous nous reposons un peu pendant l'après-midi. Et vous?

Mise en œuvre 12 C _____

Négation des verbes pronominaux

Mettez les phrases ci-dessus (Mise en œuvre 12 B) à la forme négative.

1. Nous **ne** nous adressons **pas** au professeur.

   Je **ne** m'adresse **pas** (non plus) au professeur.

PASSÉ COMPOSÉ DES VERBES PRONOMINAUX

12.4 Formation

The auxiliary verb **être** is used for all reflexive verbs. The pattern for the passé composé is always the same combination of dual pronouns (subject plus reflexive pronoun); the past participle then follows:

je me **suis**		nous nous **sommes**	
tu t'**es**	+ PP	vous vous **êtes**	+ PP
il s'**est**		ils se **sont**	
elle s'**est**		elles se **sont**	

As an example, the verb **se dépêcher (de)** *(to hurry)* is shown here:

je me suis **dépêché(e)**[2]	nous nous sommes **dépêché(e)s**
tu t'es **dépêché(e)**	vous vous êtes **dépêché(e)(s)**
il s'est **dépêché**	ils se sont **dépêchés**
elle s'est **dépêchée**	elles se sont **dépêchées**

The past participle must agree with a preceding direct object, just like the verbs using the auxiliary **avoir**. The letters shown between parentheses are those that may be added for necessary agreement. In the case of this verb, the reflexive pronoun is the PDO; agreement is made with it, which is equivalent to the subject:

Les étudiantes **se sont dépêchées**[3] de monter dans l'autocar.

Elles **se sont lavé** les mains. (DIRECT OBJECT FOLLOWS VERB.)

Ils **se sont couchés** de bonne heure.

Elle **s'est acheté** une voiture.

---

[2] If the speaker is female, use the feminine agreement. Women should adopt the habit of making this agreement automatically when they speak of themselves.

[3] Test for PDO: *They "dispatched" **what**?* Answer: *themselves;* so **se** is the PDO.

12.5 Agreement of the past participle of reflexive verbs

The past participle of a reflexive verb agrees in gender and number with a *preceding direct object* [PDO]. This is identical with the rule for verbs using the auxiliary **avoir** [9.4].

A.   If a direct object *follows* the verb, there is never agreement:

Elle s'est peigné **les cheveux.**[4]   *She combed **her** hair.*
Elles se sont brossé **les dents.**   *They brushed **their** teeth.*

Test: As before: To determine whether the reflexive pronoun is a direct object, read the subject, then the verb, then ask —**Quoi?** *(What?)* If there is an answer, that is the direct object.

Elle s'est (**reposé**).   *She rested **what?*** **se** *(herself)* is PDO.

Agreement is made: Elle s'est **reposée.**

Ils se sont (**parlé**).   *They spoke **what?***

No answer, because it is *to* each other. When *to* is added it becomes an *indirect* object. Sentence is correct as written.

B.   If the reflexive pronoun is a direct object, *and* it comes in front of the verb, the past participle agrees with the reflexive pronoun (= subject).

Elle s'est **lavée.**   She washed *what?* **se** *(herself)* is a PDO. Make agreement.

Elle s'est **lavé les mains.**   She washed *what?* **les mains** is a direct object, but not a *preceding* one. No agreement.

C.   If the reflexive pronoun is obviously an indirect object, meaning *to a person,* there is no agreement.

Ils **se** sont parlé.   *They spoke **to each other**.*

D.   If the function of the reflexive pronoun *cannot be determined,* make agreement with it. In effect, this means agreement with the subject.

12.6 Past participles that always agree with the reflexive pronoun

The past participles of the following verbs *always agree* with the reflexive pronoun in gender and number; this is the same as agreement with the subject.

---

[4] Ask *"she combed **what?"*** (—**Elle s'est peigné** *quoi?*) The answer (her hair) *follows* the verb, so there is no agreement.

s'amuser	*to have a good time*
s'arrêter	*to stop*
se coucher	*to go to bed*
se dépêcher (de [INF])	*to hurry (to do something)*
se douter (de) (que)	*to suspect*
se fâcher (de)	*to become angry (at/about)*
s'installer	*to settle down*
se laver	*to wash up*
se lever	*to get up*
se mettre à	*to begin to*
s'occuper de	*to be engaged in; to take care of*
se promener	*to take a walk*
se reposer	*to rest*
se réveiller	*to wake up*
se tromper (de)	*to get the wrong [N]; to be mistaken (about)*

Elle s'est **installée** dans un fauteuil.
She settled down in an armchair.

Jeanne s'est **trompée** de livre.
Jeanne got the wrong book.

Nous nous sommes **dépêchés** de fermer la porte.
We hastened to close the door.

12.7 Past participles that never agree

Past participles of the following verbs never agree with the reflexive pronoun: they are invariable.

se demander (si)	*to wonder (if)*
se parler	*to talk (to one another)*
se ressembler	*to resemble*
se sourire (PP: souri)	*to smile at each other*
se succéder	*to succeed one another*

Ils se sont **demandé** si la voiture marcherait.

Les deux amies se sont **souri.**

Les événements se sont **succédé** très rapidement.

Mise en œuvre 12 D _____

Passé composé

Mettez les phrases suivantes au passé composé. (Attention! Il y a dans cet exercice des verbes qui ne sont pas pronominaux!) Ensuite, refaites l'exercice en remplaçant **Paul** par un nom féminin.

EXEMPLES

Paul se couche à minuit.
Paul **s'est couché** à minuit.
Il dort bien.
Il **a** bien **dormi.**

1. Paul se réveille à six heures et demie.
2. Il se lève tout de suite.
3. Il s'habille en vitesse.
4. Il se lave les mains et la figure.
5. Il prend son petit déjeuner.
6. Il sort pour aller à l'université.
7. Il arrive en classe à huit heures.
8. Il s'installe à sa place.
9. Après la classe il se repose un peu.
10. Il déjeune à midi.
11. Il fait du tennis avec un ami.
12. Il se repose après le match.
13. Il dine avec sa famille à sept heures.
14. Il s'occupe de ses devoirs.
15. Il se couche vers onze heures.

Mise en œuvre 12 E _____

Un jour actif

Racontez ce que vous avez fait pendant une journée bien remplie. Servez-vous des verbes pronominaux de la liste 12.1, en employant autant de ces verbes que possible.

Mise en œuvre 12 F _____

Accord du participe passé

Mettez les phrases suivantes au passé composé, en faisant attention à l'accord du participe passé.

EXEMPLE

Marie se lave avant le petit déjeuner.

Marie **s'est lavée** avant le petit déjeuner.

1. Marie se lève de bonne heure.
2. Elle se lave les mains.
3. Elle se dépêche de faire la vaisselle.
4. Voilà la voiture que Robert s'achète.
5. Jeanne se procure une boite en bois.
6. Nous nous occupons de la maison.
7. La famille se réveille vers sept heures.
8. Cette belle jeune fille se marie avec Jean-Paul Masson.
9. Les étudiants s'installent dans la bibliothèque.
10. Ils se demandent si le professeur se fâche.

SORTIR ET VERBES DU MÊME TYPE

12.8   Present tense

Six important verbs conjugated in the same way are listed below. They have the peculiarity in the present tense of using only the *first three letters* as a stem (forms 1,2,3), and the regular stem (infinitive minus **-ir**) for the plural forms (4,5,6):

sortir

1	je **sors**	4	nous **sort**ons
2	tu **sors**	5	vous **sort**ez
3	il **sort**	6	ils **sort**ent

FIRST 3 LETTERS ONLY   FULL STEM

Other verbs using the same system are:

INFINITIVE	SINGULAR STEM	PLURAL STEM
partir (**de**)	je **pars**	nous **partons**
sortir (**de**)	je **sors**	nous **sortons**
sentir	je **sens**	nous **sentons**
servir	je **sers**	nous **servons**
dormir	je **dors**	nous **dormons**
mentir	je **mens**	nous **mentons**

Je **pars** pour Londres.

Nous **sentons** les effets de la pollution atmosphérique.

Cette machine **sert** à plier des feuilles de papier.

12.9   Passé composé des verbes de la famille de *sortir*

Although the past participle of regular -ir verbs ends in -u (**vendre, vendu**), the past participle of these verbs ends in -i. Just drop the final -r of the infinitive. The auxiliary is **avoir** except for **partir**[5] and **sortir**, which use **être.**

partir (être)

je **suis parti**(e)	nous **sommes parti**(e)s
tu **es parti**(e)	vous **êtes parti**(e)(s)
il **est parti**	ils **sont partis**
elle **est partie**	elles **sont parties**

servir (avoir)

j'**ai servi**	nous **avons servi**
tu **as servi**	vous **avez servi**
il **a servi**	ils **ont servi**
elle **a servi**	elles **ont servi**

[5] See the complete paradigm of **partir*** in Appendix C, Verb Table 20.

Mise en œuvre 12 G

sortir et sa famille

Remplacez chaque verbe en italique par le passé composé.

EXEMPLE

Je *pars*.

Je **suis parti**.

1. Je *dors* tard.
2. Je *sens* un courant d'air.
3. Je *cours* à la fenêtre pour la fermer.
4. Je m'*habille* tout de suite.
5. Je *descends* à la salle à manger.
6. Ma mère *sert* le petit déjeuner.
7. Je *prends* du café et des œufs.
8. Maman *sort* une cuillère, une fourchette et un couteau du tiroir.
9. Quand je *dis* que j'aime les œufs, je *mens*.
10. Je *sors* de la salle à manger et j'*entre* dans le couloir.
11. Je *pars* de la maison vers sept heures et demie.
12. Je me *sens* très bien.

Mettez le verbe au présent:

13. Alexandre *est parti* à huit heures.
14. Marie *est sortie* avec Alexandre.
15. Nous *sommes partis* avant midi.
16. Giovanni *a menti* au douanier à la frontière.
17. Tu *as senti* que Renée avait raison.
18. Jacques *a dormi* jusqu'à onze heures.
19. Tout le monde *a couru* voir le film d'Elvis.
20. Évidemment ce vendeur *a menti* au sujet de la voiture.

13

Imparfait
Narration au passé
Plus-que-parfait

IMPARFAIT (IMPERFECT TENSE)

13.1 General

The **imparfait** is a past tense. It indicates continuing action (or state of being) in the past, action that was *habitual* or occurred repeatedly. A key to deciding whether to use this tense is that there is *no clear indication of the time of beginning or ending* of the action described. (The word *imperfect* means not completed.)

In narration the imperfect is used to describe *background* information, while the **passé composé** indicates specific actions and events carried out against the background.

13.2 Formation

The imperfect is the most regularly formed tense. Both regular and irregular verbs (except **être**) follow the same system. For the stem (**le radical**), use the **nous**-form of the present tense, dropping the **-ons** ending, and add the following endings of the imperfect:

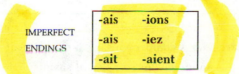

IMPERFECT ENDINGS	-ais	-ions
	-ais	-iez
	-ait	-aient

As an example of the imperfect tense, the verb **travailler** uses the stem **travaill-** (from **nous travaill**-ons):

je travaill**ais**	nous travaill**ions**	*was/were working,*
tu travaill**ais**	vous travaill**iez**	*used to work,*
il travaill**ait**	ils travaill**aient**	*worked*

Pronominal verbs are formed in the same way, with the addition of the regular reflexive pronouns:

je me lev**ais**	nous nous lev**ions**	*was/were getting up,*
tu te lev**ais**	vous vous lev**iez**	*used to get up,*
il se lev**ait**	ils se lev**aient**	*got up*

The formation of the imperfect is so regular that even irregular verbs follow the system of using the present tense **nous**-form, minus **-ons**, as the stem of the imperfect. The only exception is **être*** (imperfect stem **ét-**):

REGULAR VERBS

VERB TYPE	EXAMPLE	STEM DERIVED FROM	IMPERFECT FORM (IL-FORM)	
-er	**entrer**	nous **entr**ons	il **entr**ait	*he was entering*
-ir	**finir**	nous **finiss**ons	il **finiss**ait	*he was finishing*
-re	**vendre**	nous **vend**ons	il **vend**ait	*he was selling*
REFLEXIVE	**se lever**	nous nous **lev**ons	il se **lev**ait	*he was getting up*
REFLEXIVE	**s'amuser**	nous nous **amus**ons	il s'**amus**ait	*he was having a good time*

IRREGULAR

	venir	nous **ven**ons	il **ven**ait	*he was coming*
	prendre	nous **pren**ons	il **pren**ait	*he was taking*
	aller	nous **all**ons	il **all**ait	*he was going*
	mettre	nous **mett**ons	il **mett**ait	*he was putting*
	partir	nous **part**ons	il **part**ait	*he was leaving*
	dire	nous **dis**ons	il **dis**ait	*he was saying*
	pouvoir	nous **pouv**ons	il **pouv**ait	*he could*

		(LIMITED MEANINGS [13.3])	
comprendre	nous **compren**ons	il **compren**ait	*he understood*
savoir	nous **savons**	il **savait**	*he knew*
devoir	nous **devons**	il **devait**	*he was supposed to*

EXCEPTIONS	**être**	STEM: **ét-**	il **ét**ait	*he was, used to be*
	falloir	STEM: **fall-**	il **fall**ait	*he had to, it was necessary*

Je **m'amusais bien** le samedi soir.
I used to have a good time Saturday nights.

13.3 English equivalents

In giving English equivalents for the imperfect there are three possible choices. They should be tried out in the order given below to determine which one is most appropriate in the context.

(a) *was (do)ing* something   ⎧ *he was finishing*
(b) *used to (do)* something **il finissait** ⎨ *he used to finish*
(c) *(did)* something   ⎩ *he finished*

For certain verbs such as the following, English requires the one-word equivalent (c).

il **était**	*he was*	(*never he was being*)
il **savait**	*he knew*	(*never he was knowing*)
il **comprenait**	*he understood*	(*never he was understanding*)

13.4 Habitual action in the past

Actions or situations that were habitual or usual in the past (*used to* happen) are easily identified because of the frequent inclusion of such adverbials as **souvent, toujours, tous les jours, parfois, quelquefois, rarement, jamais.**

Nous **allions souvent** au théâtre quand nous étions à Paris.
We often went (used to go, would go) to the theater when we were in Paris.

Jeanne **prenait toujours** le métro.
Jean always used to take (would take) the subway.

Je **ne finissais jamais** avant midi.
I never used to finish (finished) before noon.

Notice that the English word *would* is sometimes used with the meaning *used to*. The word *would* is also an important indicator of the conditional tense [25.1]. You should test English sentences containing *would* to see if *used to* means the same thing. If so, the imperfect is correct for French. But, for example, in the sentence *I would like to go downtown tomorrow*, the test fails, and the imperfect cannot be used.

Mise en œuvre 13 A

Formation de l'imparfait

Mettez les phrases suivantes à l'imparfait en ajoutant à la phrase la locution **quand je suis parti.** (Vous êtes libre d'inventer une autre locution pour remplacer celle-là.)

EXEMPLE

Jean-Paul **lit** un roman.

Jean-Paul **lisait** un roman quand je suis parti.

1. J'ai soif.
2. Il fait chaud.
3. Tu te reposes.
4. Je m'amuse bien.
5. Vous mettez la table.
6. Je sais la vérité.
7. Nous finissons de déjeuner.
8. Édouard a envie de sortir.
9. Maurice est de mauvaise humeur.
10. Les jeunes filles écoutent des disques.

Mise en œuvre 13 B

Action en train de se faire

Combinez les deux phrases pour que le premier verbe se trouve à l'imparfait et le second au passé composé ou à l'imparfait, selon le cas.

EXEMPLE

Georges lit. / J'arrive.

Georges **lisait** quand je **suis arrivé.**

1. Maman se repose. / Je sors.
2. Béatrice met la table. / Pierre arrive.
3. Charles écrit une poésie. / Il entend un bruit.
4. Le général de Gaulle est dans le salon. / Il meurt.
5. Il fait très froid. / Napoléon est à Moscou.
6. Le président est à Paris. / Il fait la connaissance du premier ministre.
7. Mon grand-père est à la maison. / On attaque Pearl Harbor.
8. Le pilote est dans le désert. / Le petit prince se fait voir.
9. Emma habite à la campagne. / Charles Bovary la trouve.
10. Ces deux hommes attendent Godot. / Pozzo et Lucky arrivent.

NARRATION: THE IMPERFECT—PASSÉ COMPOSÉ TEAM

13.5   Narration: interplay of imperfect and passé composé

Narration of past events consists of two main parts: *actions* and *background descriptions*. In French, use the **passé composé** for the actions, and the imperfect for the background descriptions, which correspond to stage settings in the theater.

In setting a scene, the imperfect is used for the "stage settings," to tell of the *size, shape, color,* and *other physical attributes* of *buildings, people, clothing, the weather,* and even *habitual mental attitudes (mental stage settings)*. These things are "habitual" for the duration of a scene, as opposed to the movements of the actors (**passé composé**).

> La fenêtre **était** ouverte, parce qu'il **faisait** très chaud. J'ai ouvert doucement les persiennes et j'ai entendu une voix. J'ai saisi mes clefs et j'ai descendu l'escalier en hâte. Jacques **était** là devant la porte. Il **avait** l'air fatigué et découragé. J'ai ouvert la porte.

In this passage you can distinguish between "background" in the imperfect, and actions in the **passé composé**.

TEST YOURSELF

Select the **imparfait** (*ti*) or the **passé composé** (*tpc*) for each verb in italics in the left-hand column. (Cover the answers in the right-hand column until you have decided.)

1. Last week the weather *was* fine.	1. (*ti*)	Weather: "durable" condition
2. Mr. Dupont *was sleeping*.	2. (*ti*)	No time indicator
3. Suddenly the alarm clock *sounded*.	3. (*tpc*)	Sudden action

4.	Mr. Dupont *woke up.*	4. *(tpc)*	Sudden action
5.	He *got out* of bed.	5. *(tpc)*	Sudden action
6.	He *was* in a good mood.	6. *(ti)*	Mental background
7.	He *took* a shirt out of the drawer.	7. *(tpc)*	Action
8.	It *was* a blue shirt.	8. *(ti)*	Clothing: durable condition
9.	He *liked* that shirt very much.	9. *(ti)*	Mental attitude
10.	He *put it on.*	10. *(tpc)*	Action
11.	He *finished* dressing.	11. *(tpc)*	Action
12.	He *went* downstairs.	12. *(tpc)*	Action

13.6   Action in progress when another event occurred

In the sentence *I was reading when Alain came in*, the imperfect is used for the ongoing event *(was reading)*, and the **passé composé** for the spontaneous event *(came in)* occurring during the ongoing event. This combination of imperfect and **passé composé** is very frequent.

In the diagram below representing time, the head of the arrow is the present moment *(present tense,* and the idiom **être en train de**). On the shaft of the arrow the ⊗ represents an event at a *specific* (or specifically understood) *time*, conveyed by the **passé composé.** The wavy lines on the arrow shaft, joined by a bracket, represent the *indistinct times of beginning and ending* of an action, typical of the imperfect.

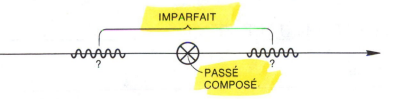

(1) Je **lisais** quand Marie **est entrée** dans la salle.
    I was reading [∿] when Marie came into [⊗] the room.

(2) Robert **regardait** la télévision quand vous avez **téléphoné.**
    Robert was watching television [∿] when you telephoned [⊗].

Sometimes both verbs may be in the imperfect:

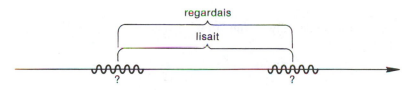

(3) Je **regardais** la télévision pendant que Paul **lisait** le journal.
    I was watching television [∿] while Paul was reading the paper [∿].

Mise en œuvre 13 C

Une journée d'Albert

Mettez les verbes en italique au passé composé ou à l'imparfait, selon le cas.

1. Hier matin Albert *(dormir)* quand le réveil-matin *(sonner)*. Le soleil *(briller)* déjà; il *(faire)* beau.

2. Il *(se lever)* mais il *(être)* toujours fatigué.

3. Il *(aller)* à la salle de bains et il *(se laver)* les mains et la figure.

4. Ensuite il *(s'habiller)* et il *(se peigner)*.

5. Il *(vouloir)* choisir une cravate. Il *(regarder)* sa collection de cravates qui *(se trouver)* dans un placard.

6. Il en *(choisir)* une qui lui *(sembler)* convenable. C'*(être)* une cravate bleue.

7. Alors il *(descendre)* à la cuisine où sa mère *(être)* en train de préparer le petit déjeuner.

8. Il *(prendre)* du café et *(beurrer)* des tartines.

9. Pendant qu'il *(manger)*, il *(réfléchir)* au travail qui l'*(attendre)* au bureau. Soudain il *(avoir)* une idée.

10. Il *(remonter)* au premier; il *(remettre)* la cravate bleue dans le placard, et *(décider)* de rester au lit jusqu'à cinq heures, quand le travail serait fini.

PLUS-QUE-PARFAIT (PLUPERFECT)

13.7   General

The pluperfect is a compound tense indicating action or situation in the past *prior to another past event* mentioned. The auxiliary verb is in the imperfect and always means *had*:

J'avais fini mon examen quand vous **êtes arrivée.**
I had finished my exam when you arrived.

ANTERIOR EVENT (PP) ☒   PASSÉ COMPOSÉ ⊗

Represented schematically on the "time" arrow:

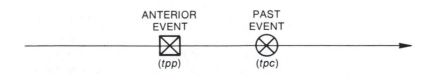

ANTERIOR   PAST
EVENT   EVENT
☒   ⊗
(tpp)   *(tpc)*

13.8   Formation

The auxiliary verb is in the imperfect, followed by the past participle. Agreement of past participles remains as before: for **avoir,** agreement is with the PDO [9.4]; and for **être,** agreement is with the subject [10.2]. The English equivalent for the auxiliary is *had* in every case.

finir *(to finish)*

j'	avais	fini	nous	avions	fini
tu	avais	fini	vous	aviez	fini
il	avait	fini	ils	avaient	fini

——AUXILIARY VERB IN IMPERFECT——

2 past events use imperfect + passé composé (reg. past tense)

VERB	EXAMPLE	MEANING
parler	J'avais **parlé** au professeur.	I **had spoken** to the teacher.
bâtir	Il **avait bâti** la maison.	He **had built** the house.
répondre	Ils **avaient répondu** à la lettre.	They **had answered** the letter.
aller	Elle **était allée** en ville.	She **had gone** downtown.
venir	Ils **étaient venus** nous voir.	They **had come** to see us.
mettre	J'avais **mis** la table.	I **had set** the table.
avoir	Nous **avions eu** besoin d'un renseignement.	We **had needed** some information.
attendre	J'avais **attendu** devant la gare.	I **had waited** in front of the station.

Mise en œuvre 13 D

Plus-que-parfait en action

Combinez en une seule phrase les phrases suivantes. Mettez l'une et l'autre au passé. La phrase (a) signale l'événement antérieur à (b). Mettez la première phrase au plus-que-parfait et la seconde au passé composé selon l'exemple.

EXEMPLE

(a) Je vois un film italien.   PREMIER ÉVÉNEMENT

(b) Vous m'invitez au cinéma[1].   DERNIER ÉVÉNEMENT

J'avais (déjà) vu ce film italien quand vous **m'avez invité** au cinéma.
*I **had already seen** that Italian film when you **invited** me to the movies.*
PLUS-QUE-PARFAIT   PASSÉ COMPOSÉ

[1] For the position of object pronouns like **me,** see section 7.5. They appear in front of the inflected verb, i.e., in front of the auxiliary if there is one.

1. (a) Jacques écrit une lettre à ses parents.
   (b) Vous lui téléphonez.
2. (a) Nous prenons les billets.
   (b) On annonce le départ du train.
3. (a) Vous ne mettez pas la table.
   (b) Les invités entrent dans la salle à manger.
4. (a) Thérèse se marie avec Jean-Claude.
   (b) Je la vois à Saint-Tropez.
5. (a) Le patron sort du bureau.
   (b) L'inspecteur vient le chercher.
6. (a) Nous dressons la liste d'invités.
   (b) L'hôtesse nous demande d'ajouter des noms.
7. (a) L'avion décolle.
   (b) Ce passager arrive.
8. (a) J'achète une machine à écrire.
   (b) Mon oncle m'offre un ordinateur.
9. (a) Ils finissent leur travail.
   (b) Ils se mettent en route.
10. (a) Ces touristes retiennent une chambre.
    (b) Ils arrivent à Paris.

Reflets

Un futur diplomate en Pologne: Romain Gary raconte sa jeunesse à Varsovie.[2]

Notre classe, à l'école, avait organisé un spectacle dramatique, et, après des éliminatoires serrées, le rôle principal dans le poème dramatique de Mickiewicz, *Konrad Wallenrod,* me fut dévolu, malgré le fort accent russe que j'avais en polonais.

Mon triomphe théâtral dans *Konrad Wallenrod* fut donc éphémère, et ne résolut aucun des problèmes matériels dans lesquels ma mère se débattait. Nous n'avions plus un sou. Ma mère courait toute la journée à travers la ville à la recherche d'affaires et revenait épuisée. Mais je n'ai jamais eu ni faim, ni froid et elle ne se plaignait jamais.

Encore une fois, il ne faudrait cependant pas croire que je ne faisais rien pour l'aider. Au contraire, je me surpassais dans mes efforts pour voler[3] à son secours. J'écrivais des poèmes et je les lui récitais à haute voix: ces poèmes allaient nous rapporter la gloire, la fortune et l'adulation des foules.

M. Lucien Dieuleveut-Caulec se penchait sur mes créations poétiques avec beaucoup d'attention. Car il va sans dire que je n'écrivais pas en russe ou en polonais. J'écrivais en français. Nous n'étions à Varsovie que de passage, mon pays m'attendait, il n'était pas question de me dérober. J'admirais beaucoup Pouchkine, qui écrivait en

---

[2] Romain Gary, *La Promesse de l'Aube,* copyright © 1960, Gallimard.
[3] voler: Ce mot a deux sens: *voler* comme les oiseaux, ou *voler* comme un cambrioleur.

russe, et Mickiewicz, qui écrivait en polonais, mais je n'avais jamais très bien compris pourquoi ils n'avaient pas composé leurs chefs-d'œuvre en français. Ils avaient pourtant, l'un et l'autre, reçu une bonne éducation et ils connaissaient notre langue. Ce manque de patriotisme me paraissait difficile à expliquer.

Je ne cachais jamais à mes petits camarades polonais que je n'étais parmi eux que de passage et que nous comptions bien rentrer chez nous à la première occasion. Cette naïveté obstinée ne me facilitait pas la vie à l'école.

Avez-vous bien compris?

Chacune des phrases suivantes contient au moins une erreur. Corrigez-les. Employez au moins deux phrases et une variété de formes négatives en corrigeant les fautes et en rectifiant l'information.

1. Le poème dramatique russe s'appellait *Kamarad Mickiewicz.*
2. Romain parlait bien le polonais.
3. On choisissait toujours les acteurs sans égard à leurs accents.
4. La mère de Romain travaillait dans un bureau commercial.
5. On n'avait pas de difficulté à se procurer de quoi vivre.
6. Romain aidait sa mère en volant quelques sous.
7. Sa mère se plaignait, surtout quand il lui lisait des poèmes.
8. Un professeur polonais s'intéressait à ses poèmes parce qu'ils étaient en russe.
9. Romain pense qu'il faut que chaque écrivain écrive en sa langue maternelle.
10. Romain et sa mère avaient grand envie de rester pour toujours à Varsovie.

Communiquons!

1. Quand vous étiez élève, est-ce que vous vous intéressiez au théâtre? à la poésie? à la musique? au cinéma? à collectionner des timbres-poste? aux sports? aux voitures? à l'haltérophilie[4]? Expliquez.
2. Racontez les choses que vous préférez ne pas faire, et que vous préférez que d'autres ne fassent pas. Employez des phrases qui contiennent **pas, plus, jamais, rien, personne,** et une combinaison.

[4] **l'haltérophilie** = *working out with weights, etc.*

14

Subjonctif au présent
voir

14.1 Use

The subjunctive mood consists of two commonly used tenses, present and past subjunctive. These forms are used mainly in subordinate clauses beginning with **que** (and certain other conjunctions) when the main clause contains verbs of *wishing*, *doubting*, or *emotion*. The decision to use the subjunctive in the **que**-clause depends upon the content of the *main clause*, not upon the information contained in the subordinate clause.

14.2 Classes of subordinate clauses

For purposes of learning the use of the subjunctive, main clauses may be divided into three classes:

CLASS	MAIN CLAUSE INDICATES	AFTER **que** USE:
A	A *fact* will follow [14.3]	INDICATIVE (any tense)
B	What follows is *not a fact*, but rather *desirable, possible, doubtful* [14.4]	SUBJUNCTIVE
C	*Emotional content* expressed before **que** [14.5]	

168

14.3   Class A: Main clause indicating fact

If the main clause states or indicates that what is to follow is an undisputed *fact* (or so considered by the speaker), use the indicative after **que.** Any tense of the indicative may be appropriate, depending upon the time expressed (present, passé composé, future, etc.).

> **Je sais que** Marie *est* malade.
> *I know that Mary is ill.*
>
> **Il est probable que** Marie *est* malade.
> *It is likely that Mary is ill.*

MAIN CLAUSE INDICATES FACT:

Je sais que		
Je suis sûr(e) que		
Il est vrai que		
Il est probable que	Marie *est* heureuse.	
Il dit que	INDICATIVE	
Il parait que		
Il semble que		
Je pense que		
Je crois que		

Notice that **Il est probable** is in Class A, while **Il est possible** is in Class B and requires the subjunctive. For an explanation of the cases of **penser** and **croire*** see section 14.6.

14.4   Class B: Main clause indicating non-fact

If the main clause indicates that what is to follow is not yet a fact, but is only *desirable* (not yet fulfilled), *possible, hypothetical,* or even *doubtful* or *false,* then the subordinate clause will contain a verb in the subjunctive.

Note that the main clause indicates *non-fact.*

A. Desirability

Il faut que
Il est bon que
Il est juste que
Il vaut mieux que   Marie *soit* heureuse.
Je veux que   SUBJUNCTIVE
Je ne veux pas que
Je désire que
Je ne désire pas que
Je tiens à ce que

Other main clauses implying that what is to follow is desirable, though not yet a fact, include:

Il est essentiel que   **Il préfère** que
Il est important que   **Il demande** que
Il est nécessaire que   **Il tient à** *ce*[1] que
Il est préférable que   **Il insiste** *pour*[1] que
Il est temps que   **Il souhaite** que
Il aime mieux que

B. Possibility

Il **est possible** que   Marie **soit** malade.
Il **se peut** que   SUBJUNCTIVE

It is possible that Mary is ill.

C. Doubtful or contrary to fact

Je doute que
Il ne parait pas que
Il ne semble pas que   Marie **soit** malade.
Il ne dit pas que   SUBJUNCTIVE
Je ne crois pas que
Je ne pense pas que

Croyez-vous que
Êtes-vous sûr(e) que   Marie **soit** malade?
Pensez-vous que

[1] Notice the special antecedent for **que** in these structures.

Notice that this category includes the negative and interrogative forms of some verbs from Class A (**penser, croire, paraître**). When such verbs are used to contradict (**Je ne crois pas . . .**) or to express doubt or uncertainty (**Croyez-vous . . .**) the subjunctive is called for in the **que**-clause.

Among other main clauses implying doubt or lack of factuality with regard to the following **que**-clause are:

Il est faux que	**Il n'est pas vrai** que
Il est impossible que	**Il n'est pas probable** que
Il est incroyable que	**Il n'est pas certain** que
	Je ne suis pas certain(e) que

14.5 Class C: Main clause having emotional content

If the main clause contains an impression of emotional content such as *surprise, regret, fear, anxiety, embarrassment,* the **que**-clause should contain a verb in the subjunctive.

MAIN CLAUSE HAS EMOTIONAL CONTENT

Je regrette que

Je suis désolé(e) que

Je suis content(e) que

Je suis heureux(-se) que } les inspecteurs **soient** ici.

Je suis surpris(e) que   SUBJUNCTIVE

Je suis étonné(e) que

Je suis fâché(e) que

J'ai peur que } **Marie ne parte.**[2]

Je crains que

14.6 Penser, croire, espérer°, sembler

These verbs are followed by the indicative when used positively, and by the subjunctive when used *negatively* or *interrogatively*. When a French speaker says **je pense** or **je crois,** he is reflecting factuality so far as he is concerned, hence the indicative follows:

[2] **Avoir peur** and **craindre que** require **ne** before the verb in the **que**-clause. It has *no negative meaning* unless **pas** is also used. (This rule is now often ignored.)

J'ai **peur que** vous **ne** tombiez.	*I am afraid you will fall.*
Il **craint que** Marie **ne** parte.	*He is afraid Mary will leave.*

The negative meaning takes effect if both **ne** and **pas** are present:

J'ai **peur que** Marie **ne** vienne pas.	*I am afraid that Mary will not come.*

Je pense que Marie **est** malade.	*I think Mary is ill.*
Je crois que vous **comprenez.**	*I believe you understand.*
J'espère que Claude **viendra.**	*I hope Claude will come.*

However, if these verbs are used in the *negative* or *interrogative* forms, the subjunctive is used after **que:**

Je ne pense pas que Marie **soit** malade.	*I don't think Mary is ill.*
Je ne crois pas que vous **compreniez.**	*I don't believe you understand.*
Espérez-vous que Claude **vienne?**	*Do you hope Claude is coming?*

14.7   Conjunction *que* mandatory

The conjunction **que** (*that*) is required in French, although often omitted in English. Observe the English equivalents in the foregoing examples. Notice that the conjunction *that* is omitted (or may be added without changing the meaning); in French, the conjunction **que** is always present.

14.8   Time indication, present subjunctive

The present subjunctive indicates either *present* or *future* meaning. Thus the verb **que je finisse** in the present subjunctive may mean either *that I am finishing* (present) or *that I will finish* (future). The context of the conversation or text, and/or the presence of an adverb of time (**maintenant, demain**) indicate which is meant:

PRESENT TIME	Il se peut que nous **comprenions** maintenant. *It is possible that we **understand** now.*
FUTURE TIME	Il se peut que nous **comprenions** plus tard. *It is possible that we **will understand** later.*

Compare the following sentences in which the future time of the subordinate clause is conveyed in different ways:

INDICATIVE	Je sais que je **finirai** le travail demain.
SUBJUNCTIVE	Je doute que je **finisse** le travail demain.
. . .	*I will finish the work tomorrow.*

Mise en œuvre 14 A

Emploi du subjonctif

Complétez chaque phrase par **Marie *est* malade** ou par **Marie *soit* malade**, selon le cas.

EXEMPLES

Je suis sûr que . . .
Je suis sûr que **Marie *est* malade.**

Je doute que . . .
Je doute que **Marie *soit* malade.**

1. Il est vrai que . . .
2. Je pense que . . .
3. Jacques ne pense pas que . . .
4. Il est possible que . . .
5. Paul a dit que . . .
6. Nous regrettons vivement que . . .
7. Croyez-vous que . . .
8. Il paraît que . . .
9. Je crains que . . .
10. Il est probable que . . .
11. Le professeur doute que . . .
12. Nous sommes certains que . . .

Mise en œuvre 14 B

Choix du subjonctif ou de l'indicatif

Ajoutez à la proposition principale la phrase entre parenthèses, en choisissant la forme convenable (indicatif ou subjonctif) du verbe.

EXEMPLE

(Lucien est / soit content.) Je veux que . . .

Je veux que Lucien soit content.

1. (Vous parlez / parliez français.) Il faut que . . .
2. (Sylvie finit / finisse son travail.) Il vaut mieux que . . .

3. (Nous vendons / vendions notre voiture.) Il se peut que . . .
4. (Il dit / dise la vérité.) Il est essentiel qu' . . .
5. (Tu écris / écrives la lettre.) Je tiens à ce que . . .
6. (Marie met / mette la table.) Maman veut que . . .
7. (Il part / parte à midi.) Je doute qu' . . .

FORMATION DU SUBJONCTIF

14.9   Formation of the present subjunctive

For most verbs, the **ils**-form of the present indicative, stripped of its **-ent** ending, is
the stem of the present subjunctive. All verbs, both regular and irregular (except
avoir and **être**), add the following endings:

-e	-ions
-es	-iez
-e	-ent

VERB	INDICATIVE ils-FORM	SUBJUNCTIVE
parler	ils **parl**ent	que je parle
finir	ils **finiss**ent	que je finisse
vendre	ils **vend**ent	que je vende
dire	ils **dis**ent	que je dise
écrire	ils **écriv**ent	que j'écrive
mettre	ils **mett**ent	que je mette
partir	ils **part**ent	que je parte
offrir	ils **offr**ent	que j'offre
conduire	ils **conduis**ent	que je conduise
connaître	ils **connaiss**ent	que je connaisse
paraître	ils **paraiss**ent	que je paraisse

Model conjugations in the present subjunctive

regarder (*to look at*)

Il faut que je **regarde**	que nous **regardions**
que tu **regardes**	que vous **regardiez**
qu'il **regarde**	qu'ils **regardent**

Notice the similarity with the *present indicative* of the -er verbs:

je **regarde**	nous *regardons*
tu **regardes**	vous *regardez*
il **regarde**	ils **regardent**

finir (*to finish*)

Il se peut que je **finisse.**	que nous **finissions.**
que tu **finisses.**	que vous **finissiez.**
qu'il **finisse.**	qu'ils **finissent.**

répondre (*to answer*)

Je doute que je **réponde.**	que nous **répondions.**
que tu **répondes.**	que vous **répondiez.**
qu'il **réponde.**	qu'ils **répondent.**

dire (*to say*)

Croit-on que je **dise** cela?	que nous **disions** cela?
que tu **dises** cela?	que vous **disiez** cela?
qu'il **dise** cela?	qu'ils **disent** cela?

14.10   *avoir* and *être*

These two verbs have irregular forms in the present subjunctive.

avoir (*to have*)

que j'**aie**	que nous **ayons**	**ay** - STEM
que tu **aies**	que vous **ayez**	
qu'il **ait**	qu'ils **aient**	← **ai** - STEM

être (*to be*)

que je **sois**	que nous **soyons**	**soy** - STEM
que tu **sois**	que vous **soyez**	
qu'il **soit**	qu'ils **soient**	← **soi** - STEM

Mise en œuvre 14 C

Formation et emploi du subjonctif

Ajoutez à la phrase principale la phrase entre parenthèses. Faites les changements nécessaires.

EXEMPLE

(Nous mettons la table.) Il faut que . . .

Il faut que nous **mettions** la table.

1. (Jacques achètera un ordinateur.) Il est possible que . . .
2. (Ses parents ont assez d'argent.) Je doute que . . .
3. (Son père est mécanicien.) Il semble que . . .
4. (Ses parents font des économies.) Il faut que . . .
5. (Ils ont besoin d'une voiture.) Pensez-vous qu' . . .
6. (Nous prenons le métro pour aller en ville.) Tu sais que . . .
7. (Le père de Jacques prend le train pour aller au travail.) Crois-tu que . . . ?
8. (Ta mère est malade.) Je regrette que . . .
9. (Son père connaît le doyen.) Il n'est pas probable que . . .
10. (Jacques vend sa voiture.) Il est essentiel que . . .

VERBE IRRÉGULIER **VOIR** ET D'AUTRES VERBES DE PERCEPTION

14.11   Verbe irrégulier *voir* (*to see*)

The complete forms of this verb can be found in Appendix C, Verb Table 32.

PRÉSENT	je **vois**	nous **voyons**	} **voy**-STEM
	tu **vois**	vous **voyez**	
	il **voit**	ils **voient**	← **voi**-STEM

IMPARFAIT   REGULAR: stem **voy-** from present tense

Autrefois je **voyais** les bateaux qui **arrivaient.**
*Formerly I **used to see** the ships that **were arriving.***

PASSÉ COMPOSÉ   PP. **vu** (avoir)

Hier **j'ai vu** une comédie de Molière.

La comédie que **nous avons vue** était *L'Avare.*

PASSÉ SIMPLE   STEM: **v-** + **is** system of endings.

En entrant dans le bureau **je vis** le gérant.

FUTUR   FC STEM: **verr-** (+ future endings)

Si je vais en ville **je verrai** la nouvelle exposition.

CONDITIONNEL   FC STEM: **verr-** (+ imperfect endings)

Si j'avais le temps **je verrais** ce film suédois.

SUBJONCTIF   STEMS: **voi-** / **voy-** (2-stem verb)

que je **voie**	que nous **voyions**
que tu **voies**	que vous **voyiez**
qu'il **voie**	qu'ils **voient**

Il faut que **tu voies** notre voiture neuve.

14.12   Signal seeking and reception: pairs of verbs

The two most important senses are **la vue, l'ouïe** (*sight, hearing*). Each is represented by two verbs: one representing the preparation for receiving a signal, and another for the actual reception:

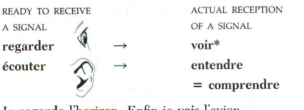

READY TO RECEIVE A SIGNAL		ACTUAL RECEPTION OF A SIGNAL
regarder	→	**voir***
écouter	→	**entendre**
		= comprendre

Je **regarde** l'horizon.   Enfin je **vois** l'avion.

J'**écoute**.   Enfin j'**entends** le train qui vient.
　　↑   ↑
SEEKING SIGNAL   RECEPTION OF SIGNAL

By extension, both verbs representing reception of a signal also mean *to understand*. To see or hear the signal is to understand.

Il **voit** ce que vous voulez dire.
*He **understands** (sees) what you mean.*

J'**entends** ce que vous dites.
*I **understand** (hear) what you are saying.*

Mise en œuvre 14 D

Reconstituez les phrases à partir des éléments donnés:

1. il / possible // que / Robert / avoir / besoin / argent
2. nous / regretter // que / tu / partir / demain
3. tu / penser // que / nous / écrire / composition / en classe / ?
4. il / falloir // que / je / finir / expérience / chimie / demain
5. je / douter // que / ce[3] / étudiante / comprendre / ce problème

---

[3] **ce, cette, ces** [5.7].

6. il / probable // que / ils / écouter / poliment

7. elle / ne pas croire // que / ils / avoir / besoin / manuels

8. il / essentiel // que / ils / répondre / précisément / à / questions / de / professeur

9. il / falloir // que / vous / se dépêcher / s'habiller

10. nous / être / surpris[4] // que / grand-père / conduire / son / voiture

11. il / sembler // que / ce philosophe / dire / vérité

12. nous / être / content // que / Jean-Claude / promettre / suivre / cours / informatique

13. son / amie / désirer // que / il / devenir[5] / programmeur

14. je / ne pas être / certain // que / nous / prendre / assez / temps / étudier / cours / de / Bourse

15. employés / peur // que / patron / se mettre / colère

16. il / ne pas sembler // que / je / finir / analyse / économie / aujourd'hui

17. il / bon // que / nous / regarder / plan / de / ville / soin

18. il / probable // que / tu / voir / ton / copains / ville

19. je / ne pas penser // que / nous / comprendre / problème

20. Paul / écouter // mais / il / ne pas entendre / train

Mise en œuvre 14 E

Sujet de composition ou de conversation:
Vous devenez cosmonaute

Ayant fait le voyage dans la lune (ou dans une planète de votre choix), vous réfléchissez sur votre situation. Qu'est-ce que vous voyez? Qu'est-ce que vous entendez? Qu'est-ce qui est intéressant? Qu'est-ce qui est important pour maintenir la vie? Qu'est-ce qui vous surprend? Qu'est-ce qu'il faut pour rendre la qualité de la vie plus agréable? Qu'est-ce qu'il faut pour le transport? le domicile? la nourriture? les distractions? Pour la respiration? Combien de temps est-ce que vous comptez y rester?

Décrivez votre arrivée et les problèmes que vous rencontrez. Employez **le temps présent** (indicatif ou subjonctif, selon le cas). En préparant votre rapport, utilisez (1) au moins six fois, des propositions principales parmi les trois catégories qui exigent le subjonctif; (2) au moins deux fois, des formes de **penser, croire, espérer** ou **sembler**; (3) au moins trois idiotismes. Contrastez parfois votre situation actuelle avec celle d'autrefois.

---

[4] After a form of **être,** be sure that the adjective agrees with the subject [5.1].

[5] If you don't know the needed form, check the Verb Tables.

Mise en œuvre 14 F

Révision générale

1. When we lived in London we often used to take a walk in Green Park.
2. Last week there was a French exam, so (therefore) we went to the language laboratory to use the computer.
3. While I was carefully reading an article in the **Grande Encyclopédie,** one of my friends came into the reading room.
4. I had been assiduously writing a paper on business management for an hour and a half when I felt like having a bite to eat.
5. John had already bought some stock in Michelin when I saw his broker at the stock market.

15

Subjonctif (suite)
Subjonctif des verbes irréguliers
savoir

SUBJONCTIF (SUITE)

15.1 Additional uses of the subjunctive

The subjunctive mood is automatically used in clauses that follow certain *conjunctions* [15.2] and *superlatives* [19.2], and after verbs expressing *purpose, wish*, or *expectation* when the specifications of a desired item are not stipulated and are purely theoretical [15.4].

15.2 Conjunctions followed by a verb in the subjunctive

The subjunctive is automatically used in clauses after these conjunctions:

avant que	*before, until*
à moins que (ne)[1]	*unless*
pourvu que	*provided that*
pour que, afin que	*so that, in order that*
bien que, quoique	*although*
jusqu'à ce que	*until (a **future** event)*

[1] This "pleonastic," or unnecessary, **ne** is now used less often before the following verb. It has no negative meaning.

Il ne se couchera pas **avant que** vous **reveniez.**
He won't go to bed before (until) you come back.

Il travaille **pour que** je **devienne** médecin.
He is working so that I may become a doctor.

Nous partons maintenant, **à moins que** vous **ne soyez** trop fatiguée.
We are leaving now, unless you are too tired.

Nous allons regarder la télévision **jusqu'à ce que** Paulette **revienne.**
We are going to watch TV until Paulette comes back.

15.3 Superlatives are followed by the subjunctive

When a **que**-clause follows a superlative or the equivalent (**le seul, l'unique, le premier, le dernier,** etc.), the verb of the **que**-clause should be in the subjunctive mood.

L'Étranger est **le meilleur roman** que nous **ayons lu.**

Georges est le garçon **le plus intelligent** que je **connaisse.**

C'est la pièce **la plus passionnante** que j'**aie** jamais **vue.**

C'est **le seul dictionnaire** qu'on **puisse** obtenir en ce moment.

The effect of using the subjunctive is to soften the statement, thus avoiding too dogmatic a statement, and allowing for different opinions.

However, if the fact described in a superlative statement is clearly unquestionable, the indicative may be used:

Aujourd'hui, en 1991, la Tour Maine-Montparnasse est **le plus haut édifice** qu'on **peut** trouver en Europe.

15.4 Quest for a theoretical object

When a verb of purpose, wish, or expectation such as **chercher** *(to look for)* is followed by a subordinate clause indicating theoretically desirable qualities of the object sought, use the subjunctive to express the desirability and lack of factuality:

Je cherche **une** assistante **qui comprenne** l'arabe.
*I am looking for **an** assistant who understands Arabic.*

Nous cherchons **une** voiture **qui ait** huit cylindres.
*We are looking for **an** eight-cylinder car.*

In the event the thing sought is *not* merely theoretical but an actual identifiable person or thing, use the indicative:

> Je cherche **la** personne **qui est arrivée** hier soir.
> *I am looking for **the** person who arrived yesterday evening.*
>
> Je cherche **la** dactylo **qui comprend** l'arabe. Est-elle occupée?
> *I am looking for **the** stenographer who understands Arabic. Is she busy?*

15.5   Replacement of the subjunctive by other structures

When the subject of the main clause is the same as that of the subordinate clause, use an infinitive expression to replace the **que**-clause:

> $\boxed{\text{She}}$ is glad that $\boxed{\text{she}}$ is in Paris this summer.
> ↑   IDENTICAL SUBJECT   ↑

Since the subject of both clauses is the same, rephrase using the infinitive:

> Elle est contente d'**être** à Paris cet été.

A.   Main clause indicating *wishing, desiring, preferring.* Verbs in this category (such as **vouloir, préférer°, aimer mieux, aimer**) are followed directly by the infinitive when the subject of both clauses would be the same:

> Nous **voulons** *prendre* l'avion.[2]
>
> Je **préfère** *diner* au restaurant.
>
> Il **aime mieux** *assister* au match de tennis.

B.   Emotional content of main clause. When the main clause includes a *verb indicating emotional content* or an *adjective*, use **de** + [INFINITIVE]:

> Il est **étonné** *de voir* son ancien collègue.
>
> Je suis **fâché** *d'avoir* oublié le nom de cette personne.
>
> Nous **regrettons** *de ne pas pouvoir* assister à la conférence.
>
> Il est **important** *d'étudier* tous les exemples.

However, if the subjects of the two clauses are different, the subjunctive cannot be avoided:

---

[2] Instead of something like *"We want that we take the plane."*

Je veux **que** *tu* **finisses** ton travail.
I want you to finish your work.[3]

Il aime mieux **que** *vous* **preniez** l'avion.
He prefers (that) you take the plane.

C.   Conjunctions replacing *que* by [*de* + INFINITIVE]. When both clauses of a compound sentence have the same subject, the conjunctions **avant que** and **afin que** may be replaced. The **que** becomes **de** plus the infinitive of the next verb.

Il fait ses devoirs **avant de** *regarder* la télévision.

Il étudie **afin de** *réussir* à ses cours à l'université.

D.   *Pour que* replaced by [*pour* + INFINITIVE]. When the subject of both clauses is the same, this substitution may be made:

Il parle lentement **pour** *être* compris.
He speaks slowly **in order** *to be understood.*

He *speaks slowly so that* **he** *will be understood.*

E.   *Bien que* [+ PRESENT PARTICIPLE] *although*. When the subject of both clauses is the same, use **bien que** plus the present participle [25.6].

Bien que *jouant* mal de la guitare, je peux accompagner des chansons.
Although I play the guitar poorly, I can accompany songs.

If the verb after **bien que** is **être**, the present participle **étant** may be omitted:

Bien que fatigué, j'assiste aux cours aujourd'hui.

F.   Conjunctions replaced by preposition plus noun. When **avant** or **après** are used, the subjunctive may often be replaced by a noun such as the following:

NOUN	PREPOSITIONAL PHRASE	EXAMPLE
le départ	avant **le départ**	**avant le départ du train**
l'arrivée	après **l'arrivée**	**après l'arrivée du prof**
le retour	avant **le retour**	**avant son retour**
le commencement	avant **le commencement**	**avant le commencement du film**
la fin	avant **la fin**	**avant la fin de la pièce**
l'ouverture	avant **l'ouverture**	**avant l'ouverture du musée**
le fermeture	après **la fermeture**	**après la fermeture du magasin**

---

[3] Literally *"I want that you finish your work."* This is a trap for English speakers, since *"I want you to . . ."* cannot be rendered directly in French.

Parlons jusqu'à **ce que le patron revienne.** *may become*

Parlons jusqu'**au retour**[4] du patron.

Nous avons dîné avant **que la pièce soit commencée.** *becomes*

Nous avons dîné avant **le commencement** de la pièce.

G.   Replacement of *il faut que* **by** *il faut* **+** [INFINITIVE]. When **il faut** is followed by a **que**-clause, it is clear who is required to do something:

Il faut **que j'étudie.**	*I must study.*
Il faut **qu'ils partent.**	*They must leave.*
Il faut que **Jean prenne** les billets.	*Jean must buy the tickets.*

When followed by an infinitive alone, it is assumed that the speaker or his companions are those who must do something, or that it is merely a general observation:

Il faut **étudier.**   Il faut **partir.**   Il faut **prendre** les billets.

This arrangement may be directed at a particular person by inserting an indirect object pronoun [7.3] before **faut** (or other tense of **falloir**):

Il **me** faut étudier.	*I must study.*
Il **leur** faut partir.	*They must leave.*
Il **lui** faut prendre les billets.	*He must buy the tickets.*

Mise en œuvre 15 A

Emploi du subjonctif

Combinez la phrase entre parenthèses avec la phrase incomplète, en mettant le verbe de la proposition subordonnée au subjonctif s'il le faut.

EXEMPLE

Vous réussirez pourvu que . . . (vous ne faites pas de fautes)

Vous réussirez pourvu que vous ne **fassiez** pas de fautes.

1. J'attendrai ici jusqu'à ce que . . . (tu finis tes devoirs)
2. Il faut que . . . (j'écris une composition)
3. Ils viendront pourvu que . . . (vous leur dites la nouvelle)
4. Je parle lentement afin que . . . (vous me comprenez)

[4] Notez la contraction **au** pour **à** + **le.**

5. Elle fait beaucoup de fautes bien que . . . (elle est intelligente)

6. Nous étudierons en attendant que . . . (le professeur revient)

7. Vous réussirez à moins que . . . (vous faites trop de fautes)

8. Ne parlez pas avant que . . . (les faits sont connus)

9. Il a apporté son cahier pour que . . . (je vois son travail)

10. Il fermera la porte avant que . . . (nous pouvons sortir)

11. C'est le meilleur dictionnaire que . . . (je connais)

12. C'est le seul fait historique que . . . (Philippe sait)

13. C'est la plus longue promenade que . . . (nous avons fait)

14. Ce roman est le plus court que . . . (vous avez dans votre collection)

15. Ce match était le plus passionnant que . . . (on peut imaginer)

Mise en œuvre 15 B

Moyens d'éviter le subjonctif

Combinez les deux phrases au moyen d'un infinitif.

EXEMPLE

Jean est content. Il visite Chartres.

Jean est **content de visiter** Chartres.

1. Nous sommes heureux. Nous allons au ballet.

2. Je suis désolé. Je fais des fautes d'orthographe.

3. Les étudiantes voudraient le faire. Elles vont au centre.

4. Le docteur Broussard est content. Il possède une voiture neuve.

5. Pierre regrette. Il nous quitte.

Mise en œuvre 15 C

Remplacement du subjonctif

Combinez les deux phrases au moyen des mots entre parenthèses. Évitez le subjonctif si c'est possible. La deuxième phrase deviendra la proposition subordonnée.[5]

[5] **la proposition subordonnée** = *subordinate clause*

EXEMPLE

Jean-Claude a déjeuné. **Il va aller au cinéma.** (*avant*)

Jean-Claude a déjeuné *avant* **d'aller** au cinéma.

1. On travaille. On gagne de l'argent. (*pour*)
2. Thierry étudie. Son père est content. (*pour*[6])
3. J'ai écrit à mes parents. Ils m'envoient de l'argent. (*afin*)
4. Jacques est allé au bistrot du coin. Il a fini son travail. (*après*)
5. Chantal va acheter un ordinateur. Elle suit un cours d'informatique. (*après*)
6. Il a fait une partie de tennis. Il est allé à la bibliothèque. (*avant*)
7. Gérard va louer un appartement. Ses parents ont assez d'argent. (*pourvu*)
8. Notre ordinateur est toujours en panne. Nous faisons des réparations. (*bien que*[7])
9. Le courtier a vendu mes actions[8]. Je suis parti de son bureau. (*après*)
10. Mon père est allé au bureau aujourd'hui. Il est malade. (*bien que*[7])
11. Je suis entrée dans le cinéma. J'ai pris mon billet. (*après*)

Récrivez les phrases suivantes pour éviter le subjonctif en employant le nom qui convient. Servez-vous de la liste [15.5F].

12. J'y suis entré avant que le film ait commencé.
13. Nous avons joué aux cartes avec Suzanne jusqu'à ce qu'elle soit partie.
14. Elle se tient devant la boutique jusqu'à ce que les portes soient ouvertes.
15. Les clients restent dans le magasin jusqu'à ce que les portes soient fermées.
16. Nous étudions jusqu'à ce que le professeur revienne.
17. Les étudiants quittent la salle de classe après que la conférence soit finie.
18. Bien que nous ayons faim, nous continuons à travailler.[9]

SUBJONCTIF DES VERBES IRRÉGULIERS

15.6 Present subjunctive of *faire, savoir, pouvoir*

These three important verbs have one-stem present subjunctive forms:

---

[6] Use *in order to please* (*to please* [P] **plaire à** [P])
[7] **Bien que** uses the present participle rather than the infinitive. See [15.5E].
[8] **le courtier** = *stockbroker;* **les actions** = *shares*
[9] For **bien que** see [15.5E].

VERB	STEM	PRESENT SUBJUNCTIVE	
faire	**fass-**	que je fasse	que nous fassions
		que tu fasses	que vous fassiez
		qu'il fasse	qu'ils fassent
savoir	**sach-**	que je sache	que nous sachions
		que tu saches	que vous sachiez
		qu'il sache	qu'ils sachent
pouvoir	**puiss-**	que je puisse	que nous puissions
		que tu puisses	que vous puissiez
		qu'il puisse	qu'ils puissent

Il veut que je **fasse** mes devoirs.
He wants me to do my homework.

Je veux que tu **saches** la vérité.
I insist that you know the truth.

Je doute que Paul **puisse** ouvrir cette valise.
I doubt that Paul can open that suitcase.

15.7   Two-stem irregular verbs

Some irregular verbs use a stem derived from the **ils**-form (present indicative) for the "L-area" (silent ending) forms of the subjunctive, and use a different stem for the **nous-** and **vous**-forms.

The stem of the **nous-** and **vous**-forms of the present subjunctive usually conforms to the spelling of the infinitive stem. For example, **prendre** has the following forms in the present subjunctive:

que je **prenne**	que nous **prenions**	**pren-**STEM
que tu **prennes**	que vous **preniez**	
qu'il **prenne**	qu'ils **prennent**	

prenn-STEM

Verbs that have two stems in the subjunctive are listed below.

VERB	STEM FOR **JE, TU, IL, ILS**	STEM FOR **NOUS, VOUS**
aller	que j'**aill**-e	que nous **all**-ions
prendre	que je **prenn**-e	que nous **pren**-ions
tenir	que je **tienn**-e	que nous **ten**-ions
venir	que je **vienn**-e	que nous **ven**-ions

VERB	STEM FOR JE, TU, IL, ILS	STEM FOR NOUS, VOUS
vouloir	que je **veuill**-e	que nous **voul**-ions
voir	que je **voi**-e	que nous **voy**-ions
devoir	que je **doiv**-e	que nous **dev**-ions

Mise en œuvre 15 D

Subjonctif des verbes irréguliers

Refaites les phrases suivantes en commençant par les mots entre parenthèses.

EXEMPLE

Je fais mes devoirs. (Il vaut mieux que . . .)

Il vaut mieux que je **fasse** mes devoirs.

1. Tu sais tes formules de chimie. (Il faut que . . .)
2. Je puis finir ce travail aujourd'hui. (Le patron doute que . . .)
3. Les garçons font la vaisselle. (Ma mère ne croit pas que . . .)
4. Jeanne veut aller au bord de la mer. (Pensez-vous que . . .)
5. Nous voyons beaucoup de jeunes gens à la plage. (Il est possible que . . .)
6. Mon amie Sophie vient aussi. (Il est bon que . . .)
7. Elle veut nager dans l'eau salée de l'Atlantique. (Êtes-vous sûre que . . .)
8. Nous prenons la voiture du père de Robert. (Il est préférable que . . .)
9. Ma sœur tient à conduire. (Je crains que . . .)
10. Je dois emprunter de l'argent pour le trajet. (Je regrette que . . .)
11. Vous ne savez pas combien cela va coûter. (Il se peut que . . .)
12. Tous les autres vont par le train. (Je suis surpris que . . .)

VERBE IRRÉGULIER **SAVOIR**

15.8   Review the forms of *savoir (to know, to be able)*, Verb Table 25

PRÉSENT	je **sais** / nous **savons**
PASSÉ COMPOSÉ (PP. SU)	il **a su** la vérité[10]
PASSÉ SIMPLE	ils **surent** les faits

Formation: STEM s- [+ -us ending system]

---

[10] *He found out the truth.*

IMPARFAIT	il sav*ait*
FUTUR	il sau*ra*
CONDITIONNEL	il sau*rait*
SUBJONCTIF PRÉSENT	que je **sache** / que nos **sach*ions***

15.9   Remarks on *savoir*

This verb has various uses and meanings.

A. Followed by a ***noun,*** **savoir** means *to know* [A FACT]:

Tout le monde **sait** *la date* de la prise de la Bastille.

Nous **savons** *la leçon* pour aujourd'hui.

Savez-vous l'adresse de cette personne?

Carefully distinguish between this use, with *definable facts*, and the use of **connaître** [Verb Table 4], which means *to be acquainted with, to be familiar with* (even though it may be used as *to know* in English):

Connaissez-vous cette jeune fille?

Nous **connaissons** bien la France.

B. Followed by an ***infinitive,*** the meaning of **savoir** is *to know how to* [I], often transformed into *can (do something)*. (The ability involved deals with intellectual or learned things, and not with **P**hysical ability or **P**ermission, which would be **pouvoir**.)

Mes amis **savent** *jouer* aux échecs.
My friends can (know how to) play chess.

Nous ne **savons** pas *danser.*
We can't (don't know how to) dance.

If physical *ability* or *permission* is implied in *can*, use **pouvoir**:

Je ne **peux** pas *ouvrir* cette porte.
I can't open this door. [ABILITY]

Est-ce que nous **pouvons** *emprunter* cet ordinateur?
May we borrow this computer? [PERMISSION]

C. In the passé composé, **savoir** means *found out:*

J'**ai su** que mes parents allaient acheter une voiture neuve.
I found out that my parents were going to buy a new car.

D. Idiomatic uses:

Je ne sais que faire.   *I don't know what to do.*
Il en sait plus long que moi. *He knows more about it than I.*

> **P** is for **P**hysical ability, **P**ermission, and *pouvoir*.
> **S** is for **S**avvy, mental **S**kills and *savoir*.

Mise en œuvre 15 E

Subjonctif de *savoir, pouvoir, connaître*

A. Refaites les phrases en commençant par l'expression entre parenthèses.

1. Tu sais tes verbes. (Il est essentiel que . . .)
2. Nous pouvons finir ce travail aujourd'hui. (Je doute que . . .)
3. Ils savent la vérité. (Il est possible que . . .)
4. Le patron prend une décision bientôt. (Croyez-vous que . . .)
5. Nous visitons la Tour Eiffel. (Il est temps que . . .)

B. Donnez la form convenable de **savoir** ou de **connaître**.

6. Cette forme du verbe irrégulier, je la . . .
7. Ce professeur, nous le . . .
8. Cette partie de la ville, Paul la . . . bien.
9. L'adresse de la Bourse, mon père la . . .
10. La cotation d'aujourd'hui, je la . . .

C. Choisissez entre **savoir** et **pouvoir**.

11. Ce meuble est très lourd; je ne — pas le lever.
12. Il faut que mon amie reste à la maison; elle ne — pas sortir ce soir.
13. Cet exercice est long, mais je ne — pas taper à la machine.
14. Cette chanteuse a mal à la gorge; elle ne — pas chanter aujourd'hui.
15. Ces touristes sont Italiens; ils ne — pas parler français.

Mise en œuvre 15 F

Thème

1. We are going to go to the movies unless you prefer to stay home.
2. Let's take the subway so that we will arrive early.
3. We feel like seeing *Le Pont de la rivière Kwaï* although it is in English.

4. Our friends are looking for a movie in Swedish with subtitles in Italian!
5. Don't go to a seat until the usherette comes to get you.
6. It is important to give the usherette a tip before you sit down.
7. Keep your ticket until you are seated.
8. One can't go into the theater after the film has started[11].
9. It is preferable to arrive a few minutes before the film begins.
10. If one arrives late, it is necessary to wait until the next show.

[11] *(After the beginning of . . .)*

16

Passé du subjonctif
faire

16.1 Use of the past subjunctive

This tense is used in subordinate clauses requiring the subjunctive when the *time is in the past*. The present subjunctive expresses present and future times [14.8]; the past subjunctive expresses any past time.

PRESENT TIME: **Il est possible que** Robert **arrive** aujourd'hui.

FUTURE TIME: **Il est possible que** Robert **arrive** demain.

PAST TIME: **Il est possible que** Robert **soit arrivé** hier.

The past subjunctive (**soit arrivé**) is a compound tense corresponding in formation to the passé composé: it consists of the auxiliary verb in the present subjunctive, plus the past participle:

INDICATIVE (passé composé)   elle **est** arrivée

SUBJUNCTIVE (passé)   qu'elle **soit** arrivée

The past subjunctive is used in the subordinate clauses after main clauses expressing *doubt, possibility, desirability,* or *emotional content* (Classes B and C) [14.4–14.5]; after certain *conjunctions* [15.2]; and after *superlatives* [15.3] when the time of the **que**-clause is in the past.

192

16.2   Formation of the past subjunctive

The past subjunctive consists of the appropriate auxiliary verb in the present subjunctive plus the past participle. There is no change in the list of verbs using the auxiliary *être* [10.3] nor in the rules for agreement of past participles. Review the present subjunctive of the auxiliaries *avoir* and *être* [14.10], since they are a part of every verb in the past subjunctive.

Compare the passé composé with the past subjunctive on the following chart:

AUXILIARY VERB	INDICATIVE PASSÉ COMPOSÉ	SUBJUNCTIVE PASSÉ DU SUBJONCTIF	MEANINGS (IDENTICAL)
avoir	il **a fini**	qu'il **ait fini**	*he finished*
	vous **avez lu**	que vous **ayez lu**	*you read*
	ils **ont fait**	qu'ils **aient fait**	*they did*
	j' **ai trouvé**	que j' **aie trouvé**	*I found*
	il **a eu**	qu'il **ait eu**	*he had*
être	elle **est arrivée**	qu'elle **soit arrivée**	*she arrived*
	ils **sont partis**	qu'ils **soient partis**	*they left*
	je me **suis reposé**	que je me **sois reposé**	*I rested*
	il s' **est levé**	qu'il se **soit levé**	*he got up*

MODEL CONJUGATIONS IN THE PAST SUBJUNCTIVE

parler (avoir)

que j' **aie parlé**	que nous **ayons parlé**
que tu **aies parlé**	que vous **ayez parlé**
qu'il **ait parlé**	qu'ils **aient parlé**

finir (avoir)

que j' **aie fini**	que nous **ayons fini**
que tu **aies fini**	que vous **ayez fini**
qu'il **ait fini**	qu'ils **aient fini**

entrer (être)—typical of verbs using auxiliary *être*

que je **sois entré(e)**	que nous **soyons entré(e)s**
que tu **sois entré(e)**	que vous **soyez entré(e)(s)**
qu'il **soit entré**	qu'ils **soient entrés**
qu'elle **soit entrée**	qu'elles **soient entrées**

s'amuser (être) — typical of reflexive verbs

que je **me sois amusé(e)**	que nous **nous soyons amusé(e)s**
qu tu **te sois amusé(e)**	que vous **vous soyez amusé(e)(s)**
qu'il **se soit amusé**	qu'ils **se soient amusés**
qu'elle **se soit amusée**	qu'elles **se soient amusées**

The forms of the past subjunctive correspond to those of the passé composé:

PAST SUBJUNCTIVE	PASSÉ COMPOSÉ
Je doute qu'**il ait fini** son travail.	Je sais qu'**il a fini** son travail.
Penses-tu qu'**elle soit arrivée?**	Je pense qu'**elle est arrivée.**
Il est content qu'**ils se soient amusés.**	Il est vrai qu'**ils se sont amusés.**

Meanings are likewise identical:

qu'il ait fini = qu'il a fini   *that he finished, that he has finished*

Mise en œuvre 16 A

Formation du passé du subjonctif

Mettez les verbes au passé du subjonctif. Commencez chaque phrase par **Il est possible que** . . .

1. Jean-Paul est allé à la bibliothèque pour faire des recherches.
2. Il a étudié jusqu'à la fermeture.
3. Suzanne est sortie de la bibliothèque avec Jean-Paul.
4. Ils se sont rendus au café pour prendre quelque chose.
5. On s'est bien amusé au dancing.

Commencez les phrases suivantes par **Pensez-vous que** . . .

6. André et Stéphane sont allés au terrain de tennis?
7. Barbara s'est souvenu de son rendez-vous avec Gilles?
8. Hélène a reçu une lettre du doyen?
9. On s'est dépêché de répondre à la lettre?
10. Les profs ont négligé de donner une bonne note aux athlètes?

Commencez les phrases suivantes par **Je regrette que** . . . ou par **Je suis heureux que** . . . , selon le cas.

11. Tu n'as pas réussi à l'examen de psychologie.

12. Nous avons eu le temps d'aller au café après l'examen.

13. L'agent m'a arrêté(e) pour ne pas avoir respecté un feu rouge.

14. Vous avez donné une petite fête au troisième étage.

15. Je me suis trompé(e) d'étage.

Mise en œuvre 16 B

Emploi du passé du subjonctif

Commencez la phrase par le fragment entre parenthèses et mettez le verbe au subjonctif s'il y a lieu.

EXEMPLE

Marie est arrivée. (Il se peut que . . .)

Il se peut que Marie **soit arrivée.**

1. Le gardien a fermé la porte. (Je sais que . . .)

2. La concierge a ouvert la porte. (Je ne suis pas sûr(e) que . . .)

3. Ton petit frère s'est lavé les mains. (J'espère que . . .)

4. Ma mère est descendue. (Je ne crois pas que . . .)

5. Le directeur est parti. (Je crains que . . .)

6. Nous avons eu de la chance. (Il est vrai que . . .)

7. Tu n'as pas eu de chance. (Nous regrettons que . . .)

8. Lucien a déjà fini ses devoirs. (Je suis étonné(e) que . . .)

9. Son ami Poirot l'a aidé. (Je me doute que . . .)

10. Jill est descendue à l'Hôtel du Louvre. (Je me demande si . . .)

11. Elle a rendu visite à une amie à Saint-Cloud. (Il est possible que . . .)

12. Vous avez réussi à l'examen. (Le professeur est heureux que . . .)

13. L'avocat est parti en vacances. (Je regrette que . . .)

14. Le ministre a proposé une nouvelle formule. (Il est bon que . . .)

15. Vous avez fait trop de fautes. (Vous réussirez à moins que . . .)

16. Nous l'avons vue. (C'est la plus belle voiture que . . .)

17. Paul l'a écrite. (C'est la lettre la plus intéressante que . . .)

18. Les jeunes filles sont rentrées. (Il ne semble pas que . . .)

19. Nous avons vu une pièce de Giraudoux. (Le professeur est content que . . .)

20. Vous avez dit la vérité. (L'agent ne croit pas que . . .)

VERBE IRRÉGULIER **FAIRE**

16.3   Review the forms of *faire* [*to make, to do*]

Review all of the forms of **faire** on Table 14 in Appendix C. Pay particular attention to the following tenses already reviewed:

PRÉSENT	Vous **faites** bien vos devoirs.
IMPARFAIT	Je **faisais** mon lit quand j'étais jeune.
PLUS-QUE-PARFAIT	Tu **avais fait** la vaisselle quand je suis rentré.
PASSÉ COMPOSÉ	Elle **a fait** les courses en ville.
SUBJONCTIF PRÉSENT	Je doute qu'il **fasse** ses devoirs.
SUBJONCTIF PASSÉ	Il est possible qu'il **ait fait** une partie de tennis.

The future / conditional stem is **fer-** (*will do, would do*) and the stem of the passé simple is just **f-** (+ **-is** endings [20.2]). Refer to future tense [24], conditional [25], passé simple (past definite) [20].

The verb **faire** is used in connection with various activities, some of which are shown below.

A.   Domestic tasks (*le travail domestique; le ménage*)

faire **le ménage**	*to keep house, to do the housework*
faire **des courses**	*to go shopping; to run errands*
faire **la cuisine**	*to cook, do the cooking*
faire **la vaisselle**	*to wash the dishes*
faire **le lit**	*to make the bed*
faire **les devoirs**	*to do one's homework*

B.   Trips and transportation (*les voyages et le transport*)

faire **un voyage**[1]	*to take a trip*
. . . **à pied**	*on foot*
. . . **à cheval**	*on horseback*
. . . **en auto**	*by car*
. . . **en autocar**	*by interurban bus*

[1] Although *voyage* in English usually designates a trip by sea, it is used for all kinds of trips in French.

. . . en avion	*by plane*
. . . par le train	*by train*
faire **un voyage d'affaires**	*to take a business trip*
faire **un voyage d'agrément**	*to take a pleasure trip*
faire **le trajet de x à y**	*to go from x to y*
faire **une promenade**	*to take a walk (for pleasure)*
. . . **à bicyclette**	*to go for a bike ride*
. . . **à cheval**	*to go horseback riding*
. . . **en auto**	*to go for a ride (in a car)*
. . . **en bateau**	*to go for a boat ride*
faire **de l'auto-stop**	*to hitch-hike*
faire **sa valise**	*to pack one's suitcase*

C.   Social events (*la vie mondaine*)

faire **la connaissance de [P]**	*to meet*[2] *[PERSON]*
faire **une visite à [P]**[3]	*to visit [A PERSON]*
faire **attention à [N]**	*to pay attention to [NOUN]*
faire **semblant de [I]**	*to pretend to [DO SOMETHING]*

D.   Sports and amusements (*les sports et les divertissements*)

faire **du sport**	*to do sports*
faire **du football**	*to play soccer*
. . . **du football américain**	. . . *football*
. . . **du basket**	. . . *basketball*
. . . **du tennis**	. . . *tennis*
. . . **du golf**	. . . *golf*
faire **du jogging**	*to go jogging*
. . . **de l'alpinisme**	. . . *mountain climbing*
. . . **de l'aérobique**	*to do aerobics*
. . . **de l'haltérophilie**	. . . *weight lifting*

Note that certain nouns may be used with **faire** for particular activities: **faire une partie / un set / un match / de** (tennis, etc.).

[2] This is used for the first meeting to make someone's acquaintance. Thereafter use **rencontrer** or **retrouver.**

[3] You can alternatively use **rendre visite à [P]**.

E.   Weather (*le temps qu'il fait*). The pronoun **il** in these expressions is always the impersonal *it*.

Il fait beau / mauvais.	*The weather is nice / bad.*
Il fait chaud / frais / froid.	*It is hot / cool / cold.*
Il fait du soleil / du vent.	*It is sunny / windy.*

Other expressions about the weather are:

Il pleut. (*from* pleuvoir)	*It is raining.*
Il neige. (*from* neiger)	*It is snowing.*
Il fait gris.	*It is overcast.*
Il fait un temps de chien.	*It is rotten weather.*

J'ai fait le trajet de Paris à Londres en avion.
I made the trip from Paris to London by plane.

Hier Gilles **a fait la connaissance** d'une Suédoise.
Yesterday Gilles met a Swedish girl.

Mon chat **fait semblant de** dormir.
My cat is pretending to sleep.

— Quel **temps fait-il?**   —**Il fait très froid.**
"How's the weather?"   "It's very cold."

— Je veux fermer la fenêtre; **ça ne vous fait rien?**   —**Faites!**
"I want to close the window; is that okay with you?" "Go ahead!"

ATTENTION! Do *not* use **faire** for *to make* someone happy / angry / sad; the verb for this is **rendre**.

Il **a rendu** sa mère très **heureuse**.
He made his mother very happy.

Mise en œuvre 16 D

Emploi de *faire*

Répondez aux questions suivantes en vous servant d'une expression avec **faire**.

1. Comment faites-vous le trajet de chez vous à l'université?
2. Comment allez-vous faire vos courses?
3. Comment fait-on le trajet du centre de Paris à la banlieue[4]?

---

[4] suburbs

4. Comment les touristes font-ils le trajet de Douvres[5] (en Angleterre) à Calais (en France)?

5. Comment font-ils le trajet de Paris à Vienne (sans prendre l'avion)?

6. Si vous faites une promenade, la faites-vous en bateau?

7. De qui avez-vous fait la connaissance la semaine passée?

8. Avez-vous fait une visite récemment? Expliquez.

9. Quand est-ce que vous faites semblant de dormir?

10. Quels sports est-ce que vous faites?

11. Quels sports est-ce que vous faisiez autrefois? Pourquoi avez-vous cessé d'y participer?

12. Quand vous ne savez pas la réponse en classe, qu'est-ce que vous faites semblant de faire?

13. Jean-Claude fait un voyage à Honolulu. Quelle sorte de voyage fait-il?

14. Que faites-vous pour vous amuser?

15. Quand est-ce qu'on fait un voyage en autocar au lieu de le faire en avion?

Reflets

Les chemins de fer

1. La Société nationale des chemins de fer français (la **S.N.C.F.**) est un réseau (*system, network*) nationalisé qui joue un rôle important dans la vie économique de la France.

2. Il y a plusieurs **gares** à Paris. Les plus importantes sont la Gare du Nord (pour les trains à destination de Calais et de Bruxelles), la Gare de l'Est (à destination de Bâle, capitale de la Confédération Helvétique), la Gare Saint-Lazare (à destination du Havre), la Gare de Lyon (pour Dijon et Nice), la Gare d'Austerlitz et la Gare Montparnasse.

3. On a le choix entre deux classes de train, dont la première coûte plus cher. Les trains de luxe comme *le Mistral* entre Paris et Nice sont entièrement composés de voitures de première classe. Ces trains s'appellent les **T.E.E.** (Trans-Europe Express).

4. Les trains européens sont toujours à l'heure. Bien entendu, les lignes sont électrifiées. On les classe ainsi: le plus rapide s'appelle le **T.G.V.** (train à grande vitesse) qui roule à 270 km/h. Ensuite il y a **un rapide** (*express*) qui ne s'arrête qu'aux plus grandes gares. Moins rapide est l'**express**, train ordinaire qui s'arrête aux grandes villes. Enfin le train **omnibus** (*local*) s'arrête à toutes les gares.

5. Au **guichet** (*ticket window*) on peut réserver une place en première pour le

[5] Dover

T.G.V. ou le T.E.E., ou demander **un billet simple** ou un **aller (et) retour.** Il faut indiquer la classe: —Un aller-retour pour Rouen en seconde, s'il vous plaît.

6. Les bagages. Dans la gare on peut laisser ses bagages à **la consigne** (*check-room*) ou à **la consigne automatique** (*coin-operated lockers*).

7. **Le trajet, le voyage** (trip). Le **voyage** n'est pas limité à la mer comme en anglais. On fait le voyage de Paris à Lyon en avion, en auto, ou par le train.

8. **Le métro** (chemin de fer **métro**politain) est un chemin de fer complètement ou partiellement souterrain, à traction électrique, qui dessert les divers quartiers d'une grande ville. A Paris les rames se composent de cinq voitures, dont la troisième seulement est de première classe. C'est la **R.A.T.P.** (régie autonome des transports parisiens) qui gère[6] le métro de la capitale.

9. Un **autocar** fait des trajets entre deux villes. On l'appelle aussi **le car.** Un **autobus** parcourt les rues d'une seule ville; il ne fonctionne qu'à l'intérieur d'une ville.

Thème

1. I doubt that your friend made the trip to Portugal by bus. It's a business trip.
2. Do you think[7] he bought some Michelin stock before he left?
3. It's probable that your students took several hours to solve this problem.
4. It is possible that they used the mainframe computer for data processing.
5. I was waiting for the train when Professor Broussard arrived.
6. I am glad that you met Professor Broussard. He's a physicist.
7. Before the lecture began, the Dean took the floor for a few minutes.
8. I am not sure he knew the subject of the professor's lecture.
9. It is essential that the students pay attention.
10. I doubt that we will have time to play tennis after the lecture ends.

VOCABULAIRE

le doyen	*dean*
la conférence	*lecture*
un ordinateur universel	*mainframe computer*
le physicien	*physicist*
le problème	*problem*
résoudre	*solve, to*
le sujet	*subject*

[6] **gérer** = *to manage*
[7] Remember that the conjunction **que** is required in French.

Sujets de composition ou de causerie _____

Passé du subjonctif, *faire*, chemins de fer

Décrivez un voyage (réel ou imaginaire) en France, ou vous avez dû choisir la destination, aller à la gare pour prendre un billet et faire d'autres préparatifs. Ensuite faites le voyage en prenant divers moyens de transport; si vous vous arrêtez en route pour voir les curiosités, décrivez-les brièvement.

NOTE: Il faut que vous racontiez tout cela au passé; servez-vous du passé du subjonctif à plusieurs reprises, aussi bien que de *faire;* montrez également ce que vous savez du transport ferroviaire.

Pour vos recherches, consultez une encyclopédie, QUID[8], ou des brochures (ou dépliants) touristiques.

---

[8] **QUID,** published annually, is a one-volume compendium of facts and general information in every field, similar to the *World Almanac.* It is published by Éditions Robert Laffont, 6, place St-Sulpice, Paris VI. Your library may have a copy.

17

*faire** causatif
laisser + INFINITIF
Pronoms toniques

FAIRE CAUSATIF
_____

17.1 Causative *faire*

Review the forms of **faire** (Appendix C, Verb Table 14). When an infinitive follows a form of **faire,** it indicates that the action was accomplished by a person other than the subject. The English equivalent is *to have someone (do something).*

> Elle **fait** *construire* une maison.   *She is having a house built.*

The expression **je fais construire** means literally *I am causing to be built*, rather than that I am doing the actual building myself. In English a person who says "I am building a house," is understood to mean that he is having it done for him; but if the matter needs clarification, he could say *"I am having a house built."* The ambiguity disappears. The **faire** [INFINITIVE] construction shows that the speaker is not the person doing the work, but has merely directed that it be done.

The selected form of **faire** must be followed directly by an infinitive, and then the noun. Compare the word order:

> Elle **fait** *planter* des arbres.   *She is having some trees planted.*

This is quite different from English word order, in which the noun follows the form of *to have* being used. Because of the distinctive word order in French, you must pay special attention to the structure.

Il **fait** *chanter* Marie.	*He has Marie sing.*
Il **fait** *chanter* la chanson.	*He has the song sung.*
Il **a fait** *lire* cette histoire.	*He had this story read.*
Il **s'est fait**[1] *couper* les cheveux.	*He had his hair cut.*

Expressions that are frequently used:

faire venir	*to send for*
faire savoir	*to inform*
faire remarquer	*to point out*
faire chercher [N]	*to have someone get* [N]
se faire couper les cheveux	*to have one's hair cut*
se faire photographier	*to have one's picture taken*

17.2   Object nouns and pronouns with *faire* + [INFINITIVE]

When there is an agent (the person actually doing the work), the agent may be shown by the prepositional phrase à or **par** [AGENT] may be used:

Il **fait** *chanter* la chanson **par Marie** (ou à **Marie**).
(*He* **causes** *the song* **to be sung** *by Marie.*) = *He has Marie sing the song.*
Il **fait** *lire* la phrase **par** l'étudiant.
He has the student read the sentence.

Since the substitution of à **l'étudiant** for **par l'étudiant** in the above sentence would cause some ambiguity, it is better to use **par** [AGENT], remembering that since an à-phrase is possible, the agent may be replaced by the *indirect* object pronoun [7.3]:

Il **fait chanter** la chanson   **par** Marie.
↓ *equals*
à Marie
↓ *equals*
lui (IND OBJ)

Il **lui** fait chanter la chanson.
  He has **her** *sing the song.*

---

[1] When **se faire** is used, the auxiliary is **être**.

The *direct* object may also be replaced by a direct object pronoun [6.3]. For word order: [7.5].

> Il **la** lui fait chanter.   *He has her sing it.*

The **faire** + [INFINITIVE] structure is inseparable. Noun objects follow it; when used, pronoun objects precede it.

TEST YOURSELF

Try the following, in writing. Cover the answer until you have written your solution.

1. I am having a house built.
   Je **fais construire** une maison.
2. I am having a sentence read.
   Je **fais lire** une phrase.
3. I am having the teacher read a sentence.
   Je **fais lire** une phrase **par** le professeur (*or* **au** professeur).
4. I am having him read a French sentence.
   Je **lui fais lire** une phrase française (une phrase en français).
5. Mary is having her car repaired (**réparer**).
   Marie **fait réparer** sa voiture (son auto).
6. She is having it repaired by a mechanic (**le mécanicien**).
   Elle **la fait réparer** par un mécanicien.
7. She is having a shelf made.
   Elle **fait faire** une étagère.

In compound tenses as part of a causative, the past participle of **faire** is invariable:

> Quels livres avez-vous **fait** venir?   *What books did you have sent?*
>
> Où est la voiture que vous avez **fait** réparer?   *Where is the car you had repaired?*

Mise en œuvre 17 A

faire causatif

Remplacez le verbe par **faire** causatif en y ajoutant l'agent entre parenthèses. Ensuite remplacez l'agent par le pronom approprié.

EXEMPLE

J'ai fermé la porte. (à Robert)

J'ai fait fermer la porte à (**par**) **Robert.**

Je **lui** ai fait fermer la porte.

1. J'ai choisi un dictionnaire. (par mon professeur)
2. Le professeur a lu une poésie. (par Jacques)
3. Ma mère a mis la table. (à ma sœur)
4. Le patron a écrit une lettre au maire. (par la dactylo)
5. J'ai nettoyé le garage. (par mon cousin)
6. Le ministre a construit une maison magnifique. (par Brissac et Cie)
7. Avez-vous monté les valises? (par le chasseur)
8. Le professeur a remarqué une faute. (aux étudiants)
9. Ma mère a fait une robe de soie. (à la couturière)
10. Le metteur en scène (*director*) a répété le dialogue. (aux acteurs)

Mise en œuvre 17 B

faire causatif remplaçant *demander de, dire de*

Remplacez **demander de** ou **dire de** par **faire** causatif.

EXEMPLE

Le professeur demande aux étudiants de **lire une phrase.**

Le professeur *fait* **lire une phrase** (par les) (aux) étudiants.

1. Le professeur dit à Paul de lire son exposé.
2. Papa demande à son ami de prendre trois billets.
3. Le douanier dit au conducteur de la voiture d'ouvrir le coffre.
4. Le douanier dit au passager de montrer son passeport.
5. J'ai demandé au mécanicien de réparer ma voiture.
6. Le patron dit à l'employé de mettre une lettre à la poste.
7. Ta mère demande à ta sœur de laver la vaisselle.
8. Les Dupont disent à leur architecte de construire une maison pratique.
9. Le directeur demande à une secrétaire de photocopier plusieurs pages.
10. Le touriste demande au chasseur de monter ses bagages.

Mise en œuvre 17 C

Thème

1. Geneviève had a shelf made.
2. The manager had three typewriters taken (**transporter**) to another office.
3. My father had the newspaper brought up to our room.
4. He had the bellhop bring a few magazines up, also.
5. The boss had one of the secretaries write a letter to the mayor.
6. Jean-Paul had the waiter bring us two bottles of red wine.

7. We had two rooms reserved (**retenir**) for May 23.
8. I had my new shirts washed by the hotel laundry. (**la blanchisserie**)
9. Then I had my secretary write a letter to professor Legrand.
10. You had the concierge call a taxi, didn't you?

LAISSER, ENTENDRE, VOIR, REGARDER + INFINITIVE

17.3 *laisser* + [INFINITIVE]

The verbs **laisser, entendre, voir,** and **regarder** may be followed immediately by an infinitive, forming an inseparable unit when the English equivalent *ends in a verb:*

Le douanier │ **a laissé** *passer* │ le fermier.
*The customs official **let the farmer pass.***

Nous │ **avons entendu** *chanter* │ Mlle Sills.
*We **heard Miss Sills sing.***

Je le │ **vois** *venir* │.
*I **see him coming.***

Nous │ **avons regardé** *jouer* │ le chat.
*We **watched the cat playing.***

English speakers must be careful *not* to place the noun directly after these four verbs; to do so would break up the inseparable verbal unit.

On the other hand, if the English equivalent does not end in a verb, but instead *ends in a noun or prepositional phrase*, the word order is the same in French as English:

*The customs official **let the farmer cross the border.***
Le douanier │ **a laissé** │ le fermier │ **passer** │ **la frontière.**

*We **heard Miss Sills sing at the Paris opera.***
Nous │ **avons entendu** │ Mlle Sills │ **chanter** │ à l'Opéra.

*I **see the teacher coming into the room.***
Je │ **vois** │ le professeur │ **entrer** │ dans la salle.

Mise en œuvre 17 D

laisser, entendre, voir + [INFINITIVE]

Donnez l'équivalent français des phrases suivantes.

1. We let Jacques buy the tickets.
2. I hear the lecturer speaking.

3. Do you see the teacher coming?
4. I have heard that said.
5. My father let my little brother drive.
6. I heard the policeman shout to the driver.
7. Did you see the train leave?
8. We heard the pilot speak to the crew.
9. The employee allowed us to pass.
10. He let the passengers go into the terminal.

PRONOMS TONIQUES

17.4 Table of disjunctive pronouns *(pronoms toniques)*

The following table shows the personal pronouns called *disjunctive* or stressed pronouns. Their uses are described in section [17.5].

DISJUNCTIVE PRONOUN	MEANING	CORRESPONDS TO SUBJECT PRONOUN
moi	*I, me*	je
toi	*you*	te
lui	*him*	il
elle	*her*	elle
(soi)	*(oneself, himself, herself, itself)*	
nous	*us*	nous
vous	*you*	vous
eux	*them* (m.pl.)	ils
elles	*them* (f.pl.)	elles

When plural nouns of mixed genders are used, the masculine plural form **eux** applies:

Voilà **Paul** et **Marie.** Je vais au cinéma **avec eux.**

17.5 Summary of uses of disjunctive pronouns

The disjunctive pronouns are separated from the rest of the sentence (hence *disjoined*), unlike all other pronouns, which cling to the verb. The uses of these pronouns are:

A. Alone or after **C'est** or **Ce sont:**   **Lui.** *C'est* **lui** qui parle.

B. After a preposition: Elle va en ville *avec* **moi.**

C. Part of a compound subject: **Lui** et **moi,** nous partons.

D. Emphasis of subject: **Moi,** je comprends.

E. After **que** in comparisons: Il est plus riche *que* **toi.**

F. To clarify **son, sa, ses:**   Voilà sa maison *à* **lui.**

G. With **C'est** [DJ PN] **qui** (**que**):   *C'est* **moi** *qui* ai parlé.

17.6 Application of disjunctive pronouns

A. Used alone or after *C'est (Ce sont).*

— Qui est là?   — **Moi.**

Voilà ces deux garçons. **Ce sont eux** qui travaillent à la librairie.

B. After a preposition.

Mon petit frère? Je vais au cinéma **sans lui.**

Mme Brun? Je me souviens **d'elle.**

Chacun **pour soi.**

NOTE: Certain verbal structures use the régime **à** + [PERSON]. These particular ones do not permit substitution of an indirect object pronoun for **à** + [P]. Instead, you must keep the preposition and use a disjunctive pronoun for [P]. The most frequently encountered are the following:

penser à   faire attention à

songer à   s'habituer à

s'intéresser à

Le professeur s'intéresse **à ses étudiants.**
Le professeur s'intéresse **à eux.**

Tu penses **à ton amie.**
Tu penses **à elle.**

However, if it is a *thing* that follows **à** with these verbs, you may use **y** to replace the prepositional portion beginning with **à:**

Le professeur s'intéresse **à la musique.**
Le professeur s'y intéresse.

C.   Part of a compound subject. When there are two subjects, either one or both may be disjunctive pronouns. No regular subject pronoun can be used for either one in the case of a compound subject:

> **Lui** et **elle** parlent français.
>
> Marie et **lui** vont au théâtre.
>
> Mon père et **moi,** nous allons en ville.

As in the last example, when **moi** is a part of the compound subject, sum up the subject using the subject pronoun **nous** and the corresponding form of the verb.

D.   Emphasis of the subject. Emphasis is placed on the subject by placing the appropriate disjunctive pronoun at the beginning or end of the sentence, separated from the rest by a comma. (The English equivalent is achieved by using italics in writing, or oral emphasis. Because of the French intonation patterns, stress cannot be shown orally as it is in English.)

> **Moi,** je comprends le japonais.   *I understand Japanese.*
>
> Daniel est riche, **lui.**   ***Daniel** is rich.*
>
> Hélène est belle, **elle.**   ***Hélène** is beautiful.*
>
> **Nous,** nous allons au parc.   ***We** are going to the park.*

When the subject is a noun, place the disjunctive pronoun at the end of the sentence.

E.   After *que* in comparisons [19.1].

> Alain écrit **mieux que moi.**   *Alain writes **better than I.***
>
> **J'ai plus** de disques **que lui.**   *I have **more** records **than he.***

F.   To clarify or emphasize *son, sa, ses.* These possessive adjectives mean *his, her, its.* As a result, **sa maison** could mean either *his house* or *her house.* To eliminate this difficulty when it seems necessary, add **à lui** or **à elle:**

> Voilà Jeanne et Georges. Voilà sa maison **à lui.**   (***his** house*)
>
> Voici son dictionnaire **à elle.**   (***her** dictionary*)

The addition of a disjunctive pronoun may be for purposes of emphasis:

> Votre école est grande, mais notre école **à nous** est plus grande.
> *Your school is large, but **our** school is larger.*

G. ***C'est*** [DJ PRONOUN] ***qui*** [VERB]. Emphasis[2] is placed on the subject of a sentence by selecting the appropriate disjunctive pronoun and placing it between **C'est** and **qui.** The verb must agree in person and number with the selected pronoun.

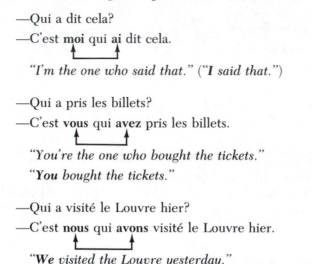

—Qui a dit cela?

—C'est **moi** qui **ai** dit cela.

   "I'm the one who said that." (*"**I** said that."*)

—Qui a pris les billets?

—C'est **vous** qui **avez** pris les billets.

   "You're the one who bought the tickets."
   *"**You** bought the tickets."*

—Qui a visité le Louvre hier?

—C'est **nous** qui **avons** visité le Louvre hier.

   *"**We** visited the Louvre yesterday."*

C'est [DJ PRONOUN] **que** is used the same way, except that **que** is a direct object. As a result the disjunctive pronoun is selected to refer to someone previously mentioned. The verb follows **que,** and then the real subject of the verb.

Vous connaissez **Bernard**?

C'est **lui** que cherchent les clients.
He's the one the customers are looking for.

Voilà **les athlètes des Jeux olympiques.**

Ce sont **eux** que nous admirons.
They are the ones we admire.

Mise en œuvre 17 E

Pronoms toniques

Répondez aux questions par **C'est** [DJ] ou **Ce sont** [DJ]:

EXEMPLE

Qui arrive? Georges?

C'est **lui.**

[2] l'insistance: L'on insiste sur [quelque chose].

1. Qui parle français?
   Albert? / Marie? / mes parents? / les étudiantes?
2. Qui a fini le devoir?
   Albert? / Albert et Georges? / Marie et Jeanne?
3. Qui est là?
   Mme Dubois? / les enfants? / le facteur? / M. et Mme Smith?

Répondez aux questions en vous servant d'une proposition avec **qui** ou **que.**

EXEMPLE

Est-ce vous qui avez fermé la porte?

Oui, c'est **moi. C'est** *moi* **qui** *ai* **fermé** la porte.

4. Est-ce Jean-Louis qui a cherché le dictionnaire?
5. Est-ce Mme Jacotin qui me cherche?
6. Est-ce le patron qui a téléphoné?
7. Est-ce vous qui avez emprunté l'annuaire? (C'est **moi** qui . . .)
8. Est-ce moi qu'on demande au bureau?
9. Est-ce votre famille qui dine au restaurant?
10. Est-ce moi qui ai fait trop de bruit?
11. Est-ce vous qui avez mis la lettre à la poste?
12. Est-ce vous qui avez vu la nouvelle pièce?
13. Est-ce vos amis qui ont l'air timide?
14. Est-ce Sylvie qui joue si bien du violon?
15. Est-ce votre camarade de chambre qui a joué au poker hier?
16. Est-ce René qui a gagné tout l'argent?
17. Est-ce nous qui avons fait tant de bruit?
18. Est-ce moi qui doit prendre les billets?
19. Est-ce l'avocat qui s'est acheté une Rolls?
20. Est-ce vous qui vous occupez de la cuisine?
21. La locution «est-ce» est-elle une forme de «c'est» ?

Insistez sur le sujet au moyen d'un pronom tonique.

EXEMPLE

Je parle français.

Moi, je parle français.   *ou*   Je parle français, **moi.**

22. Jean-Paul comprend l'arabe.
23. Mes amis ont visité l'Australie.
24. Pierre déteste les chats.
25. Tu es toujours à l'heure.
26. Marguerite est vraiment très gentille.
27. J'aime bien les mathématiques.

Remplacez les mots en italique par un pronom.

28. Voilà le médecin. Sa femme et *le médecin* vont à Genève en auto.
29. *Mlle Fontenay* et *M. Leclerc* viennent d'entrer.
30. Gérard et (*la personne qui fait cet exercice* [vous!]) allons en ville.

Reflets

Circulation routière

1. Avant de **se mettre au volant,** il faut un **permis de conduire.** Si l'on ne sait pas conduire, il y a des auto-écoles.

   A 18 ans on peut faire une demande de permis. Il faut passer un **examen théorique** audiovisuel et collectif (le code), et un **examen pratique** de conduite. Une **visite médicale** est obligatoire si l'on déclare quelque incapacité.

2. Les **règlements de la route** (le code) ressemblent à ceux des États-Unis. Par exemple, il faut éviter les **excès de vitesse.** On peut utiliser la file de gauche seulement pour dépasser, ou pour préparer un changement de direction. On ne doit pas accélérer au moment d'être dépassé. Il faut **respecter les feux rouges,** ne pas franchir une ligne continue[3], et surtout éviter de conduire quand on est intoxiqué par l'alcool ou la drogue. Les conducteurs qui sont condamnés pour **un délit** risquent des punitions strictes, y compris la suspension du permis, une amende et la prison. Par exemple, un condamné pour un **délit de fuite**[4] risque une amende de 500 à 8000 F et une peine d'un mois à un an de prison.

3. Parmi les moteurs il y a le moteur **à injection,** le moteur **diesel,** et le moteur **à piston rotatif.** Pour changer de vitesse on se sert de la **boîte de vitesses.** En Amérique la plupart des voitures ont une **boîte de vitesse automatique,** tandis qu'en France il y en a moins de six pour cent.

   Pour augmenter la puissance d'un moteur, on ajoute parfois la **suralimentation par compresseurs.**

   On se procure le **carburant**[5] à une **station-service.** Si la voiture cesse de marcher on appelle **une dépanneuse.**

4. Les catégories de voitures: la **voiture de tourisme**[6], le **break**[7], et la **voiture de sport** sont les plus courantes; on peut ajouter la **décapotable** et la voiture à **toit ouvrant** pour les amateurs de plein air. La plus populaire en France était la petite 2CV[8] de Citroën. (Cette voiture-ci va devenir un objet de collectionneur

---

[3] On dit aussi **couper la jaune** (*cross the center line*).
[4] = **ne pas rapporter un accident** (*hit-and-run,* or *leaving the scene of an accident*)
[5] Pour la plupart des voitures, c'est **l'essence.**
[6] = *Four door sedan*
[7] = *Station wagon*
[8] = *Two horsepower* (**cheval-vapeur**)

car la production s'est arrêtée.) Les diplomates et d'autres personnages de marque[9] se font transporter en de longues voitures qui s'appellent les **limousines.** Le président des États-Unis en a une.

5. Les **camions** comprennent le plus grand, le **poids-lourd** (le camion-tracteur et la remorque), et le plus petit, la **camionnette.** Pour le transport des liquides et des gaz on utilise un **camion-citerne.**

   Pour le transport du personnel, on a le **minibus** (VW), le **fourgon**[10], **l'autocar** (le **car long-courrier**), et, à l'intérieur de la ville, **l'autobus.**

6. La **marque.** Les constructeurs en France sont Citroën, Renault, Peugeot; on se sert beaucoup de Fiat[11] (voiture italienne) et des voitures allemandes, japonaises, suédoises et américaines.

   Toutes les marques de voiture sont du genre féminin: la Ford, la Toyota, la Volkswagen, la Volvo.

Le transport routier

Répondez, en ajoutant quelque explication ou élaboration.

1. Est-ce que tu as une voiture? Quelle en est la marque?
2. Quelle sorte de voiture le président a-t-il?
3. Pour transporter de l'essence, quelle sorte de camion faut-il?
4. Quels examens faut-il passer pour obtenir un permis de conduire?
5. Pourquoi est-il dangereux de conduire après avoir consommé au bar?
6. Si ta voiture a un pneu à plat, est-ce que tu peux mettre le pneu de rechange toi-même? Sinon, que faut-il faire?
7. Si tu conduis dans la file de gauche, pour quelle raison la police de la route peut-elle t'arrêter? Pour quelles raisons est-il permis d'utiliser la file de gauche?
8. Si tu es condamné pour ne pas avoir respecté un feu rouge, que faut-il payer?
9. Comment s'appelle la plus petite voiture française? La plus petite voiture allemande? japonaise? américaine?
10. Tu entres en collision avec une autre voiture et tu manques de rapporter l'accident à la police, comment s'appelle le délit? Que peut en être la conséquence?

Thème

1. Gabriel went into the bistro and ordered a beer[12].
2. He also had the waiter bring him a croissant.
3. He is having his father send him some money.

---

[9] *V.I.P.s*
[10] *panel truck,* or *medium van*
[11] **Fiat** représente l'ancien nom ***Fabbrica Italiana Automobili Torino.***
[12] **un demi**

4. In the kitchen, Sonia is having Pierre rinse the glasses.
5. The policeman had the driver take a practical test.
6. I am going to have my car washed this afternoon.
7. I doubt that the government can have taxes reduced.
8. Pierre needs to have his hair cut.
9. It is necessary that you have the doors opened on time.
10. I remember my German teacher. I remember her because she had us write sentences on the board.

18

Emploi de l'infinitif
celui
Pronoms possessifs

L'INFINITIF

18.1 Prepositions followed by infinitive

When a verb occurs after a preposition, use the infinitive. (When the preposition is **après** or **en,** special structures are required, as indicated in [18.7] and [18.8].)

> Le professeur quitte la salle **sans dire** au revoir.
> *The teacher leaves the room without saying goodbye.*
> Il est facile **de faire** des fautes de grammaire.
> *It is easy to make grammatical errors.*
> Nous promettons à Paul **de conduire** prudemment.
> *We promise Paul to (we'll) drive carefully.*

Use the preposition **pour** to indicate purpose (*in order to*):

> Nous étudions **pour apprendre** le français.
> *We are studying (in order) to learn French.*

18.2 Government of infinitives: nothing, *à*, or *de* before an infinitive

When an inflected verb is followed by an infinitive, one must decide whether to insert *nothing,* **à,** or **de** before that infinitive. This decision depends upon the inflected verb, *not* upon the infinitive. For example, if the inflected verb **commence** is followed by the infinitive **lire:**

$$\text{Je } \mathbf{commence} \begin{Bmatrix} (\text{---})? \\ (\grave{a})? \\ (\mathbf{de})? \end{Bmatrix} \textit{lire} \text{ le journal.}$$

the selection of the correct structure depends upon **commencer.** An examination of the following lists ([18.3] for verbs followed directly by the infinitive, [18.4] for those requiring à before a following infinitive, and [18.5] for those requiring **de**) shows that **commencer à** is the solution. The only correct way to make the statement is therefore:

> Je **commence** à *lire* le journal.

There is no evident logic involved in the selection of à, except that **commencer à** [I] *sounds* right to a French speaker, just as an English speaker finds certain combinations correct (*to comply with, to engage in, to infer from*) and others incorrect (*to comply at, to be oblivious from*). The choice of the correct preposition is based on practice and familiarity with the structures. Concentrate on those in the following lists, using them frequently. A more complete reference list, for use when you are in doubt, is given in Appendix D.

18.3   Verbs followed directly by an infinitive

Certain inflected verbs may be followed directly by an infinitive:

> Je **vais** *étudier* ce soir.   (*étudier* follows **vais** directly)

Among the verbs that may be followed directly by an infinitive are:

aimer	*to like*	Paul **aime** jouer au tennis.
aller	*to go*	Nous **allons** faire un voyage.
entendre	*to hear*	J'ai **entendu** arriver le taxi.
faire	*to have (done)*	Jean **a fait** réparer sa voiture.
falloir[1]	*one must*	**Il faut** étudier ce soir.
laisser	*to allow, let*	L'agent **laisse** passer le touriste.
venir	*to come*	Robert **vient** voir le professeur.
vouloir	*to want*	**Voudriez-vous** voir ce film?

[1] **falloir** is a "defective" verb, in that it exists only with the impersonal subject **il.** The following meanings should be noted:

PRÉSENT	il faut	*one must* [I], *it is necessary* [I]
	il ne faut pas	*one must not* [I]
IMPARFAIT	il fallait	*it was (used to be) necessary* [I]
PASSÉ COMPOSÉ	il a fallu	*it was necessary* [I]
CONDITIONNEL	il faudrait	*it would be necessary* [I]

The meaning *it is necessary* must be changed in the negative to *must not*:
> Il **ne faut pas** fumer.   You *must not* smoke.

18.4   Verbs requiring *à* before a following infinitive

Certain verbs may be followed by an infinitive only if à is placed before the infinitive.

> Nous **apprenons** à *parler* français.

Some of these verbs are listed below (see Appendix D for a more complete list).

apprendre à	*to learn*	J'**apprends** à écrire le russe.
avoir à	*to have*	J'**ai** à **travailler** ce soir.
chercher à	*to try*	Paul **cherche** à ouvrir cette porte.
commencer° à[2]	*to begin*	Ils **commencent** à réussir.
continuer à	*to continue*	Alain **continue** à lire.
hésiter à	*to hesitate*	Hans **hésite** à parler français.
inviter à	*to invite*	Je **t'invite** à danser.
tenir à	*to be eager*	Je **tiens** à voir Versailles.

18.5   Verbs requiring *de* before an infinitive

Certain verbs may be followed by an infinitive only when **de** is inserted before the infinitive.

> Jean-Paul **refuse de** faire la vaisselle.

Among the verbs in this category are:

accepter de	*to agree*	Il **accepte de** nous aider.
cesser de	*to cease*	Il **cesse de** travailler à quatre heures.
décider de	*to decide*	Nous **avons décidé de** voir ce film italien.
éviter de	*to avoid*	Ma mère **évite de** conduire la camionnette.
essayer° de	*to try*	Philippe **essaie de** finir son projet.
finir de	*to finish*	J'**ai fini de** lire le journal.
oublier de	*to forget*	Marie **a oublié de** lire cette poésie.
refuser de	*to refuse*	Georges **refuse de** sortir.
tâcher de	*to try*	Philippe **tâche de** terminer son film.
venir de	*to have just*	Le conférencier **vient d'**entrer dans la salle.

[2] The symbol ° indicates a stem-changing (slightly irregular) verb, discussed in [26.1–26.7].

18.6   After *avant de* (*before —ing something*)

The infinitive is used after **avant de,** according to the general rule that the verb after a preposition must be in the infinitive form. Special attention to this structure is required because of its contrast with the English equivalent. In English the expression *Before **we** closed the door, **we** . . .* uses an inflected verb with *before.* In French the structure is *Before closing the door, we . . .:* **avant de** + [INFINITIVE].

> Nous étudions **avant de quitter** la maison.
> *We study before leaving (before we leave) the house.*
>
> **Avant d'aller** au cinéma, Marie fera la vaisselle.
> *Before she goes to the movies, Marie will do the dishes.*

18.7   After *après:* INFINITIVE *AVOIR* or *être* + PAST PARTICIPLE

The preposition **après** cannot be followed by a personal pronoun, as is the case in English. Instead, use **après avoir** + PAST PARTICIPLE.

> **Après avoir fini** mes devoirs, je suis allé au cinéma.
> *After having finished my homework, I went to the movies.*   or
> *After I finished my homework, I went to the movies.*

Verbs using the auxiliary **être,** including all reflexive verbs, require the structure **après être** + PAST PARTICIPLE. In addition, the past participle must then agree in gender and number with the subject [10.2]:

> **Après être arrivée,** Marie a regardé la télévision.
> *After Mary arrived, she watched television.*   or
> *After having arrived, Mary watched television.*

18.8   After *en:* PRESENT PARTICIPLE

After the preposition **en** (*by, while*) the present participle [25.6] is used instead of the infinitive:

> On apprend le français **en parlant.**
> *One learns French by speaking.*
>
> Jean écoute la radio **en lisant** le journal.
> *John listens to the radio while reading the paper.*

18.9   Infinitives of reflexive verbs

When the infinitive form of a pronominal verb is used after a preposition, the re-flexive pronoun **se** is made to agree with the person involved in the action described by the verb.

INFINITIVE

Nous sommes allés à Tivoli **pour *nous amuser.***
We went to Tivoli to have a good time.

Il nous demande **de *nous lever.***
He is asking us to get up.

Vous êtes parti **sans *vous procurer*** les matériaux?
You left without getting the materials?

Mise en œuvre 18 A

Emploi de l'infinitif

A.   Gouvernement de l'infinitif. Achevez chaque phrase par les mots entre parenthèses, en faisant les changements nécessaires [18.3–18.5].

EXEMPLE

(parler français)   Jacques commence . . .
Jacques commence à parler français.

1. (aller au théâtre) Nous aimons bien . . .
2. (prendre un taxi) Paul et Suzanne vont . . .
3. (les accompagner) Sven refuse . . .
4. (essayer de le persuader) Il faut . . .
5. (travailler avec les autres) Tout le monde apprend . . .
6. (comprendre la valeur des arts) Nous avons commencé . . .
7. (prendre les billets en avance) Hans a oublié . . .
8. (parler anglais) Ces étrangers savent . . .
9. (communiquer en allemand) Est-ce que vous hésitez . . . ?
10. (voir la pièce *En attendant Godot*) Nous venons . . .
11. (danser) Je doute que Pozzo ait appris . . .
12. (parler à son voisin) La touriste se met . . .
13. (déranger les spectateurs) Cette femme bavarde a continué . . .
14. (critiquer la représentation) Mon professeur tient . . .
15. (s'expliquer en français) Wilhelm refuse . . .
16. (se retrouver au café après le film) Nous avons accepté . . . [18.9]

B.   Et avant cela? Et après? Employez **avant de** et **après** avec chacune des paires de locutions suivantes. Employez le passé composé pour le verbe principal.

EXEMPLE

lire le journal / éteigner la lumière

Après avoir lu le journal, j'ai éteint la lumière.

Avant d'éteindre la lumière, j'ai lu le journal.

1. ouvrir la porte / sortir de la maison
2. fermer la porte / aller au coin de la rue
3. attendre l'autobus / monter dans l'autobus
4. monter dans l'autobus / prendre mon ticket
5. arriver à l'université / aller en classe
6. prendre ma place / écouter le professeur
7. écouter le professeur / sortir du bâtiment
8. rencontrer un(e) ami(e) / aller au café
9. prendre quelque chose / se promener dans le parc
10. choisir un film / aller au cinéma

Mise en œuvre 18 B

A vous la parole!

Choisissez un sujet qui vous intéresse sur lequel vous composerez un récit suivi en employant les locutions ci-dessous, ou d'autres, si cela est nécessaire.

Faites attention au gouvernement des infinitifs [18.3, 18.4, 18.5]. Soyez prêt(e) à présenter votre causerie oralement en classe.

Au moins trois fois, ajoutez un commentaire logique utilisant **avant de** ou **après** (**avoir/être**) selon les exemples [18.6, 18.7].

EXEMPLES

Nous voulons . . .
Nous **voulons** *aller* à Paris.
Je **tiens** à *voir* le Louvre.
Avant d'aller à Paris, nous allons étudier le plan de la ville.
Après être allés à Paris, nous allons rejoindre nos parents à Londres.

André tient . . .
André **tient** à *voir* Disneyworld.
Avant de voir Disneyworld, il va lire ces brochures [18.6].
Après l'avoir vu il va visiter Marineland [18.7].

1. Je tiens . . .
2. Je voudrais . . .
3. J'ai l'intention . . .
4. Je viens . . .

5. Mon ami a besoin . . .
6. J'ai décidé . . .
7. Il faut . . .
8. Nous aimons . . .
9. J'ai évité . . .
10. Nous nous sommes dépêchés . . .
11. Nous pouvons . . .
12. Je ne regrette pas . . .

Mise en œuvre 18 C

Emploi de l'infinitif après une préposition

Refaites les phrases suivantes en employant la forme convenable des locutions entre parenthèses [18.6–18.7].

EXEMPLE

(Elle va au cinéma.)   Marie fait ses devoirs avant . . .

Marie fait ses devoirs **avant d'aller** au cinéma.

1. (Nous apprenons.)   Nous sommes à l'université pour . . .
2. (Il prépare ses leçons.)   Jean-Paul réussit en . . . [18.8]
3. (Il ne comprend pas.)   Bruno lit beaucoup sans . . . [18.1]
4. (Je paie mes frais scolaires.)   Je demande de l'argent à mon père pour . . .
5. (Il a vu mes bonnes notes.)   Mon père m'a envoyé un chèque après . . .
6. (J'arrive en classe.)   Je vais au laboratoire de langues avant . . .
7. (Il n'a pas parlé.)   Mon camarade de chambre est sorti sans . . .
8. (Il fait des exercices en maths.)   Albert cherchait un ordinateur pour . . .
9. (Il a fini le travail.)   Il est rentré au dortoir après . . .
10. (Nous nous sommes couchés.)   Nous avons regardé la télé avant . . .

PRONOM CELUI

18.10 Use

The pronoun **celui** (*the one*) enables you to avoid repeating a noun just mentioned. There are four forms of this pronoun and the one selected must match the gender and number of the replaced noun. A form of **celui** is always followed by either (1) *a relative pronoun*, (2) **de** + [N] to show possession, or (3) **-ci** or **-là**.

(1) le livre	Voici **celui que** j'ai acheté. [18.12]	
	*Here's **the one** I bought.*	
(2) la montre	**Celle de Robert** est sur la table. [18.13]	
	***Robert's** (= **the one of Robert**) is on the table.*	
(3) le stylo	**Celui-ci** est rouge. [18.14]	
	***This one** is red.*	

18.11   Agreement

The four forms of **celui** are shown below. The form selected must agree in gender and number with the noun replaced.

	MASCULINE	FEMININE	MEANING
SINGULAR	celui	celle	*the one*
PLURAL	ceux	celles	*the ones (those)*

Je cherche mon	**livre**	et	**celui**	de Robert.
J'ai lavé ma	**chemise**	et	**celle**	de mon frère.
J'ai mes	**livres**	et	**ceux**	de Marie.
J'ai lavé mes	**chemises**	et	**celles**	de mon frère.

⌐——REPRESENTING——⌐

18.12   *celui* + RELATIVE PRONOUN

J'ai trouvé mon billet et **celui que** vous avez pris.
*I found my ticket and **the one** you bought.*

(. . . les étudiants) **Ceux qui** ont passé l'examen sont partis.
*(. . . the students) **Those who** took the exam have left.*

(. . . la jeune fille) C'est **celle dont** je vous ai parlé.
*(. . . the girl) She's **the one** I spoke to you about.*

18.13   *celui* followed by *de* (or other preposition) + NOUN

J'ai ma clef et **celle d'**Eric.
*I have my key and **Eric's**.*

Marie apporte mon dictionnaire et **celui de** Francine.
*Mary is bringing my dictionary and **Francine's**.*

Jacques a vu vos parents et **ceux de Benoît.**
*Jacques saw your parents and **Benoît's.***

Voilà mon livre et **celui auquel** vous pensiez.
*There is my book and **the one** you were thinking **about.***

18.14   *celui + -ci or -là* (this one, that one)

By adding the suffix **-ci** to any form of **celui**, the meaning is changed from ***the*** *one* to ***this*** *one*; in the plural, to ***these***. By adding **-là** the meaning is changed to ***that*** *one*, ***those***. The following table shows all the forms using suffixes:

		SINGULAR		PLURAL	
-ci	MASCULINE	**celui-ci**	{ *this one,*	**ceux-ci**	{ *these,*
	FEMININE	**celle-ci**	{ *the latter*	**celles-ci**	{ *the latter*
-là	MASCULINE	**celui-là**	{ *that one,*	**ceux-là**	{ *those,*
	FEMININE	**celle-là**	{ *the former*	**celles-là**	{ *the former*

Ce livre-**ci** est neuf; **celui-là** est vieux.
This book is new; that one is old.

Ces maisons-**là** sont belles; **celles-ci** ne le sont pas.
Those houses are beautiful; these are not.

Notice that by adding **-ci** or **-là** to a noun, the meaning of **ce** can be specified:

ce livre	*this* or *that book*	**ce livre-ci**	*this* book
		ce livre-là	*that* book

18.15   *celui-ci (the latter), celui-là (the former)*

When two nouns have been mentioned, the next clause or sentence may refer to them as *the former . . . the latter*. In French, however, the order of reference is reversed: *the latter* (**celui-ci**) *. . . the former* (**celui-là**). Use the form of **celui** that agrees in gender and number with the nouns referred to:

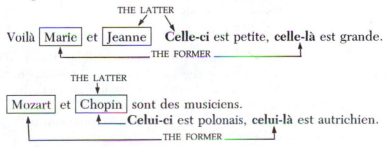

Mise en œuvre 18 D _____

Pronom *celui*

Remplacez les mots en italique par la forme convenable de **celui.**

1. Voilà un ordinateur. C'est *l'ordinateur* que nous avons essayé hier.
2. Les ordinateurs personnels sont plus petits que *les ordinateurs* qui se trouvent dans les bureaux.
3. J'ai installé mon programme et *le programme* de M. Delaplane également.
4. Ces instructions-ci sont trop longues; *ces instructions*-là sont imprécises.
5. Le tube aux rayons cathodiques est parfois remplacé par *le tube* à fibres optiques.
6. Pour me distraire j'écoute souvent la musique de Mozart ou *la musique* de Haydn.
7. Les jeunes gens préfèrent assister aux concerts de jazz-hot ou *aux concerts* de rock.
8. Voici une machine IBM et une machine Olivetti. *La machine IBM* est américaine; *la machine Olivetti* est italienne.
9. Voilà le doyen et le professeur qui arrivent au restaurant. *Le doyen* a soif; *le professeur* ne veut qu'un sandwich.
10. Mes parents font un voyage en Espagne. *Les parents* de Pierre visitent l'Angleterre.

PRONOMS POSSESSIFS _____

18.16   Use

A possessive pronoun may replace a noun group beginning with a possessive adjective (like **son livre, ma table**). It may also replace a noun group showing possession by a **de**-phrase (**le livre de mon père**) [3.15].

The possessive pronoun must agree in gender and number with the noun group it replaces.

> Avez-vous **mon dictionnaire français?** (*m.s.*)
> Avez-vous **le mien?** (*m.s.*)

As with all pronouns, the noun replaced must have been mentioned so recently that it is fresh in the hearer's mind as the main topic of discussion. In the foregoing example, **le mien** could not be used intelligibly unless someone had been talking about **mon dictionnaire français** just previously.

The essential criterion for the use of possessive pronouns is the idea of *ownership*. Compare the following:

NO POSSESSION	Est-ce que vous regardez **la maison?**	
POSSESSION	Est-ce que vous regardez ⃞**ma**⃞ maison?	
POSSESSIVE PRONOUN	Est-ce que vous regardez **la mienne?**	

18.17   Word order

Possessive pronouns are located in the same "slot" vacated by the replaced noun structure. The order is generally the same as in English.

Il a vendu **sa maison.**	*He sold **his house.***
Il a vendu **la sienne.**	*He sold **his.***
J'ai gardé **ma maison.**	*I kept **my** house.*
J'ai gardé **la mienne.**	*I kept **mine.***

18.18   Forms of the possessive pronouns

A possessive pronoun must agree in gender and number with the possessive noun group it represents, that is, with the antecedent. (The *antecedent* is merely the previous mention of the noun group being replaced.) The possessive pronoun always requires two words: (1) the appropriate definite article, and (2) the pronoun itself.

	GENDER OF THE REPLACED NOUN GROUP		MEANING
	MASCULINE	FEMININE	
SINGULAR	**le mien** [lə mjɛ̃] **le tien** [lə tjɛ̃] **le sien** [lə sjɛ̃]	**la mienne** [la mjɛn] **la tienne** [la tjɛn] **la sienne** [la sjɛn]	*mine* *yours* *his, hers*
	le nôtre [lə notrə] **le vôtre** [lə votrə] **le leur** [lə lœr]	**la nôtre** [la notrə] **la vôtre** [la votrə] **la leur** [la lœr]	*ours* *yours* *theirs*
PLURAL	**les miens** [le mjɛ̃] **les tiens** [le tjɛ̃] **les siens** [le sjɛ̃]	**les miennes** [le mjɛn] **les tiennes** [le tjɛn] **les siennes** [le sjɛn]	*mine* *yours* *his, hers*
	les nôtres [le notrə] **les vôtres** [le votrə] **les leurs** [le lœr]		*ours* *yours* *theirs*
	Pronunciation: The masculine forms rhyme with **bien,** using the nasal sound [ɛ̃]. The corresponding feminine forms end in [ɛn] with no nasal sound.		

Vos fenêtres sont fermées mais **nos fenêtres** sont ouvertes.
Vos fenêtres sont fermées mais **les nôtres** sont ouvertes.
*Your windows are closed but **ours** are open.*

Jean apprend sa leçon et Paul apprend **sa leçon.**
Jean apprend sa leçon et Paul apprend **la sienne.**
*John is learning his lesson, and Paul is learning **his.***

Mes devoirs sont courts; **leurs devoirs** sont longs.
Mes devoirs sont courts; **les leurs** sont longs.
*My homework is short; **theirs** is long.*

Notre maison est petite, mais **la maison des Morel** est grande.
Notre maison est petite, mais **la leur** est grande.
*Our house is small, but **theirs** is big.*

In each example, the first sentence contains a repetitious noun with a possessive adjective. This noun structure [POSS. ADJ. + N] is the only kind replaceable by a possessive pronoun. The second sentence in each example illustrates this substitution.

Mise en œuvre 18 E

Pronom possessif

Remplacez les mots en italique par le pronom possessif approprié.

EXEMPLE

ma voiture et *ta voiture*
ma voiture et **la tienne**

1. mon cousin et *ton cousin*
2. ma cousine et *votre cousine*
3. ta mère et *ma mère*
4. mon livre et *votre livre*
5. mes classes et *leurs classes*
6. vos vacances et *nos vacances*
7. votre appartement et *l'appartement des Smith*
8. ta tante et *ma tante*
9. vos amies et *mes amies*
10. votre voiture et *la voiture de Paul*
11. Sa voiture est bleue; *ma voiture* est jaune.
12. Votre appartement est petit, *notre appartement* est assez grand.
13. La bicyclette de Pierre est toute neuve, *ta bicyclette* est vieille.
14. Mes professeurs sont sympathiques, et *tes professeurs*?
15. Je vais au théâtre avec les Brun. J'ai mes billets et *leurs billets*.

Mise en œuvre 18 F

Est-ce *celui* ou le pronom possessif?

Remplacez les mots en italique par **celui** ou par le pronom possessif approprié. Par exemple, on peut remplacer **le livre** par **celui**; mais **votre livre** doit être remplacé par le pronom possessif **le vôtre**.

1. Voici mon livre à moi. C'est *votre livre* qui est perdu.
2. Voici ma montre. C'est *la montre* que vous m'avez vendue.
3. Paul a pris mon billet et *votre billet à vous*.
4. Paul a apporté mon sandwich et *le sandwich* que vous avez commandé.
5. Je cherche les disques (*m.*) de Johnny Hallyday et *les disques* d'Édith Piaf.
6. Je cherche mes disques et *tes disques à toi*.
7. Mes parents et *les parents* de Robert assisteront au concert ce soir.
8. Mes parents et *les parents de Robert* assisteront au concert ce soir.
9. Ma valise est usée, mais *la valise de René* est neuve.
10. Ma valise est usée, mais *la valise* de René est neuve.

Reflets

Le Passe-muraille[3]

Il y avait à Paris un homme d'un certain âge, Monsieur Dutilleul, employé au Ministère de l'Enregistrement. Il avait un patron qui n'approuvait que les méthodes modernes, et qui considérait celles de Dutilleul vieux jeu. Par conséquent ce patron maltraitait Dutilleul et le rendait très malheureux. Il avait même relégué son employé dans un tout petit bureau qui ressemblait à un placard.

　　Souffrant d'un mal de tête, Dutilleul s'est rendu chez un médecin de son quartier. Celui-ci lui a prescrit un médicament que l'employé a avalé avant de rentrer chez lui. Au moment où il arrivait devant son appartement, il y avait une panne d'électricité. Dans l'obscurité Dutilleul a tâtonné dans les ténèbres; soudain il s'est trouvé à l'intérieur de l'appartement sans avoir ouvert la porte!

　　Profitant de ce pouvoir, Dutilleul a eu l'idée de se venger sur son patron en lui jouant de mauvais tours, si bien que celui-ci a bientôt perdu la raison et qu'on l'a emmené à l'hôpital psychiatrique. Dès lors, Dutilleul s'est mis à profiter de son faculté extraordinaire pour s'amuser (il a commencé à rendre visite à toute heure chez des amies) et pour s'enrichir des il a commis toute une série de cambriolages. Il passait facilement à travers les murs des banques, prenant de l'argent et sortant après avoir signé « Garou-Garou ».

　　Lassé[4], il s'est laissé prendre par la police. Mis en prison, il en sortait à volonté

---

[3] Marcel Aymé, adapted from *Le Passe-muraille* (Paris: Gallimard, Éditions Livres de Poche, 1943).
[4] **lasser** = *to tire, to weary, to exhaust (patience)*

pour aller reprendre ses visites, et même pour entrer dans la maison du directeur de la prison. Là, il empruntait des livres. Il rentrait dans sa cellule pour les lire, et les gardiens étaient étonnés de les y retrouver le lendemain.

Un soir Garou-Garou rentrait dans sa cellule après avoir donné une sérénade à sa petite amie en s'accompagnant d'une guitare. Les effets du médicament mystérieux ont disparu au moment même où il traversait une épaisse muraille. Hélas! Il s'est trouvé emprisonné à l'intérieur de cette muraille; on dit que les passants peuvent toujours l'entendre jouer de la guitare.

Sujets de conversation ou de composition

1. En lisant cette histoire, qu'est-ce que vous y trouvez qui montre (1) le fantastique, (2) l'humour, (3) le caractère de Dutilleul, (4) l'attitude de Dutilleul envers la vie, les affaires, l'amour? Expliquez.

2. Qu'est-ce que vous feriez si vous aviez un don extraordinaire semblable à celui de Dutilleul? Quel don est-ce que vous voudriez? (celui de Midas? de l'invisibilité? de Superman? de pouvoir vous transporter dans le passé ou dans l'avenir? de pouvoir vous transformer en animal? d'autres?)

19

Comparaisons
tout
mener°

COMPARAISON DES ADJECTIFS ET DES ADVERBES

19.1 Comparative forms

To obtain the comparative form of adjectives and adverbs, place **plus** (*more*), **moins** (*less*), or **aussi** (*just as*) before the adjective or adverb, and **que** after it.

A. Adjectives:

Louise est **plus** *intelligente* **que** Paul	+ **plus**	
Paul est **moins** *intelligent* **que** Louise.	− **moins**	[ADJ] **que**
Jean est **aussi**[1] *intelligent* **que** Suzanne.	= **aussi**	

B. Adverbs:

Ce train marche **plus** *vite* **que** l'autocar.	+ **plus**	
L'autocar marche **moins** *vite* **que** le train.	− **moins**	[ADV] **que**
Ma voiture marche **aussi** *vite* **que** la voiture de Jean.	= **aussi**	

[1] **Si** may be used instead of **aussi** after a negative verb:
   Jean n'est **pas** *si* **intelligent** que Suzanne.

229

C. **Quantities compared:** *de* + NOUN:

J'ai **plus de** *livres* que vous.   + **plus de** [N]   ⎫

Tu as **moins d'***argent* que moi.   − **moins de** [N]   ⎬ **que**

Il a **autant de** *talent* que Jean.   = **autant de** [N] ⎭

NOTE: For equality of *quantities*, **aussi** is replaced by **autant de.**

19.2 Superlatives

The superlative is formed by adding the appropriate definite article (**le, la, les**) to the comparative of the adjective. The superlative of adverbs is formed by prefixing invariable **le** to the comparative form. Either **plus** or **moins** may be used.

		UNCOMPARED FORM	COMPARATIVE	SUPERLATIVE
ADJECTIVES		intelligente (*f.s.*)	{ **plus** intelligente { **moins** intelligente	*la* **plus** intelligente *la* **moins** intelligente
		belles (*f.pl.*)	{ **plus** belles { **moins** belles	*les* **plus** belles *les* **moins** belles
ADVERBS		vite	**plus** vite **moins** vite	*le* **plus** vite *le* **moins** vite

A. **With a following adjective:**

Voici un livre **intéressant.**

Voici un livre **plus intéressant.**

Voici **le** livre **le plus intéressant.**   Note repeated article **le.**

C'est une maison **chère.**

C'est une maison **plus chère.**

C'est **la** maison **la plus chère.**   Note repeated article **la.**

B. **With a preceding adjective [5.9]:**

Voilà une **grande** maison.

Voilà une **plus grande** maison.

Voilà **la plus grande** maison du quartier.

C.   With an adverb:

> Notre voiture marche **vite.**
> Notre voiture marche **plus vite** que celle de Jean.
> Notre voiture marche **le plus vite.**

19.3   Repetition of definite article with superlative adjectives

The definite article is repeated when the superlative adjective follows the noun.

> Voice *le* livre *le* **plus intéressant.**   *Here is **the most interesting** book.*

19.4   General class

After a superlative, **de** is used for *in* or *of* when the general class is mentioned.

> Voilà **la plus grande** maison *de* la ville.
> Marie est la jeune fille **la plus intelligente** *de* la classe.
> Henri marche **le plus vite** *de* tous les élèves.

19.5   With numbers

When a number follows the words **plus** or **moins,** use **de** rather than **que.**

> J'ai **plus de deux** dollars.   *I have more than two dollars.*
> Il a **moins de seize** ans.   *He is less than 16 years old.*

19.6   Irregular comparisons

Learn the following special comparisons for **bon** (*adjective*) and **bien** (*adverb*).

A.   The adjective *bon, bonne.* It *agrees* in gender and number with the noun modified, and it *precedes* the noun.

ADJECTIVE	COMPARATIVE		SUPERLATIVE
bon (*m.*)	**un** meilleur	**le** meilleur	**les** meilleurs
bonne (*f.*)	**une** meilleure	**la** meilleure	**les** meilleures

un bon livre, **un meilleur** livre, **le meilleur** livre, **les meilleurs** livres
une bonne auto, **une meilleure** auto, **la meilleure** auto, **les meilleures** autos

Notice that **un, une** is used in the comparative, and **le, la**, or **les** is used in the superlative.

NOTE: Remember to use **de** after comparative forms when a noun follows [19.4]:

C'est **la meilleure** étudiante *de* la classe.

B.   The adverb *bien*. It has only two other forms as shown below. An adverb follows the verb and is invariable.

ADVERB	COMPARATIVE	SUPERLATIVE
bien	**mieux**	**le mieux**

Elle parle **bien;** Georges parle **mieux;** Suzanne parle **le mieux.**

Common expressions using **mieux:**

aimer mieux   = préférer   J'aime mieux la bière.
il vaut mieux   = il est préférable de   Il vaut mieux étudier.

"Better"—**mieux** or **meilleur?** The French equivalents for *better* and *best* are often confused. One way to remember the distinction between **mieux** and **meilleur** is that the word *adverb* is a *short* word, and that all the adverbs in this comparison are *short*; on the other hand, *adjective* is a *long* word, and the adjectives are *long* (**bon-ne, meilleur, meilleure,** etc.).

ADVERB (SHORT WORD)	ADJECTIVE (LONG WORD)
Didier travaille **bien.**	Il a fait du **bon** travail.
Emile travaille **mieux** que Didier.	Elle a fait une **meilleure** étude que Didier.
Marc travaille **le mieux.**	C'est **le meilleur** travailleur **de** tous.

C.   Summary of irregular comparisons.

ADVERB [INVARIABLE]		COMPARATIVE		SUPERLATIVE	
bien	*well*	mieux	*better*	le mieux	*the best*
mal	*badly*	pis, plus mal	*worse*	le pis	*the worst*
peu	*very little*	moins	*less*	le moins	*the least*
beaucoup[2]	*a lot*	plus	*more*	le plus	*the most*

[2] For *very much* use **énormément: Il a énormément de talent.**

ADJECTIVE	COMPARATIVE	SUPERLATIVE
bon, bonne	un meilleur	le meilleur
	une meilleure	la meilleure
		les meilleur(e)s

ADVERBS:

Je gagne **peu**; Jean gagne **moins**; Hans gagne **le moins**.

Tu écris **mal**; les avocats écrivent **pis** (**plus mal**); ce médecin écrit **le pis**.

Suzanne parle **beaucoup**. Jacqueline parle **plus**. Henri parle **le plus**.

QUANTITIES:

Elle a **beaucoup de** disques.	ADVERB OF QUANTITY
Jean a **plus de** disques **que** Marie.	COMPARATIVE
Jean-Paul a **le plus de** disques.	SUPERLATIVE

Mise en œuvre 19 A

Comparatif des adjectifs

Comparez les deux noms en vous référant à la qualité signalée entre parenthèses. Faites attention à l'accord de l'adjectif [5.1] avec le **premier** nom mentionné.

EXEMPLE

(la beauté: beau)   la rose et le mimosa

La rose est **plus belle que** le mimosa.

Le mimosa est **moins beau que** la rose.

1. (la douceur: doux)   une orange et un citron
2. (l'intelligence: intelligent)   un homme et un chien
3. (l'âge: jeune / vieux)   un fils et son père
4. (la force: fort / faible)   un éléphant et un cheval
5. (la grandeur: grand)   une maison et un hôtel
6. (la vitesse: vite / lent)   une Renault 16 et un cheval
7. (l'excellence: bon)   le cinéma et la télévision
8. (l'épaisseur: épais / mince)   le mur et une planche
9. (la taille: grand / petit)   Napoléon et de Gaulle
10. (la difficulté: difficile / facile)   un thème et une version

Mise en œuvre 19 B

Superlatif des adjectifs

Employez le superlatif de l'adjectif. Ajoutez **de** (ou une contraction de **de**) pour indiquer la classe générale.

EXEMPLE

Cet appartement est **bon.** (quartier)

Cet appartement est **le meilleur du quartier.**

1. Cette maison est bonne. (quartier)
2. Cette école est grande. (ville)
3. Cette femme est généreuse. (village)
4. Ce boulevard est long. (Paris)
5. Ce spectacle est intéressant. (saison)
6. Ce grand magasin est commode. (ville)
7. Ces ouvriers sont bons. (usine)
8. Ces tables sont bonnes. (restaurant)
9. Cette frontière est longue. (pays)
10. Cette robe est chère. (collection)

Mise en œuvre 19 C

Comparatif des adverbes

Répondez aux questions suivantes en employant le comparatif de l'adverbe.

EXEMPLE

Nathalie travaille **beaucoup.** Et vous?

Moi, je travaille **plus que** (ou **moins que**) Nathalie.

1. Le président voyage *beaucoup.* Et vous?
2. Le chien mange *peu.* Et le chat?
3. L'étudiant écrit *bien.* Et le journaliste?
4. Votre père prend *souvent* la voiture. Et vous?
5. Mon professeur parle *fort.* Et ce comédien?
6. Votre bicyclette roule *vite.* Et le mobylette?
7. Un chat comprend *bien.* Et un chien?
8. Une infirmière étudie *longtemps.* Et un médecin?
9. Antoine regarde *peu* la télévision. Et son frère?
10. Éric conduit *lentement.* Et cette vieille dame?

TOUT

19.7 Forms of the adjective *tout*

As an adjective, **tout** precedes the noun it modifies, and agrees with it in gender and number. Notice that the meaning of the singular (**tout, toute**) varies with the addition or omission of the article. The article **les** (or a possessive like **mes**) *must* be used with the plural.

	MASCULINE	FEMININE	MEANING
SINGULAR	**tout**	**toute**	*any (every)* [N] NO ARTICLE
	tout le	**toute la**	*the whole* [N] WITH ARTICLE
PLURAL	**tous les**	**toutes les**	*all (of) the* [N] WITH ARTICLE

A. Masculine

Tout soldat est brave.	*Any (Every) soldier is brave.*
Tout le cours est bon.	*The whole course is good.*
Tous les livres sont utiles.	*All of the books are useful.*
Tous mes livres sont utiles.	*All my books are useful.*

B. Feminine

Toute saison est belle.	*Any (Every) season is beautiful.*
Toute la saison est belle.	*The whole season is beautiful.*
Toutes les saisons sont belles.	*All of the seasons are beautiful.*

19.8 Adverbial *tout*

Used as an adverb, **tout** is invariable and means *quite, very:*

Ce livre est **tout** usé.	*(m.s.) This book is quite worn.*
Elle est **tout** effrayée.	*(f.s.) She is quite frightened.*
Elle est **tout** émue.	*(f.s.) She is very moved.*
Cela est **tout** décidé.	*(m.s.) That is completely decided.*
Ce chat est **tout** jeune.	*(m.s.) That cat is very young.*

19.9 Expressions with *tout*

The following expressions are invariable:

tous les jours	*every day*
(pas) du tout	*(not) at all*
tout à fait	*completely, entirely*
tout à l'heure	*just now; in a moment*
tout de suite	*immediately, at once*
tout le monde	*everybody*
tout à coup	*suddenly*
tout d'un coup	*in one try, all at once*
tout de même	*anyway, all the same*

Je ne comprends **pas du tout**.	*I don't understand **at all**.*
Je l'ai vu **tout à l'heure**.	*I saw him **just a moment ago**.*
Il reviendra **tout à l'heure**.	*He will be right back.*
A **tout à l'heure**!	*See you **soon**.*
La porte s'ouvrit **tout à coup**.	*The door **suddenly** opened.*
Le vent emporta le toit **tout d'un coup**.	*The wind carried off the roof **in one fell swoop**.*

Mise en œuvre 19 D

Emploi de l'adjectif *tout*

Remplacez le singulier de **tout** par la forme appropriée du pluriel.

EXEMPLE

Toute langue vit, travaille, respire.
Toutes les langues viv**ent**, travaill**ent**, respir**ent**.

1. Tout homme est mortel.
2. Tout travail mérite un salaire.
3. Toute vérité n'est pas bonne à dire.
4. La nuit, tout chat est gris.
5. Tout Français admire Napoléon.

Mise en œuvre 19 E

Emploi de *tout* au sens d' « entier »

Remplacez **une partie de** par le singulier de **tout,** suivi de l'article approprié.

EXEMPLE

Une partie de la saison est belle.

Toute la saison est belle.

1. Une partie de cette maison est blanche.
2. Une partie de ce cours est difficile.
3. Une partie de la route est dangereuse.
4. Une partie de la collection a été vendue.
5. Une partie de ce roman est intéressante.

Mise en œuvre 19 F

Emploi de *tout* (= très)

Commentez les phrases suivantes en ajoutant **tout** à l'adjectif employé.

EXEMPLE

MARIE:—Que le ciel est bleu aujourd'hui!

FABIEN:—Mais oui, il est **tout bleu.** Il fait beau!

1. La terre est ronde.
2. Cette route est droite.
3. Ces garçons sont seuls.
4. Ce garçon est étonné.
5. Hélène est contente.
6. Ma leçon de français est prête.
7. Les pneus de cette auto sont usés.
8. Mais la voiture est neuve!

VERBE IRRÉGULIER **MENER**°

19.10   Verbe irrégulier *mener*° (*to lead*)

This verb is irregular only in the present indicative, present subjunctive, and FC-stem. The present tenses (indicative and subjunctive) are two-stem tenses, using **mèn-** in the L-area, and **men-** in the **nous-** and **vous-**forms. This added accent also appears in all forms of the future and conditional tenses. **Amener**° (*to bring* [*a person*]), **emmener**° (*to take* [*a person*]), and **se promener**° (*to take a walk*) are conjugated in the same way.

PRÉSENT

je **mène**	nous **menons**	} men- STEM
tu **mènes**	vous **menez**	
il **mène**	ils **mènent**	← mèn- STEM

IMPARFAIT   REGULAR STEM: **men-** from the **nous**-form of the present tense.
Autrefois je **menais** une vie tranquille.
*Formerly I **used to lead** a quiet life.*

PASSÉ COMPOSÉ   PP: **mené** AUXILIARY: (**avoir**)
Hier **j'ai emmené** ma femme au restaurant.

PASSE SIMPLE   STEM: **men** + **ai** system of endings.
Il **amena** sa petite amie à la soirée.

FUTUR   FC STEM: **mèner-** (+ future endings)
Si je te rends visite, **j'amènerai** les enfants.

CONDITIONNEL   FC STEM: **mèner-** (+ imperfect endings)
Si j'avais le temps **j'emmènerais** Pierre au cirque.

SUBJONCTIF   STEMS: **mèn-** / **men-** (2-stem verb)

que je **mène**	que nous **menions**	} men- STEM
que tu **mènes**	que vous **meniez**	
qu'il **mène**	qu'ils **mènent**	← mèn- STEM

Je doute **qu'il mène** par deux sets.
*I doubt **that he is leading** by two sets.*

19.11   Verbs related to *mener*

Four verbs conjugated in the same way as **mener** are the compounds dealing with movement of *persons*.

NOTE: The verbs meaning movement *towards* the speaker begin with **a** (related to **à**), and movement *away* from the speaker is indicated by the prefix **em-** (as in **emigrate**, related to the Latin **ex-**, *out of*).

Verbs like **mener** are:

amener°	to bring (PERSON) (*to [à] the speaker's location*)
emmener°	*to take* (PERSON) (*away from the speaker's location*)
ramener°	*to bring* (PERSON) *back*
se promener°	*to take a walk*

Amenez votre amie chez moi ce soir.

Tu vas au cinéma? **Emmène** les enfants.

J'ai emmené Marguerite au concert hier soir.

Ramenez le malade demain, a dit le médecin.

Il **se promène** avec son chien.

Les filles **se sont promenées** en bateau hier.[3] [1.6A]

When *things* are involved instead of people, the verbs used for the same kind of movement are variations of **porter**:

porter	*to wear (clothing); to carry*
apporter	*to bring (to or towards the speaker)*
emporter	*to take, to take away*
rapporter	*to bring back again*

Apportez du pain quand tu reviendras à la maison.

Emportez cette table quand tu partiras.

Elle **portait** un tailleur gris.

Mise en œuvre 19 G

Est-ce *emmener*° ou *amener*°?

Choisissez le mot juste. Employez la forme appropriée dans votre réponse.

1. Vous êtes à l'appareil. Vous invitez un ami à venir chez vous. Vous dites:
   —(Amenez) (Emmenez) votre camarade de chambre.
2. Vous sortez pour aller faire des commissions en ville. Votre frère vous accompagnera. Vous dites: —Je vais (amener) (emmener) mon frère.
3. Vous êtes à la porte de votre maison. Vous voyez venir Paul, accompagné de son oncle Jules. Vous vous dites: —Tiens! Paul (amène) (emmène) son oncle Jules!

[3] The girls went for a boat ride yesterday.

4. Paul vous dit en arrivant avec son oncle: —Salut! J'ai (amené) (emmené) mon oncle Jules.
5. Quand nous quittons Paris pour les grandes vacances, nous allons au bord de la mer. Nous (amenons) (emmenons) toujours notre chien Tonton.

Mise en œuvre 19 H

Thème

1. Henri is the most generous student in our school. He took us to the Folies-Bergère and he bought all the tickets.
2. Come to our apartment after the show, and bring your friends.
3. All the stockholders are waiting for the highest price.
4. My father is completely discouraged; he has the blues because he doubts that he can ski better than I.
5. He went skiing in Switzerland, but he fell and hurt himself.
6. "You must bring your father back here next week," said the doctor.
7. Mr. Dumont's sister took the children to the marionette show[4] at the Jardin du Luxembourg yesterday morning.
8. All the students have been waiting for the teacher for ten minutes. He is later than usual.
9. To solve this problem, we need the best computer in the university.
10. This is a good program, but the one we used yesterday was better.
11. That professor explained these lessons well; I understand them better now.

Mise en œuvre 19 J

Comparaisons et décisions

Jacques, Chantal, Robert, Jacqueline et Gérard sont étudiants à l'université. Ils travaillent tous, et ils ont tous un compte en banque et une voiture. Le tableau indique leur nom, leur nombre d'heures de travail par semaine, leur salaire horaire, la note qu'ils ont reçue en anglais, et la marque de voiture qu'ils possèdent. Faites les comparaisons demandées, en expliquant vos décisions.

NOM	HEURES	COMPTE	SALAIRE	NOTE[5] EN ANGLAIS	VOITURE
Jacques	10	2.300 F	30 F	12,5	VW
Chantal	20	3.500 F	20 F	17	Escort
Robert	9	10.000 F	50 F	16,5	BMW
Jacqueline	20	3.000 F	35 F	11,5	Fiat
Gérard	12	15.000 F	75 F	14	Mercedes

[4] **Au théâtre des marionnettes**
[5] Les notes sont **excellent** (17 à 20), **bien** (15, 16), **assez bien** (12 à 15), **moyen** (11), **suffisant** ou **passable** (10), et **insuffisant** (0 à 9).

1. Comparez les voitures de Jacques et de Gérard. (prix? qualité?)
2. Comparez les salaires de Chantal et de Robert.
3. Comparez les notes en français de Jacques et de Gérard.
4. Comparez les comptes en banque de Chantal et de Jacqueline.
5. Qui a la meilleure voiture? Pourquoi cette voiture a-t-elle tant de prestige?
6. Qui a la plus petite voiture? Quels en sont les avantages?
7. Qui est le meilleur étudiant ou la meilleure étudiante en anglais?
8. Qui est le mieux payé? Qui gagne le moins?
9. Qui est le plus sérieux, selon les notes? le moins sérieux?
10. Qui a eu le plus grand succès? Le moins de succès? Comment est-ce que vous décidez?

20

Passé simple
Prépositions: cas spéciaux
Verbe irrégulier *devoir*

PASSÉ SIMPLE TENSE

You will encounter the **passé simple** (or *Past Definite*) tense frequently in your readings. It is identical in meaning with the **passé composé.** Both tenses deal with the past (**passé**); the latter is compound (**composé**), while the other is a single word (**simple**). Their meanings are interchangeable, but while the **passé composé** is used both in speech and in writing, the **passé simple** is limited to written forms.

20.1 Uses of the passé simple

The passé simple is used in literature but not in conversation or other spoken forms. It is used under the same circumstances as the passé composé: (a) the action is *fully completed* in the past, and (b) the *time of its happening* is either *specified* or clearly implied.

The meaning of the **passé simple** is the same as that of the **passé composé:**

PASSÉ SIMPLE	PASSÉ COMPOSÉ	MEANING
il **travailla**	il **a travaillé**	*he worked*
ils **arrivèrent**	ils **sont arrivés**	*they arrived*
elle **se leva**	elle **s'est levée**	*she got up*
nous **écoutâmes**	nous **avons écouté**	*we listened*

242

The formation of the **passé simple** makes it very convenient for writers, since there is neither an auxiliary verb to select, nor a past participle agreement to consider.

In narration, the **passé simple** is used for *movement* and *actions* that advance the plot, while the **imperfect** is used to describe *settings* and *backgrounds* that remain the same for some segment of the plot. (This is the equivalent of the roles of the passé composé and imperfect previously seen [13.5].)

20.2   Formation

The passé simple is formed by dropping the infinitive ending of a regular verb, and adding the appropriate tense endings. The following chart shows the three ending systems: the **-ai** system for regular **-er** verbs like **parler**; the **-is** system for regular **-ir** and **-re** verbs. A third system using the **-us** endings is for certain irregular verbs only.

Below the endings you will find the irregular verbs using each system.

	REGULAR VERBS		SOME IRREGULAR VERBS
	-er	-ir and -re	
je	-ai	-is	-us
tu	-as	-is	-us
il	-a	-it	-ut
nous	-âmes	-îmes	-ûmes
vous	-âtes	-îtes	-ûtes
ils	-èrent	-irent	-urent

IRREGULAR VERBS USING THE ABOVE SYSTEMS		
-ai SYSTEM	-is SYSTEM	-us SYSTEM
all- (aller)	d- (dire)	d- (devoir)
	f- (faire)	f- (être)
	m- (mettre)	e- (avoir)
	v- (voir)	p- (pouvoir)
	pr- (prendre)	s- (savoir)
	naqu- (naître)	voul- (vouloir)
	écriv- (écrire)	véc- (vivre)
		mour- (mourir)

MODEL REGULAR VERBS

je parlai	je finis	je vendis
tu parlas	tu finis	tu vendis
il parla	il finit	il vendit
nous parlâmes	nous finîmes	nous vendîmes
vous parlâtes	vous finîtes	vous vendîtes
ils parlèrent	ils finirent	ils vendirent

MODEL IRREGULAR VERBS

(-ai SYSTEM)	(-is SYSTEM)	(-us SYSTEM)
aller	**dire**	**pouvoir**
j'allai	je dis	je pus
tu allas	tu dis	tu pus
il alla	il dit	il put
nous allâmes	nous dîmes	nous pûmes
vous allâtes	vous dîtes	vous pûtes
ils allèrent	ils dirent	ils purent

In practice, the third person (**il**-form) is more often seen than other forms. The third-person forms of some often used irregular verbs are shown below, but can always be accessed in the verb tables.

INFINITIVE	STEM	SYSTEM [20.2]	**il**-FORMS	**ils**-FORMS
écrire	**écriv-**	-is	il **écrivit**	ils **écrivirent**
dire	**d-**	-is	il **dit**	ils dirent
faire	**f-**	-is	il **fit**	ils firent
mettre	**m-**	-is	il **mit**	ils mirent
naître	**naqu-**	-is	il **naquit**	ils **naquirent**
ouvrir	**ouvr-**	-is	il **ouvrit**	ils **ouvrirent**
prendre	**pr-**	-is	il **prit**	ils **prirent**
sortir	**sort-**	-is	il **sortit**	ils **sortirent**
voir	**v-**	-is	il **vit**	ils virent
avoir	**e-**	-us	il **eut**	ils **eurent**
devoir	**d-**	-us	il **dut**	ils **durent**
être	**f-**	-us	il **fut**	ils **furent**
mourir	**mour-**	-us	il **mourut**	ils **moururent**
savoir	**s-**	-us	il **sut**	ils **surent**
vivre	**véc-**	-us	il **vécut**	ils **vécurent**
vouloir	**voul-**	-us	il **voulut**	ils **voulurent**

Elle **entra** dans la salle. = Elle **est entrée** dans la salle.

Il **finit** de travailler. = Il **a fini** de travailler.

Nous **vendîmes** la voiture. = Nous **avons vendu** la voiture.

J'**allai** voir mon ami. = Je **suis allé(e)** voir mon ami.

Ils me **dirent** bonjour. = Ils m'**ont dit** bonjour.

Ils **durent** partir. = Ils **ont dû** partir.

The irregular verbs **venir** and **tenir** have unusual forms in the passé simple, because they omit the **-i-** of all the endings in the **-is** system. Because of this similarity it is convenient to learn them together.

venir	STEM: **vin-**		**tenir**	STEM: **tin-**
je	vins (*came*)		je	tins (*held*)
tu	vins		tu	tins
il	vint		il	tint
nous	**vînmes**		nous	**tînmes**
vous	**vîntes**		vous	**tîntes**
ils	vin**rent**		ils	tin**rent**

20.3 Passé simple of reflexive verbs (verbes pronominaux)

The passé simple of reflexive verbs is formed exactly as for other verbs; the reflexive pronoun is included as usual. There are no problems of agreement.

Elle **se réveilla, se leva, se lava** les mains et la figure, et **s'habilla**[1].

20.4 Non-use of the passé simple

There are three exceptions to the identical use of the passé simple and the passé composé. Do not use the passé simple for the following:

A. Recent past.

Hier j'ai vu[2] le professeur Jolivet au musée.

The passé simple is for events not so close to the present.

---

[1] **Elle s'est réveillée, s'est levée, s'est lavé les mains et la figure, et s'est habillée.**
[2] Not **je vis.**

B.   Present related to the past.

Voici la bicyclette que **j'ai achetée.**

C.   *Depuis* structure. The **depuis** construction [6.4A] is normally used with the present tense (*have been doing something*) or the imperfect tense (*had been doing something*). It is also possible to use the passé composé *but **not** the **passé simple*** with **depuis** in a negative sentence, as follows:

Je ne t'**ai** pas **vue** *depuis* longtemps.
I have not seen you for a long time.

Mise en œuvre 20 A

Passé simple

Composez une phrase en utilisant les fragments ci-dessous. Changez le passé composé en passé simple, et ajoutez quelques mots pour compléter l'idée.

EXEMPLE

elle s'est reposée

Après le match, elle se reposa parce qu'elle était fatiguée.

1. il a parlé au vendeur
2. j'ai dit bonjour
3. ils ont pris les billets
4. il a pris un taxi
5. les étudiants ont pris quelque chose
6. les touristes ont cherché un agent
7. Gérard a téléphoné à son père
8. il a reçu[3] une contravention
9. il a vendu sa voiture
10. vous avez voulu partir
11. il est venu à la porte
12. ils sont allées à la Bourse
13. je suis monté(e) au premier
14. nous avons été surpris
15. Jean a eu rendez-vous
16. Éric a écrit une lettre
17. nous nous sommes levés tard
18. j'ai acheté une cassette
19. elle a eu un accident
20. ils sont venus chez moi

Mise en œuvre 20 B

Chez le médecin

Mettez les verbes au passé simple là où c'est possible. S'il y a des verbes qu'il ne faut pas changer, expliquez pourquoi.

[3] **reç-** plus **-us** system

1. Vers neuf heures du matin le docteur Lemaistre est entré dans le grand bâtiment qui se trouvait 24, rue de Galliéra.
2. Il a pris l'ascenseur pour monter au cinquième étage.
3. La porte de la cabine s'est ouverte au cinquième, et le docteur en est sorti.
4. Il s'est approché de la porte de son cabinet. Il l'a ouverte et est entré dans la salle d'attente.
5. Il y avait déjà plusieurs patients qui attendaient depuis dix minutes.
6. Un jeune homme s'est levé pour parler au médecin; les autres lisaient ou somnolaient.
7. Le docteur a salué la secrétaire et est entré dans son cabinet.
8. Bientôt il a appelé le premier patient, qui avait mal à la tête.
9. M. Lemaistre lui a posé plusieurs questions; ensuite il a pris sa tension artérielle.[4]
10. Le docteur a décidé que ce patient avait plutôt mal au cheveux[5], et il lui a prescrit[6] une aspirine.

PRÉPOSITIONS: CAS SPÉCIAUX

20.5   Emploi de *de: quelques-uns de(s)*, *la plupart de(s)*, *bien de(s)*

To say *some of* or *a few of* some item, use **quelques-un(e)s de(s)**. The gender of the following noun determines whether **un** or **une** is used at the end of this word. The article or possessive is used after **de**, and contractions apply:

Quelques-uns de *ces* livres sont en allemand.

Quelques-unes de *ses* robes sont très élégantes.

With **la plupart de** (*most of*) use the article or a possessive adjective before the noun. If the article is plural, the contraction **des** appears:

La plupart des étudiants ne sont pas riches.
Most of the students are not rich.

La plupart de mes livres sont en français.
Most of my books are in French.

The expression **bien des** should be used only before plural nouns. (It is equivalent to **beaucoup de**, which, however, can be used regardless of the number of the noun):

---

[4] = **pression du sang**
[5] = *a hangover*
[6] = *prescribed.* **Prescrire** est conjugé comme **écrire.**

Pierre a **bien des problèmes.** = Pierre a **beaucoup de problèmes.**
Pierre has many problems.

Bien des gens partent en vacances en aout.
Many people go on vacation in August.

20.6 Materials or purpose: distinguishing prepositions

The purpose for which an object is intended is often expressed using **de** with another noun, and sometimes with **à** plus an infinitive:

la salle de réunion	*the meeting room*
la salle de classe	*the classroom*
une machine à écrire	*a typewriter*
du papier à écrire	*stationery*
la salle à manger	*the dining room*

Both **de** and **en** are used for materials of which things are made:

une maison en bois	*a wooden house*
une bague en or massif	*a solid-gold ring*

Notice the distinction between the following:

une tasse **à thé**	*a teacup*	PURPOSE
une tasse **de thé**	*a cup of tea*	CONTENTS

20.7 Geographical special use: *from* a country

When a country's name is feminine, the preposition **de** is used alone, with no article, to mean *from* that country:

Jean-Claude arrive **de France.**	*Jean-Claude is arriving from France.*
Les Smith viennent **d'Angleterre.**	*The Smiths are coming from England.*
Lars est **de** Suède.	*Lars is from Sweden.*

The article is retained for compound names, plural names, and all masculine singular names of countries and states. Contractions are used when appropriate:

Lucien arrive **du** Canada.   *Lucien is arriving from Canada.*

Il vient **de la** Nouvelle-Zélande.   *He comes from New Zealand.*

Pete vient **du** Texas.   *Pete comes from Texas.*

Tex vient **des** États-Unis.   *Tex is from the United States.*

20.8   Verb structures requiring *de* alone. « Régimes »

The following verb structures include **de** plus a noun. No article is used with the noun [y].

charger [x] **de** [y]	*to load* [x] *with* [y]
entourer [x] **de** [y]	*to surround* [x] *with* [y]
remplir [x] **de** [y]	*to fill* [x] *with* [y]
écraser [x] **de** [y]	*to crush* [x] *by* [y]
fournir [x] **de** [y]	*to supply* [x] *with* [y]
discuter (**de** [x])	*to discuss* (*something*)

L'ouvrier **a chargé** le camion **de** bois.   *The worker loaded the truck with wood.*

La maison **est entourée de** jardins.   *The house is surrounded by gardens.*

Le garçon **a rempli** les verres **de** vin.   *The waiter filled the glasses with wine.*

Nous **avons discuté d'**économie.   *We discussed economics.*

Mise en œuvre 20 C

Prépositions: cas spéciaux

Employez **quelques-uns, la plupart** ou **bien** en répondant aux questions suivantes. Ajoutez une explication.

EXEMPLE

Est-ce que tous les étudiants aiment la musique classique?

Quelques-uns des étudiants l'aiment, mais **la plupart** préfèrent le rock.

1. Est-ce que toutes les Américaines sont riches?
2. Est-ce que tous tes amis possèdent des voitures?
3. Vos professeurs parlent-ils tous le français?
4. Est-ce que tous les actionnaires gagnent de l'argent à la Bourse?
5. Est-ce que tu déposes ton argent à la banque?
6. Est-ce que tous tes manuels sont en anglais?
7. Est-ce que tous les trains français sont des trains rapides?

8. Les trains européens marchent-ils très vite?
9. Vos amis passent-ils leurs vacances en Floride?
10. Les étudiants se servent-ils d'ordinateurs personnels?
11. Est-ce que toutes les machines à écrire sont électroniques aujourd'hui?
12. Vos notes sont-elles très bonnes?

20.9   Verbe irrégulier *devoir*

The meanings of this verb vary according to the time and the intent of the speaker. The top line in the following diagram indicates that the subject *is* (*was/will be*) required to do something that he intends to do—"conformity."

The second line indicates that the subject was supposed to do something, but probably did not (or will not) do it—"But won't."

The form of **devoir** used is followed by the infinitive of the main verb.

	PAST	PRESENT	FUTURE
CONFORMITY	il **a dû** ❶ *he had to, must have*	il **doit** ❷ *he must*	il **devra** ❸ *he will have to*
EXPECTED BUT WON'T	il **devait** ④ *he was supposed to*	il **devrait** ⑤ *he should*	
"LES REGRETS" HINDSIGHT	il **aurait dû** ❻ *he should have* (*and didn't*)	ALL FOLLOWED BY AN INFINITIVE	

(Numbers refer to those in the above chart)

❶ Il **a dû** étudier hier soir.

He **had to** *study last evening.* or
He **must have** *studied last evening.*

❷ Il **doit** travailler.

He **must** *work.*

❸ Il **devra** travailler samedi.

He **will have** *to work Saturday.*

④ Il **devait** voir le doyen, mais il ne l'a pas fait.

He **was supposed** *to see the dean, but he didn't do it.*

⑤ Il **devrait** étudier, mais il va au cinéma.

He **should** *study, but he is going to the movies.*

❻ Il a échoué à l'examen: il **aurait dû** étudier.

He *flunked the examination; he* **should have** *studied.*

The tenses are (1) passé composé, (2) present, (3) future, (4) imperfect, (5) conditional, and (6) past conditional.

AUTRES EXEMPLES

1. **Hier** soir Jean **a dû** *étudier;* aussi est-il resté à la maison.   ❶
2. Il **devait** *voir* son professeur, mais il a oublié son rendez-vous.   ④
3. Il **aurait dû** *regarder* sa montre.   ❻
4. Claude **doit** *passer* un examen aujourd'hui.   ❷
5. Il **devrait** *revoir* ses notes et ses manuels.   ⑤
6. Demain il **devra** *expliquer* sa note à ses parents.   ❸
7. Il **aurait dû** *étudier* avant l'examen.   ❻

When a form of **devoir** is followed by a noun, it means *to owe:*

M. Masson me **doit** cinq cents francs.

Mise en œuvre 20 D

devoir en action

Refaites chaque phrase en employant une forme convenable de **devoir**.

EXEMPLE

Il faut que j'aille en ville demain.

Je **devrai aller** en ville demain.

1. Il faut que Paul revienne ce soir.
2. Il sera obligé de préparer un examen.
3. Hier il a été obligé de faire réparer sa voiture.
4. La voiture aurait mieux marché s'il l'avait entretenue.[7]   ❻
5. Jean-Paul était obligé de travailler hier.
6. Le lendemain il avait l'intention de sortir avec Marie, mais il était trop fatigué.
7. Il faut que je paie mille francs à mon avocat.
8. Il est probable qu'il fait très chaud au Maroc.
9. Mon père a rendez-vous à la Bourse demain.
10. Il me faudra faire la vaisselle.

Mise en œuvre 20 E

Thème

1. I should write my friends in Vienna, but I'm going to the movies.
2. We should have asked them for some photos.
3. I have to take my father to the airport this afternoon.

[7] (He should have maintained it . . .)

4. He will have to wait for the plane for an hour and a half.
5. He must be annoyed when he has to wait so long.
6. It is useless for him to complain; most of the flights are on time.
7. We were surrounded by tourists from Spain and Portugal.
8. The attendants supplied the travelers with books and magazines.
9. I doubt that the American's cup is filled with tea. It must be coffee.
10. The engineers are sitting at a table in the restaurant discussing computers.
11. The flight for Warsaw just left; we should have taken that one.

Narration: Une histoire personnelle

Racontez ce qu'une personne réelle ou imaginée a fait un jour au passé. Montrez que vous savez employer le passé simple. Vous devez inclure (1) au moins quatre adjectifs et deux adverbes, (2) la construction avec **depuis** au moins une fois, (3) deux ou trois emplois du subjonctif, (4) l'imparfait et (5) des exemples de l'indication de l'heure et de la chronologie.

Libre à vous d'inventer.

21

Interrogation

INTERROGATION

When all elements of a statement are present (subject, verb, and objects), questions are made by (1) *intonation*, (2) **est-ce que** at the beginning of the statement, (3) **n'est-ce pas** at the end of the statement, or (4) *inversion* of subject and verb.

21.1 Intonation

It is common in conversation to use a rising intonation at the end of a statement to make it into a question:

Tu reviens demain?	*Are you coming back tomorrow?*
Vous cherchez le professeur?	*Are you looking for the professor?*
Tu t'amuses bien?	*Are you having a good time?*
Paul s'est couché?	*Has Paul gone to bed?*
On part maintenant?	*Shall we leave now?*

21.2 *Est-ce que* method

A statement in normal word-order is made into a question by placing **est-ce que** in front of it and adding a **point d'interrogation:**

STATEMENT   Robert fait du tennis aujourd'hui.

QUESTION   **Est-ce que** Robert fait du tennis aujourd'hui?

When the subject of a sentence is **je,** it is customary to use this method rather than inversion [21.5][1]:

Est-ce que je peux sortir ce soir?

When the sentence begins with a vowel sound, the **que** becomes **qu':**

Est-ce qu'ils ont acheté une Renault?

Est-ce qu'elle s'est reposée pendant l'après-midi?

21.3   Confirmation of a statement: *n'est-ce pas?*

If you want confirmation of the accuracy of a statement you are making, add **n'est-ce pas** at the end:

Serge joue au tennis aujourd'hui, **n'est-ce pas?**   (. . . *isn't he?*)

Ils ont acheté une Renault, **n'est-ce pas?**   (. . . *didn't they?*)

Elle s'est reposée pendant l'après-midi, **n'est-ce pas?**   (. . . *didn't she?*)

Tu as faim, **n'est-ce pas?**   (. . . *aren't you?*)

Notice the variety of meanings in English, all simplified in French by this one interrogative phrase.

21.4   Inversion method: verb unit

The VERB UNIT [8.1] is important for word-order problems in interrogation and negation. Recall that the VERB UNIT consists of the verb and *all the words in front of it* except the subject. The verb is either (a) a one-word verb or (b) a compound verb. In the latter case, *only the auxiliary verb* is included in the verb unit. The past participle is *never* a part of the verb unit.

---

[1] Inversion *is* acceptable with **ai-je, dis-je, dois-je, fais-je, puis-je, sais-je, suis-je, vais-je, vois-je.**

TEST YOURSELF ON VERB UNIT IDENTIFICATION

SENTENCE	VERB UNIT IS:	
Elle **est** arrivée.	est	1
Ils **ont** bien travaillé.	ont	2
Marie **s'est** déjà levée.	s'est	3
Il **nous l'a** donnée.	nous l'a	4
Paul **fait** souvent du ski.	fait	5
Vous **vous en souvenez**.	vous en souvenez	6
C'**est** une belle église.	est	7

21.5   Subject pronoun inversion

A question by inversion is formed by putting the VERB UNIT first, followed by a hyphen, the subject *pronoun*, then the rest of the sentence. Using the examples above, these are the inverted forms which become questions:

SENTENCE: VERB UNIT IN **boldface**	QUESTION FORMED BY INVERSION	EX.
Elle **est** arrivée.	**Est**-elle arrivée?	1
Ils **ont** bien travaillé.	**Ont**-ils bien travaillé?	2
La fille **s'est** déjà levée.	*Can't be done.* [21.6]	3
Il **nous l'a** donnée.	**Nous l'a**-*t*-il donnée[2]?	4
Paul **fait** souvent du ski.	*Can't be done.* [21.6]	5
Vous **vous en souvenez**.	**Vous en souvenez**-vous?	6
C'**est** un bon travailleur.	**Est**-ce un bon travailleur?	7

Before going on, can you see how basic sentences numbers 3 and 5 differ from the other examples?[3]

---

[2] Recall that the letter **-t-** is inserted in inversion to prevent two vowel sounds coming together. This happens only in the third person singular.

[3] Ces phrases ont un nom comme sujet tandis que les autres ont un pronom comme sujet.

21.6   Noun subject: supplied pronoun

When the subject is a *noun*, that noun cannot be moved to the inverted position. Instead, leave the sentence in normal order. Determine what pronoun is appropriate to represent the subject noun; insert it after the verb unit. Taking examples 3 and 5 above, the method is:

3. La fille s'est déjà levée.
   La fille s'est-*elle* déjà levée?

   The subject pronoun is **elle.**
   (supplied pronoun in inversion)

5. Paul **fait** souvent du ski.
   Paul **fait-***il* souvent du ski?

   The subject pronoun is **il.**
   (supplied pronoun in inversion)

It is always possible to use **est-ce que** when the subject is a noun:

3. Est-ce que la fille s'est déjà levée?

5. Est-ce que Paul fait souvent du ski?

Mise en œuvre 21 A

Questions: *est-ce que* et inversion, nom sujet

Mettez les phrases suivantes à la forme interrogative selon l'exemple. Employez **est-ce que** et l'inversion.

EXEMPLE

Mon avion part à deux heures et demie.

Est-ce que mon avion part à deux heures et demie?

Mon avion **part-il** à deux heures et demie?

1. Mon patron comprit bien ma suggestion.
2. Le directeur pouvait la mettre en œuvre.
3. Le capitaine fumait une pipe.
4. Le médecin pensait que le patient buvait trop.
5. Cette personne ne pouvait pas supporter la fumée des cigarettes.
6. Ces clients ont dû sortir de l'hôtel à cause de la pollution de l'air.
7. Madame Lecuvier aurait dû se plaindre.
8. L'examen va être difficile.
9. Jacques devait préparer cet examen avant demain.
10. Ces livres appartiennent à son camarade de chambre.

Mise en œuvre 21 B

Questions avec *est-ce-que* et inversion

Changez les phrases suivantes en questions en employant: (a) l'intonation, (b) **est-ce que,** (c) l'inversion et (d) **n'est-ce pas?**

EXEMPLE

Il est mécanicien.

(a) Il est mécanicien?

(b) **Est-ce qu'**il est mécanicien?

(c) **Est-il** mécanicien?

(d) Il est mécanicien, **n'est-ce pas?**

1. Elle est catholique.
2. Il fait beau aujourd'hui.
3. Il comprend les affaires de la Bourse.
4. Il prit un T.G.V. pour Marseille.
5. Il chercha un taxi devant la gare.
6. Il descendit à l'Hôtel Métropole.
7. Il discutait de la programmation des ingénieurs.
8. Ils lui firent voir un nouveau modèle d'ordinateur.
9. On parlait français et italien pendant la réunion.
10. Ils s'intéressaient aux idées d'un professeur suédois.

21.7   Negative questions

As with regular negation, the VERB UNIT is placed inside the **ne . . . pas** "sandwich." If you wish to make a negative question, first form a question; then (always the last thing), make it negative.

EXAMPLE 1

STATEMENT	Il fait souvent de l'alpinisme.	VERB UNIT = **fait**
QUESTION	**Fait-il** souvent de l'alpinisme?	VERB UNIT = **fait-il**
NEGATIVE	**Ne** fait-il **pas** souvent de l'alpinisme?	

EXAMPLE 2

STATEMENT	Vous vous êtes couché de bonne heure.
VERB UNIT	Vous **vous êtes** couché de bonne heure.
INVERSION	**Vous êtes** -vous couché de bonne heure?

—— SUBJECT PRONOUN

NEW VERB UNIT **Vous êtes-vous** couché de bonne heure?

When a pronoun is attached by a hyphen to a verb unit, that pronoun becomes a part of the new verb unit.

NEGATIVE   Ne ⎪vous êtes-vous⎪ pas couché de bonne heure?

EXAMPLE 3

QUESTION   Claude s'est-elle déjà levée?

NEGATIVE   Claude ne s'est-elle pas encore[4] levée?

Mise en œuvre 21 C _____

Interrogation négative

Changez les phrases suivantes en (a) une question et ensuite en (b) une question négative, selon l'exemple.

EXEMPLE

Ton camarade de chambre est facile à vivre[5].

(a) Ton camarade de chambre **est-il** facile à vivre?

(b) Ton camarade de chambre **n'est-il pas** facile à vivre?

1. Il se lève quand le réveil sonne.
2. Il fait son lit tous les jours.
3. Il préparait le petit déjeuner tous les matins.
4. Nous discutons aimablement de nos problèmes.
5. Roland est très gentil aussi.
6. Il a une belle auto.
7. Il transportait ses amis à l'école.
8. Les jeunes filles aiment bien nous accompagner.
9. Nous nous sommes bien amusés au parc d'attractions[6].
10. Les étudiants ont de la chance.
11. Bernard va faire une visite à sa petite amie à Dijon.
12. Il s'est dépêché d'aller à l'aéroport.
13. Il va être irrité si l'avion est en retard.
14. Il faut que les jeunes aient une voiture.
15. Beaucoup de voisins se sont réunis au parc pour célébrer.
16. Mon camarade et moi nous nous efforçons de manger à des heures régulières.

[4] In negation **déjà** always becomes **pas . . . encore** (*not yet*).
[5] **facile à vivre** = *easy to get along with*
[6] **le parc d'attractions** = *amusement park*. One of the attractions might be **les montagnes russes** (*roller coaster*).

QUESTION WORDS BEFORE COMPLETE STATEMENTS

21.8   In search of further information: question words with *est-ce que*

The well-known questions of the reporter (**who, what, where, when, why**) are the basis of these interrogatives that may be placed before **est-ce que** + NORMAL STATEMENT. Notice that the statement contains subject and verb, and is *not subject* to a question such as **who** or **what**. *John is reading a book* is complete. You cannot ask *who*, or *what*, since that information is already contained in the statement. However, you can ask any of the questions shown below:

Pourquoi	*Why*		
Comment	*How*		
Quand	*When*		
Où	*Where*	est-ce que +	**STATEMENT** WITH SUBJECT AND VERB
(à[7]) qui	*(to) whom*		
Quel(le)[8] [NOUN]	*What*		
A quelle heure	*At what time*		

Pourquoi	est-ce que	l'ordinateur ne fonctionne pas?
Comment	est-ce que	l'informaticien s'appelle?
Quand	est-ce que	le directeur va revenir au bureau?
Où	est-ce qu'	il est allé?
Qu'	est-ce que	nous allons faire sans l'ordinateur?

21.9   Question words with inversion

The same question words may be used before a question *without* **est-ce que**, in which case *inversion must be used:*

Pourquoi	l'ordinateur ne **fonctionne-t-il** pas?
Comment	l'informaticien **s'appelle-t-il?**
Quand	le directeur **va-t-il** revenir au bureau?
Où	**est-il** allé?
Qu'	**allons-nous** faire sans ordinateur?

[7] Or any appropriate preposition: **A qui *est-ce que* Jean lit un livre?**
[8] e.g., **Quel livre est-ce que Jean lit?**

21.10   *Qui et Que* (*Who(m)* and *What*)

If your question cannot be framed as a complete statement, but starts with *who(m)* or *what*, the words to be used are **qui** (*who, whom*) and **que** (**qu'**) (*what*).

Either the inversion method or the long form can be used. See the following examples.

A.   With inversion. If you pose your question with inversion, the short forms **qui** or **que** (**qu'**) are all that is needed.

Qui a pris les billets?	*Who bought the tickets?*
Qui cherchez-vous?	*Whom are you looking for?*
Que font-ils?	*What are they doing?*
Qu'avez-vous?	*What's the matter?*

NOTE: **qui** is never elided, while **que** becomes **qu'** before a vowel.

B.   Long form with normal word order. The same questions may be formed using long forms. The four long forms incorporate **est-ce** as the middle term, a head word that conveys *meaning*, a tail word that conveys usage. The use of **est-ce** reminds you to retain normal word order (subject first, then predicate).

Qui *est-ce* **que** vous cherchez?	*Whom are you looking for?*
Qu' *est-ce* **qu'** ils font?	*What are they doing?*
Qu' *est-ce* **qui** est sur la table?	*What is on the table?*

TAIL WORD

HEAD WORD

C.   Long and short forms.

		❶	❷
MEANING	SHORT FORM	LONG FORM + NORMAL WORD ORDER	
Who?	**Qui**	**Qui** est-ce **qui** = **QUI** alone	
		Qui est-ce **que**	
What?	**Que** (**Qu'**)	**Qu'** est-ce **qui**	
		Qu' est-ce **que**	

The *head word* ❶ in the long form conveys *all* the meaning (**qui** = *who* or *whom*; **que** (**qu'**) = *what*).

The *tail word* ❷ indicates the grammatical use of the long form: for the subject of the verb use **qui.** For the direct object of the verb use **que.**

Examples of the fill-in type are useful for understanding this principle.

1. _____ regardez-vous?

- Here we see a hyphen. That short mark tells us "short form."
- To say *Whom*, use **Qui.**
  To say *What*, use **Que.**

Qui regardez-vous?   *Whom are you looking at?*

Que regardez-vous?   *What are you looking at?*

2. _____ vous cherchez? (*what*)

- No short mark (no hyphen): use the long form.
- Start with the word for *what*.
- Note that **cherchez** already has a subject (**vous**) that agrees with it. Another subject would be superfluous. Use the direct object ending **que:**

  What are you looking for?

Qu'est-ce que vous cherchez?

        └── USE (DIRECT OBJECT)

    └────── MEANING

3. _____ est dans cette boîte?

- *What* is wanted.
- No hyphen, so use long form. Start with **Qu'est-ce** for *What*.
- *Check verb:* Does **est** have a subject? Since the answer is no, the tail word supplies the subject **qui.**

Qu'est-ce qui est dans cette boîte?

        └── SUBJECT OF **est**

    └────── MEANING *what*

QUESTIONS BEGINNING WITH A PREPOSITION

21.11   Questions beginning with a preposition

After an initial preposition, use **qui** for people, **quoi** for things. This situation occurs when the verbal structure includes a preposition (such as **avoir besoin** *de*, **penser** *à*).

PREPOSITION + *WHOM*	A[9] **qui**
PREPOSITION + *WHAT*	A[9] **quoi**

[9] Or any other preposition such as **avec, de, pour.**

Avec **qui** allez-vous au concert?	*With whom are you going to the concert?*
A **qui** penses-tu?	*About whom are you thinking?*
De **quoi** as-tu besoin?	*What do you need?*
Sur **quoi** a-t-il laissé la boîte?	*On what did he leave the box?*
Pour **qui** ont-ils fait cela?	*For whom did they do that?*

The same questions may be used with **est-ce que** [21.2]. First the prepositional phrase, then **est-ce que,** then the rest of the sentence in normal order:

Avec qui *est-ce que* vous allez au concert?

A qui *est-ce que* tu penses?

De quoi *est-ce que* tu as besoin?

De qui *est-ce que* tu parles?

Mise en œuvre 21 D _____

Le détective

Posez une question à laquelle la partie en italique serait la bonne réponse. Employez l'inversion et **est-ce que.**

EXEMPLE

Lucien veut se coucher parce qu'*il a sommeil.*

Pourquoi Lucien veut-il se coucher?

Pourquoi est-ce que Lucien veut se coucher?

1. Paul étudie la littérature russe *parce qu'il s'intéresse à Tolstoï.*
2. Il parle *très bien* le russe.
3. Il discute avec des amis quand *ils sont de bonne humeur.*
4. Ses amis préfèrent étudier *dans la bibliothèque.*
5. *Son professeur* admire l'œuvre de Dostoïevski.
6. Il aime surtout *le roman « Crime et châtiment ».*
7. Les autres étudiants préfèrent *la musique russe.*
8. Le concert symphonique a lieu à la Salle Pleyel *à huit heures.*
9. Il faut prendre *les billets* tout de suite.
10. Jean doute *que Heinz veuille nous accompagner.*
11. Heinz est allé au bistrot avec[10] *des amis allemands.*
12. Nous[11] avons besoin d'*argent.*

[10] Retenez tous les mots qui ne sont pas en italique.
[11] Répondez en employant **vous.** (*What do you need?*)

13. Je dois me passer de *sandwiches*[12].
14. Bernard a laissé un pourboire sur *la table*.
15. Je pensais à *l'argent que j'avais perdu à Monte Carlo*.

Reflets

Duke Ellington[13]

Pratique: Composez douze questions basées sur les parties en italique et numérotées dans la sélection ci-dessous. Les mots en italique doivent être les réponses à vos questions.

    L'œuvre d'Ellington[1], où l'on se plaisait à retrouver la technique harmonique de Debussy, avait donc évolué lentement vers une sorte d'idéal esthétique par la parfaite adaptation de la matière et de la forme. Assez ingénument *les arrangeurs swing*[2] crurent pouvoir atteindre d'emblée au même résultat en pillant *la musique classique*[3] d'une manière fort sommaire. Dans le cas présent, ils l'ont fait en l'adaptant à la formule orchestrale du jazz et en y appliquant tout simplement *le balancement swing*[4].

    Au demeurant, *tant en Europe qu'aux Etats-Unis*[5], le jazz et la musique classique se rejoignaient. Certains compositeurs modernes, s'inspirant des formules et des accents du jazz, et certains chefs d'orchestres jazz demandaient des arrangements *à des compositeurs de musique classique*[6] (Woody Herman à Stravinsky). Pour en arriver là, *le jazz*[7] avait dû subir une évolution similaire à celle que la musique symphonique a suivie au cours des derniers siècles. Il appliquait *spontanément*[8] les qualités que *la révolution Debussyste*[9] a admirées: la recherche de l'expression directe, la fuite de toute emphase, de toute rhétorique. *Les apôtres du formalisme swing*[10] avaient tenté de modérer son expressionnisme. Néanmoins *il*[11] était devenu, sous ses aspects les plus purs, une musique romantique, lyrique ou simplement passionnée. Aussi chercha-t-on *des Stravinsky*[12].

---

[12] Répondez en employant **vous** ou **tu**.
[13] *Le Jazz*, Paris, copyright © 1959, Marabout Flash.

22

Pronoms relatifs I
Interrogatives *quel / lequel*
lire / écrire

PRONOMS RELATIFS I

22.1 Use

A relative pronoun is used to join two sentences dealing with the same subject. In the second of the two sentences, the relative pronoun replaces a noun already used in the first sentence. (We shall call this the *repetitious noun,* or RN.) For example:

TWO SENTENCES	I am looking for **my pen. My pen** was on the table.
	REPEATED NOUN
TWO CLAUSES	I am looking for my pen, **which** was on the table.
	MAIN CLAUSE subordinate clause

In this example, both original sentences deal with the same topic, *my pen.* In the new sentence, *my pen* was replaced by the relative pronoun *which.* This joins the two sentences into a single one. Each of the original sentences became a *clause:* the first is the *main clause;* the second, containing the relative pronoun, is the *subordinate clause*.

In French the same system applies, and using the same example, we have:

TWO SENTENCES	Je cherche **mon stylo. Mon stylo** était sur la table.
TWO CLAUSES	Je cherche mon stylo **qui** était sur la table.
	RELATIVE PRONOUN

264

To select the correct relative pronoun, determine whether the repeated noun in the sentence to be used as a subordinate clause is the *subject, direct object*, or *object of a preposition* in that sentence. Here we are dealing only with relative pronouns replacing a subject (**qui**) or direct object (**que**).

22.2   Subject of a clause: *qui*

If the repeated noun in the subordinate clause is the subject, it is replaced by **qui**.

Voilà le professeur. **Le professeur** arrive en ce moment.
Voilà le professeur   **qui**   arrive en ce moment.
                            ↑   ↑
                        SUBJECT   VERB

Voici un devoir. **Le devoir** est difficile.
Voici un devoir   **qui**   est difficile.

The RN may equally well be a *pronoun* representing a noun in the main clause.

Je cherche un homme. **Il** parle chinois.   (Il = un homme)
Je cherche un homme **qui** parle chinois.

22.3   Direct object of a clause: *que (qu')*

When the repeated noun in the subordinate clause is the direct object, it is replaced by **que** (in front of a vowel sound, **qu'**). This word must be moved to the beginning of the clause, while the other words remain in place.

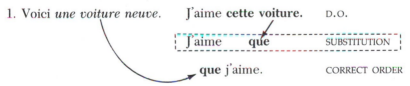

1. Voici *une voiture neuve.*   J'aime **cette voiture.**   D.O.

         J'aime   **que**   SUBSTITUTION

              que j'aime.   CORRECT ORDER

Voici une **voiture** neuve **que** j'aime.
Here's a new car that I like.

2. Où est *ce livre?*   J'ai perdu **le livre.**   D.O.

         J'ai perdu   **que**   SUBSTITUTION

              que j'ai perdu.   CORRECT ORDER

Où est **le livre que** j'ai perdu?
Where is the book [that] I lost?

If the noun replaced is plural or feminine singular, and a compound tense is being used in the subordinate clause, the past participle must now agree in gender and number with the noun. By placing the direct object **que** at the head of the subordinate clause, you are creating a PDO [1.4].

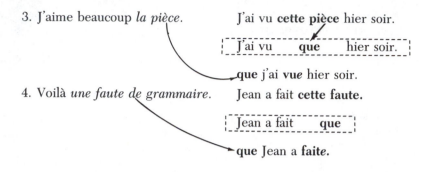

3. J'aime beaucoup *la pièce.*   J'ai vu **cette pièce** hier soir.

J'ai vu   **que**   hier soir.

que j'ai **vue** hier soir.

4. Voilà *une faute de grammaire.*   Jean a fait **cette faute.**

Jean a fait   **que**

que Jean a **faite.**

ATTENTION! Look out for the missing *that.*

English sentences often omit the direct object relative pronoun *that*; but in French the word **que** cannot be left out. Be alert for such sentences. The empty brackets below show the location of the missing *that*:

There is the man [   ] *my father employed.*
Voilà l'homme **que** mon père a employé.

The girls [   ] *you saw are students.*
Les jeunes filles **que** vous avez vues sont des étudiantes.

22.4   Position of the subordinate clause

The subordinate clause always fits into the main clause immediately after the repeated noun.

Le livre est sur la table. Vous cherchiez **ce livre.**

Here, the repeated noun is **le livre**[1]. Place a caret (∧) in the main clause after this word to remind you where the subordinate clause must be placed. The first step looks like this:

Le livre ∧ est sur la table. Vous cherchiez **que.**

The second clause must be placed in correct order by moving **que** to the beginning: *que vous cherchiez.* Then the whole subordinate clause goes into place where the caret was placed:

---

[1] It does not make any difference that this is **ce livre** in the second sentence; modifiers such as **ce, mon, ton,** etc., do not affect the choice of the relative pronoun.

Le livre *que vous cherchiez* est sur la table.

It is important to place the subordinate clause in this way; otherwise the whole meaning of the sentence may be altered.

22.5   Simplified rule: *qui* or *que*?

Although the following information is not strictly a grammatical rule, it is helpful to many students. Knowing that a subject is usually in the initial position in a sentence, use **qui** in the subordinate clause if the repeated noun is first in the sentence; if the repeated noun comes later in the sentence (after the verb), it is probably a direct object, and you may use **que** (to be switched to the beginning as outlined above).

As a mnemonic device, use the following:

REPLACING A NOUN	IN THE NEW CLAUSE IT IS:
INITIAL WORD: qu**I**	[followed by a VERB]
END WORD: qu**E**	[followed by a NOUN or PRONOUN[2]]

Thus, when combining the following sentences:

Voilà une voiture. Jean a acheté *cette voiture*.

Voiture is the repeated noun, so **que** is used because it is at the end of the sentence.

Voilà la voiture *que* Jean a acheté**e**.

22.6   Cautions in using *que*

A.   Notice that **que** becomes **qu'** in front of a vowel sound. This never happens with **qui.** An automatic PDO[3] exists when **que** (**qu'**) appears at the beginning of a clause, and you must pay attention to the agreement of the past participle.

Voilà la voiture **qu'Alain** a acheté.

———— ANTECEDENT OF **que**

---

[2] Sometimes in literature, a noun subject is inverted after **que.** Notice the following:
   Voilà le guide que les touristes cherchent. might appear as:
   Voilà le guide *que cherchent* **les touristes.**
      There is the guide that the tourists are looking for.
The verb form **cherchent** makes it obvious that the subject is plural.
Compare with: **Voilà le guide qui cherche les touristes.**

[3] (*Preceding direct object*)

B.   The difference in meaning between **qui** and **que** is critical, as in the following example, where the verb form is not helpful:

Voilà le lion **que** tua le professeur.

Voilà le lion **qui** tua le professeur.

Which was killed in which sentence? In converting to English, remember that after **que** you *must find the next noun* before stating a verb (first example). With **qui** the word order remains the same in English and French.

Mise en œuvre 22 A

Propositions subordonnées

Formez une proposition subordonnée avec chaque phrase. Commencez la proposition principale par **Voilà** + [les mots en italique]; ensuite complétez la phrase en employant le pronom relatif **qui** ou **que.**

EXEMPLE

Je regarde *les photos*.

Voilà les photos **que** je regarde.

1. *Le train* part toujours à l'heure.
2. Nous attendons *le train*.
3. Nous attendons *le train* depuis vingt minutes.
4. *Le capitaine* fume une pipe.
5. *Le patron* dort devant le café.
6. Jean a acheté *la maison blanche*.
7. *Ce client* a commandé une tarte.
8. Ce client a commandé *une tarte*.
9. Pascal a inventé *la machine à calculer*.
10. *Jacques* a posé une question difficile.
11. Jacques a posé *une question difficile*.
12. *Le professeur* vient d'arriver.

Mise en œuvre 22 B

Les phrases complexes

Combinez les deux phrases en employant un pronom relatif (**qui** ou **que**). La première phrase deviendra la proposition principale (*main clause*).

EXEMPLE

(a) Jean a une auto.

(b) L'auto a coûté cher.

Jean a une auto **qui** a coûté cher.

1. (a) Marie est une étudiante sérieuse.
   (b) Marie est absente aujourd'hui.
2. (a) La machine est dans cette boîte.
   (b) Vous cherchez la machine.
3. (a) J'ai déjà lu ce roman.
   (b) Vous m'avez prêté ce roman.
4. (a) Jean-Paul prépare son exposé.
   (b) Jean-Paul a l'air hostile.
5. (a) J'ai besoin d'argent.
   (b) Mon père m'a promis cet argent.
6. (a) Les questions sont très difficiles.
   (b) Notre professeur pose les questions.
7. (a) La clé est dans cette boîte.
   (b) Vous cherchiez cette clé hier.
8. (a) Les Lebrun ont une maison à la campagne.
   (b) Nous avons vu leur maison l'été passé.
9. (a) L'avion part de l'aéroport Charles de Gaulle.
   (b) Nous prenons cet avion.
10. (a) La pièce sera jouée à la Comédie-Française.
    (b) Nous allons voir cette pièce demain soir.

Mise en œuvre 22 C

Pronoms relatifs *qui* et *que*

Combinez les deux phrases au moyen d'un pronom relatif. La première phrase doit être la proposition principale.

EXEMPLE

L'avion est en retard. **Il vient d'atterrir.**

L'avion **qui vient d'atterrir** est en retard.

1. Le train est un T.G.V. Il va partir dans dix minutes.
2. Le billet a coûté cher. Vous avez pris le billet.
3. L'aéroport est loin de la ville. Vous cherchez l'aéroport.
4. Le vol à destination de Genève arrive. Vous attendez ce vol depuis deux heures.

5. Marie travaille dans un petit café à Marseille. Elle est serveuse.
6. Le garçon de café a vingt-deux ans. Il est en train de laver les verres.
7. Les étudiants entendent la sonnerie. La sonnerie annonce la fin de chaque classe.
8. Les calculs sont exacts. Nous les avons préparés au moyen de l'ordinateur.
9. Les affaires des bureaux du gouvernement sont facilitées par des ordinateurs. Vous avez vu ces ordinateurs à l'exposition IBM.
10. Le car arrive devant la gare. Nous devons prendre ce car pour aller à l'aéroport.

INTERROGATIFS **QUEL, LEQUEL**

22.7   Interrogative adjective *quel,-le*

The interrogative adjective **quel** has four forms (like other adjectives) so that it may agree with the noun that follows it. It is regular in formation:

	MASCULINE	FEMININE
SINGULAR	quel	quelle
PLURAL	quels	quelles

Quel **film** est-ce que tu as vu?

Quels **livres** as-tu choisis?

Quelle **voiture** as-tu prise?

Quelles **leçons** faut-il préparer pour demain?

When a form of **quel** is separated from the following noun, agreement must still be made:

Quelle est votre **adresse?**

Quel est le **prix** de ce dictionnaire?

In indirect questions, **quel** is used in such expressions as:

Dis-moi **quelle pièce de théâtre** tu as vue.

22.8   Interrogative pronoun *lequel* [*which one*]

The interrogative pronoun **lequel** has four forms. Select the proper form to agree in gender and number with the noun you are asking about.

	MASCULINE	FEMININE	MEANING
SINGULAR	lequel	laquelle	*which one*
PLURAL	lesquels	lesquelles	*which ones*

If you expect a singular noun as an answer, the singular form is used; if you expect a plural noun as an answer, use the plural form.

Vous pouvez prendre **un** de ces livres. **Lequel** voulez-vous?
*You can take one of these books. Which **one** do you want?*

Vous pouvez prendre **deux** de ces livres. **Lesquels** voulez-vous?
*You can take two of these books. Which **ones** do you want?*

Voilà trois voitures neuves. **Laquelle** préférez-vous?
*There are three new cars. Which **one** do you prefer?*

Notice that **lequel** (being a pronoun) can be used alone, while **quel** (being an adjective) must be followed by a noun.

Un de ces livres est à vous. **Lequel?**
*One of these books is yours. **Which?** (**Which one?**)*

To ask *which one of* [N *pl.*] add **de** plus the article or adjective accompanying the plural noun:

Lequel de ces romans as-tu lu?
Which [one] of these novels have you read?

Laquelle de ces pièces préférez-vous?
Which [one] of these plays do you prefer?

Lesquels de mes chats aimez-vous le mieux?
Which [ones] of my cats do you like best?

22.9   After a preposition (*dans laquelle . . . ?*)

For the interrogatives *with which, to which*, etc., use the appropriate form of **lequel** after the preposition:

Dans laquelle de ces maisons habitez-vous?
In which [one] of these houses do you live?

Avec lesquels des étudiants avez-vous parlé?
With which [ones] of the students did you speak?

Contractions of **à** and **de** occur in the usual way with the **le/les** part of **lequel, lesquels,** and **lesquelles.** Thus **à** + **lequel** results in **auquel** (*to which*); **de** + **lesquels** becomes **desquels** (*of which*), etc.

Auquel de ces romans pensez-vous?
Which one of these novels are you thinking about?

Auxquelles de ces clientes avez-vous répondu?
Which ones of those customers did you answer?

Remember that there is no contraction with **la,** hence none with **laquelle**:

A laquelle des pièces de Molière penses-tu?

Mise en œuvre 22 D

Interrogatifs *quel* et *lequel*

Complétez les questions suivantes en ajoutant la forme appropriée de **quel** ou de **lequel.**

EXEMPLE

_____ de vos tantes sont à Paris?

Lesquelles de vos tantes sont à Paris?

1. _____ de vos cours à l'université sont les plus difficiles?
2. _____ est le prix de cette revue?
3. _____ de vos amies est la plus sympathique?
4. _____ scène de Shakespeare est entièrement en français?
5. _____ des scènes de Shakespeare sont situées à Venise?
6. À _____ des poèmes de Charles Baudelaire pensez-vous? *Le Voyage?*
7. De _____ des dictionnaires as-tu besoin? *Le Petit Robert?*
8. Dans _____ des pièces avez-vous installé votre téléviseur?
9. _____ symphonies de Haydn trouvez-vous les plus belles?
10. _____ s'appelle *la Symphonie militaire?*

Mise en œuvre 22 E

Jeu d'interrogation: Quelle est la question?

Vous entendez la réponse à une question. Quelle est la question qui y correspond? Employez des formes de **quel, lequel** s'il est possible; ou, avec une préposition, **qui, quoi** [21.11].

EXEMPLE

RÉPONSE:	J'aime les chats, les chiens et les chevaux.
QUESTION:	**Quels animaux** aimes-tu?
RÉPONSE:	De tous les romans de Balzac, je pense à *Père Goriot*.
QUESTION:	**Auquel des romans** de Balzac est-ce que tu penses?

1. Mon adresse est 64, rue de Londres.
2. Mon numéro de téléphone est 333 57 92.
3. Je suis un cours d'anglais, un cours de psychologie et un cours de maths.
4. De ces trois cours je préfère le cours de psychologie.
5. Monsieur Lefèvre est mon professeur favori.
6. Le film que j'ai vu hier s'intitulait *La Belle et la bête*.
7. Les étudiantes qui m'ont accompagné étaient Jeanne, Catherine et Monique.
8. De toutes les étudiantes, il n'y a que Jeanne et Monique qui comprennent cette théorie.
9. Elles habitent dans la plus petite de ces maisons là-bas.
10. La pièce de théâtre que j'aime le mieux c'est *La Folle de Chaillot*.
11. Je pense au prochain concert rock.
12. Il y a un train à 13 h, un autre à 14 h 20 et un troisième à 20 h. Je vais prendre le train de 13 h.
13. Le prix d'un billet aller-retour est de 90 francs.
14. De tous ces romans, c'est aux romans policiers que je m'intéresse le plus.
15. Je vais lire celui de Georges Simenon qui s'intitule *Un Crime en Hollande*.

VERBE IRRÉULIER ÉCRIRE

22.10 Verbe irrégulier *écrire* (*to write*)

Review the forms of this verb in Appendix C, Table 11. Conjugated in the same way are **décrire** (*to describe*), **s'inscrire** (*to register, to sign up*), and **récrire** (*to rewrite*).

PRÉSENT	j' **écris**	nous **écrivons**
	tu **écris**	vous **écrivez**
	il **écrit**	ils **écrivent**

⌐NOTE **-v** IN PLURAL FORMS

IMPARFAIT	REGULAR STEM: **écriv-** from present tense **nous**-form

Autrefois **j'écrivais** à ma petite amie tous les jours.
*Formerly I **used to write** my girlfriend every day.*

PASSÉ COMPOSÉ	PAST PARTICIPLE **écrit** AUXILIARY: (avoir)

Hier **j'ai écrit** une composition.

PASSÉ SIMPLE	STEM: **écriv-** + **is** system of endings. [20.2]
	Il **écrivit** son nom quand il s'inscrivit.
FUTUR	FC STEM: **écrir-** (+ future endings)
	Si j'ai le temps **je t'écrirai** demain.
CONDITIONNEL	FC STEM: **écrir-** (+ imperfect endings)
	Si j'avais le temps **j'écrirais** un roman policier.
SUBJONCTIF	STEMS: **écriv-** (1-stem verb)

que j' **écrive**	que nous **écrivions**
que tu **écrives**	que vous **écriviez**
qu'il **écrive**	qu'ils **écrivent**

Je doute **qu'elle écrive** un chèque.
I doubt that she will write a check.

Qu'est-ce qu'on écrit?   Une note, un mémorandum, une lettre, une demande d'emploi, un essai, un exercice, une communication, un conte, un dialogue, un brouillon[4]. On **remplit** une fiche, un questionnaire, un formulaire. On écrit les renseignements demandés dans le questionnaire.

La personne qui écrit est l'écrivain. Il y a des noms spécialisés pour certains écrivains: le journaliste, le romancier, le poète.

22.11   Verbe irrégulier *lire* (*to read*)

Review the forms of this verb in Appendix C, Table 16.

NOTE ADDED **-s-** IN STEM

PRÉSENT	je **lis**	nous **lisons**
	tu **lis**	vous **lisez**
	il **lit**	ils **lisent**
IMPARFAIT	REGULAR STEM: **lis-** from **nous**-form present tense
	Autrefois **je lisais** le journal tous les jours.
PASSÉ COMPOSÉ	PAST PARTICIPLE: **lu** AUXILIARY: (avoir)
	Hier **j'ai lu** un poème de Mallarmé.
PASSÉ SIMPLE	STEM: **l-** + **us** system of endings. [20.2]
	Il **lut** la brochure avant de choisir cet hôtel.
FUTUR	FC STEM: **lir-** (+ future endings)
	Si j'ai le temps **je lirai** *Le Bruit et la fureur* de Faulkner.
CONDITIONNEL	FC STEM: **lir-** (+ imperfect endings)
	Si j'avais le temps **je lirais** *Guerre et paix*.

[4] = *Rough draft*

Reflets

Noir sur blanc

Dans **une librairie** on peut *acheter* des livres, tandis qu'à **la bibliothèque** on *emprunte* des livres après avoir consulté le fichier. Il y a d'habitude une bonne sélection. On peut choisir un **roman**, un **livre technique**, un **livre de référence**, une **biographie**, un **recueil de poésie** ou **de contes**, une **traité philosophique** ou **psychologique.** Il ne faut pas oublier les journaux spécialisés, les périodiques. La plupart des livres sont **reliés,** mais à la librairie il y a aussi beaucoup de livres **brochés,** comme les livres de poche. L'employé d'une librairie s'appelle **le** (ou **la**) **libraire.** Celui qui travaille à la bibliothèque est **le** (ou **la**) **bibliothécaire.**

Parmi les romans on peut choisir **un roman romantique, un roman psychologique, un roman policier, un roman historique, un roman d'aventure,** ou bien une œuvre de **science-fiction.**

Dans les livres de référence figurent les dictionnaires, les atlas, les encyclopédies, et des manuels spécialisés qui existent pour les collectionneurs, les bricoleurs, les enfants.

Sujets de composition ou de conversation

Quels livres avez-vous lus? Parlez d'un de ces livres, en employant au moins deux fois les pronoms relatifs **qui** et **que,** aussi bien que les verbes **lire** et **écrire.**

Par exemple on pourrait commencer ainsi: « La semaine passée j'ai acheté un livre que j'aime beaucoup. Le titre en est *L'Etranger.* L'auteur, qui est né en Algérie, s'appelle Albert Camus. . . .» et ainsi de suite.

Où l'action se passe-t-elle? Qui est le personnage principal? Quels autres personnages figurent dans l'intrigue? Quels sont les événements les plus intéressants? Quel problème se pose? Quel en est le dénouement? Qu'est-ce qu'on peut dire au sujet du style? Pourquoi est-ce que vous recommandez (ou ne recommandez pas) ce livre aux autres? Citez le texte pour appuyer ce que vous dites.

Libre à vous de choisir un roman, une pièce de théâtre, un conte, un poème, un essai, un journal, un article scientifique, ou n'importe quel passage littéraire ou journalistique.

23

Pronoms relatifs II
dont / où / lequel

23.1 Priority of prepositional phrases as relative connectors

We started with the relative pronouns **qui** and **que** as replacements for a repeated noun or pronoun in a subordinate clause. However, there is a consideration that *takes priority* over **qui** (subject) and **que** (direct object); if the repeated noun is *part of a prepositional phrase,* the rules in the following sections apply.

The most common preposition that may precede a RN is **de** or a form of **de** (**du, des, de l'**). The replacement is **dont** as described in 23.2. Other possibilities are then taken up in the order shown on the analysis chart [23.8].

23.2 Relative pronoun *dont*

If the repeated noun in the subordinate clause is preceded by a form of the preposition **de**, replace the entire prepositional phrase by **dont.**

EXAMPLE **1**

TO BE JOINED: Voilà le dictionnaire. J'ai besoin de ce dictionnaire.

RN IDENTIFIED: Voilà le dictionnaire∧. J'ai besoin **de *ce dictionnaire.***

276

de-PHRASE REPLACED: Voilà le dictionnaire∧. J'ai besoin . . . (**dont**)

CORRECT ORDER: Voilà le dictionnaire | **dont *j'ai besoin.*** |

EXAMPLE 2

L'université a un nouvel ordinateur. Claude s'est servi de l'ordinateur.

L'université a un nouvel ordinateur∧. Claude s'est servi **de *l'ordinateur.***

L'université a un nouvel ordinateur | **dont *Claude s'est servi.*** |

EXAMPLE 3   (Notice the importance of the caret.)

Le professeur est arrivé. Tu as parlé de ce professeur.

Le professeur∧ est arrivé. Tu as parlé | **de *ce professeur.*** |

Le professeur∧ | **dont *tu as parlé*** | est arrivé.

23.3   Use of *où* for location or time

When a prepositional phrase containing the RN expresses a location or a time, **où** may be used to replace the entire phrase.

Voilà **la maison.** Mon père est né **dans cette maison.**   PREPOSITIONAL PHRASE INDICATING LOCATION

Voilà la maison **dans laquelle** mon père est né.

or   Voilà la maison   **où**   mon père est né.

Prepositions such as **à, chez, dans, sous, sur, devant, derrière** and others introduce phrases indicating location that may be replaced by **où**:

Voilà la boutique. Paul a stationné la voiture **devant cette boutique.**

Voilà la boutique $\left\{ \begin{array}{c} \textbf{devant laquelle} \\ \textbf{où} \end{array} \right\}$ Paul a stationné la voiture.

To indicate *from where*, use **d'où:**

Voilà le musée. Alain revient **du musée.**

Voilà le musée **d'où** revient Alain.

Notice the inversion of subject and verb in the prepositional phrase of the last sentence. Inversion often occurs after a relative pronoun when the subject is a noun rather than a personal pronoun.

TIME. The word *when* is conveyed by **où** (not **quand**) directly after a noun:

NOUN

Il pleuvait $\boxed{le\ jour}$ **où** je suis allé à Chantilly.
It was raining on the day (when) I went to Chantilly.

When there is no noun antecedent, **quand** may be used:

VERB

Il $\boxed{pleuvait}$ **quand** je suis allé à Chantilly.

PRONOM DEVANT **QUI, LEQUEL**

23.4 Object of a preposition other than *de,* a time or location

If the RN in the prepositional phrase is the designation of a *person*, use **qui** after the preposition. Retain the preposition.

Voilà la bibliothécaire. J'ai parlé *avec cette bibliothécaire* hier.
Voilà la bibliothécaire **avec qui** j'ai parlé hier.

If the RN in the prepositional phrase is a *thing*, use a form of **lequel:**

La table est ronde. J'ai mis la lettre sur cette table.
La table∧ est ronde. J'ai mis la lettre *sur cette table*.
La table ∧ **sur laquelle** j'ai mis la lettre est ronde.

The form of **lequel** used must agree with the gender and number of the repeated noun. In addition, when the preposition is **à**, the usual contractions apply to the **le**- and **les**- parts of **lequel**. The available forms are listed below in section 23.5.

23.5 Forms of *lequel*

The pronoun **lequel** has two components (**le/quel**), both of which must agree in gender and number with the noun replaced in a prepositional phrase. The forms are:

	MASCULINE	FEMININE
SINGULAR	*lequel*	*laquelle*
PLURAL	*lesquels*	*lesquelles*

When the preposition **à** precedes, contraction occurs [1.3]. Thus **à** + **lequel** becomes **auquel.** The forms involved are:

m.s.	m.pl.	(f.s.)	f.pl.
auquel	*auxquels*	**à laquelle** (NO CONTRACTION)	*auxquelles*

Voilà la maison **dans laquelle** Victor Hugo est né.
There is the house Victor Hugo was born in.

Voici le roman **auquel** je pensais.
Here is the novel I was thinking about.

NOTE: After a preposition, **qui** for *persons*, a form of **lequel** for *things*.

Similar contractions exist when the preposition is **de** (such as **duquel**, **desquelles**), but they can all be replaced by **dont**.

23.6   Use of *lequel* in reference to persons

After the prepositions **entre** *(between)*, **parmi** *(among)* and **sans** *(without)*, you may use **lequel** instead of **qui.**

Voilà un professeur. Je ne réussirais pas **sans ce professeur.**

Voilà un professeur **sans lequel** je ne réussirais pas.
There is a teacher without whom I would not pass.

23.7   Supplied antecedent *ce*

When a relative pronoun does not have an antecedent, supply **ce.** Notice the difference between these two examples:

1. Voilà *la voiture* **que** je veux.   (Antecedent: *voiture*)
2. Voilà   *ce*   **que** je veux.   (Supplied antecedent: *ce*)
    *That is **what** I want.*

The meaning of **ce** + relative pronoun is always *what*. It is used only for things, not people, as in the following examples:

3. Je sais **ce qui** arrive[1].   *I know **what** is happening.*
4. Il sait **ce que** vous voulez.   *He knows **what** you want.*
5. Voilà **ce dont** tu as parlé.   *There is **what** you talked about.*

In (3), **qui** is used because the verb **arrive** needs a subject. In (4) **que** is the direct object of **voulez,** and because there is already a noun subject present; and (5) uses **dont** because **de** is needed with **parler** (**Tu as parlé** *de* **cela**). All of these relative pronouns lack an antecedent, therefore **ce** has been supplied.

If the relative pronoun appears at the beginning of a sentence, **ce** will always be the first word:

Ce que vous dites est vrai.   *What you say is true.*

Ce qui se passe est un désastre.   *What's happening is a disaster.*

Ce dont j'ai besoin c'est une chambre.   *What I need is a room.*

Sentences beginning with **ce qui, ce que,** or **ce dont** sometimes have an optional redundant **ce** in the second half:

Ce qui se passe [, **c'**]est un désastre.
Ce que vous faites [, **c'**]est votre affaire.

But this redundant **ce** *becomes mandatory* if the second clause contains **être** + a PLURAL NOUN or a PERSONAL PRONOUN:

Ce qui m'agace, **c'est lui** et sa vanité.   PERSONAL PRONOUN **lui**
What infuriates me is he and his vanity.

Ce que je cherche, **c'est [ce sont] des livres espagnols.** PLURAL NOUN
What I am looking for is some Spanish books.

---

[1] Without the **ce, Je sais qui arrive** means *I know who is arriving.*

23.8   Analytic chart for relative pronoun selection

STEP 1	Identify the RN (repeated noun in the clause) Place the ∧ marker in the main clause after the initial RN.

STEP 2	Is the RN the OBJECT OF A PREPOSITION?
	 If there is no obvious preposition, is there a "phantom[2]"?
	 If YES:
	 Is the preposition **de?** Use **dont** [23.2]
	 Does the phrase represent a
	    TIME or a LOCATION? Use **où** [23.3]
	 If neither of the above applies:
	 Use **qui** if the RN is a *person* [23.4]
	    ". . . la personne avec qui je parlais . . ."
	 Use a form of **lequel** if it is a *thing* [23.5]
	    ". . . la maison dans laquelle je suis né . . ."
	 If **NO** go to step 3.

STEP 3 Previous Chapter	Is the RN the SUBJECT of the subordinate clause? **If YES,** replace it by **qui.** [22.2] **If NO,** replace it by **que.** [22.3]
STEP 4	Place clause in correct order: relative pronoun first. Does the relative pronoun have an ANTECEDENT? (Is the word in front of the relative pronoun a noun?) If **YES,** *end of problem.* If **NO,** supply the antecedent **ce.** [23.7]

Mise en œuvre 23 A

Pronoms relatifs et prépositions

Combinez les deux phrases au moyen d'un pronom relatif (**qui, lequel, dont, où**). La phrase (a) est toujours la proposition principale.

EXEMPLE

(a) Le stylo est rouge.
(b) J'ai écrit cette lettre *avec ce stylo.*
Le stylo **avec lequel** j'ai écrit cette lettre est rouge.

[2] A "phantom" preposition is one that is required but not seen in a fill-in exercise such as:
   Voilà le livre _____ il a besoin.   Je vois la voiture _____ vous pensez.
   In each case notice that the structure after the blank contains a verbal expression requiring a preposition: **avoir besoin *de*, penser *à*.** This preposition automatically goes to the beginning of the subordinate clause: **Voilà le livre *dont* il a besoin. Je vois la voiture *à laquelle* vous pensez.** Always scan the part after the blank to see if there is a required preposition.

1. (a) Voilà la jeune fille.
   (b) J'ai dîné *avec cette jeune fille* hier soir.
2. (a) La bibliothèque est grande.
   (b) Robert a garé la voiture *derrière cette bibliothèque*.
3. (a) Jacques a acheté un dictionnaire.
   (b) Il a besoin *de ce dictionnaire* pour ses cours.
4. (a) La maison se trouve rue Royale.
   (b) Mme Legrand demeurait *dans cette maison*.
5. (a) Le théâtre est près d'ici.
   (b) Vous pensez *à ce théâtre*.
6. (a) Le professeur se trouve devant la bibliothèque.
   (b) Nous avons parlé *avec ce professeur* la semaine dernière.
7. (a) Donnez-moi le stylo, s'il vous plait.
   (b) Vous avez écrit vos devoirs avec ce stylo.
8. (a) La rue est étroite.
   (b) La maison du médecin se trouve dans cette rue.
9. (a) Voilà la valise.
   (b) J'ai oublié la clef de cette valise.
10. (a) Voilà le professeur.
    (b) Nous avons vu la femme de ce professeur à Monaco.

Mise en œuvre 23 B

Pronoms relatifs — Révision

Combinez les phrases au moyen du pronom relatif approprié.

1. (a) Voilà un homme distingué.
   (b) *Cet homme* travaille au ministère.
2. (a) Michel cherche la lettre.
   (b) Il a perdu *cette lettre* ce matin. (Attention à l'accord du PP.)
3. (a) Voilà le patron.
   (b) La femme *du patron* est actrice.
4. (a) Henri a lu une nouvelle *(short story)*.
   (b) Il aime beaucoup *cette nouvelle*.
5. (a) Voilà quelques-uns de mes amis.
   (b) *Sans ces amis* je ne parlerais jamais français.
6. (a) Alexandre est un étudiant sérieux.
   (b) Les problèmes *d'Alexandre* ne sont pas graves.
7. (a) Ce bruit est désagréable.
   (b) Mes voisins font *ce bruit*. (inversion needed [p. 267 footnote 2])
8. (a) Voilà le bus.
   (b) *Ce bus* part de la Porte Maillot à midi.

9. (a) Le directeur est dans son bureau.
   (b) Nous admirons le talent du directeur.
10. (a) Voilà le théâtre.
    (b) Monsieur Porra est le gérant de ce théâtre.
11. (a) Je connais cette dame.
    (b) La dame est assise près de la fenêtre.
12. (a) Nous cherchons le chien noir et blanc.
    (b) Mon voisin a perdu le chien.
13. (a) L'orchestre vient de commencer la symphonie.
    (b) Schubert a composé cette symphonie en 1828.
14. (a) Voilà le chien.
    (b) Le chien vous déteste.
15. (a) Voilà le chien.
    (b) Vous détestez le chien.

Mise en œuvre 23 C

Pronoms relatifs

Remplacez les tirets par le pronom relatif approprié.

EXEMPLES

Voilà la personne avec _____ vous avez parlé.

Voilà la personne **avec qui** vous avez parlé.

Le chien _____ vous a mordu est gris.

Le chien **qui** vous a mordu est gris.

1. La jeune fille _____ arrive en retard s'appelle Isabelle.
2. Le professeur _____ nous aimons bien enseigne la chimie.
3. La voiture _____ mon père a achetée est une Peugeot.
4. Voilà la tour _____ Guillaume a souvent parlé.
5. Le livre _____ j'ai besoin est une grammaire.
6. Voilà la voiture _____ je voudrais acheter.
7. Voilà _____ je voudrais acheter.
8. Je regarde _____ se passe dans la rue.
9. _____ je voudrais, c'est une motocyclette.
10. Le jeune homme avec _____ le patron parlait est avocat.
11. La maison devant _____ se tient la concierge est l'immeuble de Jean.
12. La musique _____ vous écoutez est la symphonie de César Franck.

Mise en œuvre 23 D _____

Phrases et pronoms relatifs

Composez une phrase pour la partie (a) et une autre pour la partie (b) de chaque problème, en utilisant les mots indiqués. Ajoutez les articles, partitifs, pronoms possessifs et verbes nécessaires. Faites les changements convenables. Ensuite, combinez les deux parties en une phrase (c) au moyen d'un pronom relatif. Attention aux indications de temps.

EXEMPLE

QUESTION:
(a) homme / s'appeler / Duplessis
(b) femme / de / homme / être / acteur

RÉPONSE:
(a) **Cet** homme **s'appelle M.** Duplessis.
(b) **La** femme de **cet** homme **est actrice.**
(c) Cet homme **dont la femme est actrice** s'appelle M. Duplessis.

1. (a) film / s'intituler / « Le Dernier Métro »
   (b) réalisateur / de / film / être / François Truffaut
2. (a) film / s'appeler / « Crime et Châtiment »
   (b) je / envie / voir / film
3. (a) Alfred Einstein / naître / allemagne / 1879
   (b) Albert Einstein / formuler / théorie / relativité
4. (a) lion / faim *(au passé)*
   (b) lion / tuer / gazelle *(f.)*
5. (a) voilà / lions
   (b) chasseur / tuer / lions *(au passé)*
6. (a) fusil / être / Browning *(au passé)*
   (b) chasseur / tirer / sur / lion / avec / fusil
7. (a) ingénieur / être / suisse
   (b) nous / parler / avec / ingénieur / hier
8. (a) guitare / fabriquer[3] / en bois
   (b) chanteur / accompagner / sa / chanson / avec / guitare
9. (a) tour / dominer / ville
   (b) nous / connaître / bien / tour
10. (a) exposition / universelle / 1889 / lieu / Paris
    (b) Gustave Eiffel / construire / sa / tour / pour / exposition

_____

[3] Attention au passif.

Reflets

La psychologie du chat[4]

Les chats vivent dans un monde extérieur très nettement délimité, dans un territoire établi et régi par des lois très strictes. Ce qui revient à dire que le domaine du chat peut se répartir en trois zones: 1°) la zone familière; 2°) la chasse gardée; 3°) la zone d'indépendance.

1°) *la zone familière*, son nom l'indique, c'est le fauteuil où le chat dort paisiblement, certain que, dans ce coin-là, rien de mal ne pourra[5] lui arriver. C'est la caisse où la chatte mettra ses petits au monde; c'est la pile de revues sur un radiateur; c'est mille et un endroits, insolites parfois, mais où le chat reviendra toujours d'un air satisfait.

2°) *la chasse gardée*, c'est ce que le chat voit et connaît. C'est le palier, le jardin, la terrasse. Cette zone-là, vous *devez* la lui réserver, sans quoi il se sentira vraiment en esclavage. Si vous ne pouvez le laisser courir dans la maison, si vous n'avez ni terrasse ni jardin, il existe une formule très simple: fermez régulièrement une pièce de l'appartement pour n'y laisser pénétrer votre chat que de temps à autre. Patiemment et après mille précautions, bien sûr, il s'aventurera dans cette chasse gardée. Votre chat sera heureux en étant délivré d'un complexe d'esclavage.

3°) *la zone d'indépendance*, pour les chats de ville, est évidemment réduite à un strict minimum. C'est le palier de l'étage d'au-dessus (la plupart du temps, le chat dédaigne les étages inférieurs). C'est la terrasse du voisin, les toits des maisons. C'est tout ce qui se trouve dans le voisinage immédiat, c'est le territoire de la grande aventure. Cette indépendance-là, de grâce, accordez-la-lui. Il en a tout autant besoin que de caresses, de viande et de lait!

Sa curiosité

Les chats sont curieux de ce paquet que vous déposez sur une table; à distance ils lancent un coup de patte investigateur et prudent et puis ils s'approchent en reniflant. Les chats sont curieux à chaque coup de sonnette, pour battre en retraite si le visiteur leur est inconnu!

Et le chat qui regarde à la fenêtre? Ce n'est pas par simple désœuvrement, croyez-moi. Observez-le et vous le verrez suivre des yeux une voiture, un cheval ou une personne.

Le ronron

Quel est l'amateur de chat qui n'en a pas éprouvé les délices? Lorsque, roulé en boule sur vos genoux, votre minet déclenche son petit moteur, ne vous sentez-vous pas pénétré de quiétude? Et, croyez-moi, l'éleveur le plus blasé est toujours attendri par le premier et maladroit ronron du chaton.

---

[4] *J'élève mon chat*, copyright © 1959 Marabout Flash.
[5] Negation is complete even without **pas** for **cesser, oser, pouvoir, savoir** ("COPS").

Le chat se cache pour mourir

Pas les nôtres. Pas ceux qui ont confiance et, dans un dernier abandon, meurent souvent dans nos bras. J'ai du reste connu—et plus d'une—des chattes attendant le retour de leur maîtresse pour mourir.

Les chats qui se cachent pour mourir ce sont les sauvages, les abandonnés, ceux qui n'ont plus le courage de lutter et qui n'attendent plus rien des hommes.

Sujets de conversation ou de composition

1. Quels sont les avantages et les inconvénients de posséder un animal familier?
2. Comparez le chat et le chien en ce qui regarde (a) ce qu'il faut faire pour les soigner, (b) leur indépendance, (c) leurs zones d'activité.
3. Si vous avez un chat, ou si vous avez eu l'occasion d'en observer un, décrivez ses zones d'activité.
4. Pouvez-vous citer des exemples de l'intelligence des animaux?
5. Comment les animaux montrent-ils leurs émotions (la joie, la peur, l'anticipation, le mécontentement, par exemple)? Choisissez un ou deux exemples.

24

Futur / Futur antérieur
vouloir / pouvoir

FUTUR ET FUTUR ANTÉRIEUR

24.1 Use

The future tense is used to designate actions expected to occur in the future (**dans l'avenir** ou **à l'avenir**). It is also used in the following cases:

A.   After **quand, lorsque, dès que** when the action indicated after these words is actually *in the future* [24.2].

B.   In the result clause of conditional sentences when the **si**-clause is in present tense [24.3].

24.2 After *quand, lorsque, dès que, aussitôt que*

When the action indicated after these words is actually in the future (although in English it is in the present tense), the French verb following these conjunctions *must* be in the future tense.

> J'irai à Paris **quand** je **serai** riche.
> *I will go to Paris when I am (will be) rich.*

*Je donnerai la lettre à Pierre **dès que** je le **verrai**.*
*I will give the letter to Pierre as soon as I **see** him.*

An easy rule of thumb is that if *one verb* in a sentence containing **quand** (**lorsque**, **dès que**, **aussitôt que**) is in the future, *both* must be in the future.

24.3   Conditional sentences: present-future combination

A conditional sentence is one containing a proviso (**si**-clause) and a result clause. If the **si**-clause is in the present tense, the result clause is in the future.

If I *have* time / I *will go* downtown.

| **Si** | j'ai | le temps / | **j'irai** | en ville. |

↑   ↑

PRESENT   FUTURE

The order of clauses is immaterial. **Si** is always followed by the present in this combination:

J'irai en ville **si j'ai** le temps.

24.4   Formation of the future: regular verbs

The future tense of regular verbs is formed by adding future endings to the FC STEM (future and conditional stem). The stem for all **-er** and **-ir** verbs is the *whole infinitive*. The stem for **-re** verbs is the infinitive minus the final **-e**. The endings (which resemble the present tense of **avoir** in several places) are as follows:

STEM	-ai	-ons
- R +	-as	-ez
	-a	-ont

arriver FC STEM: **arriver-** (*will arrive*)

j'	arriverai	nous arriver**ons**
tu	arriveras	vous arriver**ez**
il	arrivera	ils arriver**ont**

finir FC STEM: **finir-** (*will finish*)

je	finirai	nous finir**ons**
tu	finiras	vous finir**ez**
il	finira	ils finir**ont**

vendre FC STEM: **vendr-** (*will sell*)

je	vendrai	nous vendr**ons**
tu	vendr**as**	vous vendr**ez**
il	vendr**a**	ils vendr**ont**

s'amuser FC STEM: **s'amuser-** (*will have a good time*)

je	m'amuser**ai**	nous nous amuser**ons**
tu	t'amuser**as**	vous vous amuser**ez**
il	s'amuser**a**	ils s'amuser**ont**

24.5 Future tense of irregular verbs

Some irregular verbs have special FC STEMS, while others have regular stems. When in doubt, check Appendix C for irregular verbs in the future. Learn the FC STEMS for the irregular verbs thus far reviewed. Those having special stems are as follows:

INFINITIVE	FC–STEM	EXAMPLE
aller	**ir-**	Il **ira** en France demain.
être	**ser-**	Elle **sera** heureuse.
avoir	**aur-**	Il **aura** une voiture.
faire	**fer-**	Vous **ferez** la cuisine.
venir	**viendr-**	Il **viendra** demain.
tenir	**tiendr-**	Tu **tiendras** un livre.

Other irregular verbs form their future tense in a regular manner, using the whole infinitive, or (for **-re** verbs) dropping the final **-e:**

lire	**lir-**	Il **lira** ce roman.
écrire	**écrir-**	Elle **écrira** une poésie.
mettre	**mettr-**	Je **mettrai** la table.
prendre	**prendr-**	Il **prendra** les billets.
ouvrir	**ouvrir-**	Nous **ouvrirons** la porte.
partir	**partir-**	Il **partira** demain.

The FC STEM will be included in the review sections for further irregular verbs.

24.6 Future perfect (le futur antérieur)

The future perfect is a compound tense formed with the future of the auxiliary verb, plus the past participle of the main verb. The meaning always includes the words *will have* (*done something*).

travailler (*to work*)   PP. travaillé (avoir*)

j' **aurai travaillé**	nous **aurons travaillé**
tu **auras travaillé**	vous **aurez travaillé**
il **aura travaillé**	ils **auront travaillé**

I (you, he, we, you, they) **will have worked.**

aller* (*to go*)   PP. **allé** (être*)

je **serai allé(e)**	nous **serons allé(e)s**
tu **seras allé(e)**	vous **serez allé(e)(s)**
il **sera allé**	ils **seront allés**
elle **sera allée**	elles **seront allées**

I (you, he, she, we, you, they) **will have** *gone.*

A cinq heures j'**aurai travaillé** pendant huit heures.
*At five o'clock I **will have worked** eight hours.*

Quand vous arriverez j'**aurai fini** mon projet.
*When you arrive I **will have finished** my project.*

Mise en œuvre 24 A

Temps futur

Remplacez les mots en italique par le futur.

1. Je *vais traverser* la rue malgré la circulation intense.
2. Nous *allons faire* la vaisselle après le repas.
3. M. Bertin *va construire* une maison.
4. M. Bertin *va faire construire* une maison.
5. Le chauffeur *va arrêter* le camion au feu rouge (*red light*).
6. Paul et René *vont s'approcher* du guichet.
7. Enfin vous *allez me dire* la vérité.
8. Mes parents *vont lire* la nouvelle ce soir.
9. Nous *allons être* de retour avant minuit.
10. Tu *vas avoir* le temps de m'aider à faire la vaisselle.

Mise en œuvre 24 B

Quel temps faut-il employer?

Terminez la phrase en y ajoutant les mots entre parenthèses et en mettant le verbe au **futur**, à l'**imparfait** ou au **passé composé,** selon le cas.

EXEMPLE

(je reviens tout de suite)   Si je ne trouve pas le professeur, . . .

Si je ne trouve pas le professeur, je **reviendrai** tout de suite.

1. (il se repose)   Si François est fatigué, . . .
2. (nous parlons français)   S'il ne comprend pas l'anglais, . . .
3. (ses parents le punissent) Si l'enfant ne travaille pas en classe, . . .
4. (Jean prend les billets)   Si vous n'avez pas d'argent, . . .
5. (il est de retour à 6 h.) Si papa prend le T.G.V., . . .
6. (je viens vous voir)   Si je reste longtemps en ville, . . .
7. (vous venez nous voir)   Quand vous serez en ville, . . .
8. (vous venez nous voir)   Quand vous avez été en ville, . . .
9. (vous venez nous voir)   Quand vous étiez en ville, [*you used to come* . . .]
10. (je vais en Amérique)   Quand je serai riche, . . .
11. (ils se reposent)   Quand mes parents seront vieux, . . .
12. (nous nous amusons)   Quand nous étions jeunes, . . .

VERBES IRRÉGULIERS **VOULOIR** ET **POUVOIR**

24.7 Review of the verb *vouloir* (*to want*)[1]

This verb is frequently followed by an infinitive. Notice the similarities with **pouvoir.**

PRÉSENT[2]

je **veux**	nous **voul**ons	STEM: **voul-**
tu **veux**	vous **voul**ez	
il **veut**	ils **veul**ent	STEM: **veu-**

Je **veux** partir.   *I **want** to leave.*

Il **veut** un billet.   *He **wants** a ticket.*

IMPARFAIT   STEM: from present tense **nous**-form (**voul**-)[3]

Il **voulait** voir son cousin.   *He **wanted** to see his cousin.*

PASSÉ COMPOSÉ   PAST PARTICIPLE: **voulu**   AUXILIARY: (avoir)
Note: Special meaning [24.8B]:

Elle **a voulu** descendre sa valise.
*She **tried** to take down her suitcase.*

[1] For further review, consult Appendix C, Verb Table 33.

[2] English equivalents of tenses are as follows: **Présent:** *want;* **Imparfait:** *wanted,* **Passé Composé /** **Passé Simple:** *wanted;* **Futur:** *will want to,* **Conditionnel:** *would like to.*

[3] Recall that the imperfect stem is the **nous**-form of the present tense, minus the **-ons** ending. Hence **voul-** appears in all forms of the imperfect tense.

PASSÉ SIMPLE	STEM: **voul-** + **-us** system of endings [20.2]
	Il **voulut** partir. *He **wanted** to leave.*
FUTUR	STEM: **voudr-**
	Il **voudra** voir le Louvre. *He **will want** to see the Louvre.*
CONDITIONNEL	STEM: **voudr-**[4]
	Je **voudrais** aller au cinéma. *I **would like to** go to the movies.*
SUBJONCTIF	TWO STEMS: **veuill-** / **voul-**
	Je doute que Paul **veuille** venir. *I doubt that Paul **wants** (**will want**) to come.*

24.8   Remarks on *vouloir*

This verb resembles **pouvoir** in the present tense singular forms: **je** v**eux, tu** v**eux, il** v**eut. Vouloir** has various meanings and uses:

A.   Present tense. The present tense of **vouloir** is used for very strong expressions of will; to the French ear it is brusque and often impolite. It is preferable to use the conditional to express desires and polite requests. Compare:

Je **veux** partir.   *I insist on leaving.*
Je **voudrais** partir.   *I would like to leave.*

Que **voudriez-vous** faire maintenant?
Je **voudrais** voir des montres-bracelets, s'il vous plait.

B.   Passé composé tense. In the passé composé the meanings of **vouloir** are different from what one might expect:

J'ai **voulu** lui parler.   *I **tried to** speak to him.*
Je n'ai pas **voulu** lui parler.   *I **refused to** speak to him.*
J'ai **voulu** l'aider.   *I **offered to** help him.*

C.   Idioms with *vouloir*.

vouloir bien [I]   *to be willing*
vouloir dire [N]   *to mean*
en vouloir à [P]   *to hold a grudge against*

---

[4] This is the polite form.

Je **voulais bien** l'accompagner.
I was willing to go with him.

Voulez-vous m'accompagner? **Je veux bien.**
Do you want to go with me? Sure.

Que **voulez-vous dire?**
What do you mean?

Que **veut dire** le mot "pièce"?
What does the word "pièce" mean?

Jean **en veut à** cet agent de police.
John is holding a grudge against that policeman.

The imperative form **veuillez** is a rather formal way of saying *please:*

Veuillez fermer la porte.
Kindly close the door.

24.9   Review of the verb *pouvoir* (*to be able to*)[5]

This verb is frequently followed by an infinitive. Notice the similarities with **vouloir** [24.7].

When an infinitive follows a form of **pouvoir,** the meaning *can* is taken to mean *physical ability* or *permission.* (Remember P for these two words.)

peu- STEM

PRÉSENT (IRRÉGULIER)	je **peux**	nous **pouvons**	(*can do something*)
	tu **peux**	vous **pouvez**	
	il **peut**	ils **peuvent**	

Je **peux** ouvrir cette boîte.   *I can open this box.*
PHYSICAL ABILITY

Elles **peuvent** sortir ce soir.   *They can go out tonight.*
PERMISSION

IMPARFAIT   STEM: **pouv-**[6] (*could, used to be able to*)

Il **pouvait** flâner le samedi.
He used to be able to loaf on Saturdays.

[5] For further review, consult **pouvoir** in Appendix C, Verb Table 22.
[6] Recall that the imperfect stem is the **nous-**form of the present tense, minus the **-ons** ending. Hence **pouv-** appears in all forms of the imperfect tense.

PASSÉ COMPOSÉ	PAST PARTICIPLE: **pu** AUXILIARY: (avoir) (*was able to*)
	Ils **ont pu** faire ce travail.
	They were able to do that work.
PASSÉ SIMPLE	STEM: **p-** + **-us** system of endings [20.2]
FUTUR	IRREGULAR FC STEM: **pourr-** (*will be able to*)
	Il **pourra** partir demain.
	*He **will be able to** leave tomorrow.*
CONDITIONNEL	STEM: **pourr-** (*would be able to / could*)
	Je **pourrais** compléter ce rapport demain.
	*I **could** finish this report tomorrow.*
SUBJONCTIF	ONE STEM: **puiss-**
	Je doute que Paul **puisse** venir aujourd'hui.
	*I doubt that Paul **can** come today.*

24.10   Remarks on *pouvoir*

The verb **pouvoir** is usually followed by an infinitive, with the meaning *to be able (to do something)*. However, notice the special meaning for the passé composé, *to succeed in*. In French there are two verbs for expressing *can*, and they cannot be used interchangeably:

A. **pouvoir** [I] is used for *physical ability* or *permission*.

Pouvez-vous ouvrir cette porte?   *Can you open this door?*

Vous **pouvez partir** demain.   *You may leave tomorrow.*

B. **savoir** [I is used for *can (do something)* when *learned ability* or *skill* is implied: it means *to know how*.

Jean **sait parler** russe.   *John can speak Russian.*

Je **sais taper** à la machine.   *I can type.*

Savez-vous jouer au tennis?   *Can you play tennis?*

Mise en œuvre 24 C

Emploi de *vouloir*

Remplacez les mots en italique par une expression avec **vouloir**.

EXEMPLE

Paul *accepte de* nous accompagner.

Paul **veut bien** nous accompagner.

1. J'*accepte de* faire la vaisselle.
2. Je *désire* acheter un dictionnaire russe.
3. Roger a *essayé de* lui parler.
4. Qu'est-ce que cela *signifie?*
5. Cet étudiant *a du ressentiment contre* le répétiteur.
6. J'*ai envie d'*aller au cinéma ce soir.
7. J'étais en ville hier soir; j'*avais envie de* dîner chez Henri.
8. Le général insiste: il *commande* une Cadillac.
9. Qu'est-ce que vous *tâchez de* me dire?
10. Nous *avons réfusé de* travailler le dimanche.

Mise en œuvre 24 D

Emploi de *pouvoir*

Remplacez le verbe en italique par l'infinitif précédé de la forme appropriée de **pouvoir** ou de **savoir**, selon le cas.

EXEMPLE

Marie *accompagnera* sa mère en ville.

Marie **pourra** *accompagner* sa mère en ville.

1. Corinne *sortira* ce soir.
2. Boris *parle* russe.
3. Je *tape* ma composition à la machine.
4. Claude *arrivera* demain.
5. Nous *ouvrons* cette porte facilement.
6. Vous *conduisez* un camion.
7. Elle *téléphonera* au directeur avant midi, n'est-ce pas?
8. Quand nous serons à Paris nous *visiterons* le Louvre.
9. Si j'arrive à l'heure, j'*aiderai* ma mère.
10. M. Machin *porte* cette boîte.
11. Suzanne *fait* la cuisine.
12. Jean *lit* très bien.

Mise en œuvre 24 E _____

Reconstitution de phrases

Rétablissez des phrases complètes en employant les fragments fournis.

EXEMPLES

ce / anglais / faire / voyage / France / train

Cet Anglais **fera le** voyage **en** France **par le** train.

si / il / prendre / T.G.V. // il / traverser / tunnel / sous / Manche

S'il prend le T.G.V., il **traversera le** tunnel sous **la** Manche.

1. semaine / prochain / nous / être / vacances
2. je / pouvoir / faire / visite / à / amis / Cannes
3. si / je / avoir / assez / argent // je / faire / voyage / avion
4. quand / je / arriver / Genève // je / téléphoner / mon / oncle / et / tante
5. vous / aller / Eurodisneyland // si / vous / ne pas / obliger / travailler / ?
6. où / tu / aller // quand / classe / être / terminé / demain après-midi / ?
7. si / tu / vouloir / aller / cinéma // nous / pouvoir / y / aller / après / dîner
8. si / Suzanne / savoir / jouer / bridge // tu / pouvoir / la / amener / à / club
9. quand / elle / apprendre / taper // professeurs / pouvoir / lire / son / exercices
10. je / douter // que / patron / savoir / nom / de / tout / son / employés

Reflets _____

Eurodisneyland[7]

Depuis longtemps les parcs de la Société Disney en Californie et en Floride charment le public américain. Bientôt ce sera le tour des Européens. Le parc « Eurodisneyland » sera implanté à l'est de la région parisienne sur une centaine d'hectares qui s'étendra plus tard sur près de 2.000 ha. Ce parc sera modelé sur l'image du célèbre complexe floridien à Orlando.

Les touristes qui empruntent le T.G.V. pourront aller directement à Eurodisneyland, à l'entrée duquel on établira une gare de la SNCF qu'on appelle déjà « la gare Mickey ». Elle sera du style « très Mickey » comportant des pavillons, une rotonde et un beffroi. Il y aura un quartier d'affaires, des hôtels disposant de 5.000 chambres, et les services d'accompagnement. La ligne T.G.V. du chemin de fer sera reliée directement à Paris et à l'aéroport de Roissy-Paris. De la sorte, Eurodisneyland ne sera qu'à trente minutes du centre de la capitale.

[7] Information taken from *Journal France-Amérique*, 19–25 janvier 1989, page 4, « Eurodisneyland: En train à grande vitesse pour la « gare Mickey ».

Le tunnel sous la Manche permettra aux Anglais de se rendre directement dans la gare Mickey par T.G.V. On va établir également des interconnexions avec les grandes lignes de chemin de fer venant de Suisse, d'Italie et d'Allemagne. Deux échangeurs autoroutiers faciliteront la circulation routière aux environs du parc.

Sujets de conversation ou de composition

1. Racontez un de vos projets pour le futur: un weekend, un voyage que vous ferez, une maison que vous bâtirez, une partie de plaisir, une carrière.

2. Mettons que vous soyez très puissant(e). Qu'est-ce que vous ferez pour améliorer la situation politique (ou la vie économique, sociale, environnementale) actuelle ? (Libre à vous de choisir un sujet et un point de vue.)

25

Conditionnel
Passé du conditionnel
Participe présent
dire

CONDITIONNEL

25.1 Uses

The conditional tense (usually including the word *would* in English)[1] is used for:

A. Polite requests, statements, and questions. The use of the conditional (especially of **vouloir** and **devoir**) softens a statement that might be harsh or brusque. Compare *I want a ticket* with *I would like a ticket*.

Je **voudrais** une chemise bleue.	*I would like a blue shirt.*
Pierre **voudrait** partir à midi.	*Pierre would like to leave at noon.*
Je **devrais** étudier.	*I should (ought to) study.*

B. Future actions with relation to a past time. When a past time has been established as a base of reference, a future action relative to it is in the conditional:

[1] When in English *would* is used with the meaning *used to*, the **imparfait** is required in French [13.4].
When we lived in Paris *we would go* to the beach every summer.
Quand nous habitions à Paris, nous *allions* au bord de la mer chaque été.

298

Je savais qu'elle **comprendrait**.   *I knew that she would understand.*

Il m'a dit qu'il **viendrait**.   *He told me that he would come.*

C. Conditional sentences: imperfect—conditional combination. In a conditional sentence, the result clause must be in the conditional tense when the **si**-clause is in the imperfect [25.5].

Si j'**avais** le temps, j'**irais** en ville.
    IMPERFECT   CONDITIONAL
If I had time, I would go downtown.

Tu **comprendrais** *si* tu **faisais** attention.
You would understand if you paid attention.

D. Hypothetical, potential, or imaginary information. When a "fact" of unverified or dubious accuracy is passed on, the conditional is often used to indicate that the speaker does not take responsibility for its accuracy:

On propose de construire une fusée qui **atteindrait** Vénus.
*A rocket that **would reach** Venus is being proposed.*

C'est Michel qui **serait** malade?
*Is it Michel who is **supposed to be** (**said to be**) sick?*

25.2 Formation: regular verbs

The conditional tense of regular verbs is formed by adding the conditional endings (same as the imperfect endings) to the FC^2 STEM. As indicated previously [24.5], the FC STEM is the whole infinitive of **-er** and **-ir** verbs, and the infinitive of **-re** verbs minus the final **-e**. All FC STEMS, regular and irregular, end in **-r**. The conditional endings are:

-ais	-ions
-ais	-iez
-ait	-aient

arriver FC STEM: **arriver-** (*would arrive*)

j'arriver**ais**	nous arriver**ions**
tu arriver**ais**	vous arriver**iez**
il arriver**ait**	ils arriver**aient**

finir FC STEM: **finir-** (*would finish*)

je finir**ais**	nous finir**ions**
tu finir**ais**	vous finir**iez**
il finir**ait**	ils finir**aient**

---

^{2} FC STEM = FUTUR/CONDITIONNEL STEM.

rendre FC STEM: **rendr-** *(would give back, would return something)*

je rendr**ais**	nous rendr**ions**
tu rendr**ais**	vous rendr**iez**
il rendr**ait**	ils rendr**aient**

se lever° FC STEM: **se lèver-** *(would get up)*

je me lèver**ais**	nous nous lèver**ions**
tu te lèver**ais**	vous vous lèver**iez**
il se lèver**ait**	ils se lèver**aient**

25.3   Formation: irregular verbs

The same special FC STEMS which you learned for the future tense of certain irregular verbs [24.5] are also used for the conditional tense. The conditional endings are added to those special stems.

aller FC STEM: **ir-** *(would go)*

j'ir**ais**	nous ir**ions**
tu ir**ais**	vous ir**iez**
il ir**ait**	ils ir**aient**

PASSÉ DU CONDITIONNEL

25.4   Past conditional

The past conditional is formed by using the conditional of the appropriate auxiliary verb (always meaning *would have*) plus the past participle. Agreement of past participles must be made as usual for all compound tenses.

travailler *pp.* **travaillé** (avoir) *(would have worked)*

j'**aurais** travaillé	nous **aurions** travaillé
tu **aurais** travaillé	vous **auriez** travaillé
il **aurait** travaillé	ils **auraient** travaillé

venir *pp.* **venu** (être) *(would have come)*

je **serais** venu(**e**)	nous **serions** venu(**e**)s
tu **serais** venu(**e**)	vous **seriez** venu(**e**)(s)
il **serait** venu	ils **seraient** venus
elle **serait** venue	elles **seraient** venues

se dépêcher   *pp.* **se dépêché** (être) *(would have hurried)*

je **me serais** dépêché(**e**)	nous **nous serions** dépêché(**e**)s
tu **te serais** dépêché(**e**)	vous **vous seriez** dépêché(**e**)s
il **se serait** dépêché	ils **se seraient** dépêchés
elle **se serait** dépêchée	elles **se seraient** dépêchées

Si j'avais eu le temps, j'**aurais travaillé** à la bibliothèque.
*If I had had the time, I **would have worked** in the library.*

Si Jean avait su que le temps lui manquait, il **se serait dépêché**.
*If John had known that he lacked time, he **would have hurried**.*

25.5   Conditional sentences

The conditional sentence occurs in three standard combinations, just as in English:

A. Si Jean **a** le temps, il **ira** en ville.

   PRESENT–FUTURE COMBINATION

B. Si Jean **avait** le temps, il **irait** en ville.

   IMPARFAIT–CONDITIONAL COMBINATION

C. Si Jean **avait eu** le temps, il **serait allé** en ville.

   PLUPERFECT–PAST CONDITIONAL COMBINATION

Combination (C) is really a variety of (B), with the addition of a past participle in both halves of the sentence. The auxiliary verbs conform to the imperfect-conditional system.

The combinations are summarized in the following table:

si-CLAUSE	RESULT CLAUSE	EXAMPLE
A. *Present*	*Future*	Si Paul **est** fatigué, il **se reposera**.
B. *Imperfect*	*Conditional*	Si Paul **était** fatigué, il **se reposerait**.
C. *Pluperfect*	*Past Conditional*	Si Paul **avait été** fatigué, il **se serait reposé**.

The clauses may be in either order: the **si**-clause may be used at the end rather than at the beginning if desired.

Paul **se reposerait** s'il **était** fatigué.

Mise en œuvre 25 A

Formation du conditionnel

Recommencez chaque phrase par **Il m'a dit que** . . . suivi du conditionnel.

EXEMPLE

René *est* en retard.

Il m'a dit que René *serait* en retard.

1. M. Dupont arrive demain.
2. Les Smith viennent nous voir.
3. Claude met la table.
4. Dominique va au marché.
5. Mon oncle a besoin de trois billets.
6. Le professeur lit ma poésie.
7. Il écrit une lettre au ministère.
8. Il fait une promenade à motocyclette avec moi.
9. Vous prenez une décision.
10. Il se passe de voiture.

Mise en œuvre 25 B

Phrases conditionnelles

Faites une phrase conditionnelle sur les remarques suivantes, selon l'exemple.

EXEMPLE

Jean n'*étudie* pas; il ne *réussira* pas.

Si Jean **étudiait**, il **réussirait**.

1. Il n'écoute pas le professeur; il ne comprend pas les leçons.
2. Elle n'a pas le temps; elle ne visite pas le Louvre.
3. Nous n'avons pas de voiture; nous n'allons pas à la campagne.
4. Hans n'a rien à dire; il ne parle pas. (S'il avait quelque chose à dire . . .)
5. Hélène ne sait pas danser; elle n'a pas beaucoup d'amis.
6. Jacques n'a pas besoin d'argent; il ne travaille pas.
7. L'enfant n'est pas fatigué; il ne se couche pas.
8. Paul n'a pas d'argent sur lui; il ne prend pas les billets.
9. Le chauffeur n'a pas vu le feu rouge; il ne s'est pas arrêté.
10. Il n'est pas allé au cinéma; il ne s'est pas amusé.

PARTICIPE PRÉSENT

25.6   General

The present participle in French always ends in **-ant** (corresponding to *-ing* in English). It is used after **en** or **tout en** to indicate *a method* of doing something, or to show that its action is *simultaneous* with another.

J'ai appris le français **en étudiant.**
*I learned French **by studying.*** (METHOD)

Il a dit bonjour **en nous regardant.**
*He said hello **while looking at us.*** (SIMULTANEITY)

NOTE: The French present participle *cannot be used* for some English forms ending in *-ing*, notably the present tense, and *-ing* forms following prepositions (where the infinitive is required in French):

Il **arrive** à la gare.
*He **is arriving** at the station.* [English: present progressive tense]

Nous avons dîné **avant de quitter** la maison.
*We dined **before leaving** the house.* [English: after a preposition]

25.7   Formation of present participle

Using the present indicative **nous**-form, drop the **-ons** and add **-ant** to form the present participle. (This is the same stem used for forming the imperfect tense.)

VERB	**nous**-FORM	PRESENT PARTICIPLE [PS.P]	MEANING
travailler	nous **travaill**ons	en travaill**ant**	*by working*
finir	nous **finiss**ons	en finiss**ant**	*by finishing*
rendre	nous **rend**ons	en rend**ant**	*by giving*
aller	nous **all**ons	en all**ant**	*by going*
faire	nous **fais**ons	en fais**ant**	*by doing*
mettre	nous **mett**ons	en mett**ant**	*by putting*
prendre	nous **pren**ons	en pren**ant**	*by taking*
avoir	*Irregular*	**ayant**	*having*
être	*Irregular*	**étant**	*being*
savoir	*Irregular*	**sachant**	*knowing*

25.8   Uses of the present participle

A.   Method: *en* **+ [PS.P.].** This structure indicates the method by which something is done *(by doing something).* When **en +** [PS.P.] is used, emphasis is upon the *means* or *method* by which the action of the main verb is accomplished. The question *by doing what?* is answered by **en +** [PS.P.].

J'ai réussi **en travaillant** dur.
*I passed (succeeded) **by working** hard.*

Paul a appris sa leçon **en étudiant** toute la nuit.
*Paul learned his lesson **by studying** all night.*

B.   Simultaneous events: *en* + [ps.p.]. This structure indicates simultaneity *(while doing something)*. The events indicated by both the main verb and the present participle are happening at the same time.

Je suis tombé **en descendant.**
*I fell **while coming downstairs.***

Gérard écoutait la radio **en jouant** aux dames.
*Gérard was listening to the radio **while playing** checkers.*

C.   Concurrent events: *tout en* + [ps.p.]. This structure is used if two events occur at the same time, and it is considered *unusual* for them to do so.

François parlait **tout en écoutant** la radio.
*François was talking **while listening to** the radio.*

Elle lisait un livre **tout en regardant** la télévision.
*She was reading a book (even) **while watching** television.*

D.   Participle without *en*. The present participle used alone at the beginning of a clause indicates simultaneous events, action just prior to the main verb, or *cause* of the action indicated by the main verb.

Ouvrant les yeux, elle a dit bonjour.	SIMULTANEOUS EVENTS
Ouvrant la porte, il a vu sa femme.	JUST PRIOR *(to **il a vu**)*
Ne **sachant** que faire, il n'a rien fait.	CAUSE
Étant bien fatiguée, elle s'est couchée.	CAUSE

E.   *ayant* + [pp.] / *étant* + [pp.]. When followed by a past participle, **ayant** and **étant** indicate a marked priority of event *(having done something)*. In English this structure is often expressed as *after he finished (doing something) he (did something else)*. The structure in French uses **ayant** plus the past participle of the main verb (for verbs using **avoir*** as auxiliary), or **étant** plus the past participle (for verbs using **être***).

ayant travaillé	*having worked*
étant arrivé	*having arrived*

Ayant travaillé dur, nous sommes retournés à la maison.
Having worked hard, we went back to the house.

Ayant diné, nous sommes allés au théâtre.
Having dined, we went to the theater.
(= After we dined, we went to the theater.)

Ayant trouvé un stylo, elle a commencé à écrire.
Having found a pen, she began to write.
*(= After **she** found a pen, **she** began to write.)*

Étant entrés dans l'appartement, ils ont fermé la porte à clef.
Having gone into the apartment, they locked the door.
*(=After **they** went into the apartment, **they** locked the door.)*

Mise en œuvre 25 C

Formation du participe présent

Remplacez l'infinitif entre parenthèses par la forme appropriée du verbe.

1. En (*chercher*) mes clés, j'ai trouvé un billet de banque.
2. (*Savoir*) les faits, l'inspecteur a pu arrêter le jeune homme.
3. Bien que (*jouer*) mal de la guitare, je peux accompagner des chansons.
4. (*Être*) très intelligent, le directeur a résolu le problème.
5. (*Avoir*) besoin d'argent, Monique est passée par la banque pour toucher un chèque.
6. Il s'était endormi en (*écrire*) sa composition.
7. En (*entendre*) ces mots, l'avocat a quitté la salle en hâte.
8. Ne (*être*) pas amateur de musique, Luc s'est endormi au concert.
9. Il lisait un roman tout en (*écouter*) la radio.
10. (*Fermer*) le livre avec soin, Henri l'a remis sur la table.

Mise en œuvre 25 D

Emploi du participe présent

Combinez les deux phrases en remplaçant le verbe en italique par la forme appropriée.

EXEMPLE

J'ai réussi à l'examen. J'ai beaucoup *étudié*.

En étudiant beaucoup, j'ai réussi à l'examen.

1. Paul a fini sa composition. Il *a écrit* toute la nuit.
2. Marie est tombée. Elle *descendait* l'escalier.

3. L'agent n'a rien fait. Il ne *savait* que faire.
4. Hubert *a salué* le professeur. Il lui a donné sa composition.
5. J'ai acheté un stylo à la librairie. J'en *avais* besoin.
6. Mme Renault est rentrée à la maison. Elle *était* bien fatiguée.
7. Renée a appris la nouvelle. Elle *écoutait* la radio.
8. Cet auteur a fait grand plaisir au public. Il *a écrit* un roman passionnant.
9. Il a posé son cartable (*briefcase*) sur une table. Il *est entré* dans le salon.
10. François *avait* très faim. Il est entré dans un restaurant tout près.

COUP D'ŒIL LEXICALE

NOMS DÉRIVÉS DU PARTICIPE PRÉSENT

Plusieurs noms sont dérivés du participe présent. En voici quelques exemples:

1. le **remplaçant** (*v.* **remplacer,** *to replace*)
   Une personne qui remplace une autre s'appelle **un remplaçant.**
2. le **passant** (*v.* **passer,** *to pass by*)
   Une personne qui passe dans la rue s'appelle **un passant.**
3. le **commandant** (*v.* **commander,** *to command*)
   Un officier supérieur s'appelle **un commandant.**

Maintenant complétez les phrases suivantes en vous servant du nom dérivé du verbe indiqué.

4. (a) **assister** (*to attend*)
   Ceux qui assistent à un meeting s'appellent des . . .
   (b) **assister** (*to help, assist*)
   Celui qui aide le professeur dans le laboratoire est son . . .
5. **survivre** (*to survive*)
   Une personne qui survit à un catastrophe s'appelle un . . .
6. **correspondre** (*to correspond*)
   Un journaliste qui écrit des reportages s'appelle . . .
7. **gagner** (*to win*)
   Celui (Celle) qui gagne à la loterie s'appelle . . .
8. **représenter** (*to represent*)
   Une personne qui représente une autre s'appelle . . .
9. **négocier** (*to negotiate, to do business*)
   Une personne qui fait le commerce en grand s'appelle . . .
10. **débuter** (*to begin*)
    Une personne qui débute s'appelle . . .

VERBE IRRÉGULIER **DIRE**

25.9   Verbe irrégulier *dire* (to say, to tell)

Review the verb forms in Appendix C, Verb Table 10. This is one of three verbs that have the ending **-es** instead of **-ez** in the **vous**-form: **vous *dites*, vous *faites*, vous *êtes*.**
Conjugated in the same way are **prédire** (*to predict*), **interdire** (*to prohibit*), **contredire** (*to contradict*), **redire** (*to repeat*).

PRÉSENT	je **dis**	nous **disons**
	tu **dis**	vous **dites**
	il **dit**	ils **disent**

Il **dit** ce qu'il pense.

PASSÉ COMPOSÉ	Il **a dit** qu'il allait en ville.	PAST PARTICIPLE: dit
PASSÉ SIMPLE	Ils **dirent** qu'ils comprenaient.	

Formation: STEM **d-** + **-is** ending system [20.2]

IMPARFAIT	Il **disait** toujours la vérité.	REGULAR
FUTUR	Il **dira** ce qu'il pense.	FC STEM: **dir-**
CONDITIONNEL	Il **dirait** la vérité s'il la savait.	
SUBJONCTIF	Je doute qu'il **dise** la vérité.	ONE STEM

Jacques **dit** qu'il a pris les billets au guichet.
Jacques says that he bought the tickets at the ticket window.

Ils me **dirent** qu'ils seraient en retard.
They told me that they would be late.

Dis-moi ce que tu feras pendant les vacances.
Tell me what you will do during vacation.

Je n'y trouve rien à **redire**. *(Idiomatic)*
I don't find anything to take exception to in that.

Il **a dit** que non. Elle **a dit** que oui[3].
He said no. She said yes.

25.10   Replacements for *dire*

To avoid constant repetition of **dire,** some of the following could be used in descriptions of conversations:

---

[3] **Dire que oui; Dire que non** = To say yes (To say so); To say no. Also used in **Je pense que oui; Je pense que non.** *I think so; I think not.*

VERBE	IDÉES ASSOCIÉES
répondre	donner **une réponse** (à [N])
répliquer	**une réplique** habile
raconter[4]	**on raconte** une affaire, un conte, un événement, une histoire
expliquer	donner **une explication**
exprimer	. . . ses idées, ses sentiments, sa réaction
affirmer	**une affirmation** (que quelque chose est vrai)
chuchoter[5]	**un chuchotement**
grommeler[6]	**un grommellement**
crier[7]	**un cri**
s'exclamer	**une exclamation**
discuter de [SUJET]	on **discute de** (la politique etc.)

Reflets

Les P.T.T.

L'annuaire imprimé contient les noms et numéros de téléphone des abonnés, sauf ceux qui préfèrent être sur **la liste rouge** moyennant un redevance de 15 F par mois; les P.T.T. ne doivent pas communiquer le numéro des abonnés de la liste rouge.

On distribue plus de 24 millions de volumes de l'annuaire en papier en 104 éditions; cela représente la consommation de plus de 600.000 arbres, dont 60% importés. Cependant l'âge des ordinateurs a produit une solution économique. On fournit un Minitel à chaque abonné sans supplément d'abonnement; les entreprises reçoivent gratuitement un quota de Minitel selon le nombre de leurs lignes de P.T.T.

Le Minitel, commercialisé par France-Télécom, est le nom d'une gamme de terminaux. Au moyen d'un petit ordinateur Minitel, l'abonné peut accéder aux services Télétel. Cela comprend non seulement l'accès à l'annuaire éléctronique (dont les renseignements sont toujours tenus courants, les changements et additions étant faits instantanément) mais aussi aux banques de données de toutes sortes, y compris loisirs, arts, culture; banques et finances, économie, assurances; sports, santé; tourisme, voyages, transport; administration, politique; éducation; religion; services professionnels (agriculture, bâtiment, etc). Le service S.T.T. (Service de téléinformatique touristique) permet d'avoir accès aux centres de réservation des chemins de fer et des compagnies d'aviation.

Les P.T.T. trouvent qu'il coûte moins cher de fournir un ordinateur à chaque

[4] A related word is used in English: *a raconteur (storyteller)*
[5] *to whisper*
[6] *to mumble, grumble*
[7] *to shout, to talk loudly, to scream*

abonné que de réimprimer des annuaires en papier chaque année. Le numéro de vos correspondants usuels est composé automatiquement si vous les avez mis en mémoire. On recherche d'autres numéros sur l'écran; étant sélectionné, ce numéro est également composé automatiquement. On peut même accéder à l'annuaire d'une autre ville, par exemple pour choisir un hôtel, retenir une chambre, voir un graphisme représentant la ville, ou faire d'autres préparatifs de vacances, par exemple. En plus on pourrait employer le Minitel pour faire des calculs. Les non-voyants peuvent profiter d'un coffret Lectel (placé sur le Minitel) qui permet la traduction orale des informations écrites sur l'écran.

Interaction

Répondez aux questions.

1. Si vous vouliez que votre nom et numéro ne soient pas dans l'annuaire, que diriez-vous à l'employé des P.T.T.?

2. Quel ordinateur sera fourni aux abonnés qui désirent les services de France-Télécom? Est-ce que vous choisiriez l'annuaire électronique ou l'annuaire papier? Pourquoi?

3. Si vous changiez de numéro de téléphone, quelle différence est-ce qu'il y aurait si vous aviez l'annuaire en papier au lieu de l'annuaire électronique?

4. Si vous aviez un ami qui ne pouvait pas voir[8], et qui vous demandait que faire pour employer l'annuaire en papier, que lui répondriez-vous? S'il vous posait la même question pour l'annuaire électronique, quelle serait votre réponse?

5. A quel service devrait-on accéder pour savoir quels hôtels de luxe il y a à Marseille, quels sont les prix de chambres, à quelle distance du port ils sont situés, pour avoir d'autres renseignements et pour faire instantanément une réservation? Posez les questions nécessaires par écrit.

6. Quel service est-ce que vous choisiriez pour savoir les heures de départ et pour réserver une place sur Air France?

7. Est-ce que vous auriez envie d'avoir accès également aux services Télétel? Quelle sorte d'information répondrait le mieux à vos intérêts ou à vos besoins?

SERVICES TÉLÉPHONIQUES

l'**Eurosignal** *m.*	beeper
le **numéro vert** *m.*	800 number
le **point-phone** *m.*	public phone
le **radiocom** *m.*	mobile phone
la **réunion téléphone** *f.*	conference call
la **télécopie** *f.*	fax

[8] **Un aveugle, un non-voyant** = *a blind person;* **un borgne** = *a person who is blind in one eye*

26

Verbes à radical variable
craindre: verbes en *-ndre*

26.1 Stem-changing verbs[1]

Certain **-er** verbs have a slight spelling irregularity in the present tense L-AREA. This change is carried over into the future, conditional, and present subjunctive tenses in most cases. The present tense **nous-** and **vous-** forms conform to the stem derived from the infinitive as usual; the remaining forms (in the L-AREA) contain the change in spelling. (Stem-changing verbs are marked with a degree mark (°).)

There are three kinds of changes in the L-AREA:

A. **-è** replaces the last **-e** of the normal stem:

men/er°   je **mèn**e [26.2]

B. **-è** replaces the final **-é** of the normal stem:

préfér/er°   je **préfère** [26.3]

C. Special case for **appeler, jeter** [26.4]

appel/er°   j'**appell**e   (**ll** in the L-AREA)

jet/er   je **jett**e   (**tt** in the L-AREA)

[1] Also called *orthographic-changing* (spelling changing) verbs.

310

Learn the specific verbs in each category, since there is no other way to know which verbs are stem-changing.

26.2 *-è* replaces the last *-e* of the normal stem

In the following example, notice that the **nous-** and **vous-** forms keep the stem expected from the infinitive form, while the spelling change of the stem is in the other four forms.

INFINITIF: **mener°** (*to lead*)

PRÉSENT

je **mène**	nous **menons**	REGULAR STEM
tu **mènes**	vous **menez**	
il[2] **mène**	ils **mènent**	

The spelling change that occurs in the present tense also affects the future and conditional stem (FC STEM). Instead of the regular infinitive serving as the FC-STEM, the infinitive is altered to include the stem change. The resulting "fake infinitive" is the new FC STEM. In the case of **mener°,** the new stem is **mèner-**. This stem is used in *all six* forms of the future and conditional tenses.

FUTUR

SPECIAL FC-STEM: **mèner-**

je mènerai	nous mènerons
tu mèneras	vous mènerez
il mènera	ils mèneront

NOTE: There is no alteration of the imperfect tense. It is formed as usual from the **nous-**form, dropping the **-ons**. Since the **nous-**form of the present tense (**men**ons) is not affected by the stem change, the imperfect is regular.

IMPARFAIT (not affected)

je men**ais**	nous men**ions**
tu men**ais**	vous men**iez**
il men**ait**	ils men**aient**

[2] Only the **il** subject is shown for reasons of clarity of presentation. Of course the subjects **elle** and **on** are used with this form, and **ils** uses the same form as **elles.**

The passé composé and other compound tenses are not affected by the stem change. The past participle is regularly formed (e.g., *il a mené, nous avions mené, il aurait mené*).

Verbs in this category of stem-changing verbs:

INFINITIVE	MEANING	L-AREA	FUTUR
acheter	*to buy*	il achète	il achètera
achever	*to finish, to complete*	il achève	il achèvera
crever	*to burst; to die*	il crève	il crèvera
geler	*to freeze*	il gèle	il gèlera
lever	*to raise, to lift*	il lève	il lèvera
se lever	*to get up*	il se lève	il se lèvera
mener	*to lead*	il mène	il mènera
amener	*to bring* [P]	il amène	il amènera
emmener	*to take* [P]	il emmène	il emmènera
se promener	*to go for a walk (ride)*	il se promène	il se promènera

26.3 Verbs changing *é* to *è* in the stem

Verbs like **préférer,** in which the last vowel of the stem is **é**, change it to **è** (**préfèr-**) in the L-AREA of the present tense. The future and conditional stem (FC STEM) remains regular.

INFINITIF: **préférer°** (*to prefer*)

PRÉSENT

```
 ┌─────────────────────────────────┐
 │ je préfère   │ nous préférons  ⎫
 │ tu préfères  │ vous préférez   ⎬  REGULAR STEM
 │              └─────────────────⎭
 │ il préfère     ils   préfèrent │
 └────────────────────────────────┘
    ▲──é BECOMES è IN L-AREA
```

FUTUR (regular throughout)

je préférerai	nous préférerons
tu préféreras	vous préférerez
il préférera	ils préféreront

The spelling change in the present tense of these verbs does *not* affect the future or conditional tenses.

Verbs in this category include:

INFINITIF	MEANING	L-AREA	FUTUR
compléter	*to complete*	il complète	il complétera
espérer	*to hope*	il espère	il espérera
exagérer	*to exaggerate*	il exagère	il exagérera
posséder	*to possess*	il possède	il possédera
préférer	*to prefer*	il préfère	il préférera
protéger	*to protect*	il protège	il protégera
répéter	*to repeat*	il répète	il répétera
révéler	*to reveal*	il révèle	il révélera
succéder	*to follow*	il succède	il succédera
suggérer	*to suggest*	il suggère	il suggérera

26.4   appeler°, jeter°

These verbs double the final consonant in the stem, and an artificial infinitive (the regular infinitive, altered to include the stem change of the present tense) is used throughout the future and conditional:

INFINITIF: **s'appeler°** (*to be called*)
FC STEM: **s'appeller-**

PRÉSENT

je m'appelle	nous **nous appelons**	
tu t' appelles	vous **vous appelez**	} REGULAR STEM
il s' appelle	ils s' appellent	

FUTUR (modified infinitive)
   FC STEM: **s'appeller-**

j' appellerai	nous appellerons
tu appelleras	vous appellerez
il appellera	ils appelleront

The verb **se rappeler°** [N] (*to remember* [N]) follows the stem change for **appeler°**:

Je me rappelle l'histoire.	*I remember the story.*
Nous nous rappelons cette photo.	*We remember this photo.*
Nous nous la rappelons.	*We remember it.*

Mise en œuvre 26 A

Verbes à radical variable

Répondez par écrit aux questions suivantes. Faites des phrases complètes et vérifiez soigneusement l'orthographe.

EXEMPLE

Nous **achetons** des livres de classe. Et vous?

Moi aussi, **j'achète** des livres de classe.

1. Nous amenons des amies au théâtre. Et vous?
2. Nous crevons de faim. Et vous?
3. Vous n'exagérez jamais. Et votre camarade de chambre?
4. Appelez-vous le médecin quand vous avez mal à la tête?
5. Gelez-vous en hiver?
6. Espérez-vous réussir à l'examen?
7. Jetez-vous vos livres par terre?
8. Comment vous appelez-vous? Comment s'appellent vos meilleurs amis?
9. Comment s'appellent vos professeurs?
10. Qui emmenez-vous au cinéma?
11. A quelle heure vous levez-vous d'habitude?
12. Vous promenez-vous souvent en avion?
13. Répétez-vous toujours ce que le professeur dit?
14. Complétez-vous votre travail à l'heure?
15. Suggérez-vous souvent de bonnes solutions aux problèmes?
16. Lequel préférez-vous: un président qui joue au golf ou un président qui joue du piano?
17. Combien de dictionnaires possédez-vous?

Toujours par écrit, remplacez le futur immédiat par le temps futur.

18. Je *vais achever* mon projet avant cinq heures et demie.
19. Nous *allons compléter* notre collection de timbres.
20. Robert *va posséder* une collection magnifique de timbres-poste.
21. Le professeur *va préférer* une composition bien écrite.
22. Les Dupont *vont acheter* une nouvelle maison dans la banlieue.
23. Ils *vont appeler* un avocat pour les aider.

24. Ce vendeur *va exagérer* les qualités de sa marchandise.
25. J'espère que François *va amener* sa femme chez nous.

26.5   Verbs changing *c* to *ç* before *a, o, u*

Verbs like **commencer**° ending in **-cer** add the cedilla to **c** (**ç**) in every form where the next letter is **a, o,** or **u**. This is done to preserve the /s/ sound, which would be /k/ if the cedilla were missing.[3] This will occur whenever the ending begins with **-o** (**-ons** endings for **nous**), or with **a** (imperfect endings in the L-AREA).

INFINITIF: **commencer**° (*to start*)

PRÉSENT

je commence	nous commençons
tu commences	vous commencez
il commence	ils commencent

IMPARFAIT

je commençais	nous commencions
tu commençais	vous commenciez
il commençais	ils commençaient

Verbs in this category include:

agacer	*to annoy*	nous agaçons
déplacer	*to displace, to move*	nous déplaçons
exercer	*to exert, to exercise*	il exerçait
menacer (**de**)	*to threaten (to)*	il menaça
renoncer (**à**)	*to give up, to renounce*	elle renonça
remplacer	*to replace*	nous remplaçons[4]

The reason for this spelling change is to retain the [s] sound of the letter **c** throughout the conjugation. Since **c** becomes the hard [k] sound when followed by **a, o,** or **u,** the cedilla is added because **ç** is always pronounced [s].

---

[3] Compare with **leçon, garçon,** which preserve the /s/ sound with the cedilla.

[4] But **nous remplacions** (imperfect) does not require the cedilla. Each case must be judged separately.

COMBINATION	PRONOUNCED [k]	PRONOUNCED [s]
c + a [ka]	café, catholique	ça, commença
c + o [ko]	cousin, commander	leçon, garçon
c + u [ky]	cuisine, culture	reçu, déçu

26.6   Verbs changing *g* to *ge* before *a, o, u*

To preserve the same sound of **g** as it occurs in the infinitives, add the letter **e** when **g** comes before **a**, **o**, or **u**. This will be necessary when the ending is **-ons**, and with any tense endings beginning with **-a**, as in the **imparfait** and **passé simple**.

Verbs in this category include:

changer	*to change*	je change, nous changeons
charger	*to load*	je charge, nous chargeons
corriger	*to correct*	je corrige, nous corrigeons
exiger	*to require*	j'exige, nous exigeons
manger	*to eat*	je mange, nous mangeons
obliger	*to oblige, to require*	j'oblige, nous obligeons
nager	*to swim*	je nage, nous nageons
voyager	*to travel*	je voyage, nous voyageons

26.7   Verbs ending in *-yer*

Verbs ending in **-yer** change the **y** to **i** in the L-AREA of the present indicative and present subjunctive. The change is made in all forms of the future and conditional tenses.[5]

INFINITIF: **emplo**y*er*° (*to send*)

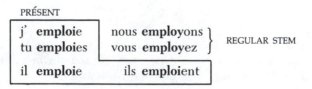

PRÉSENT

j' **emploie**	nous **employ**ons
tu **emploies**	vous **employ**ez	REGULAR STEM
il **emploie**	ils **emploi**ent

↳ **y** CHANGES TO **i** IN L-AREA

[5] The change is optional throughout for verbs ending in *-ayer*, like **essayer**.

IMPARFAIT (not affected)

j'	employais	nous	employions
tu	employais	vous	employiez
il	employait	ils	employaient

FUTUR (modified infinitive)

SPECIAL FC-STEM: **emploier-**

j'	emploierai	nous	emploierons
tu	emploieras	vous	emploierez
il	emploiera	ils	emploieront

Other stem-changing verbs in this category are:

s'appuyer (sur)	*to lean (on)*	je m'appuie, nous nous appuyons
appuyer (sur)	*to press (on), to support*	j'appuie, nous appuyons
employer	*to employ, to use*	j'emploie, nous employons
envoyer	*to send* (FC-STEM: **enverr-**)	j'envoie, nous envoyons
essuyer	*to wipe*	j'essuie, nous essuyons
nettoyer	*to clean*	je nettoie, nous nettoyons
se noyer	*to drown*	je me noie, nous nous noyons
renvoyer	*to send away, to dismiss; to refer* (FC-STEM: **renverr-**)	je renvoie, nous renvoyons

Mise en œuvre 26 B _____

Verbes à radical variable

Récrivez les phrases suivantes en remplaçant le sujet de la phrase par celui indiqué entre parenthèses. Gardez le temps du verbe. Attention aux changements d'orthographe.

EXEMPLE

Guy *commence* le travail vers huit heures. *(Nous)*

Nous commençons le travail vers huit heures.

1. Renée *déplace* des meubles dans son appartement. *(Nous)*
2. Nous *appelons* la police en cas d'urgence. *(Je)*
3. Je *renonce* aux cigarettes. *(Nous)*
4. Nous *commencions* à lire le journal. *(Il)*
5. Nous *remplacions* toujours les livres perdus. *(Paul)*

6. Jacques *agace* parfois les agents. *(Nous)*
7. Le professeur *corrige* nos fautes de grammaire. *(Nous)*
8. Les touristes *changent* leur argent à l'aéroport. *(Nous)*
9. Vous *exigiez* toujours une action immédiate. *(Pierre)*
10. Le concierge *oblige* les touristes à attendre. *(Nous)*
11. Quand vous *étiez* à la plage vous *nagiez* tous les jours. *(je)*
12. Mon père *voyage* souvent. *(Nous)*
13. Nous *employons* une machine à écrire. *(Je)*
14. Le professeur *essuie* le tableau noir. *(Nous)*
15. Nous nous *ennuyons* à la maison. *(Françoise)*
16. Nous *essayons* de réparer cette machine. *(Paul)*
17. Je *paie* toutes mes dettes. *(Nous)*
18. Nous *rayons* ces mots pour les annuler. *(Je)*
19. Mes parents *renvoient* le courrier à l'expéditeur. *(Vous)*
20. Vous *exigez* que les enfants se lavent les mains. *(Nous)*

Mise en œuvre 26 C

Thème

1. Napoléon began his march to Moscow in 1812.
2. He was beginning his campaign when Victor Hugo was ten years old.
3. A bookcase that is too high is in danger of falling (threatens to fall).
4. My uncle used to travel to Berlin every summer.
5. I will use my electric typewriter to write my homework.

PRONOMS CECI ET CELA

26.8   General

Ceci and **cela** are demonstrative pronouns. They are thus named because they indicate (*demonstrate*) the location of the *this* or *that* to which they refer. **Cela** refers to something *already mentioned;* **ceci** refers to something yet to come, something that *will be mentioned*.

$$\longleftarrow \text{cela} \ldots\ldots$$
$$\ldots\ldots \text{ceci} \longrightarrow$$

These pronouns refer to a statement or general idea already expressed (**cela**) or about to be expressed (**ceci**). They should not be confused with the adjectives *this* or *that* (**ce, cette**) used to modify a noun (as in *that house*).

26.9 Uses of *ceci* (this, the following)

Ceci may be used to refer to a statement about to be made.

> Écoutez **ceci:** je pars demain à midi.
> *Listen to **this**: I am leaving tomorrow at noon.*

It is also used in contrast with **cela.**

> J'aime **ceci**, mais je n'aime pas **cela.**
> *I like **this**, but I don't like **that**.*

In this case the meaning of the two pronouns would be clarified by the speaker's gestures, pointing to *this* and *that.*

26.10 Uses of *cela* (that, the foregoing)

The pronoun **cela** may be used as a subject, direct object, object of a preposition, or for emphasis of a subject. It refers to a whole idea already mentioned (the *antecedent).*

A. Subject

> Claude a réussi. ◄———**Cela** me plaît.

B. Direct object

> Bernard est parti. ◄——— Je ne comprends pas **cela.**

C. Object of a preposition

> Dominique a vu le directeur. ◄———Il est venu **pour cela.**

D. Emphasis of subject

> Allons au cinéma! ←   **Cela**, c'est une bonne idée!

The shortened form of **cela** is ça, frequently used in conversation:

Ça m'est égal.	*It's all the same to me. (I don't care.)*
Ça, c'est une bonne idée.	*That's a good idea.*
Comment ça va?	*How goes it? (How are things going?)*
Je lui ai parlé de ça.	*I spoke to him (her) about that.*

26.11   Four forms of *that: ce* [N] / *que* [C] / *celui* / *cela*

In English, four different uses of the word *that* call for different words in French.

A.   *that* [NOUN]   ADJECTIVE **ce, cet, cette** [N] [5.7]

> **Cet homme** parle anglais.
> ***That man** speaks English.*

B.   *that* [CLAUSE]   CONJUNCTION **que** [C] [14.7]

> Je sais **que Paul part.**
> *I know **that Paul is leaving.***

C.   *that of* [N]   PRONOUN **celui, celle** (= *the one*) [18.10]

> J'ai ma clef et **celle de Bruno.**
> *I have my key and **Bruno's.***

D.   *that* (ALONE)   PRONOUN **cela** [26.10]

> | **Cela** me plaît. | ***That** pleases me.* |
> |---|---|
> | Je sais **cela.** | *I know **that.*** |
> | Je vous ai parlé **de cela.** | *I spoke to you **about that.*** |

Mise en œuvre 26 D _____

Pronoms démonstratifs

Répétez (et écrivez) les phrases en remplaçant les mots en italique par **ceci** ou par **cela,** selon le cas.

1. Il est venu pour *nous voir*.
2. *Le fait que René a bien travaillé* me plaît.
3. Je vais vous dire *un fait important:* le maire est mort.
4. *Nous vous dirons ce qui* est évident: vous manquez de talent.
5. Avez-vous lu *l'article dans le journal* hier?

6. Regarde *ce tableau*. C'est un tableau que tu n'as pas remarqué.
7. *Que ce journaliste n'est pas d'accord avec moi* m'est tout à fait égal.
8. Jean-Pierre a réussi à l'examen. *C'est une chose qui* plaira à sa famille.
9. Ces problèmes de math sont intéressants. *Ce problème-ci* est assez facile, mais *ce problème-là* est difficile.
10. Écoutez *ce que nous allons faire*. Nous allons en vacances sur la Côte d'Azur[6].

VERBES IRRÉGULIERS EN **-INDRE**

26.12   Verbs ending in *-indre*

Several irregular verbs follow the pattern of **craindre** (*to fear*). Review the forms of this verb in Appendix C, Verb Table 7. Other important verbs following this pattern are:

atteindre	*to reach, to attain*
éteindre	*to extinguish, to put out* (*the lights*)
peindre	*to paint*
plaindre	*to pity*
se plaindre (**de**)	*to complain* (*about*)

26.13   Present indicative

Notice that all these verbs drop **-dre** from the infinitive for the singular forms (1,2,3). In the plural forms (4,5,6) the **n** of the stem becomes **gn** before the ending.

FORM		craindre	atteindre	éteindre	peindre	plaindre
1	je	crains	atteins	éteins	peins	plains
2	tu	crains	atteins	éteins	peins	plains
3	il	craint	atteint	éteint	peint	plaint
4	nous	craignons	atteignons	éteignons	peignons	plaignons
5	vous	craignez	atteignez	éteignez	peignez	plaignez
6	ils	craignent	atteignent	éteignent	peignent	plaignent
pp.		craint	atteint	éteint	peint	plaint

[6] *The Riviera.*

Nous **atteignons** notre but.	*We are attaining our goal.*
Éteignez l'électricité, s'il vous plait.	*Turn off the lights, please.*
Je vous **plains.**	*I pity you.*
Il **se plaint** du bruit.	*He is complaining about the noise.*

26.14 Compound tenses

The past participles are formed by dropping **-dre** from the infinitive and adding **-t.**
The auxiliary is **avoir** (except for the reflexive verb **se plaindre***).

Il **a atteint** son but.	*He attained his goal.*
Nous **avons éteint** la lumière.	*We turned out the lights.*
Il s'**est plaint** du bruit.	*He complained about the noise.*

Mise en œuvre 26 E

craindre et verbes apparentés

Complétez les phrases suivantes en employant le verbe entre parenthèses.

EXEMPLE

(se plaindre)   Quand je suis la victime d'une injustice, je . . .

Quand je suis la victime d'une injustice, **je me plains.**

1. Pour conserver l'énergie électrique, je . . . (éteindre les lumières)
2. Pour protéger l'extérieur, je . . . (peindre la maison)
3. Quand nous recevons de mauvaises notes, nous . . . (se plaindre)
4. Quand vous êtes malheureux, je . . . (vous plaindre)
5. Si l'on fait trop de bruit, mes voisins . . . (se plaindre)
6. Si la circulation est intense dans la rue, je . . . (craindre de la traverser)
7. Pour guider les voitures sur la route, on y . . . (peindre des lignes jaunes)
8. En partant de bonne heure le matin, je . . . (atteindre Paris avant midi)
9. En sortant d'un tunnel, les chauffeurs . . . (éteindre les phares)
10. Si l'on n'est pas satisfait de la couleur de la maison, on . . . (la repeindre)

Mise en œuvre 26 F

Reconstitution de phrases

Faites une phrase en utilisant les mots donnés. A la moitié (à votre choix)
ajoutez une phrase de votre invention qui suivrait logiquement le sens de la phrase
reconstituée.

1. nous / atteindre / notre / buts / enfin
2. je / ne pas pouvoir / atteindre / ce / livres / sur / étagère
3. mon / mère / se plaindre / bruit / de / voisins / semaine / passé
4. nous / repeindre / maison / 1988
5. si / nous / se mettre en route / de bonne heure // nous / atteindre / Paris / avant / fermeture / boutiques
6. mon / ami / Jacqueline / craindre / voyages / avion
7. nous / ne pas craindre / voyages / chemin de fer
8. en / quitter / maison / nous / éteindre / lumières / toujours
9. je / craindre / que / Jean / ne pas faire / son / travail /
10. passants / plaindre / femme / pauvre // mais / elle / ne pas / se plaindre
11. je / s'intéresser / à / romans / policier / depuis / dix / an
12. notre / avocat / lire / journal / quand / je / arriver

Reflets

Deux Auberges

Alphonse Daudet commence son conte par la description de deux auberges qui se trouvent sur le chemin d'un voyageur et qui marquent le commencement des ses aventures.

C'était en revenant de Nîmes, une après-midi de juillet. Il faisait une chaleur accablante. A perte de vue, la route blanche, embrasée, poudroyait entre les jardins d'oliviers et de petits chênes, sous un grand soleil d'argent mat qui remplissait tout le ciel. Pas une tache d'ombre, pas un souffle de vent. Rien que la vibration de l'air chaud. . . . Je marchais en plein désert depuis deux heures, quand tout à coup, devant moi, un groupe de maisons blanches se dégagea de la poussière de la route. Tout au bout, deux grandes auberges qui se regardent face à face de chaque côté du chemin.

Le voisinage de ces auberges avait quelque chose de saisissant. D'un côté, un grand bâtiment neuf, plein de vie, d'animation, toutes les portes ouvertes. A l'intérieur, des cris, des jurons, des coups de poing sur les tables, le choc des verres, le fracas des billards.

L'auberge d'en face, au contraire, était silencieuse et comme abandonnée. De l'herbe sous le portail, des volets cassés, les marches du seuil calés avec des pierres de la route. . . . Tout cela si pauvre, si pitoyable . . . En entrant, je trouvai une longue salle déserte et morne, que le jour éblouissait de trois grandes fenêtres sans rideaux fait plus morne et plus déserte encore. Quelques tables boîteuses où traînaient des verres ternis par la poussière, un billard crevé, un divan jaune, un vieux comptoir, dormaient là dans une chaleur malsaine et lourde.

Sujets de conversation ou de composition

Choisissez un des projets suivants. En faisant des contrastes, employez quantité d'adjectifs aussi bien que des expressions de la négation et de la chronologie.

1. Connaissez-vous deux édifices qui se mettent en contraste d'une façon si frappante? (deux résidences, deux hôtels, deux dortoirs, etc.) Décrivez-les, en faisant des comparaisons.

2. Choisissez deux universités ou écoles. Comparez ou contrastez leurs qualités physiques et scolaires, aussi bien que l'esprit de corps des étudiants.

27

Imparfait du subjonctif
Exclamations
Correspondance

IMPARFAIT DU SUBJONCTIF

27.1 Use of the imperfect subjunctive

The imperfect subjunctive is used when the *main clause* normally *calls for the subjunctive* [14.1] and the *main clause* is in a *past tense*.

PAST	IMPERFECT SUBJUNCTIVE	
Je doutais	**qu'il vînt.**	*I doubted / that he **would come.***
Pensais-tu	**qu'il eût** faim?	*Did you think / he **was** hungry?*
As-tu cru	**qu'il fît** ses devoirs?	*Did you believe / he **was doing** his homework?*

The imperfect subjunctive is rarely used in current French, and the present subjunctive is usually substituted:

Je doutais **qu'il vienne.**

Pensais-tu **qu'il eut** faim?

As-tu cru **qu'il fasse** ses devoirs?

27.2   Meaning

The imperfect subjunctive (*sj.i.*) is used in the same circumstances as the imperfect indicative. It indicates action in progress in the past (*was doing something*) or habitual action in the past (*used to do* or *would do something*).

Il voulait **qu'elle lui donñât** de l'argent.
He wanted her to give him some money.

L'agent a ordonné plusieurs fois **qu'on ne le laissât** pas entrer.
Several times the policeman ordered that he should not be admitted.

Elle serait partie **sans que vous le sussiez**. [15.2]
She must have left without your knowing it.

27.3   Formation of the imperfect subjunctive

The base for the imperfect form is the passé simple. Using the **je**-form of the passé simple [20.2], replace the last letter with **-sse**:

INFINITIVE	PASSÉ SIMPLE	PAST SUBJUNCTIVE
avoir	j'**eus**	que j'**eusse**
être	je **fus**	que je **fusse**
aller	j'**allai**	que j'**allasse**
faire	je **fis**	que je **fisse**
parler	je **parlai**	que je **parlasse**
vendre	je **vendis**	que je **vendisse**

The full set of endings is as follows:

-sse	-ssions
-sses	-ssiez
-^t[1]	-ssent

que je **fisse**	que nous **fissions**
que tu **fisses**	que vous **fissiez**
qu'il **fît**	qu'ils **fissent**

The circumflex accent on the form for **il, elle** and **on** always goes over the vowel just preceding the **-t** ending.

[1] The forms for **il, elle,** and **on** of the verbs **venir** and **tenir** are: **vînt** and **tînt**. These are the only irregular ones, since they do not have the circumflex on the letter immediately preceding **-t**.

EXCLAMATIONS

27.4   Comments on quality using *que* or *comme*

A declarative sentence may become an exclamation using **que** or **comme**. These are used to call attention to a certain *quality:*

COMPLETE SENTENCE

Que ce café est bondé!	*How crowded this café is!*
Que cet ordinateur est cher!	*How expensive this computer is!*
Que cette fille est belle!	*How beautiful that girl is!*
Qu' il fait froid!	*How cold it is!*
Comme ce concert est long!	*How long this concert is!*

27.5   Comments on quality using *quel*

An exclamation may begin with a form of **quel,** followed by the noun whose quality is being commented upon:

Quel toupet!	*What nerve!*
Quelle jolie voiture!	*What a pretty car!*
Quels enfants!	*What children!*
Quelles charmantes filles!	*What charming girls!*

27.6   Comments on quantity using *Que de* + NOUN

To emphasize the *quantity* of something, an exclamation may begin with **Que de** + [NOUN], where the noun is the item in question.

NOUN

Que de livres!	*What a lot of books!*
Que de fleurs!	*What a lot of flowers!*
Que de monde!	*What a crowd! (What a lot of people!)*

Mise en œuvre 27 A

Exclamations

Changez en exclamations les éléments suivants.

EXEMPLES

Cette personne est charmante.

Que cette personne est charmante! **Comme** cette personne est charmante!

livres *(beaucoup de)*
Que de livres!

1. Cette aérogare est grande.
2. Ce pilote est jeune.
3. Il est beau.
4. Cette étudiante est intelligente.
5. Elle est intelligente.
6. Ce projet est grandiose.
7. un bâtiment *(étonnant)* (quality emphasized)
8. livres *(beaucoup de)* (quantity emphasized)
9. livres *(beaux)*
10. la musique *(rythmée)*
11. La voiture est chère.
12. le prix *(trop coûteux)*
13. des fleurs *(belles)*
14. des fleurs *(beaucoup)*
15. Les fleurs sont magnifiques.

Mise en oeuvre 27 B

Imparfait du subjonctif

Donnez l'imparfait du subjonctif, **il**-form, des verbes suivants (qui sont au passé simple). Dites ce que cela veut dire en anglais.

EXEMPLE

je vins

qu'il vînt *(that he was coming, used to come, would come)*

1. je fus
2. j'allai
3. je courus
4. je fis
5. je partis
6. je dus
7. je connus
8. je dis
9. j'ouvris
10. je mis

Mise en œuvre 27 C

Imparfait du subjonctif

Donnez l'imparfait du subjonctif des verbes suivants.

EXEMPLE

ils dirent

qu'ils dissent

11. je compris
12. il sut
13. ils surent
14. il eut
15. ils étaient
16. il finit
17. il vint
18. ils mirent
19. je fis
20. ils regardèrent

Mise en œuvre 27 D

Imparfait du subjonctif

Mettez cinq des phrases suivantes au passé: employez l'imparfait de l'indicatif dans la proposition principale, et l'imparfait du subjonctif dans la proposition subordonnée.

EXEMPLE

Je doute qu'Hélène soit contente.

Je **doutais** / qu'Hélène **fusse** contente.

1. Nous regrettons que Jacques ne comprenne pas.
2. Pensez-vous que les Dumont viennent à la soirée?
3. Il dit quelques mots trop vite pour que Maigret puisse comprendre.
4. Tout est en ordre comme si rien ne s'était passé.
5. J'attends le train quoiqu'il soit en retard.
6. Catherine étudie bien qu'elle ait mal à la tête.
7. Mon copain regarde la télé quoiqu'il doive étudier.

LA CORRESPONDANCE USUELLE

This section deals with social and business correspondence and related matters.

27.7   Return address *(l'expéditeur)*

Put your own address on the back of the envelope. (**le papier à lettres**). Do not change your address into a different form (or translate it into French) because the recipient will use it to answer you, and the post office may not recognize it in altered form.

27.8   Salutation *(l'en-tête)*

For business letters the last name of the addressee is not used in the salutation, but simply **Monsieur, Messieurs, Mademoiselle,** or **Madame** followed by a comma. Some variations:

Dear Sir:	Monsieur,
Dear Madam:	Madame,
Dear Miss Burton:	Mademoiselle,
Dear Mr. Dubois:	Monsieur,
Gentlemen:	Messieurs,
Dear Professor Lebon:	Monsieur,
	Monsieur le Professeur,

Personal letters may have a less formal salutation, including the first name:

Dear Albert,	Cher ami, / Cher Albert, Mon cher Albert,
Dear Jacqueline,	Chère amie, / Chère Jacqueline, Ma chère Jacqueline,
Dear Friends,	Mes chers amis,

27.9   *Tutoiement* or *vouvoiement*

The degree of friendship already established will indicate whether to use the familiar *tu*-form (*tutoyer* is the verb meaning to use this form) or the **vous**-form in the letter. Business letters, of course, will always use the **vous**-form. Personal letters should be consistent throughout, and not switch from **tu**- to **vous**-forms.

Current trend is towards greater usage of **tutoiement,** especially between students (even though they may not have established a firm friendship as yet), and among members of the armed forces, of equal rank. **Vouvoiement** is proper in addressing superiors, older people, and strangers in general.

27.10   Complimentary closing *(formule finale)*

Complimentary closings such as those below are used verbatim in French letters as the final paragraph. They are the equivalent of *Yours very truly, Sincerely yours,* etc. Notice that the same title of address used in the salutation is repeated as part of the complimentary closing.

VERY FORMAL AND RESPECTFUL:

Veuillez agréer, Monsieur (Madame, Monsieur le Directeur, etc.) l'expression de mes salutations distinguées.

TO A BUSINESS FIRM:

Recevez, Messieurs, mes meilleures salutations.

TO A PROFESSIONAL COLLEAGUE (semi-formal):

Recevez, Monsieur, l'expression de mes sentiments distingués.

(As the bond of friendship becomes closer, **distingués** may be modulated to **sympathiques** and later to **affectueux.**)

In correspondence between students or close friends, typical complimentary closings for letters are:

Je vous envoie (Je t'envoie), mon cher ami, mes souvenirs les plus cordiaux.

Je t'envoie, mon cher Jacques, mes souvenirs les plus sympathiques.

Bien amicalement; Bien à toi; Amitiés.

27.11   Abbreviations

Do not abbreviate any part of a title on the envelope or in the salutation: spell out *Monsieur, Madame,* or *Mademoiselle.* Within the body of the letter, it is more respectful to spell out all titles of persons mentioned, in case they at some time may read the letter or see a copy.

27.12   Numbers

Spell out numbers under a hundred; use figures for dates and longer numbers:

En **1989** il y avait **dix-huit** étudiants dans la classe.

Reflets _____

Monaco

La Côte d'Azur est la côte méditerranéenne qui s'étend de Cassis (près de Marseille) à Menton. C'est un grand centre touristique dont les plages, le soleil et les possibilités de distractions attirent des visiteurs de partout. La Principauté de Monaco intéresse les touristes à cause du casino de Monte-Carlo, du Musée océanographique et du Jardin exotique; pour les fanatiques du sport automobile, il y a le Rallye de Monte-Carlo. Les collectionneurs de timbres-poste se réjouissent des productions de la poste monégasque. Les tours qui dominent le quartier commercial (*la Condamine*) témoignent de l'avantage financier qui attire les grandes entreprises dans ce minuscule paradis.

Monaco est un petit pays de 1,5 km^2 enclavé dans le département des Alpes-Maritimes; il occupe moins de territoire que Central Park à New York. On compte moins de vingt-neuf mille habitants, qui s'appellent les *Monégasques*. Leur indépendance plutôt limitée est guarantie par la France pourvu que la principauté ne fasse rien pour contrarier les intérêts français. La famille Grimaldi y règne, mais le Prince est obligé de nommer son premier ministre en choisissant un des noms sur une liste de trois candidats dressée par le gouvernement français, qui nomme également le Préfet de Police et l'administrateur de justice. La succession au trône ne pourra être dévolue qu'à une personne de nationalité monégasque ou française. Selon le traité de 1918, Monaco deviendrait un département français dans le cas où il n'y aurait pas d'héritier au trône.

La société S.B.M. (Société des bains de mer) est un monopole qui contrôle la plupart des entreprises monégasques. Elle possède deux casinos, cinq hôtels de luxe y compris l'Hôtel de Paris et l'Hermitage, des piscines, des clubs de sport, et même l'Opéra et le Ballet de Monte-Carlo. L'actionnaire principal de S.B.M. est l'État (auparavant, c'était Ari Onassis).

La sécurité à Monaco est très stricte, arrêtant et souvent détournant à la frontière les jeunes qui ne font que du camping ou les personnes suspectes; les riches et les célébrités y sont les bienvenus. Les touristes plus modestes visitent la ville pendant quelques heures seulement, tandis que les vedettes de cinéma et les millionnaires s'installent d'une façon quasi-permanente. La police a monté 60 téléviseurs télécommandés dans les rues de Monaco pour pouvoir surveiller tout ce qui se passe. Il y a partout des agents en civil qui guettent la moindre indication d'irrégularité. Il en résulte que le crime n'y existe presque pas. Monaco est un paradis pour les riches et une attraction pour tous les touristes.

Sujet de conversation ou de composition

Nommez trois autres très petits pays d'Europe en indiquant pour chacun la situation géographique. Quelle est sa situation militaire? économique? Comment est-ce que l'établissement financier profite de son existence? Quelles raisons contribuent à sa stabilité même pendant des crises mondiales? Comparez sa situation avec celle de Monaco.

Appendices

A. Cardinal and ordinal numbers

	CARDINAL	ORDINAL
1	un, une	premier, première (1er, 1re)
2	deux	deuxième, second, -e (2e)
3	trois	troisième (3e)
4	quatre	quatrième (4e)
5	cinq	cinquième (5e)
6	six	sixième (6e)
7	sept	septième (7e)
8	huit	huitième (8e)
9	neuf	neuvième (9e)
10	dix	dixième (10e)
11	onze	onzième (11e)
12	douze	douzième (12e)
13	treize	treizième (13e)

14	quatorze	quatorzième (14e)
15	quinze	quinzième (15e)
16	seize	seizième (16e)
17	dix-sept	dix-septième (17e)
18	dix-huit	dix-huitième (18e)
19	dix-neuf	dix-neuvième (19e)
20	vingt	vingtième (20e)

21	vingt-et-un (une)	vingt-et-unième (21e)
22	vingt-deux	vingt-deuxième (22e)
23	vingt-trois	vingt-troisième (23e)
30	trente	trentième (30e)
40	quarante	quarantième (40e)
50	cinquante	cinquantième (50e)
60	soixante	soixantième (60e)
70	soixante-dix	soixante-dixième (70e)
71	soixante-et-onze	soixante-et-onzième (71e)
72	soixante-douze	soixante-douzième (72e)
80	quatre-vingts[1]	quatre-vingtième (80e)
81	quatre-vingt-un	quatre-vingt-unième (81e)
90	quatre-vingt-dix	quatre-vingt-dixième (90e)

91	quatre-vingt-onze	quatre-vingt-onzième (91e)
92	quatre-vingt-douze	quatre-vingt-douzième (92e)
93	quatre-vingt-treize	quatre-vingt-treizième (93e)
94	quatre-vingt-quatorze	quatre-vingt-quatorzième (94e)
95	quatre-vingt-quinze	quatre-vingt-quinzième (95e)
96	quatre-vingt-seize	quatre-vingt-seizième (96e)
97	quatre-vingt-dix-sept	quatre-vingt-dix-septième (97e)
98	quatre-vingt-dix-huit	quatre-vingt-dix-huitième (98e)
99	quatre-vingt-dix-neuf	quatre-vingt-dix-neuvième (99e)
100	cent	centième (100e)
101	cent-un	cent unième (101e)
102	cent-deux	cent deuxième (102e)
200	deux-cents	deux centième (200e)
201	deux-cent-un	deux cent unième (201e)
1.000	mille	millième (1.000^e)
1.000.000	million	millionième (1.000.000^e)

[1] The final -s is omitted in all other forms of the 80 series: **quatre-vingt-un,** etc.

NOTE: A period is used to separate number groups (thousands, ten thousands, etc.). A comma is used for the decimal mark; for example, the metric equivalent of an inch would be 2,54 cm. Pi (π) is 3,1416.

B. Approximate numbers

The suffix **-aine** indicates *about* the number mentioned. It makes a feminine noun of the number.

une **dizaine de** filles	*about ten girls*
une **centaine de** francs	*about a hundred francs*

NOTE: **une douzaine** means exactly *12* (*a dozen*).

C. *Mille* vs. *milles*

The invariable form without a final **-s** is the word for *thousand;* with the **-s** it means *miles.* Use **mil** in dates.

cinq **mille** fleurs	*5000 flowers*
cinq **milles**	*five miles*
en l'an **mil**-neuf-cent-quatre-vingt-onze	*in 1991*

D. The use of *million* requires *de*

Paris a plus de six **millions d'**habitants.

Cet avion a coûté plus de trois **millions de** dollars.

A billion is **un milliard (de).**

E. Dimensions and statistics: *sur* = *by* or (*out*) *of*

Notice the use of **sur** in the following statements:

Neuf **sur** dix de nos étudiants parlent anglais.
*Nine **out of** ten of our students speak English.*

Cette pièce a huit mètres de long **sur quatre** de large.
This room is 8 meters long by 4 (meters) wide.

NOTE: **Avoir** rather than **être** is used in dimensions.

F.   Dates and titles

In dates and titles, use cardinal numbers except for *the first* (**premier**):

le 20 février	SPOKEN: le *vingt* février
le 17 mars	le *dix-sept* mars
BUT: **le 1er avril**	le *premier* avril

Notice the use of cardinal numbers for rulers:

Louis XIV	Louis **quatorze**
Henri IV	Henri **quatre**
BUT: **François 1er**	François **premier**

Dates including A.D. and B.C. use the following French abbreviations, which stand for **après Jésus-Christ** and **avant Jésus-Christ.**

apr. J.-C.	*A.D.*
av. J.-C.	*B.C.*
En 853 **av.** J.-C.	*In 853 B.C.*

G.   Fractional parts

la moitié de [N]	*half of* [N]
le quart ($\frac{1}{4}$) (0,250)	*a quarter*
le tiers ($\frac{1}{3}$) (0,333)	*a third*
deux tiers ($\frac{2}{3}$) (0,666)	*two-thirds*
un dix-septième ($\frac{1}{17}$)	*one seventeenth*

Demi is invariable when placed before a noun. It agrees when it follows.

demi, -e ($\frac{1}{2}$) (0,5)	*half*
une heure et demie	*an hour and a half*
une demi-heure	*a half-hour*
une demi-tasse	*a demitasse*

H.   Written forms

In writing (but not in printing), the number 7 is usually barred: **7** . The number 5 is often written **$\int$** , the combination 75 may be **$\mathcal{75}$** . The number 1 is written with a long beginning, like this **1** .

I.   Combination cardinal-ordinal

The cardinal number precedes the ordinal when both are used.

Les **deux premières** maisons sont blanches.
The first two houses are white.

APPENDIX B: MODEL REGULAR VERBS

Summary of verb tenses

Indicatif

TEMPS SIMPLES	TEMPS COMPOSÉS
Présent	**Passé composé**
il travaille	il a travaillé
il va	il est allé
Imparfait	**Plus-que-parfait**
il travaillait	il avait travaillé
il allait	il était allé
Passé simple (Passé défini)	**Passé antérieur**
il travailla	il eut travaillé
il alla	il fut allé
Futur	**Futur antérieur**
il travaillera	il aura travaillé
il ira	il sera allé
Conditionnel	**Conditionnel passé**
il travaillerait	il aurait travaillé
il irait	il serait allé

Subjonctif

Présent du subjonctif	**Passé du subjonctif**
qu'il travaille	qu'il ait travaillé
qu'il aille	qu'il soit allé
Imparfait du subjonctif	
qu'il travaillât	
qu'il allât	

PRÉSENT	IMPARFAIT	PASSÉ SIMPLE	FUTUR	CONDITIONNEL	PRÉSENT DU SUBJONCTIF

1 travailler   Model -er verb

PRÉSENT	IMPARFAIT	PASSÉ SIMPLE	FUTUR	CONDITIONNEL	PRÉSENT DU SUBJONCTIF
je travaille	travaillais	travaillai	travaillerai	travaillerais	travaille
tu travailles	travaillais	travaillas	travailleras	travaillerais	travailles
il travaille	travaillait	travailla	travaillera	travaillerait	travaille
nous **travaill**ons†	travaillions	travaillâmes	travaillerons	travaillerions	travaillions
vous travaillez	travailliez	travaillâtes	travaillerez	travailleriez	travailliez
ils travaillent	travaillaient	travaillèrent	travailleront	travailleraient	travaillent

2 entrer   Model verb requiring auxiliary être*

PRÉSENT	IMPARFAIT	PASSÉ SIMPLE	FUTUR	CONDITIONNEL	PRÉSENT DU SUBJONCTIF
entre	entrais	entrai	entrerai	entrerais	entre
entres	entrais	entras	entreras	entrerais	entres
entre	entrait	entra	entrera	entrerait	entre
entrons†	entrions	entrâmes	entrerons	entrerions	entrions
entrez	entriez	entrâtes	entrerez	entreriez	entriez
entrent	entraient	entrèrent	entreront	entreraient	entrent

3 se trouver   Model reflexive verb

PRÉSENT	IMPARFAIT	PASSÉ SIMPLE	FUTUR	CONDITIONNEL	PRÉSENT DU SUBJONCTIF
je me trouve	me trouvais	me trouvai	me trouverai	me trouverais	me trouve
tu te trouves	te trouvais	te trouvas	te trouveras	te trouverais	te trouves
il se trouve	se trouvait	se trouva	se trouvera	se trouverait	se trouve
nous nous **trouv**ons†	nous trouvions	nous trouvâmes	nous trouverons	nous trouverions	nous trouvions
vous vous trouvez	vous trouviez	vous trouvâtes	vous trouverez	vous trouveriez	vous trouviez
ils se trouvent	se trouvaient	se trouvèrent	se trouveront	se trouveraient	se trouvent

4 remplir   Model -ir verb

PRÉSENT	IMPARFAIT	PASSÉ SIMPLE	FUTUR	CONDITIONNEL	PRÉSENT DU SUBJONCTIF
remplis	remplissais	remplis	remplirai	remplirais	remplisse
remplis	remplissais	remplis	rempliras	remplirais	remplisses
remplit	remplissait	remplit	remplira	remplirait	remplisse
remplissons†	remplissions	remplîmes	remplirons	remplirions	remplissions
remplissez	remplissiez	remplîtes	remplirez	rempliriez	remplissiez
remplissent	remplissaient	remplirent	rempliront	rempliraient	remplissent

5 vendre   Model -re verb

PRÉSENT	IMPARFAIT	PASSÉ SIMPLE	FUTUR	CONDITIONNEL	PRÉSENT DU SUBJONCTIF
vends	vendais	vendis	vendrai	vendrais	vende
vends	vendais	vendis	vendras	vendrais	vendes
vend	vendait	vendit	vendra	vendrait	vende
vendons†	vendions	vendîmes	vendrons	vendrions	vendions
vendez	vendiez	vendîtes	vendrez	vendriez	vendiez
vendent	vendaient	vendirent	vendront	vendraient	vendent

† The boldface portion is the stem for the imperfect [13.2] and present participle [25.7].

IMPARFAIT DU SUBJONCTIF	PASSÉ COMPOSÉ	PLUS-QUE-PARFAIT	PASSÉ ANTÉRIEUR
travaillasse	j'ai travaillé	j'avais travaillé	j'eus travaillé
travaillasses	tu as travaillé	tu avais travaillé	tu eus travaillé
travaillât	il a travaillé	il avait travaillé	il eut travaillé
travaillassions	nous avons travaillé	nous avions travaillé	nous eûmes travaillé
travaillassiez	vous avez travaillé	vous aviez travaillé	vous eûtes travaillé
travaillassent	ils ont travaillé	ils avaient travaillé	ils eurent travaillé
entrasse	je suis entré(e)	j'étais entré(e)	je fus entré(e)
entrasses	tu es entré(e)	tu étais entré(e)	tu fus entré(e)
entrât	il est entré	il était entré	il fut entré
	elle est entrée	elle était entrée	elle fut entrée
entrassions	nous sommes entré(e)s	nous étions entré(e)s	nous fûmes entré(e)s
entrassiez	vous êtes entré(e)(s)	vous étiez entré(e)(s)	vous fûtes entré(e)(s)
entrassent	ils sont entrés	ils étaient entrés	ils furent entrés
	elles sont entrées	elles étaient entrées	elles furent entrées
me trouvasse	je me suis trouvé(e)	je m'étais trouvé(e)	je me fus trouvé(e)
te trouvasses	tu t'es trouvé(e)	tu t'étais trouvé(e)	tu te fus trouvé(e)
se trouvât	il s'est trouvé	il s'était trouvé	il se fut trouvé
	elle s'est trouvée	elle s'était trouvée	elle se fut trouvée
nous trouvassions	nous nous sommes trouvé(e)s	nous nous étions trouvé(e)s	nous nous fûmes trouvé(e)s
vous trouvassiez	vous vous êtes trouvé(e)(s)	vous vous étiez trouvé(e)(s)	vous vous fûtes trouvé(e)(s)
se trouvassent	ils se sont trouvés	ils s'étaient trouvés	ils se furent trouvés
	elles se sont trouvées	elles s'étaient trouvées	elles se furent trouvées
remplisse	j'ai rempli	j'avais rempli	j'eus rempli
remplisses	tu as rempli	tu avais rempli	tu eus rempli
remplît	il a rempli	il avait rempli	il eut rempli
remplissions	nous avons rempli	nous avions rempli	nous eûmes rempli
remplissiez	vous avez rempli	vous aviez rempli	vous eûtes rempli
remplissent	ils ont rempli	ils avaient rempli	ils eurent rempli
vendisse	j'ai vendu	j'avais vendu	j'eus vendu
vendisses	tu as vendu	tu avais vendu	tu eus vendu
vendît	il a vendu	il avait vendu	il eut vendu
vendissions	nous avons vendu	nous avions vendu	nous eûmes vendu
vendissiez	vous avez vendu	vous aviez vendu	vous eûtes vendu
vendissent	ils ont vendu	ils avaient vendu	ils eurent vendu

FUTUR ANTÉRIEUR	CONDITIONNEL PASSÉ	PASSÉ DU SUBJONCTIF	IMPÉRATIF

travailler

FUTUR ANTÉRIEUR	CONDITIONNEL PASSÉ	PASSÉ DU SUBJONCTIF	IMPÉRATIF
j'aurai travaillé	j'aurais travaillé	j'aie travaillé	
tu auras travaillé	tu aurais travaillé	tu aies travaillé	travaille
il aura travaillé	il aurait travaillé	il ait travaillé	
nous aurons travaillé	nous aurions travaillé	nous ayons travaillé	travaillons
vous aurez travaillé	vous auriez travaillé	vous ayez travaillé	travaillez
ils auront travaillé	ils auraient travaillé	ils aient travaillé	

entrer

FUTUR ANTÉRIEUR	CONDITIONNEL PASSÉ	PASSÉ DU SUBJONCTIF	IMPÉRATIF
je serai éntré(e)	je serais entré(e)	je sois entré(e)	
tu seras entré(e)	tu serais entré(e)	tu sois entré(e)	entre
il sera entré	il serait entré	il soit entré	
elle sera entrée	elle serait entrée	elle soit entrée	
nous serons entré(e)s	nous serions entré(e)s	nous soyons entré(e)s	entrons
vous serez entré(e)(s)	vous seriez entré(e)(s)	vous soyez entré(e)(s)	entrez
ils seront entrés	ils seraient entrés	ils soient entrés	
elles seront entrées	elles seraient entrées	elles soient entrées	

se trouver

FUTUR ANTÉRIEUR	CONDITIONNEL PASSÉ	PASSÉ DU SUBJONCTIF	IMPÉRATIF
je me serai trouvé(e)	je me serais trouvé(e)	je me sois trouvé(e)	
tu te seras trouvé(e)	tu te serais trouvé(e)	tu te sois trouvé(e)	trouve-toi
il se sera trouvé	il se serait trouvé	il se soit trouvé	
elle se sera trouvée	elle se serait trouvée	elle se soit trouvée	
nous nous serons trouvé(e)s	nous nous serions trouvé(e)s	nous nous soyons trouvé(e)s	trouvons-nous
vous vous serez trouvé(e)(s)	vous vous seriez trouvé(e)(s)	vous vous soyez trouvé(e)(s)	trouvez-vous
ils se seront trouvés	ils se seraient trouvés	ils se soient trouvés	
elles se seront trouvées	elles se seraient trouvées	elles se soient trouvées	

remplir

FUTUR ANTÉRIEUR	CONDITIONNEL PASSÉ	PASSÉ DU SUBJONCTIF	IMPÉRATIF
j'aurai rempli	j'aurais rempli	j'aie rempli	
tu auras rempli	tu aurais rempli	tu aies rempli	remplis
il aura rempli	il aurait rempli	il ait rempli	
nous aurons rempli	nous aurions rempli	nous ayons rempli	remplissons
vous aurez rempli	vous auriez rempli	vous ayez rempli	remplissez
ils auront rempli	ils auraient rempli	ils aient rempli	

vendre

FUTUR ANTÉRIEUR	CONDITIONNEL PASSÉ	PASSÉ DU SUBJONCTIF	IMPÉRATIF
j'aurai vendu	j'aurais vendu	j'aie vendu	
tu auras vendu	tu aurais vendu	tu aies vendu	vends
il aura vendu	il aurait vendu	il ait vendu	
nous aurons vendu	nous aurions vendu	nous ayons vendu	vendons
vous aurez vendu	vous auriez vendu	vous ayez vendu	vendez
ils auront vendu	ils auraient vendu	ils aient vendu	

APPENDIX C: IRREGULAR VERB TABLES

Irregular verbs

TABLE NUMBER	VERB	TABLE NUMBER	VERB
1	**aller** to go	29	**maintenir** to maintain
24	**apercevoir** to perceive	27	**mentir** to lie
19	**apparaitre** to appear	17	**mettre** to put
29	**appartenir** to belong to	29	**obtenir** to obtain
23	**apprendre** to learn	18	**offrir** to offer
3	**s'asseoir** to sit down	17	**omettre** to omit
7	**atteindre** to attain	18	**ouvrir** to open
2	**avoir** to have	19	**paraître** to appear
17	**commettre** to commit	20	**partir** to depart, to leave
23	**comprendre** to understand	7	**peindre** to paint
5	**conduire** to drive, to conduct	17	**permettre** to permit
4	**connaître** to be acquainted with	7	**plaindre** to pity
5	**construire** to build	21	**plaire** to please
29	**contenir** to contain	22	**pouvoir** to be able to
30	**convenir** to agree	23	**prendre** to take
6	**courir** to run	5	**produire** to produce
18	**couvrir** to cover	17	**promettre** to promise
7	**craindre** to fear	24	**recevoir** to receive
8	**croire** to believe	4	**reconnaître** to recognize
18	**découvrir** to uncover, to discover	23	**reprendre** to take back; to resume
11	**décrire** to describe	29	**retenir** to retain
5	**détruire** to destroy	30	**revenir** to come back (again)
30	**devenir** to become	25	**savoir** to know
9	**devoir** to owe, to be obliged to	27	**sentir** to feel
10	**dire** to say	26	**servir** to serve
19	**disparaître** to disappear	27	**sortir** to go out
27	**dormir** to sleep	18	**souffrir** to suffer
11	**écrire** to write	30	**se souvenir (de)** to remember
23	**entreprendre** to undertake	28	**suivre** to follow; to take (a course)
12	**envoyer°** to send	23	**surprendre** to surprise
7	**éteindre** to put out (the lights)	31	**survivre** to survive
13	**être** to be	29	**tenir** to hold
14	**faire** to make, to do, to cause	5	**traduire** to translate
15	**falloir** to be necessary	30	**venir** to come
11	**s'inscrire** to register	31	**vivre** to live
10	**interdire** to forbid	32	**voir** to see
5	**introduire** to introduce	33	**vouloir** to want
16	**lire** to read		

° stem-changing verb

PRÉSENT	IMPARFAIT	PASSÉ COMPOSÉ	PASSÉ SIMPLE	FUTUR	CONDITIONNEL

1   aller *to go* PP. **allé** (AUX **être**) PS.P. **allant**

je vais	allais	je suis allé(e)	allai	irai	irais
tu vas	allais	tu es allé(e)	allas	iras	irais
il va	allait	il est allé	alla	ira	irait
nous allons	allions	nous sommes allé(e)s	allâmes	irons	irions
vous allez	alliez	vous êtes allé(e)(s)	allâtes	irez	iriez
ils vont	allaient	ils sont allés	allèrent	iront	iraient

2   avoir *to have* PP. **eu** (AUX. **avoir**) PS.P. **ayant**

j'ai	avais	j'ai eu	eus	aurai	aurais
tu as	avais	tu as eu	eus	auras	aurais
il a	avait	il a eu	eut	aura	aurait
nous avons	avions	nous avons eu	eûmes	aurons	aurions
vous avez	aviez	vous avez eu	eûtes	aurez	auriez
ils ont	avaient	ils ont eu	eurent	auront	auraient

3   s'asseoir *to sit down* PP. **assis** (AUX. **être**) PS.P. **s'asseyant**

je m'assieds	m'asseyais	je me suis assis(e)	m'assis	m'assiérai	m'assiérais
tu t'assieds	t'asseyais	tu t'es assis(e)	t'assis	t'assiéras	t'assiérais
il s'assied	s'asseyait	il s'est assis	s'assit	s'assiéra	s'assiérait
elle s'assied	s'asseyait	elle s'est assise	s'assit	s'assiéra	s'assiérait
nous nous asseyons	nous asseyions	nous nous sommes assis(e)s	nous assîmes	nous assiérons	nous assiérions
vous vous asseyez	vous asseyiez	vous vous êtes assis(e)(s)	vous assîtes	vous assiérez	vous assiériez
ils s'asseyent	s'asseyaient	ils se sont assis	ils assirent	ils assiéront	s'assiéraient
elles s'asseyent	s'asseyaient	elles se sont assises	elles assirent	elles assiéront	s'assiéraient

4   connaître *to be acquainted with* PP. **connu** (AUX. **avoir**) PS.P. **connaissant**

je connais	connaissais	j'ai connu	connus	connaîtrai	connaîtrais
tu connais	connaissais	tu as connu	connus	connaîtras	connaîtrais
il connaît	connaissait	il a connu	connut	connaîtra	connaîtrait
nous connaissons	connaissions	nous avons connu	connûmes	connaîtrons	connaîtrions
vous connaissez	connaissiez	vous avez connu	connûtes	connaîtrez	connaîtriez
ils connaissent	connaissaient	ils ont connu	connurent	connaîtront	connaîtraient

5   construire *to construct* PP. **construit** (AUX. **avoir**) PS.P. **construisant**

je construis	construisais	j'ai construit	construisis	construirai	construirais
tu construis	construisais	tu as construit	construisis	construiras	construirais
il construit	construisait	il a construit	construisit	construira	construirait
nous construisons	construisions	nous avons construit	construisîmes	construirons	construirions
vous construisez	construisiez	vous avez construit	construisîtes	construirez	construiriez
ils construisent	construisaient	ils ont construit	construisirent	construiront	construiraient

NOTE: In the present subjunctive, a stem change in the **nous-** and **vous-**forms is shown by boldface.

PLUS-QUE-PARFAIT	PRÉSENT DU SUBJONCTIF	IMPARFAIT DU SUBJONCTIF	IMPÉRATIF
j'étais allé(e)	que j'aille	*que j'allasse*	
tu étais allé(e)	que tu ailles	allasses	va
il était allé	qu'il aille	allât	
nous étions allé(e)s	que nous **allions**	allassions	allons
vous étiez allé(e)(s)	que vous **alliez**	allassiez	allez
ils étaient allés	qu'ils aillent	allassent	
j'avais eu	*que j'*aie	*que j'*eusse	
tu avais eu	aies	eusses	aie
il avait eu	ait	eût	
nous avions eu	**ayons**	eussions	ayons
vous aviez eu	**ayez**	eussiez	ayez
ils avaient eu	aient	eussent	
je m'étais assis(e)	que je m'asseye	*que je* m'assisse	
tu t'étais assis(e)	que tu t'asseyes	t'assisses	assieds-toi
il s'était assis	qu'il s'asseye	s'assît	
elle s'était assise	qu'elle s'asseye	s'assît	
nous nous étions assis(e)s	que nous nous asseyions	nous assissions	asseyons-nous
vous vous étiez assis(e)(s)	que vous vous asseyiez	vous assissiez	asseyez-vous
ils s'étaient assis	qu'ils s'asseyent	s'assissent	
elles s'étaient assises	qu'elles s'asseyent	s'assissent	

Also: **reconnaître** *to recognize*

j'avais connu	*que je* connaisse	*que je* connusse	
tu avais connu	connaisses	connusses	connais
il avait connu	connaisse	connût	
nous avions connu	connaissions	connussions	connaissons
vous aviez connu	connaissiez	connussiez	connaissez
ils avaient connu	connaissent	connussent	
j'avais construit	*que je* construise	*que je* construisisse	
tu avais construit	construises	construisisses	construis
il avait construit	construise	construisît	
nous avions construit	construisions	construisissît	construisons
vous aviez construit	construisiez	construisissiez	construisez
ils avaient construit	construisent	construisissent	

PRÉSENT	IMPARFAIT	PASSÉ COMPOSÉ	PASSÉ SIMPLE	FUTUR	CONDITIONNEL

6 courir *to run* PP. **couru** (AUX. **avoir**) PS.P **courant**

je cours	courais	j'ai couru	courus	courrai	courrais
tu cours	courais	tu as couru	courus	courras	courrais
il court	courait	il a couru	courut	courra	courrait
nous courons	courions	nous avons couru	courûmes	courrons	courrions
vous courez	couriez	vous avez couru	courûtes	courrez	courriez
ils courent	couraient	ils ont couru	coururent	courront	courraient

7 crain/dre *to fear* PP. **craint** (AUX. **avoir**) PS.P. **craignant**

je crains	craignais	j'ai craint	craignis	craindrai	craindrais
tu crains	craignais	tu as craint	craignis	craindras	craindrais
il craint	craignait	il a craint	craignit	craindra	craindrait
nous craignons	craignions	nous avons craint	craignîmes	craindrons	craindrions
vous craignez	craigniez	vous avez craint	craignîtes	craindrez	craindriez
ils craignent	craignaient	ils ont craint	craignirent	craindront	craindraient

8 croire *to believe* PP. **cru** (AUX. **avoir**) PS.P. **croyant**

je crois	croyais	j'ai cru	crus	croirai	croirais
tu crois	croyais	tu as cru	crus	croiras	croirais
il croit	croyait	il a cru	crut	croira	croirait
nous croyons	croyions	nous avons cru	crûmes	croirons	croirions
vous croyez	croyiez	vous avez cru	crûtes	croirez	croiriez
ils croient	croyaient	ils ont cru	crurent	croiront	croiraient

9 devoir *to be obliged to; to owe* PP. **dû** (AUX. **avoir**) PS.P. **devant**

je dois	devais	j'ai dû	dus	devrai	devrais
tu dois	devais	tu as dû	dus	devras	devrais
il doit	devait	il a dû	dut	devra	devrait
nous devons	devions	nous avons dû	dûmes	devrons	devrions
vous devez	deviez	vous avez dû	dûtes	devrez	devriez
ils doivent	devaient	ils ont dû	durent	devront	devraient

10 dire *to say* PP. **dit** (AUX, **avoir**) PS.P. **disant**

je dis	disais	j'ai dit	dis	dirai	dirais
tu dis	disais	tu as dit	dis	diras	dirais
il dit	disait	il a dit	dit	dira	dirait
nous disons	disions	nous avons dit	dîmes	dirons	dirions
vous dites	disiez	vous avez dit	dîtes	direz	diriez
ils disent	disaient	ils ont dit	dirent	diront	diraient

PLUS-QUE-PARFAIT	PRÉSENT DU SUBJONCTIF	IMPARFAIT DU SUBJONCTIF	IMPÉRATIF
j'avais couru	*que je* coure	*que je* courusse	
tu avais couru	coures	courusses	cours
il avait couru	coure	courût	
nous avions couru	courions	courussions	courons
vous aviez couru	couriez	courussiez	courez
ils avaient couru	courent	courussent	

Also: **atteindre** *to reach*   **peindre** *to paint*   **se plaindre** *to complain*
éteindre *to extinguish*   **plaindre** *to pity*

j'avais craint	*que je* craigne	*que je* craignisse	
tu avais craint	craignes	craignisses	crains
il avait craint	craigne	craignît	
nous avions craint	craignions	craignissions	craignons
vous aviez craint	craigniez	craignissiez	craignez
ils avaient craint	craignent	craignissent	

j'avais cru	*que je* croie	*que je* crusse	
tu avais cru	croies	crusses	crois
il avait cru	croie	crût	
nous avions cru	**croy**ions	crussions	croyons
vous aviez cru	**croy**iez	crussiez	croyez
ils avaient cru	croient	crussent	

j'avais dû	*que je* doive	*que je* dusse	
tu avais dû	doives	dusses	
il avait dû	doive	dût	—
nous avions dû	**dev**ions	dussions	
vous aviez dû	**dev**iez	dussiez	
ils avaient dû	doivent	dussent	

Also: **contredire** *to contradict* **interdire** *to forbid* **prédire** *to predict*

j'avais dit	*que je* dise	*que je* disse	
tu avais dit	dises	disses	dis
il avait dit	dise	dît	
nous avions dit	disions	dissions	disons
vous aviez dit	disiez	dissiez	dites
ils avaient dit	disent	dissent	

PRÉSENT	IMPARFAIT	PASSÉ COMPOSÉ	PASSÉ SIMPLE	FUTUR	CONDITIONNEL

11   écrire *to write* PP. **écrit** (AUX. **avoir**) PS.P. **écrivant**

j'écris	écrivais	j'ai écrit	écrivis	écrirai	écrirais
tu écris	écrivais	tu as écrit	écrivis	écriras	écrirais
il écrit	écrivait	il a écrit	écrivit	écrira	écrirait
nous écrivons	écrivions	nous avons écrit	écrivîmes	écrirons	écririons
vous écrivez	écriviez	vous avez écrit	écrivîtes	ecrirez	écririez
ils écrivent	écrivaient	ils ont écrit	écrivirent	écriront	écriraient

12   envoyer° *to send* PP. **envoyé** (AUX. **avoir**) PS.P **envoyant**

j'envoie	envoyais	j'ai envoyé	envoyai	enverrai	enverrais
tu envoies	envoyais	tu as envoyé	envoyas	enverras	enverrais
il envoie	envoyait	il a envoyé	envoya	enverra	enverrait
nous envoyons	envoyions	nous avons envoyé	envoyâmes	enverrons	enverrions
vous envoyez	envoyiez	vous avez envoyé	envoyâtes	enverrez	enverriez
ils envoient	envoyaient	ils ont envoyé	envoyèrent	enverront	enverraient

13   être *to be* PP. **été** (AUX. **avoir**) PS.P. **étant**

je suis	étais	j'ai été	fus	serai	serais
tu es	étais	tu as été	fus	seras	serais
il est	était	il a été	fut	sera	serait
nous sommes	étions	nous avons été	fûmes	serons	serions
vous êtes	étiez	vous avez été	fûtes	serez	seriez
ils sont	étaient	ils ont été	furent	seront	seraient

14   faire *to make, to do* PP. **fait** (AUX. **avoir**) PS.P. **faisant**

je fais	faisais	j'ai fait	fis	ferai	ferais
tu fais	faisais	tu as fait	fis	feras	ferais
il fait	faisait	il a fait	fit	fera	ferait
nous faisons	faisions	nous avons fait	fîmes	ferons	ferions
vous faites	faisiez	vous avez fait	fîtes	ferez	feriez
ils font	faisaient	ils ont fait	firent	feront	feraient

15   falloir *to be necessary (to)* PP. **fallu** (AUX. **avoir**)

il faut	il fallait	il a fallu	il fallut	il faudra	il faudrait

PLUS-QUE-PARFAIT	PRÉSENT DU SUBJONCTIF	IMPARFAIT DU SUBJONCTIF	IMPÉRATIF

Also: **décrire** *to describe*   **s'inscrire** *to register*

PLUS-QUE-PARFAIT	PRÉSENT DU SUBJONCTIF	IMPARFAIT DU SUBJONCTIF	IMPÉRATIF
j'avais écrit	*que j'*écrive	*que j'*écrivisse	
tu avais écrit	écrives	écrivisses	écris
il avait écrit	écrive	écrivît	
nous avions écrit	écrivions	écrivissions	écrivons
vous aviez écrit	écriviez	écrivissiez	écrivez
ils avaient écrit	écrivent	écrivissent	

Also: **renvoyer°** *to dismiss*

PLUS-QUE-PARFAIT	PRÉSENT DU SUBJONCTIF	IMPARFAIT DU SUBJONCTIF	IMPÉRATIF
j'avais envoyé	*que j'*envoie	*que j'*envoyasse	
tu avais envoyé	envoies	envoyasses	envoie
il avait envoyé	envoie	envoyât	
nous avions envoyé	**envoy**ions	envoyassions	envoyons
vous aviez envoyé	**envoy**iez	envoyassiez	envoyez
ils avaient envoyé	envoient	envoyassent	

PLUS-QUE-PARFAIT	PRÉSENT DU SUBJONCTIF	IMPARFAIT DU SUBJONCTIF	IMPÉRATIF
j'avais été	*que je* sois	*que je* fusse	
tu avais été	sois	fusses	sois
il avait été	soit	fût	
nous avions été	**soy**ons	fussions	soyons
vous aviez été	**soy**ez	fussiez	soyez
ils avaient été	soient	fussent	

PLUS-QUE-PARFAIT	PRÉSENT DU SUBJONCTIF	IMPARFAIT DU SUBJONCTIF	IMPÉRATIF
j'avais fait	*que je* fasse	*que je* fisse	
tu avais fait	fasses	fisses	fais
il avait fait	fasse	fît	
nous avions fait	fassions	fissions	faisons
vous aviez fait	fassiez	fissiez	faites
ils avaient fait	fassent	fissent	

PLUS-QUE-PARFAIT	PRÉSENT DU SUBJONCTIF	IMPARFAIT DU SUBJONCTIF	IMPÉRATIF
il avait fallu	qu'il faille	qu'il fallût	—

PRÉSENT	IMPARFAIT	PASSÉ COMPOSÉ	PASSÉ SIMPLE	FUTUR	CONDITIONNEL

16 lire *to read* PP. **lu** (AUX. **avoir**) PS.P **lisant**

je lis	lisais	j'ai lu	lus	lirai	lirais
tu lis	lisais	tu as lu	lus	liras	lirais
il lit	lisait	il a lu	lut	lira	lirait
nous lisons	lisions	nous avons lu	lûmes	lirons	lirions
vous lisez	lisiez	vous avez lu	lûtes	lirez	liriez
ils lisent	lisaient	ils ont lu	lurent	liront	liraient

17 mettre *to put* PP. **mis** (AUX. **avoir**) PS.P. **mettant**

je mets	mettais	j'ai mis	mis	mettrai	mettrais
tu mets	mettais	tu as mis	mis	mettras	mettrais
il met	mettait	il a mis	mit	mettra	mettrait
nous mettons	mettions	nous avons mis	mîmes	mettrons	mettrions
vous mettez	mettiez	vous avez mis	mîtes	mettrez	mettriez
ils mettent	mettaient	ils ont mis	mirent	mettront	mettraient

18 ouvrir *to open* PP. **ouvert** (AUX. **avoir**) PS.P. **ouvrant**

j'ouvre	ouvrais	j'ai ouvert	ouvris	ouvrirai	ouvrirais
tu ouvres	ouvrais	tu as ouvert	ouvris	ouvriras	ouvrirais
il ouvre	ouvrait	il a ouvert	ouvrit	ouvrira	ouvrirait
nous ouvrons	ouvrions	nous avons ouvert	ouvrîmes	ouvrirons	ouvririons
vous ouvrez	ouvriez	vous avez ouvert	ouvrîtes	ouvrirez	ouvririez
ils ouvrent	ouvraient	ils ont ouvert	ouvrirent	ouvriront	ouvriraient

19 paraître *to appear* PP. **paru** (AUX. **avoir**) PS.P. **paraissant**

je parais	paraissais	j'ai paru	parus	paraîtrai	paraîtrais
tu parais	paraissais	tu as paru	parus	paraîtras	paraîtrais
il paraît	paraissait	il a paru	parut	paraîtra	paraîtrait
nous paraissons	paraissions	nous avons paru	parûmes	paraîtrons	paraîtrions
vous paraissez	paraissiez	vous avez paru	parûtes	paraîtrez	paraîtriez
ils paraissent	paraissaient	ils ont paru	parurent	paraîtront	paraîtraient

20 partir *to depart* PP. **parti** (AUX. **être**) PS.P. **partant**

je pars	partais	je suis parti(e)	partis	partirai	partirais
tu pars	partais	tu es parti(e)	partis	partiras	partirais
il part	partait	il est parti	partit	partira	partirait
nous partons	partions	nous sommes parti(e)s	partîmes	partirons	partirions
vous partez	partiez	vous êtes parti(e)(s)	partîtes	partirez	partiriez
ils partent	partaient	ils sont partis	partirent	partiront	partiraient

PLUS-QUE-PARFAIT	PRÉSENT DU SUBJONCTIF	IMPARFAIT DU SUBJONCTIF	IMPÉRATIF
j'avais lu	*que je* lise	*que je* lusse	
tu avais lu	lises	lusses	lis
il avait lu	lise	lût	
nous avions lu	lisions	lussions	lisons
vous aviez lu	lisiez	lussiez	lisez
ils avaient lu	lisent	lussent	

Also: **commettre** *to commit* **omettre** *to omit* **permettre** *to permit* **promettre** *to promise*

j'avais mis	*que je* mette	*que je* misse	
tu avais mis	mettes	misses	mets
il avait mis	mette	mît	
nous avions mis	mettions	missions	mettons
vous aviez mis	mettiez	missiez	mettez
ils avaient mis	mettent	missent	

Also: **couvrir** *to cover* **découvrir** *to discover* **offrir** *to offer* **souffrir** *to suffer*

j'avais ouvert	*que j'*ouvre	*que j'*ouvrisse	
tu avais ouvert	ouvres	ouvrisses	ouvre
il avait ouvert	ouvre	ouvrît	
nous avions ouvert	ouvrions	ouvrissions	ouvrons
vous aviez ouvert	ouvriez	ouvrissiez	ouvrez
ils avaient ouvert	ouvrent	ouvrissent	

Also: **apparaître** *to appear* **disparaître** *to disappear*

j'avais paru	*que je* paraisse	*que je* parusse	
tu avais paru	paraisses	parusses	parais
il avait paru	paraisse	parût	
nous avions paru	paraissions	parussions	paraissons
vous aviez paru	paraissiez	parussiez	paraissez
ils avaient paru	paraissent	parussent	

Also: **dormir** *to sleep* **sentir** *to feel*

j'étais parti(e)	*que je* parte	*que je* partisse	
tu étais parti(e)	partes	partisses	pars
il était parti	parte	partît	
nous étions parti(e)s	partions	partissions	partons
vous étiez parti(e)(s)	partiez	partissiez	partez
ils étaient partis	partent	partissent	

PRÉSENT	IMPARFAIT	PASSÉ COMPOSÉ	PASSÉ SIMPLE	FUTUR	CONDITIONNEL

21   plaire *to please* PP. **plu** (AUX. **avoir**) PS.P. **plaisant**

PRÉSENT	IMPARFAIT	PASSÉ COMPOSÉ	PASSÉ SIMPLE	FUTUR	CONDITIONNEL
je plais	je plaisais	j'ai plu	plus	plairai	plairais
tu plais	tu plaisais	tu as plu	plus	plairas	plairais
il plaît	il plaisait	il a plu	plut	plaira	plairait
nous plaisons	nous plaisions	nous avons plu	plûmes	plairons	plairions
vous plaisez	vous plaisiez	vous avez plu	plûtes	plairez	plairiez
ils plaisent	ils plaisaient	ils ont plu	plurent	plairont	plairaient

22   pouvoir *to be able* PP. **pu** (AUX. **avoir**) PS.P. **pouvant**

PRÉSENT	IMPARFAIT	PASSÉ COMPOSÉ	PASSÉ SIMPLE	FUTUR	CONDITIONNEL
je peux (puis)	pouvais	j'ai pu	pus	pourrai	pourrais
tu peux (puis)	pouvais	tu as pu	pus	pourras	pourrais
il peut	pouvait	il a pu	put	pourra	pourrait
nous pouvons	pouvions	nous avons pu	pûmes	pourrons	pourrions
vous pouvez	pouviez	vous avez pu	pûtes	pourrez	pourriez
ils peuvent	pouvaient	ils ont pu	purent	pourront	pourraient

23   prendre *to take* PP. **pris** (AUX. **avoir**) PS.P. **prenant**

PRÉSENT	IMPARFAIT	PASSÉ COMPOSÉ	PASSÉ SIMPLE	FUTUR	CONDITIONNEL
je prends	prenais	j'ai pris	pris	prendrai	prendrais
tu prends	prenais	tu as pris	pris	prendras	prendrais
il prend	prenait	il a pris	prit	prendra	prendrait
nous prenons	prenions	nous avons pris	prîmes	prendrons	prendrions
vous prenez	preniez	vous avez pris	prîtes	prendrez	prendriez
ils prennent	prenaient	ils ont pris	prirent	prendront	prendraient

24   recevoir *to receive* PP. **reçu** (AUX. **avoir**) PS.P. **recevant**

PRÉSENT	IMPARFAIT	PASSÉ COMPOSÉ	PASSÉ SIMPLE	FUTUR	CONDITIONNEL
je reçois	recevais	j'ai reçu	reçus	recevrai	recevrais
tu reçois	recevais	tu as reçu	reçus	recevras	recevrais
il reçoit	recevait	il a reçu	reçut	recevra	recevrait
nous recevons	recevions	nous avons reçu	reçûmes	recevrons	recevrions
vous recevez	receviez	vous avez reçu	reçûtes	recevrez	recevriez
ils reçoivent	recevaient	ils ont reçu	reçurent	recevront	recevraient

25   savoir *to know* PP. **su** (AUX. **avoir**) PS.P. **sachant**

PRÉSENT	IMPARFAIT	PASSÉ COMPOSÉ	PASSÉ SIMPLE	FUTUR	CONDITIONNEL
je sais	savais	j'ai su	sus	saurai	saurais
tu sais	savais	tu as su	sus	sauras	saurais
il sait	savait	il a su	sut	saura	saurait
nous savons	savions	nous avons su	sûmes	saurons	saurions
vous savez	saviez	vous avez su	sûtes	saurez	sauriez
ils savent	savaient	ils ont su	surent	sauront	sauraient

PLUS-QUE-PARFAIT	PRÉSENT DU SUBJONCTIF	IMPARFAIT DU SUBJONCTIF	IMPÉRATIF
j'avais plu	*que je* plaise	*que je* plusse	
tu avais plu	plaises	plusses	plais
il avait plu	plaise	plût	
nous avions plu	plaisions	plussions	plaisons
vous aviez plu	plaisiez	plussiez	plaisez
ils avaient plu	plaisent	plussent	
j'avais pu	*que je* puisse	*que je* pusse	
tu avais pu	puisses	pusses	
il avait pu	puisse	pût	—
nous avions pu	puissions	pussions	
vous aviez pu	puissiez	pussiez	
ils avaient pu	puissent	pussent	

Also: apprendre *to learn; to teach* **comprendre** *to understand*   **entreprendre** *to undertake* **reprendre** *to take back; to resume*   **surprendre** *to surprise*

j'avais pris	*que je* prenne	*que je* prisse	
tu avais pris	prennes	prisses	prends
il avait pris	prenne	prît	
nous avions pris	**pren**ions	prissions	prenons
vous aviez pris	**pren**iez	prissiez	prenez
ils avaient pris	prennent	prissent	

Also: apercevoir *to perceive*

j'avais reçu	*que je* reçoive	*que je* reçusse	
tu avais reçu	reçoives	reçusses	reçois
il avait reçu	reçoive	reçût	
nous avions reçu	recevions	reçussions	recevons
vous aviez reçu	receviez	reçussiez	recevez
ils avaient reçu	reçoivent	reçussent	

j'avais su	*que je* sache	*que je* susse	
tu avais su	saches	susses	sache
il avait su	sache	sût	
nous avions su	sachions	sussions	sachons
vous aviez su	sachiez	sussiez	sachez
ils avaient su	sachent	sussent	

PRÉSENT	IMPARFAIT	PASSÉ COMPOSÉ	PASSÉ SIMPLE	FUTUR	CONDITIONNEL

26   servir *to serve* PP. servi (AUX. avoir) PS.P. servant

PRÉSENT	IMPARFAIT	PASSÉ COMPOSÉ	PASSÉ SIMPLE	FUTUR	CONDITIONNEL
je sers	servais	j'ai servi	servis	servirai	servirais
tu sers	servais	tu as servi	servis	serviras	servirais
il sert	servait	il a servi	servit	servira	servirait
nous servons	servions	nous avons servi	servîmes	servirons	servirions
vous servez	serviez	vous avez servi	servîtes	servirez	serviriez
ils servent	servaient	ils ont servi	servirent	serviront	serviraient

27   sortir *to go out* PP. sorti (AUX. être) PS.P. sortant

PRÉSENT	IMPARFAIT	PASSÉ COMPOSÉ	PASSÉ SIMPLE	FUTUR	CONDITIONNEL
je sors	sortais	je suis sorti(e)	sortis	sortirai	sortirais
tu sors	sortais	tu es sorti(e)	sortis	sortiras	sortirais
il sort	sortait	il est sorti	sortit	sortira	sortirait
nous sortons	sortions	nous sommes sorti(e)s	sortîmes	sortirons	sortirions
vous sortez	sortiez	vous êtes sorti(e)(s)	sortîtes	sortirez	sortiriez
ils sortent	sortaient	ils sont sortis	sortirent	sortiront	sortiraient

28   suivre *to follow* PP. suivi (AUX. avoir) PS.P. suivant

PRÉSENT	IMPARFAIT	PASSÉ COMPOSÉ	PASSÉ SIMPLE	FUTUR	CONDITIONNEL
je suis	suivais	j'ai suivi	suivis	suivrai	suivrais
tu suis	suivais	tu as suivi	suivis	suivras	suivrais
il suit	suivait	il a suivi	suivit	suivra	suivrait
nous suivons	suivions	nous avons suivi	suivîmes	suivrons	suivrions
vous suivez	suiviez	vous avez suivi	suivîtes	suivrez	suivriez
ils suivent	suivaient	ils ont suivi	suivirent	suivront	suivraient

29   tenir *to hold* PP. tenu (AUX. avoir) PS.P. tenant

PRÉSENT	IMPARFAIT	PASSÉ COMPOSÉ	PASSÉ SIMPLE	FUTUR	CONDITIONNEL
je tiens	tenais	j'ai tenu	tins	tiendrai	tiendrais
tu tiens	tenais	tu as tenu	tins	tiendras	tiendrais
il tient	tenait	il a tenu	tint	tiendra	tiendrait
nous tenons	tenions	nous avons tenu	tînmes	tiendrons	tiendrions
vous tenez	teniez	vous avez tenu	tîntes	tiendrez	tiendriez
ils tiennent	tenaient	ils ont tenu	tinrent	tiendront	tiendraient

PLUS-QUE-PARFAIT	PRÉSENT DU SUBJONCTIF	IMPARFAIT DU SUBJONCTIF	IMPÉRATIF

Also: courir *to run*   **dormir** *to sleep*   **partir** *to depart*   **sentir** *to feel*   **sortir** *to go out*

PLUS-QUE-PARFAIT	PRÉSENT DU SUBJONCTIF	IMPARFAIT DU SUBJONCTIF	IMPÉRATIF
j'avais servi	*que je* serve	*que je* servisse	
tu avais servi	serves	servisses	sers
il avait servi	serve	servît	
nous avions servi	servions	servissions	servons
vous aviez servi	serviez	servissiez	servez
ils avaient servi	servent	servissent	

Also: dormir *to sleep*   **mentir** *to lie*   **sentir** *to feel*

PLUS-QUE-PARFAIT	PRÉSENT DU SUBJONCTIF	IMPARFAIT DU SUBJONCTIF	IMPÉRATIF
j'étais sorti(e)	*que je* sorte	*que je* sortisse	
tu étais sorti(e)	sortes	sortisses	sors
il était sorti	sorte	sortît	
nous étions sorti(e)s	sortions	sortissions	sortons
vous étiez sorti(e)(s)	sortiez	sortissiez	sortez
ils étaient sortis	sortent	sortissent	

PLUS-QUE-PARFAIT	PRÉSENT DU SUBJONCTIF	IMPARFAIT DU SUBJONCTIF	IMPÉRATIF
j'avais suivi	*que je* suive	*que je* suivisse	
tu avais suivi	suives	suivisses	suis
il avait suivi	suive	suivît	
nous avions suivi	suivions	suivissions	suivons
vous aviez suivi	suiviez	suivissiez	suivez
ils avaient suivi	suivent	suivissent	

Also: appartenir *to belong to*   **contenir** *to contain*   **maintenir** *to maintain*   **retenir** *to retain*   **obtenir** *to obtain*

PLUS-QUE-PARFAIT	PRÉSENT DU SUBJONCTIF	IMPARFAIT DU SUBJONCTIF	IMPÉRATIF
j'avais tenu	*que je* tienne	*que je* tinsse	
tu avais tenu	tiennes	tinsses	tiens
il avait tenu	tienne	tînt	
nous avions tenu	**ten**ions	tinssions	tenons
vous aviez tenu	**ten**iez	tinssiez	tenez
ils avaient tenu	tiennent	tinssent	

PRÉSENT	IMPARFAIT	PASSÉ COMPOSÉ	PASSÉ SIMPLE	FUTUR	CONDITIONNEL

30 venir *to come* PP. **venu** (AUX. **être**) PS.P. **venant**

PRÉSENT	IMPARFAIT	PASSÉ COMPOSÉ	PASSÉ SIMPLE	FUTUR	CONDITIONNEL
je viens	venais	je suis venu(e)	vins	viendrai	viendrais
tu viens	venais	tu es venu(e)	vins	viendras	viendrais
il vient	venait	il est venu	vint	viendra	viendrait
nous venons	venions	nous sommes venu(e)s	vînmes	viendrons	viendrions
vous venez	veniez	vous êtes venu(e)(s)	vîntes	viendrez	viendriez
ils viennent	venaient	ils sont venus	vinrent	viendront	viendraient

31 vivre *to live* PP. **vécu** (AUX. **avoir**) PS.P. **vivant**

PRÉSENT	IMPARFAIT	PASSÉ COMPOSÉ	PASSÉ SIMPLE	FUTUR	CONDITIONNEL
je vis	vivais	j'ai vécu	vécus	vivrai	vivrais
tu vis	vivais	tu as vécu	vécus	vivras	vivrais
il vit	vivait	il a vécu	vécut	vivra	vivrait
nous vivons	vivions	nous avons vécu	vécûmes	vivrons	vivrions
vous vivez	viviez	vous avez vécu	vécûtes	vivrez	vivriez
ils vivent	vivaient	ils ont vécu	vécurent	vivront	vivraient

32 voir *to see* PP. **vu** (AUX. **avoir**) PS.P. **voyant**

PRÉSENT	IMPARFAIT	PASSÉ COMPOSÉ	PASSÉ SIMPLE	FUTUR	CONDITIONNEL
je vois	voyais	j'ai vu	vis	verrai	verrais
tu vois	voyais	tu as vu	vis	verras	verrais
il voit	voyait	il a vu	vit	verra	verrait
nous voyons	voyions	nous avons vu	vîmes	verrons	verrions
vous voyez	voyiez	vous avez vu	vîtes	verrez	verriez
ils voient	voyaient	ils ont vu	virent	verront	verraient

33 vouloir *to want* PP. **voulu** (AUX. **avoir**) PS.P. **voulant**

PRÉSENT	IMPARFAIT	PASSÉ COMPOSÉ	PASSÉ SIMPLE	FUTUR	CONDITIONNEL
je veux	voulais	j'ai voulu	voulus	voudrai	voudrais
tu veux	voulais	tu as voulu	voulus	voudras	voudrais
il veut	voulait	il a voulu	voulut	voudra	voudrait
nous voulons	voulions	nous avons voulu	voulûmes	voudrons	voudrions
vous voulez	vouliez	vous avez voulu	voulûtes	voudrez	voudriez
ils veulent	voulaient	ils ont voulu	voulurent	voudront	voudraient

PLUS-QUE-PARFAIT	PRÉSENT DU SUBJONCTIF	IMPARFAIT DU SUBJONCTIF	IMPÉRATIF

Also: **convenir** *to agree* **devenir** *to become* **revenir** *to come back* **se souvenir (de)** *to remember*

PLUS-QUE-PARFAIT	PRÉSENT DU SUBJONCTIF	IMPARFAIT DU SUBJONCTIF	IMPÉRATIF
j'éais venu(e)	*que je* vienne	*que je* vinsse	
tu étais venu(e)	viennes	vinsses	viens
il était venu	vienne	vînt	
nous étions venu(e)s	**ven**ions	vinssions	venons
vous étiez venu(e)(s)	**ven**iez	vinssiez	venez
ils étaient venus	viennent	vinssent	

Also: **survivre** *to survive*

PLUS-QUE-PARFAIT	PRÉSENT DU SUBJONCTIF	IMPARFAIT DU SUBJONCTIF	IMPÉRATIF
j'avais vécu	*que je* vive	*que je* vécusse	
tu avais vécu	vives	vécusses	vis
il avait vécu	vive	vécût	
nous avions vécu	vivions	vécussions	vivons
vous aviez vécu	viviez	vécussiez	vivez
ils avaient vécu	vivent	vécussent	

Also: **revoir** *to see again*

PLUS-QUE-PARFAIT	PRÉSENT DU SUBJONCTIF	IMPARFAIT DU SUBJONCTIF	IMPÉRATIF
j'avais vu	*que je* voie	*que je* visse	
tu avais vu	voies	visses	vois
il avait vu	voie	vît	
nous avions vu	**voy**ions	vissions	voyons
vous aviez vu	**voy**iez	vissiez	voyez
ils avaient vu	voient	vissent	

PLUS-QUE-PARFAIT	PRÉSENT DU SUBJONCTIF	IMPARFAIT DU SUBJONCTIF	IMPÉRATIF
j'avais voulu	*que je* veuille	*que je* voulusse	
tu avais voulu	veuilles	voulusses	veuille
il avait voulu	veuille	voulût	
nous avions voulu	**voul**ions	voulussions	
vous aviez voulu	**voul**iez	voulussiez	veuillez
ils avaient voulu	veuillent	voulussent	

APPENDIX D: GOVERNMENT OF INFINITIVES

A.   Verbs followed directly by an infinitive

aimer	to like to
aimer mieux	to prefer to
aller*	to be going to
compter	to expect to
courir*	to run to
croire*	to believe (*one is doing*)
daigner	to condescend to
descendre	to go downstairs to
désirer	to want to
détester	to hate to
devoir*	to have to, to be obliged to
écouter	to listen (*to sthg being done*)
entendre	to hear (*sthg being done*)
envoyer°	to send
envoyer° chercher	to send for
espérer°	to hope to
faillir* (j'ai failli [I])	to nearly (*do sthg*)
faire*	to cause (*sthg to be done*)
falloir* (il faut *only form*)	to be necessary (*to do sthg*)
laisser	to allow (*sthg to be done*)
oser	to dare to
paraître*	to appear to
penser	to plan to
pouvoir*	to be able to
préférer°	to prefer to
prétendre	to claim to
regarder	to watch (*sthg being done*)
rentrer	to return home to
retourner	to go back (in order) to
revenir*	to come back (in order) to

* = irregular verb
° = stem-changing verb

savoir*	to know how to
sembler	to seem to
sentir*	to feel (*sthg happening*)
souhaiter	to wish to
valoir* mieux	to be preferable to
venir*	to come to (*do sthg*)
voir*	to see (*sthg being done*)
vouloir*	to want to

B.   Verbs requiring *à* before a following infinitive

aimer à	to like to
s'amuser à	to have fun (*doing sthg*)
s'appliquer à	to apply oneself to
apprendre* à	to learn to
avoir* à	to have to
avoir* [N] à	to have (*sthg*) to (*do*)
se borner à	to limit oneself to
chercher à	to seek to
commencer° à	to begin to
consentir* à	to consent to
consister à	to consist of (*doing sthg*)
continuer à	to continue to
se décider à	to decide to
se déterminer à	to determine to
déterminer [P] à [I]	to persuade [P] to
se disposer à	to prepare to
employer° [N] à	to use [N] to (*do sthg*)
enseigner [N] à	to teach [N] to
exciter [N] à	to instigate [N] to
s'exercer° à	to practice (*doing sthg*)
se fatiguer à	to wear oneself out (*doing sthg*)
forcer° [N] à	to force [N] to
s'habituer à	to become accustomed to
hésiter à	to hesitate to
inviter [N] à	to invite [N] to (*do sthg*)

se mettre* à	to begin to
obliger° [N] à	to oblige, force [N] to
s'occuper à	to busy oneself in (*doing sthg*)
parvenir* à	to succeed in
pencher à	to be inclined to
penser à	to consider (*doing sthg*)
persister à	to persist in (*doing sthg*)
se plaire* à	to take pleasure in
se préparer à	to prepare to
procéder° à	to proceed to
provoquer [N] à	to provoke [N] to
recommencer° à	to begin (*doing sthg*) again
réduire* [N] à	to reduce [N] to (*doing sthg*)
renoncer° à	to give up (*doing sthg*)
se résigner à	to resign oneself to
se résoudre* à	to resolve to
réussir à	to succeed in
servir* à	to serve to
songer° à	to consider (*doing sthg*)
tarder à	to delay in
tenir* à	to be anxious to
travailler à	to work to
viser à	to aim to

C. Verbs requiring *de* before a following infinitive

achever° de	to finish (*doing sthg*)
s'arrêter de	to stop (*doing sthg*)
avertir [P] de	to warn [P] to
cesser de	to stop (*doing sthg*)
choisir de	to choose to
commander [N] de	to order [N] to
conseiller [P] de	to advise [P] to
se contenter de	to be content to
convaincre* [P] de	to convince [P] to
convenir* de	to agree to

craindre* de	to fear to
crier de	to shout to
décider de	to decide to
défendre [à P] de	to forbid [P] to
demander [à P] de	to ask [P] to
se dépêcher de	to hurry to
déterminer de	to determine to
dire* [à P] de	to tell [P] to
écrire* [à P] de	to write [P] to
s'efforcer° de	to make an effort to
empêcher [N] de	to prevent [N] from (*doing sthg*)
s'empresser de	to make haste to
essayer° de	to try to
éviter de	to avoid (*doing sthg*)
(s') excuser [P] de	to excuse [P] from (*doing sthg*)
finir de	to finish (*doing sthg*)
forcer° [N] de	to force [N] to
inspirer [N] de	to inspire [N] to
interdire* [à N] de	to forbid [N] to
jouir de	to enjoy (*doing sthg*)
jurer de	to swear to
manquer de	to fail to
menacer° de	to threaten to
mériter de	to deserve to
négliger° de	to neglect to
obtenir* de	to obtain permission to
offrir* de	to offer to
ordonner [à N] de	to command [N] to
oublier de	to forget to
pardonner [à N] de	to pardon [N] for (*doing sthg*)
parler de	to talk about (*doing sthg*)
permettre* [à N] de	to permit [N] to
persuader [N] de	to persuade [N] to
prendre* garde de	to be careful *not* to
prendre* soin de	to take care to
se presser de	to hurry to

prier [N] **de**	to ask [N] to
promettre* [à P] **de**	to promise [P] to
proposer de	to propose to
refuser de	to refuse to
regretter de	to regret to
remercier [N] **de**	to thank [N] for (*doing sthg*)
reprocher [N] **de**	to reproach [N] for
risquer de	to run the risk of
soupçonner [N] **de**	to suspect [N] of
se souvenir* de	to remember (*to do sthg*)
tâcher de	to try to
tenter de	to try to
venir* de	to have just (*done sthg*)

Vocabulaire

A

abonné *m.* subscriber
abonnement *m.* subscription
abord: d'— first, first of all
aborder *v.* to approach, to broach
accablant,-e *adj.* overpowering
accepter (**de** [I]) to agree (to [I])
accéder *v.* to access
accompagnement *m.* accompaniment; escort
accompagner (**de** [N]) *v.* to accompany (by); go with
accord *m.* agreement
achat *m.* purchase
acheter° *v.* to buy
acquis *pp.* **acquérir*** acquired
acteur *m.* actor
actif, active *adj.* active
action *f.* share (stock); (literature) plot, action
actionnaire *m.* stockholder
actrice *f.* actress
actualités *m. pl.* news

actuel,-le[†] *adj.* current, present-day
actuellement[†] *adv.* currently, at present
admettre* *v.* to admit
admirer *v.* to admire
adresse *f.* address
adresser v. to address
adresser: s'— à [P] to speak to [P]
aérogare *f.* air terminal
aéroport *m.* airport
affaire *f.* affair; case
affaires *m.pl.* business
afin de *conj.* in order to
agacer° *v.* to annoy
âge: d'un certain — middle-aged
agence *f.* agency
agent *m.* policeman; agent
agir *v.* to act; **il s'agit de** it is a matter of
aimer *v.* to like; to love; **— mieux** to prefer
ainsi *adv.* thus;**— de suite** and so forth, etc.
ajouter *v.* to add
allemand,-e *adj.* German
aller* *v.* [1.6] to go; **— au bord de la mer** to go to the beach (shore)
aller-retour: un billet — *m.* round-trip ticket
allumer *v.* to light
allure *f.* speed; **à toute —** at full speed
alpinisme *m.* mountaineering
amende *f.* fine (penalty)
amener° *v.* to bring [P]
américain,-e *adj.* American
ami *m.* friend (male); **petit —** *m.* boyfriend
amie *f.* friend (female); **petite —** *f.* girlfriend
amoureux,-se *adj.* in love
amusant,-e *adj.* amusing
amuser: s'— to have a good time
an *m.* year (use with numbers)
an: avoir [x] ans to be [x] yrs old
ancien,-ne *adj.* ancient; (before noun) former; **ancien combattant** *m.* veteran; **anciens élèves** *m.pl.* alumni
anglais,-e *adj.* English
Angleterre *f.* England
année *f.* year (not for exact measure); **— scolaire** academic year
anniversaire *m.* birthday, anniversary
annoncer° *v.* to announce
annuaire *m.* telephone directory

annuler *v.* to cancel

antérieur,-e *adj.* preceding

apôtre *m.* apostle

appareil *m.* apparatus; camera

appartement *m.* apartment

appartenir* (à) *v.t.* 29 to belong (to)

apporter *v.* to bring (a thing)

apprendre* *v.t.* 23 to learn; to teach

approcher: s' — de to approach

appuyer° *v.* to support, to prop up

après *prep.* after

après-midi *m.* afternoon

arabe *m.* Arabic (language)

arbre *m.* tree

argent *m.* money; silver

arrière: en — backwards; towards the back

arrêt *m.* stop (bus, etc.)

arrêter *v.* to stop; to arrest

arrêter: s' — (**de** [1]) to stop (doing sthg)

arrivée *f.* arrival

arrondissement *m.* arrondissement; ward

ascenseur *m.* elevator

asseoir: s' — *v.* to sit down

assez *adv.* enough; (before adj.) rather

assis,-e *adj.* seated

assister† (**à** [N]) *v.* to attend

assourdissant,-e *adj.* deafening

assurance *m.* insurance

athlète *m.* athlete

attaquer *v.* to attack

atteindre* (à) *v.* to attain, to reach

attendant: en — que + *sj. conj.* until

attendre [N] *v.* to wait for [N] (sthg)

attente *f.* waiting; **salle d' —** *f.* waiting room

atterrir *v.* to land

attraper *v.* to catch

auberge *f.* inn

aucun(e) [N]: **ne —** [8.4] no, not any [N]

augmenter *v.* to increase

aujourd'hui *adv.* today

auquel, -le *rel. pn.* [23.5] to which

aussi *adv.* also; **— +** INVERTED VERB [11.9] therefore; **— bien que** as well as

aussitôt que *adv.* [24.2] as soon as

autant *adv.* as much, as many

auteur *m.* author
auto-stop: faire* de l' — to hitch-hike
autobus *m.* bus (city)
autocar *m.* bus (interurban)
automne *m.* fall, autumn
autre *adj.* other
autrefois *adv.* formerly; in the past
Autriche *f.* Austria
autrichien,-ne *adj.* Austrian
avaler *v.* to swallow
avance: en — *adv.* in advance
avant *prep.* before; — **de** [I] before [. . .] ing; — **que** *conj.* before
avec *prep.* with
avenir: l' — *m.* the future
avion *m.* airplane
avis *m.* opinion; **être de l'** — **que** to be of the opinion that
avocat,-e *m./f.* lawyer
avoir* *v.t.* 2 to have; **avoir lieu** to take place
avouer *v.* to admit

B

baisser *v.* to go down, decrease
banlieue *f.* suburb
banque *f.* bank (finance); **en** — in the bank
banquette *f.* bench
bas,-se *adj.* low
basket *m.* basketball
bateau *m.* boat
bavard,-e *adj.* talkative
Bâle Basle (capital of Switzerland)
bâtiment *m.* building
bâtir *v.* to build
beau: avoir — [I] to [I] in vain; **il fait** — the weather is nice
beau, bel, belle *pr. adj.* beautiful
beau-père *m.* father-in-law
beaucoup *adv.* a lot; much, many
beffroi *m.* belfry
bel *alt. of* **beau** handsome, beautiful
belle *adj. f.* beautiful
belle-mère *f.* mother-in-law
berline *f.* sedan (auto)
besoin: avoir — **de** [N] to need [N]
beurre *m.* butter
béton *m.* concrete (material)

bête *f.* animal, beast; *adj.* stupid
bibliothécaire *m. ou f.* librarian
bibliothèque *f.* library
bien *adv.* well; **être —** to be comfortable (person); **C'est —** [N]? Is this really [N]?
bien sûr of course, certainly
bientôt *adv.* soon
bière *f.* beer
bijou *m.* jewel
billet *m.* ticket; **— aller-retour** *m.* round-trip ticket; **— simple** one-way ticket
bistrot; bistro *m.* bar, pub, café
blanc,-he *adj.* white
bleu *adj.* blue
boire* *v.* to drink
Bois de Boulogne *m.* name of a large park in Paris
bois *m.* wood(s)
boite *f.* can, box; **— de nuit** *f.* night club; **— de vitesse** *f.* gear shift (auto)
bon,-ne *pr. adj.* good
bondé *adj.* crowded, packed
bonne: de — heure *adv.* early
bord *m.* edge; **à —** on board; **au — de la mer** at (to) the shore
bouche *f.* mouth
boucherie *f.* butcher shop
boulangerie *f.* bakery
boulevard *m.* boulevard
bouquet[†] *m.* clump
Bourse (des valeurs) *f.* Stock Exchange
bourse *f.* purse; scholarship
bout *m.* end; **tout au —** at the very end
bouteille *f.* bottle
boutique *f.* shop
bricoleur *m.* putterer, tinkerer
briller *v.* to shine
briquet *m.* cigarette lighter
broché paperback book
brosse *f.* brush
brosser to brush
brouillard *m.* fog
bruit *m.* noise
brun,-e *adj.* brown
bruyamment *adv.* noisily
bulletin d'informations *m.* newsletter
bureau *m.* office; office building; desk
but[†] *m.* purpose; goal; **avoir pour —** to have as a purpose or goal
buv- *vst* **boire*** to drink

C

cabine *f.* elevator car; booth
cabinet *m.* doctor's office
cacher ([N] à [P]) *v.* to hide ([N] from [P])
cadeau *m.* gift
cadre *m.* framework
cahier *m.* notebook
Caire, Le Cairo
camarade de chambre *m. ou f.* roommate
cambriolage *m.* burglary
cambrioleur *m.* burglar
camion *m.* truck
camionnette *f.* van
campagne *f.* country (not city)
car[†] *m.* interurban bus
car *conj.* because, for
carburant *m.* fuel
carrière *f.* career
cas *m.* case; situation
cathédrale *f.* cathedral
cause: à — de because of
causerie *f.* informal talk, speech
ce, cet, cette, ces *pr. adj.* this, that
cela *pn.* that
célèbre *adj.* famous
celle *pn., f. s.* [5.7] the one
celle-ci (-là) [18.14] this one (that one)
cellule *f.* cell
celui *pn.* [18.10] the one
celui-ci (-là) [18.14] this one (that one)
cendrier *m.* ash tray
cent *num.* hundred; **pour —** percent (%)
centaine: une — de [N] about a hundred [N]
cependant *conj.* however
ce qui, ce que [23.7] what
cercle *m.* circle; club (social)
ces *pr. adj.* [5.7] these
cesser (de) *v.* to cease
cet *adj. m.* [N] [5.6] this, that
cette *adj.f.* [5.7] this, that
ceux *pn., m.pl.* [18.10] the ones, those
chaise *f.* chair (without arms)
chaleur *f.* heat

chambre *f.* room (bedroom)

chance[†] *f.* luck; **avoir de la —** to be lucky

change: bureau de — *m.* money changer

changement *m.* change

changer° (**de** [N]) *v.* to change [N]

chanson *f.* song

chanter *v.* to sing

chanteur, chanteuse *m./f.* singer

chapeau *m.* hat

chapitre *m.* chapter

chaque *adj.* each

charger ([N] **de** [N]) *v.* to load sthg with [N]

charmant,-e *adj.* charming

chasseur *m.* bellhop; hunter

chat *m.* cat

château *m.* château, castle

chaud,-e *adj.* warm

chauffeur *m.* driver

chaumière *f.* cottage

chaussures *f.* shoes

chef-d'œuvre *m.* masterpiece

chef d'orchestre *m.* conductor (music)

chemin *m.* path; **— de fer** *m.* railroad; train

chemise *f.* shirt

chemisier *m.* blouse

chêne *m.* oak tree

chèque *m.* check (banking)

cher, chère *pr. adj.* [5.9] (before noun) dear; (after noun) expensive

chercher [N] [6.5] to look for [N]; to get [N]

cheval (pl. **chevaux**) *m.* horse

cheveu *m.* hair; **cheveux: avoir mal aux —** to have a hangover; **se faire couper les —** have one's hair cut

chez [N] *prep.* at the home of; at the place of business of; in the case of [N]

chien *m.* dog

chimie *f.* chemistry

chinois,-e *adj.* Chinese

chose *f.* thing; **quelque —** something [4.5]

choisir *v.* to choose

choix *m.* choice

ciel (pl. **cieux**) *m.* sky

ci-dessous below

ci-dessus above

cigale *f.* cicada

cinéma *m.* movie theater; art of film

cinquième fifth; — **étage** sixth[1] floor
circulation[†] *f.* traffic
cirque *m.* circus
citation *f.* quotation
citerne *f.* tank (container)
citron *m.* lemon
clair,-e *adj.* [5.15] (after a color) light-
clé, clef *f.* key
client *m.* customer
clou (pl. **clous**) nail
coffre *m.* trunk (of car)
coffret *m.* small box
coin *m.* corner
colère *f.* anger; **se mettre* en** — to get angry
collectionner *v.* to collect
collision *f.* collision; **entrer en** — **avec** to collide with
combien de [N] how many [N]
combinaison *f.* combination
comédien[†] *m.* actor
commandant *m.* major; commandant
commande *f.* order; — **d'achat** buy order
commander *v.* to order
comme *adj.* as; like
commencement[†] *m.* beginning
commencer° *v.* to begin
comment *adv.* [21.8] how
commettre* *v.* to commit
commis *m.* clerk
commissions: faire des — to do some errands
commode[†] *adj.* convenient
communiquer *v.* to communicate
compagne de chambre *f.* roommate
complaire: se — **à** [I] *v.* to take pleasure in [I]
complet, complète *adj.* complete; full
compléter° *v.* to complete
compliqué,-e *adj.* complicated
comporter *v.* to include
composer *v.* to compose; (telephone) to dial; **se** — **de** to be composed of
compositeur *m.* composer
comprendre* *v.t.* 23 to understand; include
compris *pp.* **comprendre*** understood
compte *m.* account; — **en banque** bank account

---

[1] The ground floor is *le rez-de-chaussée*. The floor above the ground floor is *le premier étage*. Thus add one to get the U.S. equivalent. A two-story house is *une maison à un étage*.

comptoir *m.* counter
concierge *m.* ou *f.* concierge (manager)
condamné *adj.* convicted
conducteur *m.* driver
conduire* *v.t.* 5 to drive; to conduct
conférence[†] *f.* lecture, conference
conférencier,-ière *m./f.* lecturer
confiance *f.* confidence
congé *m.* holiday, day off
connaissance *f.* acquaintance; **faire* la — de** [P] to make [P's] acquaintance
connaître* *v.t.* 4 to be acquainted with
connu *pp.* **connaître*** known
conséquent: par — consequently
consommation *f.* consumption
constatation *f.* verification
constructeur *m.* manufacturer
consigne *f.* check-room
conte *m.* short story
contenir* *v.t.* 29 to contain
contravention *f.* citation, "ticket"
contre *prep.* against
contredit: sans — without question
contrôle *m.* control
contrôleur *m.* conductor (train, bus)
convenable *adj.* appropriate
convenir* *v.* to be appropriate
copie *f.* copy; exercise
copain *m.* pal, buddy
corps *m.* body
correction[†] *f.* correction; correctness
corriger° *v.* to correct
cosmonaute *m.* astronaut
côté *m.* side
cotation *f.* quotation (stock)
coucher: se — *v.* to go to bed
couleur *f.* color
coup *m.* stroke, blow, **— d'état** revolution; **— de téléphone** *m.* telephone call; **tout à —** *adv.* suddenly; **tout d'un —** *adv.* all at once
couper *v.* to cut
courrier *m.* mail; **long —** long distance
court,-e *adj.* short
courant *m.* current; **tenu au —** kept up-to-date
courageux,-se *adj.* brave, courageous
courir* *v.t.* 6 to run
cours *m.* course (academic); (stocks) stock prices; **au — de** in the course of

courses: faire* les — to go shopping
court,-e *pr. adj.* short
courtier *m.* stock broker
cousin *m.* cousin (male)
cousine *f.* cousin (female)
coût *m.* cost
coûter *v.* to cost; **— cher** (≠ **bon marché**) to be expensive (≠ cheap)
couteau *m.* knife
couturier/-ière *m./f.* dressmaker
couvercle *m.* cover
couvert,-e *adj.* (*pp.* **couvrir***) covered; **il est —** it is cloudy, overcast
couvrir* (**de** [N]) *v.t.* 18 to cover (with, by)
crever *v.* to die
craie *f.* chalk
craindre* [26.12] to fear
crayon[†] *m.* pencil
cravate *f.* necktie
crime *m.* crime
critiquer *v.* to criticize
croire* *v.t.* 8 [14.6] to believe
cuillère *f.* spoon
cuisine *f.* kitchen; cooking; **faire* la —** to do the cooking
cuisinier,-ière *m./f.* cook, chef
curiosité de la ville *f.* the "sights" of the city
cyclomoteur *m.* moped

D

d'abord *adv.* first, first of all
d'ailleurs besides, moreover
dame *f.* lady
danois,-e *adj.* Danish
dans *prep.* in; on (street); **dans [x] minutes** [x] minutes from now
d'après according to; adapted from
davantage *adv.* more
début *m.* beginning
décapotable *f.* convertible (car)
déchirant,-e *adj.* ear-splitting
déclarer *v.* to declare
décoller *v.* to take off
découvrir *v.t.* 18 to uncover; discover
dégager: se — *v.* to emerge
déjà *adv.* already
déjeuner *m.* lunch; **petit —** *m.* breakfast
déjeuner *v.* to have lunch
délit *m.* offense; infraction

demain *adv.* tomorrow

demander[†] [N] *v.* to ask for [N]; **demander à** [P] **de** [I] to ask [P] to [I]; **se —** (**si**) to wonder (whether, if)

démêler *v.* to untangle, to solve

déménager *v.* to move (residence)

demeurant: au — for all that

demeurer *v.* to live, to dwell

demi,-e *adj.* (*invar.* before a noun) half

demi-heure *f.* a half-hour

dénouement *m.* ending (of a story); solution

dent[†] *f.* tooth; **avoir mal aux —** s to have a toothache

départ *m.* departure

dépanneuse *f.* tow truck, wrecker

dépasser *v.* to pass; to exceed

dépense *f.* expense

dépêcher: se — (**de** [I]) to hurry (to [I])

dépenser *v.* to spend (money)

déplacer°: se — to move from one place to another

déposer *v.* to deposit

depuis [2.4] for; since

déranger *v.* to disturb

dernier, dernière *pr. adj.* last

dérober: se — *v.* to evade; to hide

déroulement *m.* progression of events

derrière *prep.* behind

désagréable *adj.* disagreeable, unpleasant

descendre *v.* to go down, to get off; **— dans** (**un hôtel**) to stay (at a hotel)

dès [TIME] from [TIME] on; **— que** *conj.* [24.2] as soon as; **— lors** from that time on

désert,-e *adj.* deserted

déshabiller: se — to get undressed

désirer *v.* to want, to desire

désolé,-e *adj.* very sorry

dessert *m.* dessert

desservir* *v.t.* 26 to serve

dessin *m.* sketch

destination *f.* destination; **à — de** for; going to

détendre: se — *v.* to relax

devant *prep.* in front of

devenir* *v.t.* 30 to become

devoir *m.* duty

devoir* *v.t.* 9 [20.9] to be obliged to

devoirs *m.pl.* homework

dévolu,-e *adj.* devolved; fell upon

dictionnaire *m.* dictionary

difficile *adj.* difficult

dire* *v.t.* 10 to say
diriger: se — à (vers) to go (towards)
discuter (de [N]) *v.* to discuss [N]
disparaître* *v.t.* 19 to disappear
disparu *pp.* **disparaître*** disappeared
disponible *adj.* available, at one's disposal
disposer de [N] *v.* to have [N] at its disposal
disposition: à (leur) — *f.* at their disposal
disque *m.* disk, records; **— fixe** *m.* hard disk (computer)
distraire*: se — *v.* to relax, to amuse oneself
dit *pp.* **dire*** said, told
divers,-e *adj.* various
divertir: se — *v.* to amuse oneself
diviser *v.* to divide
dîner *v.* to dine; to have supper
doit *from* **devoir*** *v.t.* 9 owes; must [I]
dominer *v.* to dominate
donc *adv.* therefore, so
dont *rel. pn.* [23.2] of whom
dormir* *v.t.* 27 to sleep
dortoir *m.* dormitory
douane *f.* customs
douanier *m.* customs official
doucement *adv.* gently
douceur *f.* sweetness
doute: sans — *adv.* certainly
douter *v.* to doubt; **se — que** [C] to suspect that, to be practically certain that
doux, douce *adj.* gentle; sweet
doyen *m.* dean
drapeau *m.* flag
dresser une liste to make a list
drogue *f.* drug
dû *pp.* **devoir*** [20.9] must have, had to
dur,-e *adj.* hard

E

E.-U. (les États-Unis) *m.pl.* United States
eau *f.* water
éblouir *v.* to dazzle
échangeur *m.* interchange
échecs *m.pl.* chess
échelle *f.* scale
échouer (à) *v.* to fail
écouter [N] *v.* [6.5] to listen to [N]
écran *m.* screen

écraser *v.* to crush; to run over

écrire* *v.t.* 11 to write; **machine à —** *f.* typewriter

écrit *pp.* **écrire*** written

écrivain *m.* writer

écurie *f.* stable

éditeur[†] *m.* publisher

édition électronique *f.* desktop publishing

effacer *v.* to erase

effectuer *v.* to carry out

effet *m.* effect; **en —**[†] in fact

efforcer°: s' — de *v.* to make a great effort to

effrayer° *v.* [26.7] to frighten

égal,-e *adj.* equal

également *adv.* also; equally

égard *m.* regard; **à l' — de** with regard to

église *f.* church

élégant,-e *adj.* elegant

élève *m.* student (grade school)

élévé,-e *adj.* high; raised

éliminatoire *m.* elimination (audition)

éliminer *v.* to eliminate

embarquement *m.* loading; embarkation

emblée: d' — *adv.* right away; at once

embrasé,-e *adj.* blazing

emmener° *v.* [19.11] to take (a person)

emphase *f.* pomposity; **fuite de toute —** *f.* simplicity

emporter *v.* to carry off, take away

emploi *m.* job, employment

emprunter *v.* (≠ **prêter**) to borrow (≠ to lend) **— le train** to take the train

ému,-e *adj.* moved (emotion)

encore *adv.* still, again; **— une fois** once again; **pas —** not yet

encre *f.* ink

endormir*: s' — *v.t.* 27 to go to sleep

endroit *m.* place

enfant[†] *m.* or *f.* child

enfantin,-e *adj.* childlike

enfin *adv.* finally

enfoncé *adj.* sunken

ennuyé,-e *adj.* bored

énoncer° *v.* to state, to set forth

énormément *adv.* (comp. of **beaucoup**) enormously

enrichir *v.* to enrich

enseigner *v.* to teach

enseignement *m.* instruction, teaching

ensemble *m.* collection; *adj.* together

ensuite *adv*,. then, next

entendre *v*. to hear

entendu *pp*. **entendre** heard; understood; **bien —** of course

enterrement *m*. burial

entier,-ière *adj*. entire

entièrement *adv*. entirely

entourer (de) *v*. to surround (by)

entraîner *v*. to drag along

entre *prep*. between; among

entrée *f*. entrance

entreprendre* *v*. to undertake

entreprise *f*. enterprise

entrevue *f*. interview

énumérer *v*. to enumerate

envers *prep*. with regard to; towards

envie: avoir — de [I] to feel like (doing sthg)

environ *adv*. about, approximately

envoler: s' — *v*. to take off

envoyer° *v*. to send; **— chercher** [P] to send for [P]

épais,-se *adj*. thick

épaisseur *m*. thickness

épicerie *m*. grocery store

épineux,-se *adj*. thorny, prickly

épuisé,-e *pp*. exhausted

équipage *m*. crew

escalier *m*. stair

Espagne *f*. Spain

espagnol,-e *adj*. Spanish

espérer° *v*. [26.3] to hope

essayer° (de [I]**)** *v*. to try (to do sthg)

essence *f*. gas, gasoline

essentiel,-le *adj*. essential

est *m*. east

esthétique *adj*. aesthetic

établir *v*. to establish

établissement *m*. establishment

étage *m*. (≠ **le plancher**) floor (building level); **au premier étage** on the second floor

étalage *m*. display (store window)

état *m*. state; condition

été *pp*. **être*** been

été *m*. summer

éteindre* [26.13] to extinguish

étendre: s' — *v*. to extend

étonné,-e *adj*. astonished, surprised

étranger, étrangère *adj*. foreign

être* *v.* [10.6] to be; (aux. with verbs in house of **être**) to have; — **de retour** to be back

étroit,-e *adj.* narrow

étudiant,-e *m./f.* student

étude *f.* study

étudier *v.* to study

eu *pp.* **avoir*** had

eux *dj.* them

européen,-ne *adj.* European

évaluer *v.* to evaluate

événement *m.* event

évidemment *adv.* obviously

éviter [N] *v.* to avoid (sthg); — **de** [I] to avoid (doing sthg)

évoluer *v.* to evolve

examen *m.* examination; **examiner** *v.* to examine

excès *m.* excess

excuser: s' — **de** to beg pardon for

exemple *m.* example; **par** — for example

exercer° *v.* [26.5] to exercise

exercice *m.* exercise

explication *f.* explanation

expliquer *v.* to explain

exposition *f.* exhibition; — **universelle** *f.* World's Fair

exagérer° *v.* to exaggerate

exemple *m.* example; **par** — for example

F

fabriquer *v.* to make, to fabricate

fâché,-e *adj.* angry; sorry

fâcher: se — (**de** [N]) to become angry (about)

facile *adj.* easy; — **à vivre** easy to get along with

faciliter *v.* to facilitate, to make easier

façon *f.* way, manner

facteur *m.* postman

faculté[†] *f.* college

faible *adj.* weak

faim: **avoir** — to be hungry

faire remarquer (**que** [C]) *v.* to point out (that [C])

faire* *v.t.* 14 to make, to do; — **voir** to show; — **marcher** to operate; — **une promenade** [16.3] to take a walk

fait *m.* fact

fait *pp.* **faire*** made, done

familier, -ère *adj.* domestic

famille *f.* family

fatigué,-e *adj.* tired

fauché,-e *adj.* broke, penniless
faut: il — [10.3] it is necessary [I]; **il — dire** it must be said
faute *f.* fault, error
fauteuil *m.* armchair
faux, fausse *adj.* false
femme *f.* woman; wife
fenêtre *f.* window
fer *m.* iron; **chemin de —** *m.* railroad
fermer *v.* to close; **— à clé (clef)** to lock
fermeture *f.* closing
fermier *m.* (= **agriculteur**) farmer
feu *m.* fire; **feu rouge** *m.* red (traffic) signal
feuille *f.* leaf; sheet (paper)
fichier *m.* card catalogue; files
fier, fière *adj.* proud
figuier *m.* fig tree
figure[†] *f.* face
file *f.* lane (highway)
fille *f.* girl; daughter; **jeune —** *f.* girl
film *m.* movie, film
fils *m.* son
fin *f.* end
financièrement *adv.* financially
finir *v.* to finish; **— par** to end up by (doing sthg)
fixer *v.* to set, to establish
flâner *v.* to loaf; to lounge about
flatter *v.* to flatter
fleur *f.* flower
fois *f.* time (recurrence)
foncé *adj.* (after a color) dark
fond: au — in the background
fonctionnement *m.* operation, functioning
fonctionner *v.* to operate, to function
fonds *m.pl.* funds
fontaine *f.* fountain
force *f.* strength
forcément *adv.* necessarily
forme *f.* form
formation[†] *f.* formation; training
formidable! *adj.* "swell!" "great!"
formule *f.* formula; form
fort (+ *adj.*) very (+ adj.)
fort,-e *adj.* strong
fou, folle *adj.* mad, crazy
foule *f.* crowd, masses

fourchette *f.* fork
fournir *v.* to furnish, to supply
fraîcheur *f.* freshness
frais, fraîche *adj.* fresh; cool
frais *m.pl.* expenses, fees
français,-e *adj.* French
franchir *v.* to cross; — **une muraille** to pass through a wall
frapper to strike, to hit
fréquenter *v.* to frequent, to "hang out" at
frère *m.* brother
fripé,-e *adj.* crumpled
froid *adj.* cold
fromage *m.* cheese
frontière *f.* frontier, border
fruit *m.* fruit (*not a collective*)
fuir *v.* to flee
fuite *f.* flight, escape
fumée *f.* smoke
fumer *v.* to smoke
fusée *f.* rocket
fusil *m.* rifle

G

gagner to earn; to win; to gain
gallois *m.* Welsh (language)
gamme *f.* line; range; gamut
gant *m.* glove
garçon *m.* boy; waiter
garde: prendre — **de** watch out for, be careful of
garder[†] *v.* to keep, to retain
gardien *m.* guard
gare *f.* station
garer *v.* to park
gaspiller *v.* to waste
gâteau *m.* cake
gauche *adj.* left; **à** — on (to) the left
gaz *m.* gas (gaseous materials)
gazon *m.* lawn
geler° *v.* [26.2] to freeze
généreux, -se *adj.* generous
Genève Geneva
gentil, -le *adj.* nice
genou *m.* knee
genre *m.* gender; kind, sort
gens *m.pl.* people; **jeunes** — , **les** *m.pl.* young people

gentil, -le *adj.* nice, kind
gérant *m.* manager
gloire *f.* glory
grammaire *f.* grammar
grand,-e *pr. adj.* large; (person) tall
grandeur *f.* size
grandir *v.* to grow larger
grand-mère *f.* grandmother
grand-père *m.* grandfather
grange *f.* barn
graphisme *m.* graphic; picture
grappe *f.* bunch
gratte-ciel *m.* skyscraper
gratuitement *adv.* gratis; free
grave *adj.* serious
gris,-e *adj.* gray
guère: ne — [19.3] scarcely, hardly
guetter *v.* to watch closely
guichet *m.* ticket-window

H

* indicates aspirate *h*
ha. *abbr.* **hectare** *cf* hectare
hâte *f.* haste; **en —** *adv.* hastily
habile *adj.* clever, talented, skillful
habiller: s' — *v.* to get dressed
habitation *f.* dwelling
habiter *v.* to live
habitude: d' — *adv.* usually, habitually
habituer: s' — à *v.* to get accustomed to
haltérophilie *f.* weight-lifting
harmonieux, -se *adj.* harmonious
haut,-e *pr. adj.* high; **à haute voix** aloud, out loud
hectare *m.* (metric area measurement, about 2.471 acres)
hélas! darn it! (alas!)
hésiter (à [1]**)** *v.* to hesitate (to do sthg)
heure *f.* time, hour; **de bonne —** *adv.* early; **à l' —** on time
heureusement *adv.* fortunately
heureux, heureuse *adj.* happy; fortunate
hésiter *v.* to hesitate
*hibou *m.* owl
hier *adv.* yesterday
histoire *f.* history; story
hiver *m.* winter
*honte *f.* shame

hôpital *m.* hospital; — **psychiatrique** psychiatric hospital
horaire *adj.* hourly
horaire *m.* schedule
hôtesse *f.* hostess; stewardess
huile *f.* oil
huit eight; — **jours** a week
humeur† *f.* mood

I

ici *adv.* here
idée *f.* idea
il y a [TIME] [2.5, 9.11] [TIME] ago
île *f.* island
îlot *m.* small island
immeuble *m.* apartment house
important,-e *adj.* large; important
importe; n' — quel(le) [N] any [N] at all
impôt *m.* tax
imprécis,-e *adj.* imprecise
imprimante *f.* printer (computer)
imprimer *v.* to print
inattendu,-e *adj.* unexpected
incapacité *f.* disability; handicap
incommodé,-e *adj.* inconvenienced
incomplet, -ète *adj.* incomplete
inconnu,-e *adj.* unknown, unidentifiable
inconnu,-e *m./f.* stranger
inconvénient† *m.* disadvantage
incroyable adj. unbelievable
indiquer *v.* (= **signaler**) to indicate
individu *m.* individual
infirmière *f.* nurse
informaticien *m.* data-processor
informatique *f.* computer science
informatisé *adj.* computerized
ingénieur *m.* engineer
ingénument *adv.* ingenuously
inimitié *f.* hostility, enmity
insistance *f.* emphasis
insister (sur) *v.* to emphasize
inspecteur *m.* detective
installer: s' — to settle down
instituteur *m.* teacher (grade school)
institutrice *f.* teacher (grade school)
intelligent,-e *adj.* intelligent

intéressant,-e *adj.* interesting
intéresser: s' — à [ɪ ou ɴ] to be interested in
intérieur *m.* interior
intituler: s' — *v.* to be titled
investissement *m.* investment
invité,-e *m./f.* guest
irais: j' — (**aller***) [25.1] I would go
irrégulier, -ière *adj.* irregular
issue *f.* exit; way out
italien,-ne *adj.* Italian
ivre *adj.* drunk

J

jaloux,-se *adj.* jealous
jamais: ne . . . — *adv.* [8.3] never
jambe *f.* leg
japonais,-e *adj.* Japanese
jardin *m.* yard; garden; — **zoologique** *m.* zoo
jaune *adj.* yellow
jeu: vieux — old-fashioned
jeune *pr. adj.* young
jeune fille *f.* girl
jeunes gens *m.pl.* young men
jeunesse *f.* youth
joli,-e *pr. adj.* pretty
jouer *v.* to play à (game); — **de** (instrument)
jour *m.* day (specific measure)
journal *m.* newspaper, journal
journée *f.* day (social content)
jours: tous les — *adv.* every day
juin June
jupe *f.* skirt
jus *m.* juice
jusqu'à *prep.* until; — **ce que** *conj.* (+ *sj.*) until
juste *adj.* just, right

L

l'air: avoir — [+ *adj. m.s.*] to seem (*adj.*)
là-bas *adv.* over there
laboratoire *m.* laboratory
laisser *v.* to allow, to let; to leave
laitue *f.* lettuce
lambeau *m.* rag
lancer *v.* to toss

langue *f.* language
large[†] *pr. adj.* wide
laver *v.* to wash
laver: se — *v.* to wash up (self)
leçon *f.* lesson
lecture *f.* reading
léger,-ère *adj.* light (weight)
légèrement *adv.* slightly
légume *m.* vegetable
lendemain: le — *m.* the next day
lent,-e *adj.* slow
lentement *adv.* slowly
lequel, -le *rel. pn.* [23.5] which, that
lequel des [N pl.] which one of the
lesquelles *adj.* which ones
lettre *f.* letter
leur *poss. adj.* (*before* a noun) their
leur *i.o. pn.* (*before* a verb) to them
leur: le (la) — *poss. pn.* [18.16] theirs
lever° *v.* [26.2] to raise; to lift
lever°: se — *v.* to get up
libraire *m. ou f.* bookseller
librairie[†] *f.* bookstore
libre *adj.* free; **— à vous de** [I] feel free to [I]
lieu *m.* place; **avoir —** [9.12] to take place
ligne *f.* line
lire* *v.t.* 16 to read
lis- *vst* **lire***
liste *f.* list
lit *m.* bed
livraison *f.* delivery; **— des titres** delivery of certificates
livre *m.* book
locution[†] *f.* expression
logiciel *m.* software program
logiquement *adv.* logically
loi *f.* law
loin de *prep.* far from
lointain *m.* distance
lointain,-e *adj.* distant
loisir *m.* leisure
long, -ue *pr. adj.* long
longtemps *adv.* for a long time
lorsque *conj.* [24.2] when
lourd,-e *adj.* heavy
lu *pp.* **lire*** read

lui *dj.* [17.4] him
lui *i.o.pn.* [7.3] to him; to her
lumière *f.* light
lundi *m.* Monday
lune *f.* moon

M

ma *poss. adj. f.* my
machine *f.* machine
magasin *m.* store; **grand —** *m.* department store
maigre *adj.* thin
main *f.* hand
maintenant *adv.* now
maintenir* *v.t.* 29 to maintain
maire *m.* mayor
mais *conj.* but
maison *f.* house
mal à [N]: **avoir —** to have a pain in [N]; **avoir — à la tête** to have a headache; **— aux cheveux** to have a hangover
malade *m.* ou *f.* patient (ill person)
malade *adj.* ill, sick
malgré *prep.* in spite of
malheureusement *adv.* unfortunately
malheureux,-se *adj.* unfortunate, unhappy
malsain *adj.* unhealthy
maltraiter *v.* to mistreat
Manche, la English Channel
manger° *v.* [26.6] to eat; **salle à —** dining room
manière: d'une — (+ *adj.*) in a (*adj.*) way
mannequin *m.* model
manque *m.* lack
manquer *v.* to miss; **— de** [I] to fail (to do sthg)
manuel *m.* textbook
maquiller: se — *v.* to put on makeup
marchand *m.* merchant
marchande *f.* salesgirl
marchandise *f.* merchandise
marcher *v.* to run (machines)
marché *m.* market; **bon —** *adj.; adv.* cheap
mariés: les nouveaux — *m.pl.* newlyweds
marier: se — avec to marry
marque *f.* brand
marron *adj.* brown
mars March
mat *adj.* dull

matériel *m.* material

maternel,-le *adj.* maternal; **langue maternelle** *f.* native language

matin *m.* morning; **du —** A.M.

matière *f.* material

matou *m.* tom-cat

mauvais,-e *adj.* bad

mécanicien *m.* mechanic

médecin *m.* doctor (physician)

médicament *m.* medicine

meilleur,-e *adv.* (*comp.* **bon**) better; **le —** [19.6] the best

même *pr. adj.* (before noun) same; (beginning of clause) even; (after noun) very; (him/her/it) self

ménage *m.* household; **faire* le —** to do the housework

mener° *v.* [26.2] to lead

mentir* *v.t.* 27 to lie, prevaricate

mer *f.* sea

mère *f.* mother

mes *poss. adj. pl.* my

mesure: à — que as

métier *m.* trade, calling

métro *m.* subway

mettez *imp.* **mettre*** put; **mettez que** *imp.* assume that; **mettons que** *imp.* let's say that

mettre* *v.t.* 17 to put; **se — à** [I] to begin [I]; **— une lettre à la poste** to mail a letter; **— la table** to set the table; [N] **— en œuvre** to put [N] into action

meuble *m.* piece of furniture

meurt: il — (pres. **mourir***) he dies

meurtre *m.* murder

mi-semestre *m.* mid-semester

midi noon

mien, mienne *poss. pn.* [18.6] mine

mieux *adv.* (comp. **bien**) better; **aimer —** to prefer

mille *num.* thousand

mince *adj.* thin

ministère *m.* ministry (government department)

ministre† *m.* (cabinet) minister

minuit midnight

mis *pp.* **mettre*** put

mode *f.* means, method

modérer° *v.* [26.3] to moderate

modestement *adv.* modestly

moi *dj.* me

moins *adv.* less, minus; **à — que** + *sj. conj.* unless; **— de** [x] fewer than

mois *m.* month

mollet *m.* calf (of leg)

moment *m.* moment; **en ce —** at this moment
mon *poss. adj. m.* my
monde *m.* world; people; **beaucoup de —** lots of people; **tout le —** everybody
monsieur *m.* gentleman; sir; Mr.
monter *v.* to go up, to get on
montre *f.* watch
montre-bracelet *f.* wrist watch
montrer *v.* to show
monument[†] *m.* public building; monument
morceau *m.* piece
mordre *v.* to bite
Moscou Moscow
mot *m.* word
mourir* to die
moyen *m.* means; **au — de** by means of
moyennant *ps.p.* in return for
munir de *v.* to equip with
mur *m.* wall
musée *m.* museum
musique *f.* music; band
mystérieux, -se *adj.* mysterious

N

nager° *v.* to swim
naître* *v.* to be born
naturellement *adv.* naturally
né *pp.* **naître*** born
néanmoins *adv.* nevertheless
nécessaire *adj.* necessary
neiger *v.* to snow
net,-te *adj.* neat, clear
nettoyer° *v.* to clean
neuf, neuve *adj.* new
neveu *m.* nephew
nez *m.* nose
ni: ne [VERBE] **ni** [N] **ni** [N] [8.3] neither . . . nor
noir,-e *adj.* black
nom *m.* name; noun
nombre *m.* number
nombreux, nombreuse *adj.* numerous
nord *m.* north
note *f.* grade; bill
noter *v.* to note, to notice
notre *poss. adj.* our
nôtre: le (la) — *poss. pn.* ours

nourriture *f.* food, nourishment
nouveau, nouvel, nouvelle *pr. adj.* new
nouvelle *f.* news
nu,-e *adj.* bare
nuit *f.* night
numéro *m.* number

O

obéir (à) *v.* to obey
obligation *f.* bond (securities); obligation
obliger° *v.* to require; to be obliged
obscurité *f.* darkness
obstiné,-e *adj.* obstinate
obtenir* *v.t.* 29 to obtain
occupé,-e *adj.* busy
occuper: s' — de to be busy with
œil (pl. **yeux**) *m.* eye
œuf *m.* egg
œuvre *m.* work (body of work)
œuvre *f.* work (literary)
offert *pp.* **offrir*** offered, given
offrir* *v.t.* 18 to give, to offer
oiseau *m.* bird
olivier *m.* olive tree
ombre *m.* shade
omettre* *v.t.* 17 to omit
on *pn.* [8.14] one, "they"
oncle *m.* uncle
onze eleven
or *m.* gold; — **massif** solid gold
oreille *m.* ear
ordinateur *m.* computer; — **universel** *m.* mainframe
orthographe *f.* spelling
oser *v.* to dare to
ou *conj.* or
où *adv.* [23.3] where, when
oublier [N] *v.* to forget [N]; — **de** [I] to forget to [I]
ours *m.* bear
ouvert *pp.* **ouvrir*** opened
ouverture *f.* opening
ouvrables: jours — business days (open)
ouvrage *m.* work (artistic)
ouvrier,-ère *m./f.* worker
ouvrir* *v.t.* 18 to open

r

pain *m.* bread

palais *m.* palace

panne: être en panne to be broken down; — **d'électricité** *m.* electrical outage (black-out)

pantalon *m.* pair of trousers

papeterie *f.* stationery store

papier *m.* paper (material)

par *prep.* by; through; — **là** by that; that way

parcourir* *v.t.* 6 to travel through

paraît: il — que it appears that

paraître *v.t.* 19 to appear

parc *m.* park

parmi *prep.* among

parent *m.* parent; relative

parenthèses *m. pl.* parentheses

parfait,-e *adj.* perfect

parfois *adv.* sometimes

parole *f.* word; **prendre* la —** to take the floor

parler *v.* (≠ **dire***) to speak

parti *m.* party (e.g. political)

participer *v.* to participate

particulier *m.* private citizen

particulier,-ière *adj.* private

partie *f.* part; game (**de tennis**); — **de plaisir** *f.* party (social)

partir* *v.t.* 20 to leave, to depart

partout *adv.* everywhere

passage: être de — to be just passing through

passager,ère *m./f.* passenger

passant *m.* passer-by

passer par [N] to pass by [N]

passer† *v.* to pass; to take (exam)

passer: se — to happen

passer: se — de [N] (ou [I]) to get along without [N]

passerelle *f.* passenger-loading bridge; jetway

passionnant,-e *adj.* exciting

patiemment *adv.* patiently

patron *m.* boss

pauvre *adj.* [5.11] poor

payer* *v.* to pay, to pay for

pays *m.* country, nation; land

pendant [TIME] [2.6] for [TIME]; — **que** *conj.* while

pénétrer (dans) *v.* to enter

penser (à [N]) *v.* [6.6A; 17.6B] to think (about [N])

peigner*: se — to comb one's hair

peine: à — *adv.* [11.9] scarcely, hardly

peinture *f.* painting

pencher: se — **sur** [N] to bend over [N]

perdre *v.* to lose

père *m.* father

périphérique adj. peripheral

permettre* (à [P] **de** [I]) to permit [P] to [I]

permis de conduire *m.* driver's license

persienne *f.* venetian blind

personnage *m.* character

personne *f.* person; **ne** — [8.5] nobody

petit,-e *pr. adj.* small, little

peu *adv.* very little, very few; — (+ *adj.*) (antonym of the adj.); e.g. **peu profonde** = shallow; **sous** — *adv.* shortly; in a short time

peu, un — *m.* a little

peur *f.* fear; **avoir** — to be afraid

peut: il se — **que** [14.4] + *sj.* it is possible that

peut-être *adv.* (+ inversion) [11.9] perhaps

peux (pres. **pouvoir***) can

phare *f.* headlight

phrase† *f.* sentence

physique *f.* physics

pièce *f.* room; coin

pièce (de théâtre) *f.* play

pied *m.* foot; **à** — on foot

pierre *m.* stone

piller *v.* to rob; to pillage

piste *f.* runway; trail; — **d'envol** runway for takeoff; — **de circulation** taxiway

placard† *m.* closet

place *f.* space, place; square

placer: se — *v.* to be placed, located

plage *f.* beach

plaindre*: se — (**de** [N]) to complain (about)

plaire* (à [P]) *v.t.* 21 [6.6A] to please [P]

plaisir: voyage de — *m.* pleasure trip

plait *pres.* **plaire*** pleases

plan *m.* plan; plane; **au premier** — in the foreground

planche *f.* plank

plancher *m.* (≠ **étage**) floor

plat *m.* dish

plein,-e *adj.* full; — **air** open air

pleuvoir* *v.* to rain; **il pleut** it's raining / **il pleuvait** it was raining

plier *v.* to fold

plume *f.* feather; pen

plupart: la — de [20.5] most of the

plus *adv.* more; **en —** moreover; **ne . . . —** no longer; **non —** either

plusieurs *adv.* several

plutôt *adv.* rather

pneu (pl. **pneus**) *m.* tire; **— à plat** *m.* flat tire

poche *f.* pocket

poème *m.* poem

poésie *f.* poetry

poids-lourd *m.* heavy truck (semi) "eighteen wheeler"

point *m.* period; point

point: ne [VERB] **—** (negative verb)

poire *f.* pear

pois: petits — *m. pl.* green peas

poisson *m.* fish

poissonnerie *f.* seafood store, fish market

poli,-e *adj.* polite

police *f.* police

policier,-ère *adj.* pertaining to the police

polonais,-e *adj.* Polish

polycopier *v.* to duplicate

pomme *f.* apple; **— de terre** *f.* potato; **— frites** *f. pl.* french fries

pont *m.* bridge

porte *f.* door; gate

porter *v.* to carry; (clothing) to wear

poser (une question) to ask; **— une demande (de)** to apply (for)

posséder° *v.* [26.3] to possess

poste *f.* post office; **— de pilotage** *f.* flight deck, cockpit; **mettre une lettre à la —** to mail a letter

pour *prep.* [18.1; 2.6] for; in order to [I];**—que** *conj.* + *sj.* [15.2] so that, in order that

pourboire *m.* tip

pourquoi [21.8] why

pourtant however

pourvu que (+ *sj.*) *conj.* provided that

poussière *f.* dust

pratique *f.* customers

pratique *adj.* practical

précédent,-e *adj.* preceding

précis,-e *adj.* precise

préférable *adj.* preferable

préférer° *v.* to prefer

premier (étage) *m.* second floor

premier, première *pr. adj.* [17.11] first

prendre* *v.t.* 23 to take

préparatif *m.* preparation

près de *prep.* near

prescrire* *v.t.* 11 to prescribe
presque *adv.* almost
pressé: à temps — hurried tempo
presser: se — (**de** [I]) to hurry (to [I])
prêt,-e *adj.* ready
prêter *v.* to lend
prévoir* *v.t.* 32 to foresee
printemps *m.* spring (season)
pris *pp.* **prendre*** taken
prix *m.* price
problème *m.* problem
procédé *m.* process
prochain,-e *adj.* next
procurer: se — *v.* to get (for oneself)
produire* *v.t.* 5 to produce
produire*: se — to happen
profiter (**de** [N]) *v.* to take advantage of [N]
programmateur *m.* programmer
programmation *f.* programming
projet *m.* plan, project
promenade à bicyclette *f.* bicycle ride
promenade *f.* walk; **faire* une** — to take a walk
promener°: se — *v.* [12.1] to take a walk (ride)
promettre* (**à** [P] **de** [I]) *v.t.* 17 to promise [P] to [I]
proposition† *f.* clause; — **principale** *f.* main clause
propre *pr. adj.* [5.11] own; clean [17.11]
propriétaire *m.* proprietor, owner
protéger° *v.* to protect
provenance: en — **de** coming from
prudent,-e *adj.* careful
public *m.* public
puissance *m.* power
punir *v.* to punish
pur,-e *adj.* pure

Q

qualité *f.* (good) quality
quand *adv.* [24.2; 2.7B] when
quart *m.* quarter ($\frac{1}{4}$)
quartier *m.* neighborhood, section of town
que *rel. pn.* that
que *conj.* [14.7] that; . . . **ne** — [8.4] only
quel,-le [N] *adj.* what, which
quelque chose [4.5] (abbr. *qqch*) something
quelques *adj.* a few

quelques-un(e)s [20.5; 6.9] some
quinze *num.* fifteen; — **jours** two weeks, a fortnight
quitter [N] *v.* to leave [N]
quoique + *sj. conj.* [15.2] although

R

raconter *v.* tell about; recount
rafraîchissements *m.pl.* refreshments
raisin *m.* grape
raison: avoir — to be right; **perdre la** — to lose one's mind
rame *f.* train (string of cars)
ramener° *v.* [26.2] to bring [P] back
rapide *m.* express train
rapide *adj.* rapid
rapport *m.* report
rapporter *v.* to bring
rassembler *v.* to assemble
rayons cosmiques *m.pl.* cosmic rays
réacteur *m.* jet engine
réalisateur *m.* (movie) producer
rebord *m.* ledge
récemment *adv.* recently
recevoir* *v.t.* 24 to receive
recherche *f.pl.* research; **à la** — **de** [N] seeking (sthg)
recteur *m.* rector; head of university
recueil *m.* collection; anthology
redevance *m.* fee
réduire* to reduce
refaire* re-do, do again
réfléchir *v.* to reflect
refouler *v.* to be forced back
refuser (**de** [I]) *v.* to refuse (to [I])
regarder [N] *v.* to look at [N]
règle *f.* rule
règlements *m.pl.* regulations
regretter *v.* to regret; to be sorry
rejoindre*: se — *v.* to join each other
réléguer *v.* to relegate
relié *adj.* hard-bound (books)
relier *v.* to connect
remarquer *v.* to notice
remercier *v.* to thank
remettre* ([N] **à** [P]) *v.t.* 17 to remit, to give
remonter *v.* go back up again; wind (timepiece)
remorque *m.* trailer

remorquer *v.* to tow
remplacement *m.* replacement
remplacer° *v.* [26.5] to replace
remplir *v.* to fill
rencontrer *v.* to meet; to encounter
rendez-vous *m.* appointment, date; **avoir —** *id.* to have a date, appointment
rendre *v.* to give, to hand in; **— malheureux** to make unhappy
rendre: se — (à) to go (to)
rendre visite (à) to pay a visit (to)
renommé *adj.* famous, renowned
renoncer° (à [N]) *v.* to renounce [N]; to give up [N,I]
renseignements *m.pl.* information
rentrer *v.* to return home
rentrée *f.* return to classes
réparation *f.* repair
réparer *v.* to repair
repas *m.* meal, repast
répéter° *v.* to repeat
répétiteur *m.* tutor; coach
répondre (à) *v.* [7.4] to answer
reposer: se — *v.* to rest
reprendre* *v.t.* 23 to take back; **— la place** to go back to one's place
représenter *v.* to perform (a play)
représentation† *f.* performance (play, etc.)
reprises: à plusieurs — several times
résol- *vst* **résoudre*** solved
résoudre *v.* to resolve; to solve
respirer *v.* to breathe
ressembler: — à [N] [7.4] to resemble [N]
ressentiment *m.* resentment
rester *v.* to stay, to remain; **il reste** [N] [N] is left, remains
résultat *m.* result
retard *m.* delay; **en —** late
retenir* *v.t.* 29 to retain; to reserve, to remember
retentir *v.* to resound
retour *m.* return; **être de —** to be back
retourner *v.* to go back; to return
retrousser *v.* to tuck in
réunion† *f.* meeting
réunir *v.* to meet
réussir (à) *v.* to succeed (in); to pass
réveil-matin *m.* alarm clock
réveiller: se — to awaken
revenir* *v.t.* 30 to come back
rêver (**de** + [I]) *v.* to dream (about [I])

revoir* *v.t.* 32 to review; to see again
revue *f.* magazine
rez-de-chaussée *m.* ground floor
rhum *m.* rum
rideau *m.* curtain
rien [8.3; 8.5] nothing
rincer *v.* to rinse
risquer (**de** [ɪ]) *v.* [6.6B] to run the risk (of [ɪ])
rivière† *m.* river (flowing to the sea)
roi *m.* king
rôle: à tour de — in turn
robe *f.* dress
roman *m.* novel (literature); **— policier** *m.* detective novel
ronde *adj.* round
ronfler *v.* to snore
rosbif *m.* roast beef
rose *adj.* pink
rouler *v.* to roll; **— au sol** to taxi
route *f.* highway; **se mettre en — (pour)** to set out (for)
routier, -ère *adj.* highway
rouvrir* *v.* [9.9] to open again
roux *adj.* [5.15] red (hair)
rue *f.* street
ruisseau *m.* brook, stream
Russie (URSS) *f.* Russia
russe *adj.* Russian

S

sa *poss. adj. f.* his, her, its
sabot *m.* clog (shoe)
sac *m.* handbag; sack
sage *adj.* well-behaved
sagesse *f.* wisdom
saisir *v.* to seize, grab
saison *f.* season
salade *f.* salad
sale *adj.* dirty, filthy
salé,-e *adj.* salted; **eau —** salt water
salle *f.* room
salon *m.* living-room
saluer *v.* to greet
salut! (*fam.*) Howdy!
samedi Saturday
sans *prep.* without
santé *f.* health

satisfaire* à [P] [7.4] to satisfy
savant *m.* scientist
savoir* *v.t.* 25 to know; to be able to
savon *m.* soap
schéma *m.* diagram
scolaire *adj.* academic
sécher (un cours) *v.* to cut (a class)
second,-e *adj.* second
secours *m.* aid, help
sélectionner *v.* to select
self-service *m.* cafeteria
selon *prep.* depending on, according to
semaine *f.* week
semblant; faire* — **de** [I] to pretend to [I]
sembler *v.* to seem
s'en aller* to leave, to go away
sentir* *v.t.* 2 to feel; to smell
　se — to feel
ser- *vst* **être** will be, would be
série *f.* series
sérieux,-se *adj.* serious minded
serré,-e *adj.* close; tight; strict
serveuse *f.* waitress
servir* *v.t.* 26 to serve; **se** — **de** [N] to use [N]
ses *adj.* his, her, its
seul,-e *adj.* only; alone; single
si *adv.* if; whether; so
siècle *m.* century
sien,-ne: le (la) — *pn.* [18.18] his; hers
siffler *v.* to whistle
signalé *pp./adj.* indicated, pointed out
signaler *v.* to indicate
signer *v.* to sign
silencieux,-se *adj.* silent
sinon *conj.* if not; otherwise
sirène *f.* siren
SNCF[2] French National Railways
sœur *f.* sister
soi *dj.* oneself
soie *f.* silk
soif: avoir — *id.* to be thirsty
soigneusement *adv.* carefully
soin *m.* care

---

[2] Société nationale des chemins de fer français

soir *m.* evening
soirée *f.* party; evening
soit *sj.* **être** is, will be
soldat *m.* soldier
soleil *m.* sun
sommaire *adj.* summary
sommeil: avoir — to be sleepy
somnoler *v.* to doze
son *poss. adj. m.* his, her, its
son *m.* sound
songer° (à) *v.* to think (about)
sonner *v.* to ring, to sound
sorte: de la — in this way
sortir* *v.t.* 27 to go out
soudain *adv.* suddenly
souffle *m.* breath
souffrant,-e *adj.* not feeling well; suffering
soulier *m.* shoe
souligner *v.* to underline
soupe *f.* soup
sourire *v.* to smile
souterrain,-e *adj.* subterranean; underground
souvenir*: se — (de N]) *v.t.* 30 to remember [N]
souvent *adv.* often
spectateur *m.* spectator, audience
spirituel,-le *adj.* witty
stationnement *m.* parking
statue *f.* statue
stylo *m.* pen; **— à bille** *m.* ball-point pen
su *pp.* **savoir*** [15.9C] known; found out
subir *v.* to undergo
subordonné,-e *adj.* subordinate
succéder° *v.* to succeed (follow)
succès *m.* success
sucre *m.* sugar
sud *m.* south
Suède *f.* Sweden
suédois,-e *adj.* Swedish
Suisse *f.* Switzerland
suite: tout de — *adv.* immediately
suivant,-e following
suivre* *v.t.* 28 to follow
    — un cours to take a course
sujet *m.* subject; **au — de** concerning; on the subject of
supporter† *v.* to endure

supprimer *v.* to eliminate, suppress
sur *prep.* on
sûr,-e *adj.* sure
suralimentation *f.* supercharging
surtout *adv.* especially
surprendre* *v.t.* 23 to surprise
surveiller *v.* to keep watch on
sustenation *f.* suspension
sympathique† *adj.* likable

T

tabac *m.* tobacco
tableau (noir) *m.* blackboard, painting; table; **— de bord** *m.* keyboard; dashboard
tache *f.* spot
tâcher (de [ɪ]) *v.* to try (to do sthg)
taille *f.* stature
tailleur *m.* woman's suit
tandis que *conj.* whereas
tant . . . que both in . . . and in . . .
tante *f.* aunt
tantôt . . . tantôt at one time . . . at another time
taper (à la machine) *v.* to type(write)
tard *adv.* [11.6B] late
tasse *f.* cup
tâtonner *v.* to grope about
te *pn.* you; to you
technique *adj.* technical
tel,-le *adj.* such a
téléphoner (à [P]) [7.4] to telephone [P]
téléviseur *m.* television set
témoigner v. to witness
temps *m.* time; tense; weather; (music) tempo; **il fait un — de chien** the weather is miserable
ténèbres *m. pl.* dark
tenir* *v.t.* 29 to hold; **— à [ɪ]** *id.* to be eager to (do sthg); **— à [N]** *id.* to value [N] highly; **se —** *v.* to stand
tension artérielle *f.* blood pressure
tenter (de) *v.* to attempt (to)
terminer *v.* to terminate; to end
tête *f.* head; **mal de —** *m.* headache
TGV (Train à grande vitesse) *m.* high-speed train
thé *m.* tea
théâtre *m.* theater (stage)
thème *m.* translation
théorie *f.* theory

tiens! well

tigre *m.* tiger

timbre-poste *m.* postage stamp

timidement *adv.* timidly

tirer *v.* to pull out; to fire (gun)

tiret *m.* dash (punctuation)

tiroir *m.* drawer (furniture)

titre *m.* title; (stock) certificate

toi *pn.* [2.12] you

toit *m.* roof; — **ouvrant** *m.* sun roof (auto)

toiture *f.* roofing

tomber *v.* to fall

tort: avoir — to be wrong

tôt *adv.* [11.6 B] early

toucher *v.* to touch; — **un chèque** to cash a check

toujours *adv.* still, always

tour *f.* tower

tour *m.* tour; turn; **à** — **de rôle** in turn; **de mauvais** —**s** dirty tricks

touriste *m.* ou *f.* tourist

tout *adv.* [19.8] *invar.* very, quite

tout à l'heure *adv.* a moment ago; in just a moment

tout de suite *adv.* immediately

tout le monde everybody

tout,-e *adj.* [19.7] all

toutes *adj. f.pl.* all

tous les deux both

traduction *f.* translation

train *m.* train; **par le** — (= **en chemin de fer**) by train

train: être* en — **de** [ɪ] *id.* to be engaged in

traîner *v.* to drag

traitement *m.* processing; — **des données** data processing; — **de texte** word processing

trajet *m.* trip

tranche *f.* slice

transport *m.* transportation

travail *m.* work

travailler *v.* to work

travailleur *m.* worker

traverser *v.* to cross

trombone *m.* trombone; paper clip

tromper: se — (**de** N]) to be mistaken (about)

trop *adv.* too much, too many

trouver *v.* to find; **Comment trouvez-vous** [N]? What do you think of [N]?; **se** — *v.* to be, to be located

tuer *v.* to kill

tuyau: avoir un — to have a tip, inside information
TGV *m.* high-speed train (**Train à grande vitesse**)

U

un(e): l'— et l'autre both
université *f.* university
usage *m.* use
usé,-e† *adj.* worn
usine *f.* factory
utile *adj.* useful
utiliser *v.* to use

V

vacances *f. pl.* vacation; **en —** on vacation; **grandes —** , **les** summer vacation
vache *f.* cow
vaisselle *f.* dishes (collective); **faire* la —** to wash the dishes
valeur *f.* value; **la Bourse des —**s Stock Exchange; **—** s **mobilières** *f.pl.* stocks and bonds
valise *f.* suitcase
Varsovie Warsaw (Poland)
vaut *pres.* **valoir*** to be worth; **il — mieux** it is preferable
veille *f.* the day (night) before
vedette *f.* star (performer)
vélo *m.* bicycle
vendeur, -euse *m./f.* salesman; saleswoman
vendre *v.* to sell
venger: se — (sur) *v.* to avenge oneself (on)
venir* *v.t.* 30 to come; **— de** [ɪ] *id.* [7.13] to have just [ɪ] (sthg)
Venise Venice
vent *m.* wind
venu *pp.* **venir*** come
verbe *m.* verb
vérité *f.* truth
verre *m.* glass
vers *prep.* towards; about
verser *v.* to pour
version *f.* translation, foreign language to native language
vert,-e *adj.* green
veston *m.* jacket
vêtement *m.* clothing
viande *f.* meat
vide *adj.* empty
vie *f.* life
vieille *adj. f.* old

Vienne Vienna
vieux, vieil, vieille *pr. adj.* old
village *m.* village
ville *f.* city; **en —** downtown
vin *m.* wine
visage *m.* face
visite médicale *f.* medical examination
visiter to visit (place)
vite *adv.* fast; quickly
vitesse *f.* speed
vivre* *v.t.* 31 to live
voilà there is
voir* *v.t.* 32 to see
voisin,-e *m./f.* neighbor
voiture *f.* car; vehicle
voix *f.* voice
vol *m.* flight; theft, robbery
volant *m.* steering wheel
voleur *m.* robber
volonté *f.* will
volontiers *adv.* willingly, gladly
vos *poss. adj. pl.* your
votre *poss. adj. s.* your
vôtre: le (la) — *pn.* [16.18] yours
voudriez-vous *cond.* **vouloir*** would you like
vouloir* *v.t.* 33 [24.7] to want; **en — à** [P] to hold a grudge against [P]; **— bien** to be
    willing (to [I]); **— dire** to mean
vouvoyer° *v.* [26.7] to address another using "**vous**"
voyage *m.* trip; **faire* un —** to take a trip
voyager° *v.* to travel
voyant *m.* sighted person; **non —** blind person
vrai,-e *adj.* true
vu *pp.* **voir*** seen

Z

zut alors! darn it!

Index